Bloomers on the Liffey

BLOOMERS ON THE LIFFEY

Eisegetical Readings of Joyce's Ulysses

PAUL VAN CASPEL

THE JOHNS HOPKINS UNIVERSITY PRESS
Baltimore and London

This book has been brought to publication with the
generous assistance of the Andrew W. Mellon
Foundation.

The Johns Hopkins University Press
701 West 40th Street
Baltimore, Maryland 21211
The Johns Hopkins Press Ltd., London

∞ The paper used in this publication meets
the minimum requirements of American
National Standard for Information
Sciences—Permanence of Paper for Printed
Library Materials, ANSI Z39.48-1984.

Library of Congress Cataloging-in-Publication Data

Van Caspel, Paul.
  Bloomers on the Liffey.

  Includes bibliographical references and index.
  1. Joyce, James, 1882–1941. Ulysses. I. Title.
PR6019.O9U754   1986   823'.912   85-24106
ISBN 0-8018-3288-8 (alk. paper)

FOR GILA

CONTENTS

PREFACE

This book arose out of my doctoral dissertation (1980), in which I discussed the twelve episodes that constitute Book II of *Ulysses*, "Calypso" through "Circe." In that thesis I tried to convince inexperienced readers that reading *Ulysses*, though not at all easy, can be fun, urging them not to let themselves be discouraged by learned interpretative theories that tend to smother the text under a growth of metaphor. I warned them against summaries, commentaries, and annotations, which, as I demonstrated at length, are often based on careless or even downright faulty reading. In some cases I was able to show that translations may be helpful in solving—or at least making less opaque—problems of interpretation, although in this field errors proved not to be infrequent either.

Meanwhile, the material that I had collected over the years and which, needless to say, covered the other six episodes as well, kept staring me in the face. So, encouraged by the response to my thesis, both in the Netherlands and abroad, I started rewriting the work, which meant adding six chapters as well as updating the text, not to speak of weeding out errors of my own that sympathetic readers had pointed out to me. The result, as might have been expected, proved an unwieldy mass that needed—and subsequently underwent—much pruning.

In reworking the text I found that, by a natural process, the bias seemed to be shifting somewhat. While still starting out by addressing beginning readers, I gradually got involved in discussions with critics whose analyses of Joyce's text differed from mine. In hindsight, this may be all to the good, because in this way the scope of the book may have widened so as to appeal to beginning readers as well as to advanced ones.

Unless otherwise indicated, references in the text are to *Ulysses: A Critical and Synoptic Edition*, prepared by Hans Walter Gabler with Wolfhard Steppe and Claus Melchior (New York and London: Garland Publishing, 1984). The Gabler edition provides a consecutive line numbering by episodes as a reference system. In my text these references will be followed by page and line numbers of the 1961 Random House edition.

ACKNOWLEDGMENTS

Permission to quote from *Ulysses* by James Joyce was granted by the Society of Authors, London, acting on the behalf of the Trustees of the James Joyce Estate. Permission to quote from *Ulysses: A Critical and Synoptic Edition*, published by Garland Publishing, New York, was obtained from Random House, Inc., New York, and the Bodley Head, London. A brief passage from *Finnegans Wake* by James Joyce, copyright 1939 by James Joyce, renewed © 1967 by George Joyce and Lucia Joyce, is reprinted by permission of Viking Penguin Inc. For world distribution (excluding the United States) permission was given by the Society of Authors.

My thanks are due to the Suhrkamp Verlag (Frankfurt am Main) for the right to quote the German translations of *Ulysses* by Goyert (1930) and Wollschläger (1975). Permission to quote from the Catalan translation of *Ulysses* (by Mallafrè) was kindly given by the translator and the publishers, Leteradura (Barcelona). Thanks are also due to Editions Gallimard (Paris) for quotations from the French translations of *Ulysses* (by Morel) and *Finnegans Wake* (by Lavergne), and to Arnoldo Mondadori Editore (Milan) for quotations from the Italian translation of *Ulysses* (by De Angelis). Credit is given to Editorial Bruguera (Barcelona) for a few passages reprinted from the Spanish translation of *Ulysses* (by Valverde) and to De Bezige Bij (Amsterdam) for a few quotations from the Dutch translation of *Ulysses* (by Vandenbergh).

I thank the Ohio State University Press for permission to quote from *The Argument of "Ulysses"* (1964) by Stanley Sultan and from *Joyce's Moraculous Sindbook: A Study of "Ulysses"* (1978) by Suzette A. Henke. Professor Clive Hart kindly gave permission to reproduce a few brief passages from his and Leo Knuth's *Topographical Guide to James Joyce's "Ulysses"* (1981). The author and the publishers kindly granted permission to quote a few passages from *The "Ithaca" Chapter of Joyce's "Ulysses,"* copyright Richard E. Madtes, UMI Research Press, Ann Arbor, Michigan, 1983. Wilhelm Fink Verlag (Munich) allowed me to reprint a passage from *Der implizite Leser: Kommunikationsformen des Romans von Bunyan bis Beckett* (1972) by Wolfgang Iser. I thank Carl Hanser Verlag (Munich) for permission to quote a passage from *Der Kampf mit Proteus* (1970) by Glauco Cambon. Permission to include a few quotations from *James Joyce: A Student's Guide* (1978) by Matthew

J. C. Hodgart was kindly granted by the publishers, Routledge and Kegan Paul (London).

Passages from *The Sigla of "Finnegans Wake"* (1976) by Roland McHugh; from *James Joyce: "Ulysses"* (1972) by Michael Mason; and from *James Joyce: The Citizen and the Artist* (1977) by J. C. Peake are reprinted by courtesy of Edward Arnold (London). I thank Colin Smythe (Gerrards Cross, Bucks.) and Barnes and Noble Books (Totowa, N.J.) for permission to quote passages from *James Joyce: An International Perspective* (1982), edited by Suheil Badi Bushrui and Bernard Benstock. My thanks are due to the author and the publishers (Chatto and Windus, London) for permission to quote from *Character and the Novel* (1970) by W. J. Harvey. Quotations from *James Joyce's Metamorphoses* by John Gordon (copyright © John Gordon, 1981) are reproduced by courtesy of the publishers, Gill and Macmillan (Dublin), Barnes and Noble, and the kind permission of the author. The Athlone Press (London) gave permission to quote from *Tellers and Listeners: The Narrative Imagination* (1975) by Barbara Hardy.

Thanks are due to André Deutsch Ltd (London) for permission to reprint a few sentences from *Joysprick: An Introduction to the Language of James Joyce* (1973) by Anthony Burgess. I thank the publishers, George Allen and Unwin (London), for permission to reprint a few passages from *Ulysses* (1980) by Hugh Kenner. Permission to include a number of passages from *James Joyce's "Ulysses": Critical Essays* (1974, 1977), edited by Clive Hart and David Hayman, and from *The Chronicle of Leopold and Molly Bloom: "Ulysses" as Narrative* (1977) by John Henry Raleigh, is acknowledged with thanks to the University of California Press. Quotations from *Joyce's Voices* (1978) by Hugh Kenner are reprinted by permission of the University of California Press and Faber and Faber (London). A few quotes from *Proteus, His Lies, His Truth* by Robert M. Adams, copyright © 1973 by W. W. Norton and Company, Inc., were used by permission of W. W. Norton and Company, Inc. Random House, Inc., granted permission to quote from Robert M. Adams, *James Joyce: Common Sense and Beyond* (© 1966). Methuen and Co (London) kindly gave permission to quote from *The Bloomsday Book: A Guide through Joyce's "Ulysses"* (1966) by Harry Blamires, and *A Starchamber Quiry: A James Joyce Centennial Volume, 1882–1982* (1982), edited by E. L. Epstein.

The quotations from *Joyce's "Ulysses" and the Assault upon Character* by James H. Maddox, Jr., copyright © 1978 by Rutgers, The State University of New Jersey, were reprinted by permission of Rutgers University Press, and also by permission of the Harvester Press (Brighton). Both the Harvester Press and the Indiana University Press (Bloomington) gave permission to use material from an essay by Fritz

Senn in *James Joyce: New Perspectives* (1982), edited by Colin MacCabe, and to reprint a passage from an essay by Robert Adams Day in *The Seventh of Joyce* (1982), edited by Bernard Benstock. Princeton University Press granted permission to quote from Dorrit Cohn, *Transparent Minds: Narrative Modes for Presenting Consciousness in Fiction*, copyright © 1978 by Princeton University Press; from M. Groden, *"Ulysses" in Progress*, copyright © 1977 by Princeton University Press; and from Mary T. Reynolds, *Joyce and Dante: The Shaping Imagination*, copyright © 1981 by Princeton University Press. Harvard University Press kindly allowed me to quote from Marilyn French, *The Book as World: James Joyce's "Ulysses"* (1976). I am indebted to the Associated University Presses for the use of quotations from John Henry Raleigh, "On the Way Home to Ithaca: The Functions of the 'Eumaeus' Section in *Ulysses*," in *Irish Renaissance Annual* II (1981), edited by Zack Bowen, and from Cheryl Herr, "Irish Censorship and 'The Pleasure of the Text': The 'Aeolus' Episode of Joyce's *Ulysses*," in *Irish Renaissance Annual* III (1982). Faber and Faber (London) kindly gave permission to quote from *James Joyce's "Dubliners": Critical Essays*, edited by Clive Hart. Copyright © 1969 by Faber and Faber. Reprinted by permission of Viking Penguin Inc. Faber and Faber and Alfred A. Knopf, Inc. (New York) allowed me to quote from *James Joyce's "Ulysses": A Study* (© 1930) by Stuart Gilbert. Quotations from *"Ulysses" on the Liffey* (1972) and *The Consciousness of Joyce* by Richard Ellmann were reprinted by permission of Faber and Faber and Oxford University Press (New York). A short extract from *A Question of Modernity* by Anthony Cronin (London: Secker and Warburg, 1966) is reprinted by permission of A D Peters and Co Ltd (London). Passages from *Surface and Symbol: The Consistency of James Joyce's "Ulysses"* (1962) by Robert M. Adams were reprinted by permission of Oxford University Press (New York).

Passages from Don Gifford's *Notes for Joyce: An Annotation of James Joyce's "Ulysses"* (New York: Dutton, 1974) were quoted by kind permission of the author. Excerpts from Richard Morton's *"Ulysses": Notes* are reproduced by permission of the publishers, Coles Book Stores (Rexdale, Ontario). A brief passage from Edmund Wilson was excerpted from *Axel's Castle: A Study in the Imaginative Literature of 1870–1930*. Copyright 1931 Charles Scribner's Sons; copyright renewed © 1959 Edmund Wilson. Reprinted with the permission of Charles Scribner's Sons.

NOTE ON TRANSLATIONS

The following translations of *Ulysses* are cited in the text.

Catalan

Ulisses. Translation by Joaquim Mallafrè. Barcelona: Leteradura, 1980.

Dutch

Ulysses. Translation by John Vandenbergh. Amsterdam: De Bezige Bij, 1969. Several reprints.

French

Ulysse. Integral translation by Auguste Morel, with the help of Stuart Gilbert, completely revised by Valery Larbaud and the author. Paris: La Maison des Amis des Livres, 1929. Quotations are from the 1948 issue (Paris: Gallimard). Edition in two volumes. Paris: Gallimard, Collection Folio, 1976.

German

Ulysses. Definitive German edition by Georg Goyert, with the supervision of the author. Two volumes. Zürich: Rhein-Verlag, 1930. New edition, in one volume. Frankfurt am Main: Suhrkamp, 1979.

Ulysses. Translation by Hans Wollschläger. Two volumes, consecutively numbered. Frankfurt am Main: Suhrkamp, 1975. New edition, in one volume. Suhrkamp: 1979.

Italian

Ulisse. Only authorized integral translation by Giulio de Angelis. Milan: Arnoldo Mondadori Editore, 1961. Paperback, 1982.

Spanish

Ulises. Translation by José Maria Valverde. Barcelona: Bruguera-Lumen, 1976. Paperback, two volumes, 1982.

Bloomers on the Liffey

INTRODUCTION

*T*HE REMARK has been made that in all the guidebooks dealing with James Joyce "there is an open assumption that his later works, *Ulysses* and *Finnegans Wake,* cannot be read; they can only be studied" (Booth, 1961:325). Put like this, the statement may seem exaggerated, especially as far as *Ulysses* is concerned, but these works have been both read and studied for years, with a vengeance, and there is no doubt in any critic's mind that they will go on being studied for years to come.

So far, Joyce scholars have accumulated a vast mass of criticism, covering, mainly, the fields of annotation, explication, and interpretation. Because translation is (or implies) interpretation as well, translators should also be considered as having contributed their share toward the analysis and exegesis of Joyce's work. Fortunately, they have not let themselves be daunted by such considerations as Isaac Bashevis Singer voiced in a preface to one of his collections of stories, to the effect that the language into which the original work must be rendered (it was, of course, his own work he had in mind) "does not tolerate obscurity, puns, and linguistic tinsel." If the text of *Ulysses* is obscure, in places, translators simply must meet the challenge of its obscurity, which is inherent in the work—as it is in life. The only thing they should avoid at all costs is to add to the obscurity. As for puns, the translator's task seems hopeless, so the critic should not be too hard on him in judging the results of his efforts. And as to linguistic tinsel, whatever Singer might have meant by that (one thinks of episodes such as "Sirens" or "Oxen of the Sun"), translators will simply have to grapple with that aspect, too.

As Senn once remarked, critics and commentators can afford to be selective, whereas the translator cannot shirk a single issue (1970:518). Nevertheless, the critic should be granted the basic right to speak his mind at all times. If I think Vandenbergh's Dutch translation of the simple phrase "in trains and cloakrooms" (8.557/166.25) by "in treinen en het afgiftebureau" (194) is factually wrong, nonidiomatic, and rhythmically unsatisfactory, I should be allowed to say so. His translation of *Ulysses* has come in for a lot of praise, but sometimes the authors of the reviews reminded me of people claiming that body-building is a serious branch of sport. Granted, the sheer size and complexity of the book make one shudder at the thought of having to translate it. Still, it has been done, and I see no valid reason why the result should not be open to criticism.

It should be clear, however, that it would require the combined efforts of a team of expert critics to achieve an approximately complete, exhaustive commentary on *Ulysses*, resolving allusions as well as providing factual information. Such a comprehensive work of annotation, which presupposes a state of affairs in which the fundamental problems of understanding the text have been solved, would no doubt be welcomed by translators and general readers alike.

As for interpretation, before critics start analyzing or interpreting any literary text, especially a novel (for, whatever else *Ulysses* might be, it remains, basically, a realistic novel), they ought to be clear in their minds about the facts narrated in the work under discussion: the events, or that which happens in the book. Anyone, therefore, whether annotating or translating, has had to consider, primarily, the question: What does the text tell the reader about the things that happen in the book?

In the case of *Ulysses*, attempts to answer this crucial question by providing more or less extensive analyses have been made by such scholars as Kain (1947, 1959), Tindall (1959), Sultan (1964), Blamires (1966), French (1976), Peake (1977), Henke (1978), Maddox (1978), Kenner (1980), Gordon (1981a), and Hayman (1982). Summaries, in some cases accompanied by commentaries, have been drawn up by Hart (1968), Morton (1970), Mason (1972) and Hodgart (1978). Interesting new ground has been explored by Benstock and Benstock (1980), with their directory dealing with the thousands of names in Joyce's prose works (with the exception of *Finnegans Wake*), and by Raleigh (1977b), who tries to piece together the chronicle of the Blooms' lives from the bits of information distributed piecemeal throughout *Ulysses*. Full titles of the studies mentioned here and elsewhere in the text will be found in the List of References. Obviously, this list is only a select bibliography. Advanced readers who want to consult one of the latest bibliographical tools might turn to Rice (1982), a guide that even lists studies of the individual episodes of *Ulysses*.

It is not always easy to draw sharp dividing lines between the various types of studies of *Ulysses*. On the one hand, there is the page-by-page summary as worked out by Blamires, offering a minimum of comment, and on the other hand, there is the episode-by-episode analysis as found in Sultan's book, with its moralistic outlook, largely devoted to commentary and interpretation. At another level, there are such differences in approach as between Kenner (1955) and Goldberg (1961). Over the constant flow of Joycean studies we have witnessed in recent years we should not forget such classics as Gilbert (1930)—still an excellent introduction to *Ulysses*—and the reminiscences of Budgen (1934).

For *Finnegans Wake*, too, several aids have become available since it was published in 1939, such as Campbell and Robinson (1947), Hart (1962), Bernard Benstock (1965), Tindall (1969), Begnal and Senn (1974), Norris (1974), the *Censuses* (three so far) compiled by Glasheen (1956, 1963, 1977), Mink's unsurpassable *Gazetteer* (1978), and McHugh (1976, 1980, 1981).

Ulysses abounds in literary, historical, and musical allusions. Thornton (1968) and Gifford with Seidman (1974) have managed to trace and track down the bulk of these allusions, quotations, proper names, and so forth. These reference works by Thornton, who had done the groundwork, and Gifford do overlap to a certain extent even though their approaches are supposed to be different. Thornton, confining himself to allusions in the fields of literature, theology, philosophy, history, the fine arts, and music, especially popular and folk music, does not annotate any difficult or archaic words, slang or foreign phrases, whereas Gifford does (accordingly, the latter's list of notes is much longer). This is, however, a treacherous field; you must be sure of your ground, and it is not surprising, therefore, that Gifford slips up once in a while. Apart from containing much that is plainly irrelevant, his book, as Knuth (1975) remarks, has a number of shortcomings, such as factual errors and silent omissions. It is only fair to add that in the forthcoming revised edition of Gifford's *Notes* many passages will be corrected, among them some quoted by me (personal communication).

Since *Ulysses* shows us Leopold Bloom walking along the streets of Dublin for a great many hours on a sunny day (16 June 1904), names of streets, shops, offices, churches, keep cropping up, either in the narrative flow or in Bloom's stream of consciousness. It will be a great help for the reader, therefore, to have a map of Dublin handy or, better still, Hart and Knuth's excellent *Topographical Guide* (1981), with its maps, itineraries, and list of Dublin addresses, from which much useful information of an eminently practical nature may be gleaned.

An indispensable tool for anyone who wants to undertake a serious study of *Ulysses* is Hanley's *Word Index*. It suffers, however, from a few shortcomings: It does not include all the words in the book (and who is to tell a priori which word will prove to be important and which not?); furthermore, it only gives page and line references (based on the old Random House edition) for words occurring twenty-five times or less—except for proper names and such words as *father* and *mother*. This is a serious drawback if you want to study recurrent elements, a phenomenon that is highly characteristic of Joyce's novel. Fortunately, there is now a special guide to such elements in *Ulysses* (Schutte, 1982).

Faced by the overwhelming mass of studies, we should not forget that *Ulysses* is there, in the first place, to be enjoyed: it is literature, fiction, and as such it should give pleasure, aesthetic stimulation. The reader who is susceptible to its styles and moods, and sensitive to its unbelievably subtle use of language, will soon come to delight in its richness and its humor. Of course, it would be naïve to deny that *Ulysses* is a difficult book; the point is that it is worthwhile trying to overcome the difficulties.

There are three things the prospective reader should take into account: Joyce was an Irishman, a Catholic by upbringing, and a humorist. So, some knowledge of Ireland and things Irish (readers should know, for example, who Parnell was and what was his role in Irish history) as well as of Catholic ritual and dogma, will help, but essential is a keen sense of humor: if we are to believe Arthur Power (1974:89) we have Joyce's own word for it that *Ulysses* is a fundamentally humorous work.

Reading *Ulysses* is a matter of years, it is a process of reading and rereading, in the course of which understanding, enlightenment, may come in a flash, as a shock of recognition or, rather, cognition. There is no other way to get the feeling of the climate of the book, which is the climate of Ireland and, more specifically, of Dublin around the turn of the century, a climate of tensions, in which the influence of Catholicism, representing the gloomy side of life, was more or less counterbalanced by the bright world of music, of opera, sentimental songs, and heroic ballads—helped along, no doubt, by drink. To tune in to this climate the student might do well, instead of just plunging into *Ulysses,* to start with the earlier prose works, the collection of stories, *Dubliners,* and the auto-biographical novel *A Portrait of the Artist as a Young Man,* or its first draft, *Stephen Hero,* the reading of which may greatly enhance the process of assimilating the Ulyssean atmosphere.

I myself have been reading *Ulysses,* on and off, for half a century and I have made a lavish and grateful use of such critical works as mentioned above, particularly in recent years, but in doing so I was often struck by curious incongruities I encountered in such studies. On the one hand, I would look up an author's comment on a certain passage or episode in order to settle, if possible, a certain issue, and find that—in my opinion and from my knowledge and understanding of the text—this author's interpretation seemed altogether beside the point. On the other hand, I would peruse some handbook without any particular problem in mind, and in the course of my reading be brought up short by some sweeping statement—based, presumably, on a passage from *Ulysses*—which, to my taste, sounded dubious in the extreme. In either case, of course, renewed direct contact with the text was essential to decide the issue one way or another, although sometimes I had to concede that the case in hand might well be one not of *either/or* but of *both/and.*

Roughly speaking, such a situation mirrors the shift in Joycean criticism that has occurred over the years. In the early commentaries, stress was laid on the significance of the Homeric parallels and corre-spondences, in later years critics preferred to look for symbolic and allegorical dimensions, whereas recently there has been a tendency to emphasize the realistic aspect of *Ulysses*. Partly perhaps as a reaction to the latest trend, Knuth (1976), without losing sight of the realistic component, has drawn attention to the importance of what he calls "extra-realistic dimensions" in Joyce's work. My own experiences with commentaries and works of annotation—aids that often let you down— have led me to consider the question: What does a student who wants to read *Ulysses* as it should be read need in the way of equipment? The answer is, of course, simple: an as yet unwritten book, a kind of super-Gifford. As things stand, our hypothetical student has to make do with the existing tools, the majority of which consist of notes and handbooks such as have been listed above.

Obviously, what he needs first is a text in one of the current editions, which were, until recently, Bodley Head, Random House, and Penguin. None of these, however, provides a text that is entirely free from corrup-tions, the later printings not necessarily being superior to the earlier ones in all respects. Sometimes it is a matter of a simple misprint, as when the new Random House edition has "lampost" (311.23) as against the old Random House's "lamppost" (306.08), but in other cases the corruption will inevitably entail a different reading. Where the ORH edition, in the scene where Bloom scoops up his mail from the hall floor, has "He stooped" (61.29), which makes sense, the NRH (61.35) as well as the New Bodley Head (74.11) and Penguin (63.33) editions have "He stopped," which does not. Conversely, there is a paragraph in "Nau-sicaa" that in the ORH begins as follows: "Mr Bloom *stopped* and turned over a piece of paper on the strand. He brought it near his eyes and peered" (374.32–33, italics mine). As is apparent from the words that conclude the preceding paragraph ("What's that? Might be money."), Bloom must have halted already when he spotted the piece of paper; he then bends down in order to pick it up from the sand. Therefore, the reading adopted by the other editions, "Mr Bloom *stooped* and turned over a piece of paper on the strand" (italics mine), is clearly to be preferred.

This sounds reasonable, but the crucial question, of course, is: What did Joyce write? In Munich, Gabler (1984) has completed a critical and synoptic three-volume edition of *Ulysses*. It tries to answer this question in a systematical way. Gabler and his associates have produced a text in which most emendations are firmly based on holograph evidence. In the case of the "stopped/stooped" confusion, for instance, they have opted for the reading in the so-called Rosenbach manuscript, Joyce's fair copy of *Ulysses* in a certain stage of its evolution. Here, in both places (4.243

and 13.1246, respectively), we have, in Joyce's hand, "stooped."

In Gabler's edition, the lines are numbered in the margin in groups of five, starting from scratch with each new episode, a system that will probably be adopted for any forthcoming one-volume edition as well. Consequently, the text of *Ulysses* may be referred to, from now on, by episode (1–18) and line number of the critical edition. Thus, 15.3562 indicates line 3562 of episode 15 ("Circe"). In the following pages the references to *Ulysses* are to the Gabler edition, followed by the page and line numbers of the 1961 Random House edition, thus: 18.1175/771.03. For the text of the quotations from *Ulysses* only the Gabler edition has been used.

Translations may serve a twofold purpose. In the first place, they are intended, of course, as a substitute for the benefit of those readers who feel that their command of English would not permit them to read *Ulysses* in the original. Although the text, viewed as a whole, will remain impressive enough, it is clear that any translation, however congenial, will entail a loss of one kind or another. There are numberless little touches that either defy the translator's inventiveness or may be over-looked from sheer carelessness or downright ignorance on the translator's part. In either case the reader who is not acquainted with the original text will not be any the wiser; he will not, that is, realize what he has missed. To show what I mean let me quote a passage from the "Sirens" episode.

After Ben Dollard's performance of "The Croppy Boy" his cronies, bringing him with them amid general acclaim, come tramping back to the bar to quench their thirst, and Miss Douce is getting ready to wait on them.

Meanwhile the other barmaid, Miss Kennedy, has been serving two unnamed gentlemen who are drinking "tankards of cool stout" (11.542/ 270.19–20); they are referred to, throughout the scene, in such phrases as, "first gent with tank" or "second gentleman," one of them even ending up by being identified as "tankard one" or simply "tankard." Over the din caused by the men crowding around the bar to order their drinks, this gentleman apparently begs Miss Kennedy to tell him who the singer was. With an admirable economy of narrative technique this whispered conversation is presented as follows:

> Miss Mina Kennedy brought near her lips to ear of tankard one.
> —Mr Dollard, they murmured low.
> —Dollard, murmured tankard.
> Tank one believed: Miss Kenn when she: that doll he was: she doll: the tank.
> He murmured that he knew the name. The name was familiar to him,

that is to say. That was to say he had heard the name of. Dollard, was it?
Dollard, yes.

Yes, her lips said more loudly, Mr Dollard. He sang that song lovely,
murmured Mina. Mr Dollard. And *The Last Rose of Summer* was a
lovely song. Mina loved that song. Tankard loved the song that Mina.
(11.1167–77/287.36–288.07)

This passage contains some subtle difficulties, one of them being what to
do with "The Last Rose of Summer," Thomas Moore's song sung by
Lady Harriet in the opera *Martha* when asked by Lionel to sing something that comes straight from the heart. It is a debatable point whether
such titles should be translated at all; here, moreover, not only the title
but also some words of the song itself will be heard echoing in later passages.
Its opening lines are: " 'Tis the last rose of summer / *Left blooming
alone*" (italics mine), and when Bloom is presented next as having left the
bar and being troubled by flatulence there is a faint echo of part of these
words: " 'Tis the last rose of summer dollard *left bloom* felt wind wound
round inside" (11.1178–79/288.08–9, italics mine). There will be a final
echo, completing the "quotation," as it were, in the passage where Mr.
Dedalus is seen standing at the counter, "staring hard at a headless
sardine": "Under the sandwichbell lay on a bier of bread one last, one
lonely, *last sardine of summer, Bloom alone*" (11.1220–21/289.12–13,
italics mine). I shall not go into the details of the various translations, but
it is evident that it would require quite some research and ingenuity on
the translator's part if he wanted to render such subtleties in an attempt
to be loyal to the author's intentions.

From the critic's point of view there is another use translations may be
put to, a secondary one. When in doubt about the meaning of some
passage in the original and not being satisfied with what commentaries
and annotations have to offer in the way of elucidation, the critic may
turn to a translation for a second opinion. As Adams observes, "Joyce
was such a remarkable linguist in his own right, and worked so closely
with the French and German translators of *Ulysses* (especially those
turning it into French) that these versions often give us special light into
the original" (1973:136). Naturally, this should not be taken to mean
that the translators in question came to Joyce to have him approve every
turn of phrase they produced. Most probably, they sent him lists of
specific knotty points, but in the end they were responsible themselves
for what they put on paper.

Although the house at 7 Eccles Street, where the Blooms lived, no
longer exists, and many other landmarks have also disappeared, it still is a
great experience to walk the streets of Dublin following in Bloom's steps.
Failing this, the reader of *Ulysses* might do well, as a substitute, to study

illustrated works that show characteristic sights of Dublin as it was or as it is now; topical details, which *Ulysses* is full of, will then cease to be mere names. Apart from general tourist guides there are even collections of photographs especially attuned to Joyce's world, such as Hutchins's *James Joyce's Dublin* (1950) or Tindall's documentary *The Joyce Country* (1976), and Quinn's *James Joyce's Dublin* (1974), personal impressions, accompanied by passages from *Dubliners, A Portrait, Ulysses,* and *Finnegans Wake.* Some illustrated guide books of more recent years are Delaney's *James Joyce's Odyssey* (1981) and the topographic guide by Bidwell and Heffer, *The Joycean Way* (1981).

No less important than the sights of Joyce's world are its sounds. For the texts of the innumerable songs mentioned in *Ulysses* one might consult Hodgart and Worthington (1959) or later reference works such as Thornton (1968) and Gifford (1974). As to their accompanying sounds, their music, whether of popular songs, ballads, or operatic airs, records could be the answer. They may not be absolutely essential but they are invaluable to the reader who can appreciate a dash of local color. For a few years we have had an annotated collection of two hundred songs—words and music—alluded to in Joyce's work from the early poems through *Finnegans Wake* (Bauerle, 1982).

A different matter altogether is the question whether recordings of the text itself can contribute to any better understanding of the book. Many a reader will feel they can, especially where the *Wake* text is concerned. It is a unique experience, deeply moving, to hear Joyce himself reading "Anna Livia Plurabelle," and when a skilled actor or actress reads this or some other fragment from the *Wake,* the listener's grasp of the meaning of the text will certainly be reinforced. However (in this respect recordings resemble translations), it can take away the thrill of discovering the meaning for oneself, the kind of puzzling that forms part of the reader's literary enjoyment in this case. Still, it would have been interesting if we had had authentic recordings of fragments from *Ulysses* as well. We might then have known perhaps how to pronounce "swurls" in such a way as to make it sound differently from "swirls," the word that Bloom, thinking about Boylan's song of the "lovely seaside girls" (4.443/67.12) substitutes for the original "whirls" (Bowen, 1975:90). From Bloom's comment on the way Boylan sings this song, in particular the line "Your head it simply swirls," we learn that for Bloom anyway there is an audible difference: "*Swurls,* he says" (4.440/67.10). Similarly, we would have liked to hear Joyce reading the prelude to "Sirens," but on the whole we cannot maintain that recordings, of one kind or another, are really indispensable as part of the beginner's equipment.

There was a time when practically the only tool for beginners to fall back upon—apart, of course, from general reference works—was Gilbert's pioneering study of *Ulysses* (1930). Since then, the available equipment in the way of analytic studies and works of annotation has become more varied and more, let us say, sophisticated, but for the beginner who is looking for some sensible information about the Homeric framework and who wants to get an overall view of what *Ulysses* is all about, Gilbert still remains a reliable mentor. Nowadays, the problem is not so much the scarcity as rather the wealth and diversity of the critical apparatus which face the beginner. It is hard to decide what the latter needs most, but one thing at least is clear: he should start by studying the text itself, using handbooks as sparingly as possible for the time being.

As said before, one should not expect these various studies of *Ulysses* to fall more or less automatically into a number of categories with clear-cut boundary lines; there will always be a certain amount of overlapping. Still, a few main types might be distinguished.

First is the annotation, which—in theory at least—would offer line-by-line notes from the first to the last page of *Ulysses*. For readers who feel they cannot afford to miss anything, this might be the ideal tool. In practice, we have Thornton (1968) and Gifford (1974), works that are designed to save a lot of time and will certainly do so.

Second is the page-by-page summary or commentary, of which Blamires (1966) is a typical example. It is probably meant to be studied *before* the student starts reading *Ulysses* in earnest, the effect being somewhat that of studying a railway timetable as compared to making the actual train journey. Still, if you like that sort of thing, it may be useful, provided the author does not indulge in interpreting the text at the expense of summarizing it.

Third is the critical study; a number of such studies have already been referred to, others will be met with in subsequent chapters. Some attempt to present a comprehensive view of *Ulysses* only, such as French (1976), others deal with Joyce's earlier prose works as well, such as Peake (1977), and some try to focus on a specific aspect of Joyce's writings, such as Moseley (1967) or Knuth (1976). The former's study of Joyce and the Bible preaches the gospel according to Saint James, making rather a muddle of it, whereas the latter's study of Joyce's "phatic communication," stressing the significance of his riddling technique, really enters into the spirit of Joyce's work. All these studies, and many more, such as the excellent collection *Critical Essays*, edited by Hart and Hayman (1974), belong to a category that the beginner should avoid. I cannot but agree with Knuth when he states: "In principle *all* critical interpretations are dangerous for the inexperienced reader; ready-made interpretations involve the risk of some kind of brain-washing, in that they may hinder the process of reaching one's own conclusions" (1975:300). To be on the safe side in this respect at least, the beginner would do well to stick to aids that provide purely factual information, such as Thornton's *Allusions* and Gifford's *Notes*. An exception might be made for the intelligent sixty-page section on *Ulysses* in Bolt's general introduction to Joyce (1981). Even in this book there is a curious case of protracted misquotation. In the "Hades" episode, Simon Dedalus, referring to a certain moneylender, Reuben J. Dodd, says: "The devil break the hasp of *your* back!" (6.256/94.06, italics mine). Ellmann once quoted this passage—as an example of "the blurred margin"—in a slightly altered form: "The devil break the hasp of *his* back" (1959:377, corrected in the revised edition, 1982:366, italics mine), and finally Bolt quotes Ellmann on this phenomenon of the blurred margin as saying, "For example, on the way to the funeral, the mourners catch sight of Reuben J. Dodd and Mr Dedalus says, 'The devil break the hasp of *his neck*'" (1981:149, italics mine).

Dependent on the reader's mood such odd little errors may be either amusing or irritating. Some are what you might call compulsive errors, as when Adams, speaking about Haines (in "Telemachus"), observes, "The green stone in his cigarette lighter is Ireland, a casual adornment" (1962:30). Well, no, the green stone is not to be found in Haines's lighter, a "nickel tinderbox" (1.619/20.06), but in his cigarette case; the text is perfectly clear on this point (1.615–16/19.38–20.03). Or take French's remark that "in all areas of life, Stephen suffers from what Mulligan mockingly calls 'g.p.i,' general paralysis of the insane, a consequence of venereal infection" (1976:67). Actually, it is not Mulligan himself who diagnoses Stephen's case in these terms, he only reports what someone else had said: "That fellow I was with in the Ship last night, said Buck Mulligan, says you have g.p.i. He's up in Dottyville with Connolly Norman. General paralysis of the insane!" (1.127–29/6.19–21).

In such a staggering mass of notes as compiled by Thornton and Gifford something simply must go wrong from time to time. In the third episode of *Ulysses*, Stephen, strolling along the beach, recalls an Irishman he used to meet in Paris, Kevin Egan, a friend of his father's, who was fond of reminiscing about the Irish movement: "Noon slumbers. Kevin Egan rolls gunpowder cigarettes through fingers smeared with printer's ink, sipping his green fairy as Patrice his white" (3.216–18/42.36–38). Gifford notes that "'green fairy's Fang' is slang for absinthe. . . . 'White' is not clear in the context" (1974:39). Not clear? The reader has only to go back a page or so to find Stephen recalling another scene, an encounter with Kevin's son, Patrice, whose mother is French and who serves in the army: "Patrice, home on furlough, lapped warm milk with me in the bar MacMahon. Son of the wild goose, Kevin Egan of Paris" (3.163–64/41.16–18). This explains why Stephen, sitting with Egan and observing him sipping his *green* absinthe, is reminded of that other scene when he sat at a café table facing Patrice, watching him sip his milk, his *white* fairy.

The former passage ("Noon slumbers . . . ") has another aspect, which is much more interesting. The phrase "gunpowder cigarettes" primarily refers to the black, powdery tobacco Egan uses to roll his cigarettes. On another level, though, it alludes to an episode in the history of Irish rebellions in which an attempt was made to help some Irish leaders to escape from a London prison, a story told by Ellmann in his biography of Joyce (1982:125). Kevin Egan is said to have been modeled on one of the organizers, Joseph Casey, a typesetter who lived in Paris and had a French wife, a son called Patrice, and a taste for absinthe. The point of the story is that a keg of gunpowder was used to blow up part of the prison wall. Now Thornton states in the introduction to his *Allusions* that he only intends to list "words and phrases that are allusions in the sense that they necessarily bring some *context* with them." By his own standards, therefore, one would have expected him to include the "gunpowder cigarettes" phrase, but he does not. Gifford does include the phrase in his notes as part of the information summarized above (1974:37).

Because Thornton is a bit vague as to what should be termed an allusion, his list includes items that are no more than annotations and have had to be duplicated, therefore, in Gifford's *Notes*. A case in point is a passage in "Nausicaa" where we find Bloom sitting on the beach at Sandymount, watching some girls minding their little charges while sounds of an evening service in a nearby church are heard from time to time. The churchgoers, we are told, are kneeling before the Holy Virgin, "reciting the litany of Our Lady of Loreto" (13.287–88/354.08).

Both Thornton (1968:309) and Gifford (1974:318–19), the latter with a wealth of detail, explain that such a benediction service always comprises a litany of Our Lady or a hymn in honor of the Virgin Mary, and that this litany is *often* that of Our Lady of Loreto. This is all right as factual information, but neither Thornton nor Gifford spotted the allusion involved. Joyce might have chosen any other litany or hymn as long as it was devoted to Mary. Just why Our Lady of *Loreto*? This question will not be answered till we come to the scene where the three girls are leaving the beach—Cissy and Edy taking the little twins and the baby, Gerty MacDowell lingering behind in a last silent communion with Bloom. When she, too, gets up and walks away, Bloom suddenly realizes that the poor girl is lame (13.771/367.41). In order to understand the allusion contained in this passage one should have visited Loreto, a small Italian town near the Adriatic, where pilgrims flock to the cathedral to offer up their prayers of supplication to the Virgin Mary and where the streets are crowded with people in wheelchairs, pushed along by nurses and boy scouts. For, and this is the point, Our Lady of Loreto is a patron

saint of the lame and the crippled. It is hard to believe that this juxta-
position of her litany and lame Gerty's limping away could be a mere
coincidence.

As we have seen, Thornton has some trouble in defining his concept of
"allusion." A similar difficulty crops up when Gifford starts using the
notion of "pun." According to *Webster's* a *pun* is "the humorous use of a
word in such a way as to suggest different meanings or applications or of
words having the same or nearly the same sound but different meanings." The phrase "Boylan with impatience," which will be discussed
later, is a striking example of a pun in the narrow sense of the word. In a
wider sense, pun might perhaps be equated with (verbal) fun. The names,
for instance, of the members of "the picturesque foreign delegation
known as the Friends of the Emerald Isle," which are listed in the
"Cyclops" episode (12.554ff./307.17ff), are, shall we say, funny insofar
as they make use of certain characteristics of the languages concerned,
but considering them puns might be stretching the definition too far.
There is a Russian called the Grandjoker (Grandduke) Vladinmire (Vla-
dimir; vlad in mire: ruler in the mud?) Pokethankertscheff (pocket
handkerchief), a Dane called Olaf Kobberkeddelsen (Olaf Copperkettle-
son), and the like. I think the function of this list of names, in an episode
that ridicules short-sighted nationalism, is to poke fun at the various
national representatives by overtly exaggerating the characteristic linguistic features of their names and titles. Some of Gifford's notes on
these names are clearly beside the point. On the Austrian delegate, the
Archjoker (Archduke—alluding to German *Junker* as well?) Leopold
Rudolph von Schwanzenbad-Hodenthaler (12.559–60/307.24–25), he
has the following annotation: "German: 'Idle-about-bath-Inhabitant-
of-the-valley-of-testicles.' " As to the latter half of the name, Gifford is
right, but he missed the joke, surprisingly, in the former part, "Schwan-
zenbad." He must have thought of the German verb *schwänzen* (to idle,
to loiter) as in the expression, *die Schule schwänzen* (to be absent from
school without leave, to play truant). Actually, there is an allusion here
to German *Schwanz* (tail), a slang phrase for *penis*, which yields a fitting
counterpart to the "Hodenthaler" half of the Archduke's name. Note the
Christian names: Bloom's (Leopold) and his father's (Rudolph), respectively.

In "Paysayenn" (3.176/41.30) Gifford sees "a pun that combines the
letters 'P.C.N.' with *paysanne*, 'peasant' " (1974:37). This refers to the
following scene: Stephen is walking along the beach, carrying on an
imaginary conversation about his days in Paris: "My Latin quarter
hat. . . . You were a student, weren't you? Of what in the other devil's
name? Paysayenn. P. C. N., you know: *physiques, chimiques et natur-
elles*. Aha" (3.174–77/41.28–31). In order to bring in some *couleur*

locale, Stephen may have pronounced the letters "P. C. N." first the French way, and Joyce may have presented this in a kind of phonetic transcription so as to make sure the reader would understand the pronunciation to be "pay-say-en" and not "pee-see-en" as in English. Alternatively, this "paysayenn" might represent the Irish pronunciation, a sample of which is found in the "Aeolus" episode, where—as explained by Gifford (1974:112)—a certain T. P. O'Connor is referred to as "Tay Pay" (7.687/137.27). In both cases Stephen may have added "P. C. N." for good measure or as an afterthought, this time pronouncing the letters the English way. As I see it, there is no link at all with French "paysanne" here, neither as to sound nor as to meaning.

If there is one thing translators of *Ulysses* cannot avoid doing, it is creating the paradox of Dublin citizens carrying on conversations in idiomatically correct French, German, Italian, or any language other than English, a paradox inherent in any translation of literary texts. As soon, however, as the characters in the original novel start speaking (or quoting) a few lines in French or German, the translator is spared this difficulty. At the same time he may be faced by another paradox, depending on the language he is translating into. What I mean is this: within an English text a passage in French will stand out as a kind of quotation, sometimes lending local color to a scene described by the narrator or evoked in a character's interior monologue. When the English text is translated, say, into Dutch or German, the French passage need not be tampered with, for it will stand out against the non-French background, but what will happen when the same text is translated into French? Obviously, the figure-and-ground relationship of the original will break down, and the French phrase will fade into its equally French background, resulting, inevitably, in a certain loss of function. This may be illustrated by the passage from "Proteus" we have already referred to: Stephen recalls a talk he had in Paris with Patrice, Kevin Egan's French son. Because exiled Irish rebels such as Kevin Egan were nicknamed "wild geese," Stephen is reminded of a phrase from the "Ballad of Joking Jesus," a blasphemous song chanted by Mulligan that morning (1.584ff./9.03ff.). Within the framework of Stephen's interior monologue this phrase ("My father's a bird") is a direct quotation. Translators should take care, therefore, to use the identical wording in both cases. To judge from their translations, Morel and Wollschläger realized this. They have "Un oiseau mon papa" (22 *and* 43) and "Mein Paps ist ein Vogel" (28 *and* 59), respectively. Vandenbergh, on the other hand, failed to see or anyway to acknowledge the connection. In the scene where Mulligan chants the ballad, he has: "Mijn vader een vogel" (25), but in Stephen's interior monologue he translates: "Mijn vader is een vogel" (51). Another association Stephen has links Patrice's "bunny's face" and his way of *lapping* his milk with the French word for bunny or rabbit, *lapin*:

> Patrice, home on furlough, lapped warm milk with me in the bar MacMahon. Son of the wild goose, Kevin Egan of Paris. My father's a bird, he lapped the sweet *lait chaud* with pink young tongue, plump bunny's face. Lap, *lapin*. He hopes to win in the *gros lots*. About the nature of women he read in Michelet. But he must send me *La Vie de Jésus* by M. Léo Taxil. Lent it to his friend.
> —*C'est tordant, vous savez. Moi, je suis socialiste. Je ne crois pas en l'existence de Dieu. Faut pas le dire à mon père.*
> —*Il croit?*
> —*Mon père, oui.*
> *Schluss.* He laps.

> (3.163–73/41.16–27)

The Dutch, Spanish, and Catalan translations leave all the foreign phrases in this passage intact (in the Spanish translation the sentence "He hopes to win in the *gros lots*" has been omitted). The French translation only retains the German word at the end ("Schluss"), whereas in the modern German translation this "Schluss" is the only foreign phrase that had to be sacrificed as such. That is to say, it is still there on the printed page, but it has lost its foreign character (there was no need to italicize it any more), because in a German translation Stephen's interior monologue must seem to be carried on in German anyway.

As we have seen, a translator need not bother overmuch about the foreign phrases in *Ulysses*. We might even go so far as to claim a translator's right to ignore the meaning of such phrases. Take, for instance, section VI of "Wandering Rocks" (10.338–66/228–29). Here a dialogue is carried on in Italian between Stephen Dedalus and his music teacher, Almidano Artifoni, a character modeled upon a Jesuit, Father Charles Ghezzi, a native speaker, who taught Joyce Italian at University College, Dublin (Ellmann, 1982:59–60). In a passage such as the following there is only one word ("said") translators have to deal with; the rest is theirs for the copying: "*Anch'io ho avuto di queste idee*, Almidano Artifoni said, *quand'ero giovine come Lei. Eppoi mi sono convinto che il mondo è una bestia. È peccato. Perchè la sua voce . . . sarebbe un cespite di rendita, via. Invece, Lei si sacrifica*" (10.344–47/228.21–24). An annotator is, however, in a different position. Because there is no apparent allusion involved, Thornton has a right to skip these foreign phrases, but Gifford, in his attempt to give as much useful information as possible, may be expected to supply an adequate translation for the benefit of readers lacking sufficient knowledge of Italian. Gifford offers translations of all the Italian phrases in this episode, but whether they are adequate remains to be seen. This is how he renders the passage quoted above: "I too had the same idea when I was young as you are. *At that time I was convinced that the world is a beast* (i.e., a pigsty). It's too bad. Because your voice . . . would be a source of income, come now. But instead, you are sacrificing yourself" (1974:217, italics mine). To start with a minor objection, "the same idea" is much too precise. What Artifoni says is rather vague, something like "Me too, I have had such ideas." What those ideas were is not quite clear, but it is evident that this statement implies some contrast to what follows ("Eppoi mi sono convinto"), and that is just where Gifford's translation appears to be based on a faulty interpretation of the passage as a whole. When Artifoni was young, as Stephen is now, he may have had such lofty ideas as Stephen has now, perhaps of becoming a great artist, of offering mankind something radically new in the fields of music or literature. He was then, as Stephen is now in his, Artifoni's, eyes, still naïve, unspoilt, fostering the belief that the world might be waiting for whatever he had to offer. Later on, however ("Eppoi"), he became convinced or began to realize ("mi sono convinto," *not*: "ero convinto") that the world simply did not care and is, after all, not worthy of such youthful idealism. Stephen, he suggests, should give up his futile efforts at writing poetry, for they will never enable him to make a living. Instead, he should devote his time to developing his voice, not for art's sake, but as a sure way of making money as a professional singer. Gifford's translation mirrors the way Sultan views this episode: Artifoni, he contends, "in a combination of Continental politeness and affectionate solicitude, informs Stephen that he too once regarded the world as *una bestia*" (1964:216). I am not convinced that their interpretation makes sense.

I also do not believe that Henke, who pretends to be able to explain the events of Bloomsday by referring to Heidegger's philosophy, has an inkling of what Artifoni is hinting at when she says: "Artifoni was right: if Stephen perceives the world as *una bestia,* he only sacrifices himself" (1978:120). As said before, Artifoni rather *wants* Stephen to see the world for what it is, *una bestia*: by not cultivating his voice, which might become a splendid source of income, he sacrifices himself (Bloom, in the "Sirens" episode, has similar thoughts about Stephen's father, Simon Dedalus). Stephen, however, makes light of this "sacrifice," as shown by his reply, *"Sacrifizio incruento."* As Knuth remarks in his review of Gifford's *Notes,* the latter's translation of this phrase as "cold-blooded sacrifice" (1974:217) "entirely misses the point, which is an allusion to the bloodless sacrifice of the Mass" (1975:301). What Stephen means to say, of course, is that his, in the literal sense, is at least a nonbloody sacrifice.

Toward the end of the conversation it becomes clear that Artifoni is waiting for a tram. When he sees the one he wants to catch approaching he takes leave of Stephen, urging him to come and see him some time and to think about the matter seriously: "His heavy hand took Stephen's firmly. Human eyes. They gazed curiously an instant and turned quickly towards a Dalkey tram.—*Eccolo*, Almidano Artifoni said in friendly haste. *Venga a trovarmi e ci pensi. Addio, caro*" (10.356–59/228.34–38). In Gifford's annotation "Eccolo" is translated as "This is it," a phrase that, with its note of finality, is quite inappropriate here. Artifoni, seeing his tram nearing the stop (*il tram* in Italian, hence the masculine pronoun *lo*), simply means to say, "There she is" or "Here she comes now," a statement of fact, but at the same time intended as an apology for his hasty way of taking leave.

Among the various annotations that struck me as wrong or beside the point, there were some that aroused my curiosity. I could not help wondering in such cases whether there might not be some simple explanation why these errors could have been committed in the first place.

One such a case where I think I have detected the source of the error has no direct bearing on *Ulysses*, but it is so typical of the sloppy methods sometimes used in compiling notes on Joyce's works that I feel justified in giving it a place in this introduction.

In his guide to *Finnegans Wake*, Tindall comments on lines 79.25–26 in the following words: "Such progressions of four elements, common in the *Wake*, stand for Vico's process. Cf. 'Artha . . . moksa' (93.22), probably Sanskrit: *Kama* means sip or suck; *dharma* is legal, dutiful, virtuous; *moksha* is liberation or escape. *Artha* eluded me. Ever try using a Sanskrit dictionary?" (1969:95). It is hard to see in what way any reader may hope to profit from inconclusive information such as this. Even if the separate meanings offered by Tindall were correct—which they are not—the whole would not make sense at all, as anybody can see. For one thing, it must be realized that all four Sanskrit words are nouns. In the religious system of Hinduism they represent the four aims of human life, namely, the useful: the practical life of man, success in worldly affairs *(artha)*; the pleasant: love, pleasure, lust *(kāma)*; the good: the code of right conduct, duty *(dharma)*; final liberation in a religious sense *(moksha)*. These four ends of life may be summed up as the fourfold path *(catur-varga)*. Attaining *moksha* requires a rather ascetic way of life, so whoever does not feel up to it may just stick to the first triad of duties, *artha, kāma, dharma*, thus following *tri-varga*, the threefold path. As to the "elusive" *artha*, if Tindall had used the well-known Monier-Williams Sanskrit dictionary, he would have found the relevant entry. A simpler way would have been to look up the formula in Campbell and Robinson (1947:79n.4), where all the necessary information is provided.

The trouble with Sanskrit—a drawback it shares with such tongues as Russian and Hebrew—is that for practical purposes you need a method of transliteration. In the passage under discussion the current editions of *Finnegans Wake* have *kama* and *moksa*. According to the now-prevailing system as recommended by the Geneva Transliteration Committee, these words should be spelled *kāma* and *mokṣa*. Lacking an *ṣ*, compositors may resort to the combination *sh*, thus spelling *moksha*. Tindall's statement that *kama* means *sip* or *suck* baffled me at first until I realized that he may very well have consulted another reference work, Macdonell's Sanskrit dictionary, which uses the rival system of transliteration adopted by the editors of the series *Sacred Books of the East*. In the case of *artha* this would not have made any difference, but a striking feature of Macdonell's system—a most unfortunate one at that—is the use of italic *k* to represent the palatal sound [*ch*], as in "church" (it is rendered as *c* in the Geneva system adopted by Monier-Williams). It is this feature, I think, that must have caused the misunderstanding in the case of *kama*. Thus, the Sanskrit root CAM (to sip) appears in Macdonell's dictionary as KAM, only the initial letter being italicized, whereas in order to look up *kāma* (in his system *kâma*), with the [*k*] of "king," you have to turn to another page. But, and here is the rub, KAM is followed by: "I. P. kama, sip." This means that the verb in question belongs to the first thematic class (I), is only recorded in the active (*P* standing for *Parasmaipadam*, the Sanskrit term for active voice), and has kama- (or, as we would spell now, cama-) as its present-tense stem, conveying, in short, the information that (he) "sips" would be "camati" or, in Macdonell's spelling, "kamati." It is this visually highly misleading juggling with only partly italicized words, I suspect, by which Tindall—or someone he consulted—may have been deceived.

While we are on the subject let me add a few words about another passage in *Finnegans Wake* where Joyce has made use of Sanskrit. The text reads *Tasyam kuru salilakriyamu* (601.03). As Tindall reports, he had at first spotted two words he thought to be Japanese, *kuru* and *yamu*. He was told, however, that the sentence was not Japanese but Telugu, one of the languages of India. The meaning would be: "You should deal fairly with her or do her justice—advice to HCE on dealing with ALP," and Tindall goes on to explain: "*Tasyam* is by or to her; *kuru* is do; *salila* is good; *kriyamu* is act" (1969:330). I would not know about Telugu, but if we take the sentence to be Sanskrit it can be shown to make sense. Adding diacritical signs as in the passage discussed above, we get: *Tasyām kuru salilakriyām u*, in which *kuru* is the predicate, imperative singular, from the root KR (to do, to make). Derived from this same root is *kriyā* (accusative singular *kriyām*), a feminine noun, meaning act or action. *Salila* means water, and the compound *salilakriyā* (synonym of the more frequent term *salilakarman*) means "water-rite," that is, a libation of water offered to a deceased person ("Totenspende"). *Tasyām* is the locative case of the feminine personal pronoun, third-person singular. As to final *u*, in Vedic hymns *u* occurs as an enclitic particle, but the words, as Misra (1964:10) points out, were taken from an epic work, the *Rāmāyana*, so he is certainly right in assuming that *kriyamu* is just a misreading for *kriyam*. Even so I found it impossible to fit the line into the common epic meter, whose lines consist of two groups of eight syllables each. Some research brought to light that it was taken from book one of the epic. The complete line reads: "tasyām kuru mahāvāho / pitṛnām salilakriyām" (I.40.19), which means: "Perform therein, o great hero, the last rites of the ancestors" (brotherly advice to Rāma). "Therein" ("in her") refers to the river Mandākinī ("gently flowing"), one of the many names of the sacred river Ganges, feminine in Sanskrit. All this seems to relate to the preceding "offrand to the ewon of her owen" (*FW* 601.02), *owen* being Anglo-Irish for "river," as McHugh explains (1980:601). It is a pity he leaves out the Sanskrit phrase altogether in his *Annotations*. As far as I know nobody has ever corrected the tentative translation offered by Tindall; it even lives on in a modern French translation of the *Wake*. Fragments had been translated into French before; they were published under the mystifying title *Dans le sillage de Finnegan* (Paris, 1950) and later as *Fragments adaptés* (Paris, 1962). French *sillage* denotes the strip of smooth water left behind a moving ship, a vessel's *wake* in short. Did the translator, André Du Bouchet, really think *Finnegan* was a ship? Anyway, now an integral version of the *Wake* in French has been published, translated—if you can call it that—by Philippe Lavergne, who omitted the whole phrase and substituted Tindall's version mentioned above ("You should . . . do her justice"): "Tu devrais lui rendre justice!" (622.33).

In the case of "Artha kama dharma moksa," however, Tindall could not help him, as we have seen above, so he just skipped this phrase without offering any explanation, turning "And so it all ended. Artha kama dharma moksa. Ask Kavya for the kay" (*FW* 93.22) into "Et c'est comme ça que tout fut fini. Demande la clef du problème à Kay" (102.30). In the process, he managed to suppress another Sanskrit term, *kāvya*, which, incidentally, means *poetry* and not (as McHugh has it) *poet*.

In *Ulysses* the Sanskrit terms present no difficulties. In "Circe" we find *yoni* (15.2550/519.29), *lingam* (15.2550/519.30), and *yadgana*

(15.2555/520.03), the meanings of which are self-evident in the context, and in "Cyclops" (12.354/301.32) there is some mock Sanskrit: tālāfānā (telephone), ālāvātār (elevator), hātākāldā (hot and cold) and wātāklāsāt (water closet).

The Hebrew quotations in *Ulysses* are not as simple; a few instances will be discussed here. In "Ithaca" Bloom quotes from the *Song of Songs:* "*kifeloch, harimon rakatejch m'baad l'zamatejch* (thy temple amid thy hair is as a slice of pomegranate)" (17.729–30/688.06), which may be read as follows: ke'félakh (as a slice) ha-rimón (of the pomegranate) raka-t-ékh (is your temple) mi'bá'ad (in the midst) l'zama-t-ékh (of your hair). Obviously, there should not be a comma after *kifeloch*; in this respect the ORH edition happens to have the right version.

In the same episode Bloom chants the opening lines of the Zionist anthem: "*Kolod balejwaw pnimah / Nefesch, jehudi, homijah*" (17.763–64/689.05–6). Note that the commas, as Prescott already pointed out (1952a:160), should be expunged, properly speaking. The transliterated text fails, naturally, to convey an adequate idea of the meter (*pnimah*, for instance, is to be sung as a three-syllable word, of which the first two syllables have to be slurred as well). Stress, as marked here, has been adapted to the melody, which is "European" in origin, so it sometimes runs counter to the usual Hebrew pronunciation: *Kól'od* (as long as) *ba-léwaw* (in the heart) *pé-nimáh* (deep within) / *Néfesh jehúdi* (the soul of the Jew) *hómiyáh* (keeps pulsating). . . .

Quoting should be done with meticulous care—at the risk of over-doing it, as when Hayman, speaking of a statement made by Stephen to Mr. Deasy, quotes Stephen's words as "History . . . is a nightmare from which I am trying to awake" (1982:25). Presumably, the three ellipses are there to signal that a few words have been omitted, but in this case the ellipses are superfluous because the words in question ("Stephen said") do not belong to the statement proper. When quoting what Stephen *does* say, there is no need to include words not spoken by him. These words are part of the text, part of the narrative, but do not exist on the level of the character's utterance.

Still, this is a technicality, and greatly to be preferred to sloppy quoting, if that is the alternative. To give an example of the latter variety: Stephen's remark about history is also quoted by Blamires in his summary of *Ulysses*, but it is transcribed as "History is the nightmare from which I am trying to escape" (1966:12), which contains two deviations from the text and produces a clumsy metaphor into the bargain.

The more abstruse a critic's interpretation of the text is, the more cautious the reader should be of acknowledging the validity of quotations offered in support of such views. It is an irritating and frustrating experience to discover that passages cited in evidence prove to be, on closer inspection, completely irrelevant to the point the critic is trying to make.

There is another aspect to quoting that should not be overlooked. What I mean is not the quoting from Joyce's text, but what one might call cross-quoting, which goes on inevitably, it seems, among many critics. In writing about *Ulysses* these critics have namely developed a vocabulary of their own, abounding in stock phrases that tend to recur in most critical writings as faithfully as the recurrent elements in *Ulysses* itself. As Bernard Benstock remarks in his essay on the first episode: "That Stephen-Telemachus is in search of a father has become a critical commonplace. Yet there is little evidence in the first chapter of any such quest" (1974:12). Incidentally, now the inverse, "Stephen is *not* in search of a father," threatens to become a critical commonplace. Anyway, such stock phrases can hardly be avoided; it would put a terrible constraint upon critics were they to try to do so. However, it would be boring, to writers and readers alike, were critics to try and acknowledge every single phrase or every single view they share with others. Sometimes, quotation marks are a necessary evil, but even then when you use them you have to be careful. To give an example: in quoting Benstock just now I cited his words in full, giving both sentences as they appear in the original, the source, and adding particulars as to the place where the statement is to be found. For my purpose, however, I might just as well have said: As Benstock once remarked, it has become a critical commonplace that Stephen is in search of a father, although there is little evidence of any such quest in "Telemachus." I might even go beyond that: because I held this view before I ever set eyes on Benstock's essay, I might not feel obliged at all to refer to him—or to any other exponents of the same view—when using an expression that in itself has already attained the status of a commonplace. Each new book on *Ulysses* inevitably carries with it a whole load of hidden quotations, the author silently having asked for a loan of other critics' "noserags" to wipe his razor.

What I hinted at when stressing the need to be careful—and accurate—when using quotations may be illustrated by two examples from Gordon (1981a): the first concerns a quote from *Ulysses*, the second is an instance of cross-quoting.

In his discussion of the "Telemachus" episode Gordon depicts Haines "looming obscurely as a 'dark figure' (*U* 11) before accruing his Hainesness" (1981a:49). The single quote marks around 'dark figure' and the following reference to *U* 11 suggest that this phrase is to be found, literally, in *Ulysses* on a specific page. Actually, however, there is no such phrase on that page. What Gordon refers to, apparently, is the "tall figure" in the following passage: "A tall figure rose from the hammock where it had been sitting, went to the doorway and pulled open the inner doors" (1.319–21/11.32–34). Of course, we might pass this over as an irrelevant slip of the pen, but this "dark figure" plays a role in Gordon's argument, so we had better check and see if it has a basis in the text.

Up to this passage Haines has not been visible; we have only heard Buck Mulligan and Stephen Dedalus talking about him and once we have heard a voice from within the tower calling, "Are you up there, Mulligan?" (1.228/9.10), and we have surmised that this voice must be Haines's. Note, by the way, that Haines does not mention Stephen—it is Mulligan who is his host. Then, the two young men having gone downstairs into the living room, we hear Mulligan addressing Haines directly, asking him to open the door (1.318/11.30–31), and while Stephen puts Mulligan's shaving bowl on the locker a tall figure rises from a hammock and goes to the door. This is just Joyce's narrative technique of presenting things the way they tend to happen: we hear someone shouting, "Haines, open that door!" and then a tall figure gets up and goes to the doorway; a voice is heard asking for the key. We conclude from all this that the tall figure must be Haines and that the voice asking for the key must be his. Technically speaking, the whole scene is pure cinema. The fact, moreover, that Haines's name is suppressed after Stephen has entered the scene stresses the latter's state of aloofness: He is present, he is there in the room with the others, he cannot help seeing a tall figure rising from a hammock or help hearing a voice—just *a* voice—but he is not interested. Only when Mulligan shakes him out of his brooding thoughts does he come forward to assist Haines. So far there has not been any mention of a *dark* figure at all. Try as we may, it is hard to visualize Haines in his loose-collared, presumably white, tennis shirt (1.479/16.04) as such a dark figure—"looming obscurely"—as Gordon makes him out to be.

In the second instance matters are slightly more complicated. In his discussion Gordon further points out that whereas the opening episode of *Ulysses* is Stephen's the style is Mulligan's, and he then makes the following observation: "The result is 'mercurial' writing never hampered by the various hypotactic devices that enable a narrator to comment on the impact of his own narration, free of the 'varieties of embedded sentence so dear to the heart of the modern grammarian'" (1981a:48). In this passage—one sentence, actually—there are two sets of quotation marks, the first marking a single word, the second setting off a lengthy nominal phrase. The latter quotation carries a note directing the reader to the source if he is at all interested, but in the case of "mercurial" the reader cannot be sure: is this to be taken as a quote or as a signal that the author wants the word to be understood in some figurative or generally idiosyncratic meaning? In *Ulysses* the epithet is applied to Mulligan, whose Christian name, as he tells us himself (1.41/4.04) is Malachi; "Mercurial Malachi" he is called in a later passage (1.518/17.06). Annotators such as Gifford (1974:13), assuming, apparently, that "mercurial" must be derived directly from Mercury, hasten to explain that Mercury is the messenger of the gods in Roman mythology, but that is beside the point in this context, even if Malachi does mean *my messenger* in Hebrew. Mulligan is called mercurial because he is of the nature of mercury, or quicksilver, an element that is volatile, glittering, but also slippery, constantly changing its shape. Mulligan as the mythological messenger does not come in till later, with "the brims of his Panama hat quivering" (1.582/19.01), and again, when he is seen "fluttering his winglike hands, leaping nimbly, Mercury's hat quivering in the fresh wind" (1.600–602/19.21–22). But he is a messenger without a message; it is only his outward appearance that reminds Stephen of the wing-footed god.

The other quotation in the above passage from Gordon at least does not leave readers guessing, as it has this note attached by which we are referred, via the notes (181ff.), to the bibliography (195ff.). There we find that the cited phrase stems from an article on narrative technique in *Ulysses* by Levenston and when we follow this up by turning to the page referred to in the note, we discover something else: the entire adjunct from "never hampered" to the comma after "narration" is a literal quotation from Levenston, just like the nominal phrase beginning with "varieties," without, however, being acknowledged as such. I suppose that is what comes of having to wade through pages and pages of critical literature. In the numberless notes a critic makes, a single quotation mark may easily come unstuck. McHugh's phrase "the blurred margin" (1976:137) sounds vaguely familiar; indeed, Ellmann had already used this phrase in his Joyce biography (1959:377; 1982:366) and for all we know he may have coined it.

I am fully aware of the hazards involved in this kind of work, and I am afraid I myself may also be caught in the act of trying to smuggle in more or less well-camouflaged quotes here and there, phrases, mostly, that have stuck in the critic's mind somehow, no longer to be recognized as aliens, as intruders. If that really happens, I can only apologize.

The aim of this introduction has been to convey a general impression of the kind of textual difficulties to be overcome before critics and translators will be in a position to tackle the interpretation and translation of *Ulysses* with any degree of confidence. Claiming both the critic's right to be selective and the general reader's privilege to use his common sense—assuming, moreover, that the reader is at least familiar with a broad outline of the book's contents—I hope to shed some light on a number of passages in the text which, even if they had not been obscure or ambiguous from the outset, might have become so in the hands of commentators and translators. I am not going to explain the text in the sense of adding to the existing analyses or of trying to elucidate any symbolism involved. Instead, I am attempting to point out a number of demonstrably wrong readings in the works of commentators and annotators and offer alternative readings or interpretations in an effort to lead the reader *into* the text of *Ulysses*. In a word, what the reader should expect from this book is not so much exegesis—which often, as McHugh reminds us (1976:137), tends to lead away from the text—but, I hope, eisegesis.

In the process of reading and studying *Ulysses* I have tried to observe and describe my own responses to what others have said about the book; I have consulted handbooks and all kinds of students' or readers' guides and often found them lacking in guidance, apt to confuse the uninitiated reader. So I decided to follow some of the routes mapped out by those guides and to put up warnings of my own at dangerous crossroads; while I was at it I thought I might even try to uproot a misleading signpost or two. It was with this practical purpose in mind that I started writing this book.

It soon became apparent that pointing out what I considered errors of interpretation inevitably led to discussions with critics holding different views from mine—on major or minor points, as the case might be. Presenting and discussing such views may press home the point that in these matters there is not always a clear-cut yes or no, right or wrong. This means, I hope, that the following chapters, although intended, originally, for the inexperienced reader, may prove to appeal to more or less advanced readers as well.

The structure of *Ulysses* is a tripartite one, modeled on Homer's *Odyssey*. Book I (episodes 1–3) introduces Stephen Dedalus and corresponds to "Telemachia," in which young Telemachus sets out in search of his father, Odysseus—or Ulysses, as he is called in Latin. Book II (episodes 4–15, which introduce Leopold Bloom and deal primarily with him) corresponds to the *Odyssey* proper, Odysseus's adventures, and narrates what befalls Bloom in the course of his wanderings through the city of Dublin. Book III (episodes 16–18) represents "Nostos" and relates Bloom's homecoming: accompanied by Stephen Dedalus, Bloom returns to Eccles Street after a long and tiring day. He entertains his guest (who leaves after a while) and goes to sleep beside his wife, whose famous nocturnal soliloquy concludes the book.

I have followed the universally accepted custom of referring to these eighteen episodes of *Ulysses* by the Homeric titles that Joyce gave them in the manuscript (but which he discarded when the book was published) and that did not become widely known until the publication of Gilbert's epoch-making study in 1930.

EPISODE ONE
"Telemachus"

*A*ROUND eight o'clock in the morning of a sunny summer day: Buck Mulligan is going to shave—in the open air, apparently—and Stephen Dedalus (Mulligan calls him Kinch) is coming up the dark winding stairs to the top of a tower. Stephen is twenty-two years old, as the reader will learn later. He has a teaching job in a school. The tower, we shall be informed in the course of the episode, is situated on the east coast of Ireland, overlooking Dublin Bay.

There are lots of other pieces of information we have to pick up while going along with our reading. We gather, for instance, that Buck must be Mulligan's nickname; his Christian name will prove to be Malachi. He is a medical student and his behavior is that of a cynical clown. He is plump, as we are told in the opening sentence; lest we forget we are reminded of his "plump body" on the last page of the episode (1.729/23.09). Moreover, and that is the first word of the opening sentence, he is "stately": "Stately, plump Buck Mulligan came from the stairhead, bearing a bowl of lather on which a mirror and a razor lay crossed." Or, some readers may think, he *is* not a stately fellow, he merely now *walks* in a stately manner.

After all, in ordinary use adjectives ending in *-ly* have no corresponding adverbial form. More than one critic has pointed out that there is a certain irony in that the book's very first word already leaves some doubt as to interpretation. Of course, if you take it to be a predicative attribute or adjunct, which I think it is, the word may be considered a formal adjective. Still, it has a different grammatical status from "plump," and I disagree, therefore, with Ellmann, who says that Mulligan is "heralded by the adjectives 'Stately, plump' " (1972:19). Translators have had to decide whether to use an adjectival or an adverbial form, at least in languages where there is a clear-cut morphological difference. In his Spanish translation, Valverde chose the adjective (*solemne*), whereas Mallafrè, who translated *Ulysses* into Catalan, plumped for the adverb (*solemnement*). In theory, there must be such a word as *statelily*, but taken in isolation this looks and sounds rather awkward. I have only seen it used once: Anthony Burgess, in his novel *Earthly Powers*, speaks of a certain poem as being "bitterly, though statelily, ironical." Balanced as it is, in this case, by the equisyllabic "bitterly," it does not sound too bad, but Burgess may very well have put it in intentionally as an allusion to Joyce (who also figures in his novel).

Incidentally, there is a kind of code among critics in speaking about the main characters in *Ulysses*. It is usually "Mulligan" but "Stephen," and we speak of "Bloom" or at best "Mr. Bloom," but when referring to the latter's wife the code seems to call for "Molly."

Next, in this episode, a third character is mentioned; Stephen asks Mulligan how long Haines is going to stay. Haines turns out to be an English student (from Oxford), who, as Mulligan's guest, has come to Dublin to do research on Irish folklore or Celtic mythology.

We shall soon get the impression that Stephen is unhappy, but that will not necessarily endear him to us. He lost his mother over a year ago but is still suffering from the shock and has even been in mourning until now. He seems to have had a traumatic experience because he refused to kneel and pray at his mother's deathbed, and she has appeared to him in his dreams, reproaching him with her "glazing eyes, staring out of death" (1.273/10.19). It is a critical commonplace to say that Stephen is tortured by remorse, feeling guilty for not having knelt down and granted his mother her last wish. I am not so sure about that. In another passage in which Stephen thinks back on this dream, it says, "Pain, that was not yet the pain of love, fretted his heart" (1.102/5.31–32). What is the meaning of this "not yet"? I feel Stephen may actually *hate* his mother for having asked him to yield to the demands of the Church (which he had abjured), demands that threaten his sense of personal freedom and intellectual integrity, and now he feels guilty just because of this hate. The pain inflicted upon him by the memory of his mother's death may be pity but it is *not yet* the pain of love. In time, he may be able to overcome those feelings of hate and guilt but that time has not yet arrived.

Several themes that will be taken up in later episodes are already sounded in "Telemachus," including Hamlet, history, heretics and their heresies, British domination, and the father-son relationship. "Usurper," the episode's final word, symbolizes Stephen's rather vague but persistent feeling of being victimized by Mulligan.

The first episode of *Ulysses* has often been considered relatively easy to read. However, this is a most deceptive notion, for, in a sense, this episode may very well prove to be the most difficult one in that the reader has yet to be, let us say, conditioned; he must get used to more or less abrupt transitions from seemingly straightforward narrative to interior monologue and vice versa. On the very first page there is no lack of details apt to raise minor problems if you care to linger on them. Take the passage that ends in a description of Mulligan's hair as seen through

Stephen's eyes: "the light untonsured hair, grained and hued like pale oak" (1.15–16/3.17). What is the meaning of "untonsured"? In the flow of third-person narrative of an apparently conventional type, interrupted from time to time by dialogue, this word stands out at first sight as an incongruous element. So, there is no tonsure on the head that Mulligan bends down to Stephen? But why describe or even so much as mention something that is not there? The answer lies in Mulligan's masquerading as a mock-priest, acting "solemnly" and "gravely." Looking at Mulligan's hair, without any real interest ("coldly"), Stephen half expects to see a shaven crown, as of a priest or a monk. The narrator uses a most economical device to make the reader aware of Stephen's slight surprise, hardly consciously felt, at not finding this tonsure. Stephen's association is reinforced a few moments later when Mulligan's face reminds him of "a prelate, patron of arts in the middle ages" (1.32–33/3.34–35).

There has been some discussion with regard to the word (or one-word sentence) "Chrysostomos" (1.26/3.28). It is generally agreed that this Greek name (the golden-mouthed one) must be in Stephen's mind as an unspoken comment; it cannot very well be anything else. Matters of interpretation, however, are not always as simple; witness the following passage:

> And putting on his stiff collar and rebellious tie he spoke to them, chiding them, and to his dangling watchchain. His hands plunged and rummaged in his trunk while he called for a clean handkerchief. God, we'll simply have to dress the character. I want puce gloves and green boots. Contradiction. Do I contradict myself? Very well then, I contradict myself. Mercurial Malachi. A limp black missile flew out of his talking hands.
> —And there's your Latin quarter hat, he said.
>
> (1.513–19/16.42–17.08)

Here we have Mulligan finishing his dressing while Stephen is looking on and listening to Mulligan's rather incoherent monologue. In a sense, the latter is still the mock-priest of the opening scene: instead of blessing the things he puts on and putting his lips to them, as a priest does when donning his vestments before serving Mass, Mulligan is chiding them. What may puzzle the reader in this passage is the lack of any typographical or syntactical aids: there are no quote marks or supporting phrases such as "he thought." Following the two opening sentences in plain third-person narrative style, there are a few samples of what Mulligan is muttering all the time while dressing or rummaging in his trunk, his clowning ending on the final note of "Very well then, I contradict myself." This is followed by a silent comment in Stephen's mind, "Mercurial Malachi," and then the final sentence of this paragraph resumes the past-tense narrative. Mulligan's next words will make it clear to the reader that the "limp black missile" is nothing but Stephen's hat.

There are critics who take "Mercurial Malachi" to be words spoken aloud by Mulligan himself. Maddox, for instance, in discussing this character, says, "His own name for himself is apt: mercurial Malachi" (1978:22). Senn, too, describing Mulligan as an actor, on the scene throughout this opening episode, appearing in many roles, male as well as female, holds that the phrase is a name Mulligan applies to himself: "Er nennt sich 'Mercurial Malachi,' widersprüchlich, quecksilbrig, dem Götterboten Hermes ähnlich" (1977:31; see also 1972:29–46). I for one do not hold with this view; I feel this phrase to be on a par with "Chrysostomos" (1.26/3.28) as coming from Stephen, an unspoken comment on Mulligan's character and behavior.

On the beach, a few hours later, Stephen will remember this scene. Turning northeast (3.158ff./41.11ff.) he sees the *Pigeonhouse* power station looming up in the far distance. This view, or rather this name, releases a chain of associations, starting with a quotation from a book by Léo Taxil, *La Vie de Jésus*, in which Mary explains to Joseph that it is actually the pigeon's fault that she is pregnant ("C'est le pigeon, Joseph"). This reminds Stephen of his ill-starred stay in Paris, where, on one occasion, he sat in a bar with a young Irishman, Patrice Egan, who told him he should read Taxil's book. His thoughts having turned back to his days in the *Quartier latin*, he now remembers Mulligan's clownish performance after breakfast, how he raved about puce gloves and green boots and threw him what he called "your Latin quarter hat": "My Latin quarter hat. God, we simply must dress the character. I want puce gloves." This is, with some slight changes, what Mulligan had said that morning: an instance of quotation within interior monologue. Stephen must have been sufficiently impressed by Mulligan's words to remember them, even if only to ridicule them or to find fault with them, but he would surely have been equally impressed—more so, if anything—by this phrase, "Mercurial Malachi," if it had really been Mulligan's own. The sight of a dead dog on the beach, for instance, calls up in his mind the very phrase Mulligan had applied to him, not unkindly (1.112/6.02), when they were standing on top of the tower: "Ah, poor dogsbody!" (3.351/46.30). Mulligan is on his mind very much, to the extent that in his thoughts he need not even refer to him by name; a simple (emphatic) pronoun will do, as in: "He saved men from drowning and you shake at a cur's yelping" (3.317–18/45.30–31).

One of Buck's apparitions in "Circe" speaks the same words: "She's beastly dead. The pity of it! Mulligan meets the afflicted mother. (*he upturns his eyes*) Mercurial Malachi!" (15.4170–71/580.09–10), but this scene, in which Stephen's mother urges him to repent, is one of Stephen's hallucinations and therefore may contain elements originating from his own subconscious.

There is a similar problem of interpretation in the following passage: "A cloud began to cover the sun slowly, wholly, shadowing the bay in deeper green. It lay beneath him, a bowl of bitter waters. Fergus' song: I sang it alone in the house, holding down the long dark chords. Her door was open: she wanted to hear my music. Silent with awe and pity I went to her bedside. She was crying in her wretched bed. For those words, Stephen: love's bitter mystery" (1.248–53/9.32–38). The passage has been discussed by Fischer (1973:147). Up to the last sentence, she explains, Stephen's interior monologue reflects a remote memory, past tense and well-formed syntax signaling temporal as well as emotional distance. In the final sentence, however, Stephen returns to the present, realizing all of a sudden that the words of the song had caused his mother to cry.

This interpretation fails to acknowledge the paragraph as a functional self-contained unit and presupposes a sudden break in the flow of thought, a switch from past to present. Stephen, in the remembered scene, having finished the song he sang at the piano and seeing his mother in tears, may have asked her: "What are you crying for?" And she may have replied just that: "For those words, Stephen: love's bitter mystery." This, then, could very well be another instance of quotation within interior monologue.

In some cases, differences in interpretation may entail considerable differences in the factual circumstances of the story as reconstructed by the reader from material offered in the text in the form of narrative, dialogue, and flashbacks contained in snatches of interior monologue. It is always said that *Ulysses* is the story of one day and in a sense that is true, but the real story stretches far back. That is why students are sometimes told they should read *A Portrait* before tackling *Ulysses*, and this is sensible advice. If they do not take it, the implication of, say, "Cranly's arm. His arm" (1.159/7.14) will be lost on them but, of course, as far as Stephen Dedalus is concerned there is a gap between the ending of *A Portrait* and the beginning of *Ulysses*, "a blank period of time" (17.2051/729.06), and, besides, *A Portrait* does not offer much help with regard to Bloom. Still, Stephen's and Bloom's worlds do overlap and considerable background information about major and minor characters in *Ulysses* may be scraped together not only from *A Portrait* but also from *Dubliners*.

A case where the factual interpretation depends entirely on the way we read the text is the well-known passage "He wants that key. It is mine, *I paid the rent*. Now I eat his salt bread. Give him the key too. All. He will ask for it. That was in his eyes" (1.630–32/20.19–21, italics mine). In this fragment of Stephen's interior monologue two persons seem involved, referred to by the pronouns "he" (respectively, "his" and "him") on the one hand, and "I" (respectively, "mine") on the other, and, on the surface, "he" must be Mulligan and "I" must be Stephen. To get the complete picture we should recall first what has gone on before. After breakfast, Mulligan, Haines, and Stephen leave the tower. Stephen locks the iron door, pocketing the key, and the three of them descend the outside ladder. Mulligan asks, "Did you bring the key?" and Stephen replies, "I have it." Stephen walks in front; behind him he hears Haines asking, "Do you pay rent for this tower?" and Mulligan answering, straightaway, "Twelve quid." He himself then adds, "To the secretary of state for war" (1.528–40/17.17–31). There is something strange about neither Mulligan nor Stephen answering "yes" or "no" and confining themselves to giving some bare factual information. Finally, we should take into account what happens afterward, the very thing Stephen had expected:

> Stephen turned away.
> —I'm going, Mulligan, he said.
> —Give us that key, Kinch, Buck Mulligan said, to keep my chemise flat.
> Stephen handed him the key. Buck Mulligan laid it across his heaped clothes.
> —And twopence, he said, for a pint. Throw it there.
> (1.719–24/22.38–23.03)

These are the data, and the question now to be answered is simply this: Who pays the rent for the tower? Until recently, this did not seem a problem at all. It was taken for granted that Stephen, in his interior monologue, was referring to himself when saying, "I paid the rent." So we find Jones explaining that Haines, the Englishman, "has been invited by Mulligan to share the quarters paid for by Stephen" (1955:65) and Tindall stating that the patrimony of which Mulligan and Haines rob Stephen (in his role of Telemachus) "is at once the tower, for which he pays rent, and Ireland" (1959:135). Morton says that "we get the impression that Mulligan pays the rent. Only later do we learn that Stephen does" (1970:21). He thinks Mulligan's asking for the key a reasonable request, as he may want to return and change. There is, however, no evidence for such a move on Buck's part. Emerging from the tower, Buck appears, like Haines, for that matter, fully dressed for going into town after his swim; he has even put on a stiff collar and a tie, although it is only a short walk from the tower to the bathing place at the foot of the rocks (however, Mulligan would have to get rid of his bathtowel). Stephen, looking down on the heap of Mulligan's clothes while throwing two pennies on it, thinks all this dressing and undressing is a silly business: "Dressing, undressing" (1.725/23.04–5). In Mason's ultrashort summaries there is, of course, no room for such fascinating minor enigmas. He does not mention that there is rent to be paid, but simply states that Stephen "is lodging with an Irish medical student, Buck Mulligan, and Haines, an Englishman from Oxford . . . in a Martello tower at Sandycove" (1972:39). In contrast to this neutral position, both Blamires (1966:01) and Bernard Benstock (1974:11) hold that it is Stephen who has paid the rent for the tower.

If the passage in question ("I paid the rent") were straightforward, "pure" interior monologue, in which any "I" in the stream of consciousness unequivocally represents the subject of that consciousness, the critics mentioned above would have been right; after all, they apparently have Stephen's own word for it. However, common sense might have told us that it is highly improbable that a young man earning three pounds twelve a month (see 2.222/30.06) with as many debts as Stephen himself remembers (cf. 2.255–59/31.01–6) could ever have gotten together the twelve pounds needed for the rent.

It is Kenner who has given Mulligan his due, Mulligan, "who not only paid the rent and calls the tunes, but assumes *droit de seigneur* over Stephen's schoolpay as well" (1980:55), adding, in a lengthy footnote, that he owed to Arnold Goldman "the suggestion that Stephen's unspoken words 'It is mine, I paid the rent' are to be read in Mulligan's voice, between invisible quotation marks, as words Stephen can already hear Mulligan speaking when he demands the key. For it is unlike Stephen to assert ownership in consequence of payment—that is the way of the Mulligans and Deasys." From the beginning, moreover, it is obvious that Haines is Mulligan's guest; hence Stephen's question to Mulligan: "How long is Haines going to stay in this tower?" (1.49/4.13).

The words "I paid the rent," then, must be an instance of what I have called quotation within interior monologue. We have discussed such cases before, but there is a difference. In those cases, the words quoted were supposed to have been uttered by somebody at one moment or another. This specific case, however, presents an interesting variation in that the words in question will be spoken, presumably, at some moment in the near future. Actually, Mulligan will *not* speak them, which goes to show that Stephen has underrated him. There is no need for Mulligan to throw his weight around; it will be enough for him just to say, "Give us that key, Kinch."

If it is true, then, that Mulligan pays the rent, why should Stephen be so keen on pocketing the key? And why should he, in his heart, call Mulligan "usurper"? What is his real relationship with Mulligan? Leaving the tower in the morning Stephen thinks, "I will not sleep here tonight" (1.739–40/23.20), which means that he would be prepared to leave Mulligan, but later, on the beach, he thinks of Mulligan as a friend, with a hint even at a kind of homosexual relation, and apparently fears that Mulligan will leave *him:* "Staunch friend, a brother soul: Wilde's love that dare not speak its name. His arm: Cranly's arm. He now will leave me" (3.450–52/49.22–24).

From the beginning the reader has to reconcile himself to the fact that the text offers all kinds of problems which he has to solve for himself. As Hayman observes, "there are large gaps in the action of 'Telemachus,' despite the meticulous attention to details. For one thing, while Stephen thinks, the action continues. What Stephen overlooks, we too miss. Again, though we watch Mulligan shave, eat, cavort, dress, and finally bathe, we see Stephen performing only minimal actions" (1982:26).

There are details that keep nagging at our minds, such as the miraculously well-timed "two strong shrill whistles" answering Mulligan's "long slow whistle of call" (1.24–27/3.26–29), a point taken up by Benstock and Benstock (1982:19ff.), or the question as to whom Stephen alludes to when he, having first stated that he is "a servant of two masters, an English and an Italian" (1.638/20.27–28), then adds: "And a third there is who wants me for odd jobs." It is amazing to see how cocksure critics can sometimes be when offering their interpretations of such cryptic passages. For Blamires it is evident that Stephen's third master is "poor old Ireland" (1966:06). We are reminded of the old milkwoman who comes in at breakfast time (1.386ff./13.24ff.), a symbol of Ireland, "poor old woman," as the country was called "in old times" (1.403–4/14.03), but Stephen's attitude toward her is not such as to induce us to believe that he would be willing to serve her. He will even tell Bloom, late that night, that he thinks "Ireland must be important because it belongs to me" (16.1164–65/645.09–10). Now, at breakfast, Stephen listens "in scornful silence" (1.418/14.19) to Mulligan's and Haines's remarks and to the old woman's humble responses. She may have a message for him but he "scorned to beg her favour" (1.407/14.07).

Hodgart introduces another candidate for the office of third master. Stephen "does not bother to explain that the third is his Muse, to whom alone the writer must always be a devoted servant" (1978:75). The writer? What has Stephen written so far? A few poems? And would he speak of his literary efforts as "odd jobs"? We might just as well cast Mr. Deasy in the role. He is Stephen's present employer, head of the Dalkey school, where Stephen has been working as an assistant schoolmaster for a couple of months (the reader will meet him in the second episode).

Or Mulligan—why not? That is at least what Henke has come up with.

"Contradicting the biblical injunction that 'no man can serve two masters,' Stephen is in servitude to three: Britain, the Roman church, and Malachi Mulligan" (1978:30), she says.

There are more wild guesses in Henke's work. The breakfast scene in the tower is commented on by her as follows: "Themes of violence and cannibalism dominate the morning repast. When Old Mother Grogan figuratively appears in the person of an aged Irish milkwoman, Buck responds to her exclamation of 'Glory be to God' with the wry remark: 'The islanders . . . speak frequently of the collector of prepuces' (p. 13). His medical reference to the Hebrew-Christian God as a barbaric foreskin-hunter is as meaningless to the old lady as Haines's Gaelic-French. 'Are you a medical student, sir?' (p. 14), the woman inquires" (1978: 25–26). This is a willful distortion of a scene marked by sunshine and light-hearted talk. For all Stephen's occasionally gloomy thoughts there is, in this first episode, an atmosphere in which the reader is conscious, as Hodgart says, of "the bright morning, the sea, the pleasures of literary quotation and parody, the high spirits of youth" (1978:76)—a far cry from any violence or cannibalism. The equally disparaging or even offensive term "barbaric foreskin-hunter," which Henke uses to allude to a nonviolent hygienic custom, the rite of circumcision, is absolutely out of place in this context. Moreover, Mulligan's remark is not at all a *medical* reference, and the milkwoman's question is not in any way triggered by this remark. To realize just how wrong Henke is in her summary or paraphrase we have only to follow the text as closely as possible. When the old woman enters, Stephen, who is apparently sitting nearest to the locker, is asked to get the milk jug. The woman, familiar, of course, with the layout of the place, moves forward to stand "by Stephen's elbow," and in speaking to him she uses the phrase "Glory be to God." Mulligan, from across the table, just glances at her, saying, "To whom?" and "Ah, to be sure!" He then turns to Haines, in an aside, with his casual remark about the islanders and the collector of prepuces. Meanwhile the milkwoman has been waiting for Stephen to put the jug on the table, and she now asks him how much he wants her to measure out for them. Thus the odds are she has not paid any attention to Mulligan's words; she may even be a little hard of hearing, for we are told that Mulligan, when addressing her directly, speaks "somewhat loudly" (1.411/14.13). Filling the jug, she praises the quality of her Sandycove milk. She then invites Mulligan, who is already pouring milk into the tea cups, to taste it, which he does. He then tells her: "If we could live on good food like that . . . we wouldn't have the country full of rotten teeth and rotten guts. Living in a bogswamp, eating cheap food and the streets paved with dust, horsedung and consumptives' spits" (1.411–14/14.12–16). It is then and only then that the old woman, in response to Mulligan's going on about rotten teeth and consumptives' spits, asks him, "Are you a medical student, sir?" Mulligan's reply is in the affirmative, as much for her benefit as for the reader's, in case the reader had missed the hints in the passage of 1.204–15/8.25–38.

The following paragraph shows Stephen inwardly responding to the scene while Haines starts talking Gaelic to the old woman: "Stephen listened in scornful silence. She bows her old head to a voice that speaks to her loudly, her bonesetter, her medicineman; me she slights. To the voice that will shrive and oil for the grave all there is of her but her woman's unclean loins, of man's flesh made not in God's likeness, the serpent's prey. And to the loud voice that now bids her be silent with wondering unsteady eyes" (1.418–23/14.19–25). Here is Henke's comment on this passage: "The crone panders to her medicineman, and Stephen cynically envisions her 'unclean loins' as prey to the phallic serpent" (1978:26), thus reducing the solid structure of the paragraph to a mere mess of scrambled words. What she fails to see, apparently, is that there are *three voices* involved in this scene, voices of authority the old woman is used to bow her head to.

Mulligan's is the powerful voice of medical science, and for such a woman as this old milkwoman there is another voice with equal if not greater authority—the voice of the Church, the voice of the priest. Stephen, looking at her and still unable to forget his mother's deathbed, an event that must have caused a crisis in his life, is reminded of the sacrament of extreme unction to be performed by the priest. The "unclean loins" are just that part of the female body that will not be anointed; there is nothing cynical in this thought, or in the reference to Eve, who was seduced by Satan in the guise of a serpent (why "phallic"?). Stephen may call himself a "horrible example of free thought" (1.625–26/20.14), but in some respects his atheism is only skin-deep. He cannot easily shake off his Jesuit training, and he delights, as in this case, in pondering matters theological. The whole episode abounds in allusions to theology, liturgy, and Church rites. Finally, Stephen's thoughts are interrupted by the third voice, that of Haines. To the old woman it is the voice of a stranger (she thinks he speaks French!), the voice of a gentleman, who claims her attention as an undisputed right.

If there is one thing beginning readers should be wary of, it is the use and especially misuse of metaphor in studies and commentaries. More often than not metaphorical phrases only lead away from the text without offering any really deeper insight into its meaning.

Henke, for instance, seems particularly keen on exuberant metaphor. Here is an example: "The sea terrifies Stephen because it portends engulfment—a sinking down into matter and the annihilation of personal identity. It calls up womb images and metaphorically functions as a giant placenta, encompassing Ireland in viscous amniotic fluid. The unborn souls of men float paralyzed in the 'deep jelly of the water' (p. 21)'' (1978:16). Skipping the first part of this gynecological imagery as simply too clinical, we might cling to the final sentence of the passage, for here at least there is a specific fragment the reader is referred to, so we may check whether we are really talking about the same book and learn what it is all about. The three young men are going down to the place where Mulligan wants to have his swim. Haines and Stephen, who have stopped a few moments to light cigarettes, find Mulligan already undressing, while another young man, who is in the water (and whose name we are not told), is talking to him:

> They followed the winding path down to the creek. Buck Mulligan stood on a stone, in shirtsleeves, his unclipped tie rippling over his shoulder. A young man clinging to a spur of rock near him, moved slowly frogwise his green legs in the deep jelly of the water.
> —Is the brother with you, Malachi?
> —Down in Westmeath. With the Bannons.
> —Still there? I got a card from Bannon. Says he found a sweet young thing down there. Photo girl he calls her.
>
> (1.678–85/21.34–42)

It is through Stephen's eye that the reader looks at this scene, and the language in which it is described, therefore, takes on a poetic hue. The young man in the water, Stephen ''thinks,'' moves his legs like a frog in order to keep himself afloat. He moves slowly, but he is not paralyzed at all. He is alive and kicking and will soon push himself backward to reach the middle of the inlet ''in two long clean strokes'' (1.715/22.34).

Of much greater interest to the reader is the reference to Bannon and the ''sweet young thing.'' Bannon will be mentioned or alluded to several times in the course of the book (see Benstock and Benstock, 1980:51); he will even appear in the flesh (14.497, 651–55/397.14, 401.31–35). The ''sweet young thing'' will prove to be Bloom's daughter, fifteen-year-old Milly, who has a job with a photographer in Mullingar; she mentions Bannon in her letter to her father (4.406ff./66.12–13).

The young man in the water has another news item, this time about a certain Seymour, an acquaintance of Mulligan's (cf. 1.163/7.18):

> —Seymour's back in town, the young man said, grasping again his spur of rock. Chucked medicine and going in for the army.
> —Ah, go to God! Buck Mulligan said.
> —Going over next week to stew. You know that red Carlisle girl, Lily?
> —Yes.

—Spooning with him last night on the pier. The father is rotto with money.

(1.695–700/22.10–18)

It is amazing to see what Henke makes of all this. She had already declared that the "frogman," as she calls him, "never identifies Milly Bloom; he describes her as 'a sweet young thing,' the object of Bannon's male amusement" (1978:31), forgetting, apparently, that those are not the young man's words, but Bannon's, and the latter would hardly mention names on a postcard. Anyway, Henke continues: "Similarly, Seymour, the medical student turned soldier, has been 'stewing' around with female flesh, food for his sexual appetite" (1978:32). Actually, of course, Seymour has not yet been stewing; he will only start doing so, according to the young man, in a week or so, when he has to follow, presumably, a training course for officers. He will then have to "stew" (to swot, to work hard) for the exams he may have to pass to obtain an officer's rank or, simply, work hard at being drilled.

While Mulligan is unlacing his boots, another bather emerges from the water: "Buck Mulligan sat down to unlace his boots. An elderly man shot up near the spur of rock a blowing red face. He scrambled up by the stones, water glistening on his pate and on its garland of grey hair, water rilling over his chest and paunch and spilling jets out of his black sagging loincloth" (1.687–91/22.02–6). In Henke's interpretation the elderly man becomes, in turn, "an aged crab-man," something which "seems to be the ghost of a resurrected corpse," "an impotent Poseidon stripped of his powers over the sea," and a man whose loincloth is "spilling forth seedless rills of salt water" and whose "decrepit body is one step removed from that of the dead man" (1978:32), the latter being an allusion, presumably, to the "man that was drowned" (1.675/21.31).

When this man scrambles ashore after his invigorating early morning swim (which he seems perfectly able to enjoy in spite of his "decrepit body"), we see Mulligan sending meaningful glances to Haines and Stephen and then crossing himself "piously" and, no doubt, mockingly (1.692–94/22.07–9). The man's "garland of grey hair" may already have reminded us of a tonsured head, and now Mulligan's gesture reinforces our impression that the elderly man might be a priest. Sure enough, when the man's hair ("a grey nimbus") is referred to again, the text speaks of *the* (not *a*) priest (1.739/23.19); the use of the definite article implies that reader and character alike should be familiar with the figure in question.

The character in this case is Stephen, and the scene is the final one of this episode. Mulligan, who knows by now that Stephen will draw his monthly pay today (it is the sixteenth of the month), asks, or practically orders, him to leave twopence ("for a pint") before he goes, the twopence they should have paid the milkwoman (1.458/15.22). Having received Stephen's two pennies he strikes a mock-solemn attitude, saying: "He who stealeth from the poor lendeth to the Lord. Thus spake Zarathustra" (1.727–28/23.07–8). Haines, who had sat down on a stone to smoke a cigarette, his eyes on the bathing scene, presumably, now turns around to say a few civil words to Stephen, who is setting out on the path that leads up to the road: "We'll see you again, Haines said, turning as Stephen walked up the path and smiling at wild Irish" (1.730–31/ 23.10–11). Bernard Benstock here speaks of "the insensitive Sassenach Haines, who can patronize the Celts and smile at Stephen as 'wild Irish' " (1974:16). This statement does not do justice to Haines. The latter's smile was not directed at Stephen Dedalus in the first place but at those wild Irishmen, such as Mulligan, who have no scruples in parodying phrases from the Bible. When Haines turned around to address Stephen, the smile simply stuck to his face. Stephen takes note of this smile— hence his inward comment, a proverbial phrase about three things an Irishman should beware of: "Horn of a bull, hoof of a horse, smile of a Saxon" (1.732/23.12)—but he must have realized, at the same time, that the smile was not meant for him in particular.

It is interesting to see how translators have tried to render the text less ambiguous in this respect, more transparent somehow. Goyert, by displacing a clause, makes it sufficiently clear that Haines is smiling at what he thought was a sample of crazy Irish humor: "Wir treffen Sie nachher, sagte Haines, der sich umwandte und über den tollen Irenwitz lächelte, als Stephen den Pfad hinaufging" (1.36). Wollschläger keeps closer to the original text, semantically as well as syntactically, but the German punctuation may have helped to create a greater distance between Haines's smile and Stephen: "Wir sehen uns dann ja noch, sagte Haines, sich umwendend, als Stephen den Pfad hinaufschritt, und lächelnd über die wilden Iren" (34).

A most extreme example of interpretative translation is offered by Morel. Besides shifting clauses around, like Goyert does, he inserts an adverb ("encore") to impress upon the reader that Haines was *still* smiling at unbridled Irish phrases or manners ("irlandisme débridé") when he turned to Stephen: "Nous nous reverrons, dit Haines encore souriant de cet irlandisme débridé et tourné vers Stephen qui remontait le sentier" (26).

Mulligan, who has just plunged into the water, may have overheard Haines saying, "We'll see you again." He wants to make sure that Stephen, loaded with "shining sovereigns" (1.296/11.05), will be there to provide drinks in a certain pub around noon, more precisely, at half past twelve: "The Ship, Buck Mulligan cried. Half twelve. —Good,

Stephen said" (1.733–34/23.13–14). While Mulligan swims out into the bay, Stephen continues along the path: "He walked along the upward-curving path. *Liliata rutilantium. / Turma circumdet. / Iubilantium te virginum.* The priest's grey nimbus in a niche where he dressed discreetly. I will not sleep here tonight. Home also I cannot go" (1.735–40/ 23.15–20). Mulligan's peremptory command may have reminded Stephen of his old grudge against him, of how Mulligan had once said to his mother, "*O, it's only Dedalus whose mother is beastly dead*" (1.198–99/ 8.19–20). This, in its turn, may have called up, not for the first time, the memory of his mother's deathbed, which would explain the fragments of the prayer for the dying that now accompany his footsteps.

Kaiser, who made a study of the role of quotations in *Ulysses*, observed that there was something wrong with the punctuation: There should not be a full stop after "rutilantium," but there should be some kind of punctuation after "virginum" (1972:171). It should be noted that the texts were not unanimous on this point. In the form quoted by Kaiser the lines were only found in the new Bodley Head and the new Random House editions, whereas in the old Random House and the Penguin editions, as well as in Goyert's and Wollschläger's German translations and in Valverde's Spanish translation all three lines end in a full stop. There is another variant reading, found both in Morel's French and in Mallafrè's Catalan translation; these have only one full stop, after the third line this time.

We should not attach too much importance to this matter of punctuation, anyway, for there is a lot more to this passage than meets the eye. As we have seen, just why these words from the prayer for the dying should crop up in Stephen's mind this very moment is anybody's guess. Hart's hypothesis (Hart and Knuth, 1981:I.23–24) is more than a guess. He argues as follows. In a later episode, "Ithaca," Bloom and Stephen, parting, hear the bells of Saint George's church tolling the hour (17.1224–34/704.03–14). From the end of "Calypso," where Bloom, leaving his home in Eccles Street, hears the same church bells, we know that Joyce uses one pair of "heighos" to mark each quarter of an hour. Bloom, listening, is counting the peals, ticking them off, the sounds reminding him of Dignam's funeral he is going to attend that morning: "Quarter to. There again: the overtone following through the air. A third. Poor Dignam!" (4.549–51/70.14–16). The time being 8:45 A.M., the three quarters of the hour are represented in print by three lines of two "heighos" each. In "Ithaca" Bloom "hears" *two* lines of "heighos": the time may be 1:30 or 2:30 A.M. For Stephen the sound of the bells is associated with the words of the prayer, equally set out in *two* lines of print. Now, in the "Telemachus" scene, this prayer—or what remains of it—has been spread over *three* lines, the same as Bloom's paired "heighos" in "Calypso," which warrants Hart's conclusion that Stephen must be hearing church bells chiming at the same time Bloom does, only from a different source, "probably from a clock tower in Kingstown, to correspond with the chimes from St. George's Church. Both Stephen and Bloom set off to confront the world at a quarter to nine" (1981:1.24).

To the first-time reader who does not yet know all this, Stephen's murmuring (or "thinking") these lines seems a compulsive act, helping to drown or deafen the clamor of the memory of his mother's death struggle itself. Walking the path *upward*, Stephen uses the prayer as a kind of marching song: after "Liliata rutilantium" he has to catch his breath, hence the seemingly illogical full stop. With "Turma circumdet" he falls into step again, having skipped or murmured under his breath the words "te confessorum" (cf. 1.276–77/10.23–24). The first part of the prayer now being finished, adding a full stop would be justified anyhow. Stephen starts on the second part, but "Iubilantium te virginum" is as far as he gets: the church bells have stopped and his stream of consciousness is interrupted by the sight of the priest's tonsured head. As he is walking along an upwardcurving path, Stephen may have drawn level, by now, with this priest, the very man who had come up from the water, the elderly man with the "blowing red face" (1.688/22.03), who is now dressing in a niche among the rocks.

Stephen's next thought, "I will not sleep here tonight," seems rather sudden. Could there be some link between the priest's dressing and Mulligan's "Dressing, undressing" (1.725/23.04–5), or had Stephen been harboring some such thought all the time and does it dawn upon him that he has just given up the key to the tower?

EPISODE TWO
"Nestor"

*A*T THE naturalistic level—which is what we are concerned with here—the action in "Nestor" is not too hard to follow. It is staged in a boys' school in Dalkey, near Dublin (see 2.25/24.31), where Stephen is employed; the time is about ten o'clock in the morning (see 2.92/ 26.23). There are three scenes. First, we find Stephen running a class, trying to cope with an unruly bunch of boys, who do not show any appreciable interest in the subjects they are supposed to have studied. Then, the boys having rushed off to the locker room and the hockey field, Stephen is seen coaching Sargent, a boy who has stayed behind in the classroom, showing him how to solve an algebra problem. Stephen does this unbidden, it seems, beyond the line of duty, for according to the boy himself he had only been told by the headmaster, Mr. Deasy (pronounced "daisy"), to show Stephen that he had copied the sums in question from the blackboard (see 2.131–38/27.25–32). Finally, the scene shifts to the headmaster's study, where Stephen receives his monthly pay, having to listen meanwhile to Mr. Deasy's strongly biased views on historical and political issues, some of which are demonstrably wrong. The headmaster has written a letter to the press (on foot-and-mouth disease) and now hands Stephen two copies, asking him to persuade some of his "literary friends" (2.290/ 32.01) to get this letter published. Stephen, thinking of the *Evening Telegraph* and the *Irish Homestead*, the editors of which he knows, as he says, "slightly" (2.414/35.24), promises to do so. For the plot of *Ulysses* this is an important detail: In order to comply with Mr. Deasy's request, Stephen has to go first to the *Telegraph* office to see the editor, Crawford (in "Aeolus"), and later seeks out the *Homestead* editor, Russell, in the National Library (in "Scylla and Charybdis"). In both cases there is a near-meeting of Stephen and Bloom.

Stephen does not impress us as being a teacher. During the brief scene in the classroom which the reader is permitted to witness he is not seen *teaching* either history or literature, that is. He is just hearing the boys' lessons and that may explain why he seems rather ashamed of his job, treating it, as Kenner points out, "as a squalid secret, incompatible with the artist's welcome to Life" (1980:56). Apart from upgrading his salary by more than ten percent (or is Mulligan just exaggerating when he expects Stephen to touch "four shining sovereigns" [1.296/11.05] and does Stephen not care enough to correct him?), he must have boasted within Lenehan's hearing—while standing drinks in a pub in the city—that his temporary affluence was due to having received a sizable honorarium for literary work (see 11.253–65/262.26–40). In the hospital scene of "Oxen of the Sun" Stephen goes so far as to show those present the money he still has left, pretending that it represents the honorarium he received for a poem. In the narrator's voice: "And he showed them glistering coins of the tribute and goldsmith notes the worth of two pound nineteen shilling that he had, he said, for a song which he writ" (14.285–87/391.13–15). The "song" does not seem to arouse any interest but the money does: "They all admired to see the foresaid riches in such dearth of money as was herebefore." When Stephen refers to his job at all he does so in an oblique way. Being taken in tow by Bloom, well after midnight, he is accosted by a certain Corley (one of the "two gallants" in the story of that title in *Dubliners*), who tells him he has no place to sleep, being out of a job and absolutely penniless, thus trying to wheedle a few shillings out of him. Stephen ends up by letting him have a halfcrown, but first he mentions a vacancy for what he calls a "gentleman usher" (i.e., an underteacher or assistant schoolmaster), a job Corley might apply for: "There'll be a job tomorrow or next day, Stephen told him, in a boys' school at Dalkey for a gentleman usher. Mr Garrett Deasy. Try it. You may mention my name" (16.157–59/617.14–16).

Indeed, both Stephen himself and Mr. Deasy are well aware of the former's lack of interest in teaching. When Mr. Deasy shrewdly remarks, "You were not born to be a teacher, I think. Perhaps I am wrong" (2.402/35.11–12), Stephen's retort is, "A learner rather." His next thought, "And here what will you learn more?" (2.404/35.14), may be taken as a hint that he seriously considers quitting. At this stage, however, readers cannot be sure. Later, they may wonder what Stephen means when he mutters to himself, playing the piano with his eyes shut: "Must visit old Deasy or telegraph. Our interview of this morning has left on me a deep impression. Though our ages. Will write fully tomorrow" (15.2497–99/518.01–3), but not until they come upon Stephen's remark to Corley and grasp its implications will they find their suspicions confirmed and feel reasonably sure that Stephen plans to give notice one of these days.

The trivial questions and answers of the history lesson serve as a setting to Stephen's musings, a shade less suffused with self-pity than in the preceding episode and mainly concerned with the nature of history, its ultimate sense—or lack of sense. His witticisms, such as his definition of Kingstown pier ("a disappointed bridge"), are clearly lost upon the boys' dull minds, and he thinks of saving this phrase for Haines, who had asked his permission (see 1.480/16.05) to make a collection of his sayings and whom he expects to meet again that night: "For Haines's chapbook.

No-one here to hear. Tonight deftly amid wild drink and talk, to pierce the polished mail of his mind" (2.42–43/25.07–9).

Sitting at the side of Cyril Sargent, shortly afterward, Stephen shows him how to solve the algebra problem (2.155–60/28.11–18). Maddox calls this "an especially rich passage" (1978:25), in which Stephen "thinks of teachers whose work went unregarded." He quotes a few lines and raises a moot point by stating that we have here "one of those complex crosscurrents of allusion to which the reader of *Ulysses* soon becomes accustomed," but is it at all fair to tell a reader who has barely got through some twenty-five pages of the book that he will soon get used to Joyce's literary techniques? This is all very well for an experienced critic, but even if a beginning reader believes to have got the hang, more or less, of what it is all about in the first episode, there will remain passages that the reader simply cannot be expected to get to the bottom of on a first reading.

One such passage is the scene depicted in the preceding episode which Peake singles out as "the first passage of any length directly representing Stephen's thoughts" (1977:176):

> Young shouts of moneyed voices in Clive Kempthorpe's rooms. Palefaces: they hold their ribs with laughter, one clasping another. O, I shall expire! Break the news to her gently, Aubrey! I shall die! With slit ribbons of his shirt whipping the air he hops and hobbles round the table, with trousers down at heels, chased by Ades of Magdalen with the tailor's shears. A scared calf's face gilded with marmalade. I don't want to be debagged! Don't you play the giddy ox with me!
>
> Shouts from the open window startling evening in the quadrangle. A deaf gardener, aproned, masked with Matthew Arnold's face, pushes his mower on the sombre lawn watching narrowly the dancing motes of grasshalms.
>
> To ourselves . . . . new paganism . . . . *omphalos.*
>
> (1.165–76/7.21–33)

These thoughts are triggered by Mulligan offering to give Haines a ragging if he makes any trouble, "a ragging worse than they gave Clive Kempthorpe" (1.163–64/7.19). Peake, adding that Mulligan's offer "calls up the memory of an earlier ragging," describes the passage as no more than "a remembered scene vividly recalled," but other critics have pointed out that there is no evidence that Stephen had ever gone to Oxford, so how can he *remember* anything that must have happened in one of the Oxford colleges? The whole scene, described in present tense, looks like a flashback, but as such it is misleading. Mulligan seems to have been educated at Oxford and, presumably, knows what he is talking about when he declares that Stephen has "the real Oxford manner" (1.54/4.19), so it must have been

Mulligan who told Stephen such anecdotes as the story of Kempthorpe's ragging. But, the reader may well ask, how do critics know that Mulligan was educated at Oxford before taking up the study of medicine in Dublin? The answer is: they do not, they just *assume* he had, because Mulligan is modeled, evidently, upon Oliver St. John Gogarty, a contemporary of Joyce's, and it was Gogarty who spent a couple of terms in Oxford. From the text, however, the reader cannot know this. He may wonder vaguely how Mulligan had got acquainted with the Oxford man Haines without having been there himself, but Mulligan may have met Haines, who had come to Ireland for his Celtic studies, anywhere (e.g., in a Dublin pub) and he may then have invited him to share their lodgings in the tower. We are not told, besides, how long Haines had already been staying with them. So what is to prevent us from assuming that it was Haines who had been telling them such anecdotes from student life in Oxford, especially this one in which the victim was an Irish boy? When Mulligan speaks about the ragging *they* gave Clive Kempthorpe, it sounds as if he himself was not actually witnessing or taking part in that silly prank but had heard the story from others, whether or not he himself was at Oxford at that time.

Whatever the source of the story, a striking feature of the form in which the scene is reenacted in Stephen's imagination is its wealth of detail. Obviously, the bare outline of the story has greatly been embellished in the editing process. It is highly unlikely, for instance, that the original narrator, whoever he was, would have indulged in such phrases as "young shouts" and "moneyed voices" or would have used present tense, for that matter. This is Stephen writing *Ulysses*.

Another notable aspect of this passage is its shifting point of view: in the first paragraph we witness the scene from inside; in the second paragraph—a delightful little scene that can hardly have been part of the original tale—the reporter seems stationed outside, listening to the shouts coming from the open window and observing a gardener so intent upon his work that the observer concludes that he must be deaf. Finally, Stephen's thoughts return to the present, as he remembers Mulligan's saying something about Hellenizing Ireland (see 1.158/7.13): Could the Sinn Fein movement ("To ourselves") represent that "new paganism"?

Seeing that the fictional observer in the quadrangle of the Oxford college, by looking at the gardener's face, is reminded of Matthew Arnold, who once taught in Oxford, the naïve reader will probably just visualize this gardener as a man with rather impressive whiskers without giving it a second thought, but since Noon remarked that Matthew Arnold's "lawn mowing" signifies his "attempt to tidy up and eliminate all the differences between religion, poetry, and philosophy" (1957:8), critics have been reading all kinds of allusions into this passage. Arnold, pleading for what he called "Hellenism" in culture and literature, spoke of "Hebraism" and "Hellenism" as rival forces in Western culture. Stephen is assumed to reject this dichotomy as an ideology far removed from reality. How do we know? Well, the gardener is deaf, deaf to the harsh sounds of this world, and if this is not enough, Fischer even concludes (from the gardener's "watching narrowly," presumably) that the man is short-sighted as well (1973:143). We are still waiting for the critic who explains the hidden meaning of the gardener's apron, an item that seems to have escaped critical scrutiny so far.

Let us now look in some detail at the classroom scene. The boy Sargent has come forward to show Stephen the sums he had been told to copy off the blackboard (2.123ff./27.16ff.). He has to admit, however, that he is still unable to do them himself. Looking at the unprepossessing boy, Stephen reflects that one person at least, the boy's mother, must have loved and cherished him, and he asks himself if a mother's love is thus the "only true thing in life" (2.143/27.38). As Fischer rightly remarks (1973:152), there must be a turning point somewhere in Stephen's stream of consciousness: He starts by identifying himself with Sargent, seeing himself as the boy he was at Sargent's age, his thoughts dwelling on the memory of his own mother's death. The catch phrase "an odour of rosewood and wetted ashes" alone would make this clear, condensing as it does phrases from Stephen's dream which we remember from the first episode: "an odour of wax and rosewood," "a faint odour of wetted ashes" (1.104–5/5.34–36). On the whole, the tone of these fleeting memories is less intense now; there is less feeling of guilt, less pain, more pity and resignation, more emotional distance ("She was no more"). There is, however, a jarring note in this passage, the curious reference to Saint Columbanus, a sixth-century Irish missionary to the Continent: "His mother's prostrate body the fiery Columbanus in holy zeal bestrode" (2.143–44/27.38–40). It is on this point that I take issue with Fischer's interpretation of this seemingly irrelevant intrusion into Stephen's train of thought. She holds that this is a metaphorical expression in which "His mother" stands for both Sargent's and Stephen's mother, as well as for Ireland and for all Irish women, subdued as they are by the Church (1973:152).

As I see it, what Stephen means is this: A mother's love may be the only real thing in life in the last analysis, but what if that clinging love puts too heavy a claim on you, or threatens to throttle you, stunt your spiritual growth, prevent you from following your vocation, artistic or otherwise? It is said that the mother of Columbanus—in an impulse, no doubt, to protect him from the dangers of the world—tried to prevent him from setting out into that world to preach the Gospel: She threw herself on the threshold of their house, whereupon he just stepped across her prostrate body. His vocation, his "holy zeal," meant more to him, was more compelling, than his mother's love or wishes. In this view the mother is not a victim, as Fischer sees her; on the contrary, the maternal love that she embodies stands in her son's way and represents the assault upon his spiritual independence, the obstacle to be overcome at all cost. If we want to play the game—so popular among commentators—of "who is standing for whom?" Columbanus stands for Stephen, refusing to kneel at his mother's deathbed.

Next, we find Stephen showing Sargent how to solve one of the algebra problems he had to copy: "Across the page the symbols moved in grave morrice, in the mummery of their letters, wearing quaint caps of squares and cubes. Give hands, traverse, bow to partner: so: imps of fancy of the Moors. Gone too from the world, Averroes and Moses Maimonides, dark men in mien and movement, flashing in their mocking mirrors the obscure soul of the world, a darkness shining in brightness which brightness could not comprehend" (2.155–60/28.11–18). In Gordon's paraphrase, Stephen is "looking at a page of numbers and evoking gloomy Moors" (1981a:49). I do not think this quite catches the spirit of the scene. Averroes and Maimonides are visualized by Stephen as *dark* men (i.e., Oriental types); in his mind there is nothing particularly *gloomy* about these brilliant philosophers with their flashing mirrors. To him the algebraic symbols, "imps of fancy of the Moors," call up the image of a group of morrice dancers. Although their dance may be a grave one, obeying specific rules (we hear a dancing master shouting above the music, giving his directions: "Give hands . . ."), the whole presents a lively scene of dancers moving about in gay costumes with their "caps of squares and cubes" (an allusion to algebraic notations such as x^2 and y^3). What we have here is more than Stephen just looking at a page of numbers, a view that is far too static. There is *movement* here: the symbols *moved* across the page, and Stephen supervises their movements, writing out the entire sum for Sargent, explaining the necessary moves and hearing, in his imagination, a dancing master's commands accentuating the various operations as his hand traces the algebraic choreography with its plus and minus signs, its brackets and parentheses. When Stephen finishes the equation or whatever it is ("so"), his thoughts turn to the learned men who developed this branch of mathematics. According to Maddox, Stephen's thoughts here stray to "teachers whose work went unregarded," and he holds, therefore, that there is "an implicit comparison between Stephen himself and the two philosophers—all of them disregarded teachers" (1978:25). This is a dubious point, for those two scholars, an Arab and a Jew, were famous enough in their time and certainly not unregarded or disregarded; on the contrary, they are reputed to have influenced medieval thought to a considerable extent, and as to Stephen, being regarded as a teacher is not his ambition at all.

What, then, is the meaning of this phrase, "Gone too from the world"? In my view it means that those philosophers have been claimed by history; they are dead but their names and their work live on: "They are not to be thought away" (2.49/25.15–16). Preceding pages have been leading up to the phrase, starting with Pyrrhus and Caesar, who had *gone* from this world; both were murdered. Then, when Stephen had started imagining Sargent's mother loving and protecting her little son (2.139ff./27.33ff.), somewhere along the line, as said before, there must have occurred a transition, Stephen's thoughts now shifting to his own mother, who did the same for him: "She was no more . . . and had *gone*, scarcely having been. A poor soul *gone* to heaven" (2.144–47/27.40–28.02, italics mine), and finally we have these two philosophers, who also have *gone* from this world.

Such considerations may not solve the problem of how to interpret the history of mankind, but in Stephen's personal history they may at least assist Stephen in groping his way toward a state of mind in which he may come to accept his mother's death without any undue feelings of guilt and remorse.

The episode's final scene is enacted in Mr. Deasy's study, where the headmaster will pay Stephen his salary. As he has to settle some altercation among the hockey teams first, he asks Stephen to wait for him in his room. So Stephen has a moment to look around in the study. Everything is just the same as on the day when he applied for the job: "As on the first day he bargained with me here" (2.200/29.23–24). There are the familiar sights: the collection of coins and the silver spoons. The spoon handles are decorated with the heads of the apostles: "And snug in their spooncase of purple plush, faded, the twelve apostles having preached to all the gentiles: world without end" (2.202–4/29.26–28). "And" at the beginning of this sentence seems to imply that the spoon case is on the sideboard, as is the tray of coins mentioned in the preceding sentence. At the back of Stephen's mind in this paragraph, triggered perhaps by his thought "As on the first day," is a sequence from a Church hymn, the *Gloria Patri:*" as it was in the beginning, is now and ever shall be, world without end."

It is amazing to see what Fischer has made of this little vignette of the silver spoons in their plush-lined case, with its impressive economy of literary expression. She speaks of a metaphorical vocabulary that is used to describe the *faded picture* of the twelve apostles (1973:164). According to Fischer, Stephen looks upon the *frame* of this faded picture as upon a plush spoon case, and Stephen's interpretation of the objects he observes is not just a whim; the reason is, presumably, that he has perceived a kind of analogy or similarity between Mr. Deasy's attitude toward the Christian faith and the bourgeois custom of handling silver things "with care"

(1973:164). There is no need for all this rigmarole, as far as I can see. Stephen has his quarrel with history and theology; he senses that—if it comes to a discussion—Mr. Deasy, predictably, will say something such as "All human history moves towards one great goal, the manifestation of God" (2.380–81/34.27–28). For Stephen, the Stuart coins are just symbols of political history and British power, while the apostle spoons remind him of religious history and the power of the Church. The coins, true to their nature, actually represent both aspects; they bear the motto CHRISTO VICTORE TRIUMPHO: "When Christ is victorious I shall triumph." Gifford's schoolboy translation is "Christ in Victory and in Triumph" (1974:23).

When Mr. Deasy starts meting out Stephen's wages he makes quite a show of it, beginning by taking out his pocketbook and "carefully" putting down two pound notes on the table. The rest of the amount due will have to come from Deasy's savings box. Stephen knows this, hence the reflection of his thoughts in the following paragraph: "And now his strongroom for the gold. Stephen's embarrassed hand moved over the shells heaped in the cold stone mortar: whelks and money cowries and leopard shells: and this, whorled as an emir's turban, and this, the scallop of saint James. An old pilgrim's hoard, dead treasure, hollow shells" (2.212–16/29.36–40).

Stephen has gone through all this before, so he is fairly sure that Mr. Deasy, having put his pocketbook away, will say, "And now my strongroom for the gold," in keeping with the way he opens the proceedings by speaking of "our little financial settlement" (2.207/29.31). In Stephen's interior monologue the quotation, if we may call it that, has undergone a transformation (my $\Longrightarrow$ his), turning the phrase into a kind of free indirect discourse, in the terms of narrative theory. To cover his acute embarrassment at having to listen to Mr. Deasy's inane remarks, Stephen starts playing with the shells in the mortar on the headmaster's table. The narrator's voice starts in seemingly conventional third-person narrative but gradually merges into interior monologue again, the transition being signaled by the repeated "and this" and by the absence of finite verbs in the last sentence of the paragraph.

From his savings box, Mr. Deasy then shoots one sovereign, two crowns, and two shillings. Having pocketed notes and coins, Stephen returns to the shells: like money they are "symbols of beauty and of power," but the money ("A lump in my pocket") is "soiled by greed and misery" (2.226–28/30.11–13). The old man reproves him for putting the money loosely in his trousers pocket and advises him to buy one of these little savings boxes with compartments for sovereigns, crowns, shillings, and so on. Stephen is not impressed; he has heard this before and it has failed to change his outlook: "The same room and hour, the same wisdom:

and I the same. *Three times now*. Three nooses round me here. Well? I can break them in this instant if I will" (2.233–35/30.19–21, italics mine). In her discussion of this scene, Henke refers to Stephen's "third salary" (1978:42), but, as Kenner has pointed out, there can only have been one payday before the present one (1980:56n.). The first time Stephen was in the study of Mr. Deasy must have been the day the latter "bargained" with him, which was referred to earlier (2.200/29.23). Having been employed for a month, Stephen entered the headmaster's room for the *second* time, having earned his *first* salary, and so forth.

Mr. Deasy keeps harping on the importance of saving: "Money is power," he lectures, adding that an Englishman's proudest boast is: "*I paid my way. I never borrowed a shilling in my life . . . I owe nothing*" (2.253–54/30.41–42). He asks Stephen whether he can feel that. Of course, Stephen cannot share that feeling; in his mind he draws up an impressive survey of his debts, totaling £25.17.6 in cash alone, apart from such things as shoes, socks, ties, two lunches, and five weeks' board. We should not conclude, as Gordon does (1981a:49), that Stephen considers money to be useless; he is very well aware of the power it confers upon a man as long as he is free to spend it, and that is just what he is planning to do that day. What Stephen means when, in his thoughts, he employs the term "useless" is that this depressingly long list of what he owes to all these people forces him to acknowledge that the sum he has received just now will not go far in repaying any of these debts: "The lump I have is useless" (2.259/31.05–6). Indeed, at the end of the day he will already have spent more than half of it, and the chances are that from now on Mr. Deasy will not have to pay him any more wages at all.

EPISODE THREE
"Proteus"

THERE IS hardly any action in "Proteus." Stephen is alone all the time, so there is not any real dialogue either; technically speaking, there is some but that is either imagined (3.72ff./38.40ff.) or remembered (3.169–72/41.23–26). Stephen does see a few people on the beach, but they do not speak to him; he merely observes them as he observes the things around him, noting their colors, "snotgreen [a term he borrows from Mulligan, 1.73/5.02], bluesilver, rust: coloured signs" (3.03–4/37.04), and pondering problems of perception. The reader may wonder who "he" is in the opening paragraph until the Italian phrase brings the solution—if you know where to look for it. We hear the voice of Dante describing limbo, the region that is neither hell nor heaven and where Virgil shows him Aristotle in the midst of other philosophers, the thinker who is *maestro di color* (*loro* or *coloro* in modern Italian) *che sanno,* "the master of those that know."

Stephen's thoughts turn around the notions of time and space, Blake, Berkeley's theory of visual perception, and the nature of rhythm. Meanwhile, he conducts a mock experiment, walking on with closed eyes, tapping with his walking stick like blind men do. He then opens his eyes to assure himself that not all has vanished since, which it might have done if the world of reality were real only in the eye of the beholder. He has proved his point: "See now. There all the time without you: and ever shall be, world without end" (3.27–28/37.31–32). This realization that the world is not only real but eternal as well determines the trend of his thoughts about birth, death, sin, and his own parental home, when he sees two elderly women coming down to the beach (3.29ff./37.33ff.). One carries what in Stephen's view is a "midwife's bag," and consequently most commentators have identified them as midwives, although we might reflect that a man carrying an attaché case is not necessarily an attaché. Maddox keeps an open mind as to the women's identity; as he sees it, "Stephen mentally transforms (them) into midwives" (1978:31) and Kenner, too, attributes the women's midwife status to Stephen's fancy: "In the theatre of Stephen's mind women with a bag enact midwives" (1980:39). Stephen even puts a name to one of them, Florence MacCabe, a name he will use later for one of the "Dublin vestals" in his "Parable of the Plums" in "Aeolus" (7.923ff./145ff.). He persists in thinking of her as a midwife: "One of her sisterhood lugged me squealing into life" (3.35/37.40), and why shouldn't he have known her as such? Eldest son of a large family himself, he may very well have had some experience with midwives. The women will be referred to once more in one of the sections of "Wandering Rocks," a section in which Stephen is the protagonist. One is carrying a midwife's bag, but the narrator still refrains from calling them midwives: "Two old women fresh from their whiff of the briny trudged through Irishtown . . . one with a midwife's bag in which eleven cockles rolled" (10.818–20/242.07–10)—a meager result, eleven cockles, assuming that they have spent all these hours on the beach since Stephen saw them.

It has been remarked more than once, for example by Peake (1977:180), that in this episode there are repeated shifts from narrative to interior monologue, occurring in the middle of paragraphs and even sentences. A case in point is a sequence such as this: "His pace slackened. Here. Am I going to Aunt Sara's or not?" (3.61/38.28). "Here" marks the spot where Stephen takes stock of his surroundings and where he would have to leave the beach if he wanted to go to his aunt's (Aunt Sara, married to his mother's brother, Richie Goulding)—to ask her if she could put him up for the night, perhaps. He is not quite sure what to do. Walking slowly on, presumably, he imagines his father talking to his sisters, in a rather complex passage that starts with "My consubstantial father's voice" (3.61–69/38.29–37). In his interior monologue we hear him mimicking his father: "Did you see anything of your artist brother Stephen lately? No? Sure he's not down in Strasburg terrace with his aunt Sally? Couldn't he fly a bit higher than that, eh?" Then, in between, Stephen's monologue mimics Simon Dedalus in his turn mimicking the Gouldings, either Richie or Sara, when speaking to Stephen: "And and and and tell us Stephen, how is uncle Si?" This is followed, again, by Simon's scornful comments on the Goulding family: "O weeping God . . . Highly respectable gondoliers," phrases Stephen must have heard often enough. Morton, holding that Stephen's mind is full of what he calls "the triviality and the monotony of the provincial boy," says: "So, for example, a phrase from the low-brow operette *The Gondoliers* pops into his mind as readily as a quotation from *King Lear*" (1970:27). The phrase he alludes to, however, is not Stephen's but his father's as remembered by him. Next, we hear Simon Dedalus referring to Stephen's squinting cousin Walter, mimicking the way the boy addresses his father: "And skeweyed Walter sirring his father, no less. Sir. Yes, sir. No, sir," and finally Stephen has Dedalus Senior wind up with one of his characteristic, mildly blasphemous phrases: "Jesus wept: and no wonder, by Christ."

What follows (3.70–103/38.38–39.31) takes the form of a flashback (witness the consistent use of present tense) but is, most probably, a composite picture, a scene dreamed up on the basis of impressions gained in former visits to the Gouldings, a brilliant tour de force of Stephen's imaginative mind. The passage describes something that *might* happen when Stephen actually decides to call at the cottage and need not refer to a specific scene in the past.

Walking on, Stephen reflects that he has nothing to gain by staying in such houses as his parents' home or his uncle's cottage or any Irish house, for that matter: "Houses of decay, mine, his and all" (3.105/39.33), and he seems to hear a voice telling him what sounds like a quotation: "Come out of them, Stephen. Beauty is not there" (3.106–7/39.35). He remembers all kinds of youthful follies, such as his ideas about the books he was going to write: "Books you were going to write with letters for titles. Have you read his F? O yes, but I prefer Q. Yes, but W is wonderful. O yes, W" (3.139–40/40.31–33). Joyce has actually reached that stage: critics do use letters for titles of his works, such as *D* for *Dubliners*, *P* for *A Portrait of the Artist as a Young Man*, *U* for *Ulysses*, and *FW* for *Finnegans Wake*.

Stephen has sauntered on, deep in thought. He now becomes aware of some changes underfoot. He looks around, notes what there is to see, halts, realizing that he is not going to his Aunt Sara's after all—he never seriously intended to do so, probably—and turns to firmer ground:

> The grainy sand had gone from under his feet. His boots trod again a damp crackling mast, razorshells, squeaking pebbles, that on the un-numbered pebbles beats, wood sieved by the shipworm, lost Armada. Unwholesome sandflats waited to suck his treading soles, breathing upward sewage breath, a pocket of seaweed smouldered in seafire under a midden of man's ashes. He coasted them, walking warily. A porterbottle stood up, stogged to its waist, in the cakey sand dough. A sentinel: isle of dreadful thirst. Broken hoops on the shore; at the land a maze of dark cunning nets; farther away chalkscrawled backdoors and on the higher beach a dryingline with two crucified shirts. Ringsend: wigwams of brown steersmen and master mariners. Human shells.
>
> He halted. I have passed the way to aunt Sara's. Am I not going there? Seems not. No-one about. He turned northeast and crossed the firmer sand towards the Pigeonhouse.
>
> (3.147–60/40.41–41.13)

What starts as third-person narrative trails off into snatches from Stephen's thoughts, such as the not quite accurate quotation from *King Lear* (rightly, "that on the unnumbered idle pebbles chafes") and finally turns into a series of impressions, specifying things, near by and far away, viewed through Stephen's eyes. This is a brilliant description of what Stephen sees, of the process going on in his mind in an effort to shape literature out of reality, and the reader, I think, should appreciate and enjoy it as such, without feeling obliged to think of the bottle stuck in the sand as a "phallic porter-bottle" that "stands as an omen of castrated manhood" (Henke, 1978:58—a paradoxical metaphor!). Once we start groping and delving for possible interpretations there is no telling where we may end. What is the "isle of dreadful thirst" guarded by the porter bottle? Ireland, land of a hard-drinking people? In Henke's commentary, the maze of dark cunning nets "strangles creativity" (1978:58), but that is also a paradox, for when Stephen's mind shapes this phrase, "maze of dark cunning nets," that is a creative act in itself. The nets, we might as well say, serve to ensnare Proteus's manifold forms, they represent language as a creative force *par excellence*.

Another critic, French, scrambles the various details of this passage without taking into account the separate distances involved. She pictures Stephen as: "Standing among the ruins of nature and civilization washed in by the tide, among 'human shells,' a porter bottle, broken hoops, nets, discarded backdoors and two 'crucified shirts' (41), he feels his own rotting shells of teeth" (1976:81). As I see it, there are different planes to be distinguished: in the foreground there is the bottle, more or less before Stephen's feet; lifting his eyes, he discerns broken hoops and nets in what might be the middle distance; finally, as a backdrop, there are the cottages of the Dublin suburb of Ringsend, with shirts on a drying line and with back doors on which children have scrawled names and what not. Stephen has just been treading on shells—in which animals may live—and now he thinks of these seamen's and fishermen's houses ("wigwams") as shells for human beings to live in: "human shells." Stephen's rotting shells of teeth, which French refers to, do not figure in this paragraph at all; they are not going to crop up until some ten pages later.

Sometimes the unspoken associations by which such shifts from narrative to interior monologue are prompted are easy to track down, as in the following passage: "Airs romped round him, nipping and eager airs. They are coming, waves. The whitemaned seahorses, champing, brightwindbridled, the steeds of Mananaan. I mustn't forget his letter for the press. And after? The Ship, half twelve. By the way go easy with that money like a good young imbecile. Yes, I must" (3.55–60/38.22–27). Here, the opening sentence is not even pure narrative. There is some *Hamlet* in it, and that has to be traced to Stephen's stream of consciousness, presumably. Of course, as Knight (1952) already pointed out, it is an illusion to speak of the characters in *Ulysses* as actually presenting a normal stream of consciousness (and who, by the way, is to decide what is "normal"?), but this stream confronts us, anyway, with the characters' essential preoccupations. This technique as used by Joyce is, as Lukács observes, "the formative principle governing the narrative pattern and the presentation of character" (1972:475), and if we accept this view we now understand what the first part of this passage is meant to convey. It is the narrator's attempt to tell us that Stephen becomes aware of a fresh breeze from the sea and responds to it by recalling a phrase from *Hamlet*. In the midnight scene on the platform before Elsinore castle Hamlet remarks, "The air bites shrewdly; it is very cold," and Horatio assents, saying, "It is a nipping and an eager air." As the reader must be aware of by now, the air on the beach is not cold at all. On the contrary, it is a "burning scene," the time being nearly midday, "Pan's hour, the faunal noon" (3.442/49.13). The Shakespearean allusion is meant to point to something else, obviously. The reader should realize that Stephen is playing one of his roles; he is, in Kenner's words, "a young man who thinks he is enacting Hamlet's part (obstinate mourning, soliloquies, disobligingness)" (1980:69). It is true that Stephen "in his obstinate condolement" (*Hamlet* I.ii.93) wears mourning for his mother, not for his father as Hamlet does, but still, turning his "Latin quarter hat" (3.174/41.28), as Mulligan had called it, into his "Hamlet hat" (3.390/47.33), he seems intent on playing this role.

Schutte has listed ten *Hamlet* quotations in this episode (1957: 181–82) but only two are phrases actually spoken by Hamlet himself: "My tables" (I.v.107), in Stephen's adaptation: "My tablets" (3.399/48.04), and "to try conclusions" (III.iv.195; 3.50/38.16). Stephen just manipulates the phrases from the play, juggling them and adapting them freely to his own situation (an extreme case is 3.280–81/44.27–28). To allude to his hat, his walking stick, and the boots Mulligan gave him as a gift or a loan (3.16–17/37.19), he uses a pair of lines from Ophelia's song in act IV, with slight variations, resulting in: "My cockle hat and staff and hismy sandal shoon" (3.487–88/50.25–26). Elsewhere in his interior monologue he refers to the boots as "borrowed sandals" (3.411/48.19–20). Actually, Stephen wears no sandals but a sturdy pair of "broadtoed boots, a buck's castoffs" (3.446/49.17), which will arouse Mr. Bloom's appreciation later in the day: "Wonder is that young Dedalus the moving spirit. Has a good pair of boots on him today. Last time I saw him he had his heels on view" (7.984–86/147.03–5).

Stephen now turns his attention to the sea: "They are coming, waves." The present tense signals the onset of a stream of consciousness that conveys the workings of Stephen's imagination while he is gazing out at the rising tide, playing around in his mind with notions from Irish or Celtic mythology ("whitemaned seahorses," "steeds of Mananaan").

The second part of this passage has a more conspicuous interior-monologue character. It shows Stephen coming down to earth, reminding himself that some practical matters demand his attention. The imagery of the mythical seahorses has turned his thoughts back to Mr.

Deasy's study, with its pictures of famous racehorses (2.300ff./32.14–15), and to the old man's letter to the editor (*his* letter for the press), two copies of which Stephen has in his pocket. This, in turn, reminds him of his promise to meet Mulligan and Haines at half past twelve (see 1.733–34/23.13–14), a promise extracted from him by Mulligan because the latter expected him to come with his pockets full of money. The fact that Stephen remembers Mulligan's peremptory words does not necessarily mean that he plans to keep his promise. Even so, his vague resolution to "go easy with that money" will come to nothing, as the reader will learn in time. Stephen does not seem able to cope with the sordid reality so far removed from his lofty musings. He pretends that *history* is the nightmare from which he is trying to awake (see 2.377/34.22–23), instead of concentrating on the present and the future. Shari Benstock's judgment, "incapable of dealing with any of the exigencies of his day, any more than he can utilize his free afternoon for the purposes of literary composition, Stephen sinks into listless dissipation—wasting time, energy, and money" (1978:161), may seem a bit harsh (after all, Stephen will spend at least part of his afternoon expounding some sort of Shakespeare theory), but we have to concede that it is essentially irrefutable.

Toward the end of the episode, we find Stephen sitting down on a rock (3.282ff./44.29ff.), and he is still sitting there while composing a poem, scribbling the words on a piece of paper, the blank end he had torn off Mr. Deasy's letter. It is a passage (3.397–407/48.01–15) in which, as so often, interior monologue replaces narration. Having hit upon what he thinks of as a happy phrase, Stephen is frantically searching his pockets, looking, it seems, for a piece of paper on which to write down the lines he has composed, which are still fresh in his mind. This one word, "Paper," is like an impatient cry, and then, putting his hand into a pocket, he comes upon the bank notes that were part of his salary and that he cannot use now ("blast them"). We remember, indeed, that he had stowed away the entire sum in this indifferent manner: "Thank you, sir, Stephen said, gathering the money together with shy haste and putting it all in a pocket of his trousers" (2.223–24/30.07–9). The bank notes now remind him of Mr. Deasy and his letter for the press ("Old Deasy's letter"), which he must have put away in some other pocket, in his jacket, presumably. He takes it out and turns to the last page ("Here"). Finding some blank space left after the final flourish ("Thanking you for the hospitality of your columns" [2.336–37/33.16–17]), he tears the end off to write down his poem, a four-line stanza, which will not be put before the reader's eyes until later, in "Aeolus."

Until recently there has been a striking consensus among critics as to Stephen's last act in this episode. It has always been assumed that he must have got up from his rock at some point to make water, to urinate. This action has even been glorified as something akin to poetic creation, and it often inspired critics to create marvels of metaphor, mixed or otherwise, as when Henke depicted Stephen as follows: "Alone, micturating on a rock, Stephen makes water in a symbolic, lyrical stream that will eventually buoy him up above the grasp of 'old Father Ocean' " (1978:65). Opinions on the interpretation of the last pages of "Proteus" will have to be revised since Hayman demolished the generally accepted article of faith by arguing forcibly that Stephen is performing masturbation, not micturation (1977).

As a rule, readers do not turn to the opening episodes of *Ulysses* to find answers to fundamental philosophical questions about form and substance, appearance and reality, or to find solutions to theological problems involving the Persons of the Holy Trinity. What they are supposed to be interested in is Stephen's urge to ask himself such questions—without coming up with any definite answers, for that matter. In fact, as Gordon characterizes Stephen's musings in the third episode, "The result is one prolonged riddle with no good answer" (1981a:50).

From the point of view of the "story," in this episode stream of consciousness, interior monologue, and flashback serve to tell the reader some more about the time Stephen spent in Paris, to reveal his cravings for love, to recall various memories of his, not always pleasurable, and to record (3.365–69/47.04–9) a strange prophetic dream he had.

EPISODE FOUR
"Calypso"

A S WE have seen, one of the problems a reader of *Ulysses* has to grapple with is the heterogeneous nature of the interior monologue as a literary device, a carefully organized structure challenging the reader to disentangle the elements it is composed of. The act of reading, as Iser (1974) observes, becomes a constant process of selection in view of the mass of perspectives and aspects offered by the text. This does not mean that the author shows no tendency to come to the reader's aid. On the contrary, throughout *Ulysses*, and with increasing intensity, Joyce seems bent on making the reader aware of the presence of the author, a presence that becomes manifest when the interior monologue's psychological subject disappears, as happens from time to time. In Bloom's monologue, as Topia (1976) has demonstrated, a kind of hesitation is often felt, and there are points, breaking points, at which the reader is not sure to which voice the utterance should be attributed. There is a constant pendulum movement between "reactivated texts" and Bloom's own words, to such an extent that the reader may find it hard to draw a sharply defined border line between them.

The kind of breaking point in the interior monologue discussed by Topia is not the only one that an analysis of *Ulysses* has to take into account. We may distinguish at least two more types. First, there are places where narrative merges into interior monologue or stream of consciousness, and, the other way round, places where interior monologue fades out and narrative is resumed. Second, we may find interior monologue in which quotations have been incorporated, and within this category we might differentiate between cases in which the psychological subject of the stream of consciousness is quoting himself and cases in which the quotation derives from some other source. The following passage includes several instances of the first category:

> On quietly creaky boots he went up the staircase to the hall, paused by the bedroom door. She might like something tasty. Thin bread and butter she likes in the morning. Still perhaps: once in a way.
> He said softly in the bare hall:
> —I'm going round the corner. Be back in a minute.
> And when he had heard his voice say it he added:
> —You don't want anything for breakfast?

A sleepy soft grunt answered:
—Mn.

No. She didn't want anything. He heard then a warm heavy sigh, softer, as she turned over and the loose brass quoits of the bedstead jingled.

(4.49–59/56.16–28)

We see Bloom, on his way out to the butcher's, coming up from the kitchen in the basement and passing through the hall. Leading off from the hall floor is a door to the back room, which serves as the conjugal bedroom for the Blooms. The first sentence of the above passage is straight narrative; the rest of the paragraph represents what passes through Bloom's head while he halts before the closed door. With "He said softly" narrative is taken up again, and Bloom's words are reported in direct speech. Narrative then is resumed, leading up to Bloom's question. Note that Bloom, always a considerate man, allows some time to elapse, waiting for his words and the message they contain to sink in before coming up with his question. That is why the text has, "And when he *had heard his voice say it*" (italics mine). The answer Bloom gets is "Mn," a two-syllable sound interpreted by him, correctly, as having a negative connotation; it means that Molly does not want anything besides the usual homely fare of bread and butter and tea.

The next narrative sentence, quoted above, introduces a new train of thought, evoked by the jingling sounds of the bedstead, which Molly seems to have brought into the marriage: "jingled. Must get those settled really. Pity. All the way from Gibraltar. Forgotten any little Spanish she knew. Wonder what her father gave for it. Old style. Ah yes! of course. Bought it at the governor's auction. Got a short knock. Hard as nails at a bargain, old Tweedy. Yes, sir. At Plevna that was. I rose from the ranks, sir, and I'm proud of it. Still he had brains enough to make that corner in stamps. Now that was farseeing" (4.60–65/ 56.28–35). In this passage we find an example of the second category (quotation within interior monologue), the fragment: "Yes, sir . . . proud of it." Clearly, Bloom's father-in-law, Major Tweedy, who had served in the Gibraltar garrison and had married—if we are to believe what Molly tells us in the final episode—a Spanish Jewess, must have spoken like this time and again. Readers wondering about Molly's education, or apparent lack of it, may have asked themselves whether her father, the late Major Brian Cooper Tweedy, as he will be called later on (17.2082/730.03), could really have been a *major* in the British army. Burgess (1973b:33) considers both the man's rank and his marriage implausible. Could "major" have been a courtesy title given him when he spent his years of retirement in Dublin? Of course, he may have been a sergeant major or, as he is called by one of the singers in the Ormond saloon, a drum major (11.508/269.21). One way or another this would make him a noncommissioned officer, and that would explain why Bloom, his mind still on the stamp business, reflects: "Daresay lots of *officers* are in the swim *too*" (italics mine), which seems to imply that Tweedy himself is *not* an officer, strictly speaking.

Senn once listed the Tweedy enigma as one of the unsolved problems of *Ulysses* (1980). Von Phul has taken up the challenge by writing a complete *vie romancée* of the major, including his having been born of a passionate romance between a gentlewoman and a poor musician—or the other way round—and having been brought up by paid foster parents (1982), a fascinating and quite amusing account.

The next paragraph conforms to a pattern we have seen before, starting out with plain third-person narrative, merging into interior monologue, which in its turn may be relieved by narrative, and so on: "His hand took his hat from the peg over his initialled heavy overcoat and his lost property office secondhand waterproof. Stamps: stickyback pictures. Daresay lots of officers are in the swim too. Course they do. The sweated legend in the crown of his hat told him mutely: Plasto's high grade ha. He peeped quickly inside the leather headband. White slip of paper. Quite safe" (4.66–71/56.36–42). Joyce's way of describing Bloom's action of taking his hat from the peg evokes an absent-minded mechanical gesture wholly in keeping with Bloom's early morning mood. Prescott was one of the first to draw attention to this sample of stylistic realism. He quotes two more cases: "His [Bloom's] hand accepted the moist tender gland and slid it into a sidepocket. Then it fetched up three coins from his trousers' pocket and laid them on the rubber prickles" (4.181–83/60.06–8), and "His [Bloom's] slow feet walked him riverward, reading" (8.10/151.12). In such passages, Prescott observes, "a part of Bloom's body takes on independent activity while his mind is busy elsewhere. In each, the information is conveyed with admirable precision and economy" (1964:163n.4).

Turning our attention from Bloom's hand to his hat, we should remember not only that the time is early morning, before breakfast, but also that the year is 1904. In photographs from those days, especially street scenes, almost all the men are wearing hats or caps, depending on their social class. It is safe to say, therefore, that Bloom must have taken his hat from the peg unthinkingly, as a matter of course, if only for going round the corner to the butcher's on a bright June morning. This may seem an insignificant detail in itself, but the reader will soon discover its inherent relevance: toward the end of the episode he will find that Bloom, going out through his bit of a garden to the outhouse, suddenly wonders: "Where is my hat, by the way?" (4.485/68.20). Again, it must have been his hand that put it back on the peg, but his hand cannot remember. We shall have to look at that passage more closely later.

The mechanical nature of Bloom's gesture also explains the initial continuity of his stream of consciousness. The theme his mind plays around with remains the same till he reaches the front door: stamps and soldiers.

Before putting on his hat Bloom looks inside, as we have seen, in order to check whether the "white slip of paper" is safely hidden behind the headband, an action that takes his mind off stamps. What Bloom reads inside his hat—the last word of "Plasto's high grade ha" having partly worn away—figures among the "apparently trivial details" listed by Hayman as instances of potential symbols. Hayman speaks of "the missing letter on Bloom's hat band" (1982:22), but I do not think the firm's name is to be found on this leather band; the text is quite unambiguous in mentioning a legend *in the crown* of the hat. Such a legend is usually a piece of cloth into which the brand name has been woven. Besides, it is not one letter but, most probably, two letters that are missing; the hatter's label must have read: Plasto's high grade hats.

In time, readers will learn that the "slip of paper" must be some sort of (forged?) identity card, but just now its significance will probably escape them. As we see, narrative gradually merges into stream of consciousness, with the phrase "White slip of paper" as a channeling device in between. No longer pure narrative, it is not yet undisguised interior monologue, whereas the following "Quite safe" is. The absence of a finite verb form implies an underlying present tense, the meaning of the latter phrase being "it is quite safe there," which is the conclusion drawn by Bloom's mind once the presence of the slip of paper has been registered by his eyes.

Similar cases of transition are found in the next paragraph (4.72–76/ 57.01–6), where we learn that Bloom—having changed into a black suit, as he will have to attend a funeral—has left his key in the trousers he had worn the day before. He did not forget, however, to transfer his potato, an object that Bloom seems to think important ("Potato I have"). It is, we shall learn later, a hard black shriveled thing his mother used to carry in the pouch of her petticoat (see 15.287–89/438.28–30). It is "Poor mamma's panacea" (15.201–2/435.27), "A talisman. Heirloom" (15.1313/476.16), "a relic of poor mamma" (15.3513/555.17), and a "Preservative against Plague and Pestilence" (15.1952/499.03).

Note that Bloom has hung his trousers neatly in the wardrobe, whereas Molly's clothes have been scattered around, on a chair and on the bed (4.265–66; 321–23/62.16–18; 63.39–41). If dirt, as anthropologists define it, is "matter out of place" (Douglas, 1970:48), Molly may be called a dirty person indeed. True to form, she wipes her fingertips on the blanket (4.334/64.10–13), having just eaten a slice of bread and butter, and talking with her mouth full seems to come natural to her: "She doubled a slice of bread into her mouth, asking: —What time is the funeral?" (4.318–19/63.36–37).

Quotation twice removed occurs in Bloom's interior monologue when he passes Larry O'Rourke's grocery and spots the owner through the open doorway. He remembers Simon Dedalus amusing his cronies by performing a dialogue in which he imitated O'Rourke's way of talking. Next he imagines himself addressing the grocer on the subject of Dignam's death, thus quoting himself beforehand as taking part in a conversation that will never come to pass, for at the crucial moment he confines himself to the conventional "Good day" and "Lovely weather," neither of which seems to interest the shopkeeper to any marked extent. The passage runs as follows: "There he is . . . leaning against the sugarbin in his shirtsleeves watching the aproned curate swab up with mop and bucket. Simon Dedalus takes him off to a tee with his eyes screwed up. Do you know what I'm going to tell you? What's that, Mr O'Rourke? Do you know what? The Russians, they'd only be an eight o'clock breakfast for the Japanese. Stop and say a word: about the funeral perhaps. Sad thing about poor Dignam, Mr O'Rourke" (4.112–19/58.06–14).

In another passage we find quotation, still as part of an interior monologue, from a printed source. Waiting his turn in Dlugacz's butcher shop, Bloom takes up a page from a pile of sheets lying on the counter, to be used by the butcher to wrap up meat: "He took a page up from the pile of cut sheets: the model farm at Kinnereth on the lakeshore of Tiberias. Can become ideal winter sanatorium. Moses Montefiore. I thought he was. Farmhouse, wall round it, blurred cattle cropping" (4.154–57/59.15–18). First we have what looks like a caption belonging to an illustration in some Zionist leaflet or advertisement. What follows, including the name of the well-known nineteenth-century Anglo-Jewish philanthropist, could be flashes from the accompanying text. Then Bloom comments briefly on the butcher's background in relation to what he has just been reading about a Jewish planters' company promoting the purchase of land in Palestine. He is confirmed in the idea he must have entertained all along that the butcher (for all that he is a *pork* butcher!) is a Jew, as he is himself in a way. That, at least, seems to be the meaning of Bloom's "I thought he was" (with sentence stress on "thought"), and if we want some corroboration we might point to a passage farther down (4.185–87/60.10–12); the butcher has put Bloom's pennies into the till, saying: "Thank you, sir. Another time," but Bloom does not remove himself instantly. The butcher looks at him intently, and Bloom is tempted, but only for a moment, to give some sign of recognition. Then he decides not to commit himself, not yet, anyway; in his interior

monologue he echoes the butcher's "Another time," lending it a different meaning: "A speck of eager fire from foxeyes thanked him. He
withdrew his gaze after an instant. No: better not: another time."

There are, however, other ways of interpreting Bloom's phrase. It
might, for example, refer to the preceding fragments from the text of the
pamphlet, in particular to the name Montefiore. Bloom may be thinking
something such as, "Ah yes, I've read (or heard) of such plans, I thought
indeed this Montefiore was involved somehow." However, the phrase
might represent an unfinished thought ("I thought he was . . ."); perhaps
Bloom could not remember who Montefiore was and then started
wondering: "Montefiore? I thought he was a composer, not a cattle
raiser." The trouble is, of course, that we cannot be sure of the intonation
of these four words, which are, after all, unspoken—a paradoxical
situation. There is a lot of difference between "I thóúght he was (a Jew)"
and "I thought he was (a *composer*)."

There are similar cases in the book, not less subtle. When Molly gives
Bloom the novel she has been reading, asking him to bring her another
one from the library, she says: "There's nothing smutty in it" (4.355/
64.36). On the printed page, taken out of context, this may look like a
bland statement of fact, but as spoken by a human being there must be
some feeling behind these words, and it is left to the reader to interpret
the nature of this feeling. Mary Power, for instance, holds that Molly is
defending the moral tone of the book (1981:120), whereas Gilbert
believes that Molly speaks these words with some regret (1930:140). I
think he is right. I, for one, have always taken it for granted that Molly is
voicing her disappointment, not her praise.

Bloom's next thought, "Farmhouse, etc.," is no longer quotation, it
summarizes what he sees in the picture of the model farm. More
extensive quotation from the planters' company's publicity text will be
found in his inner monologue on the way home (4.191–99/60.16–26).
Bloom has apparently taken the sheet of paper with him; walking home,
he keeps reading it. Note that all editions of *Ulysses* give the company's
name as "Agendath Netaim." In Hebrew one would expect "Agudáth
Netaím" (three syllables each, stress marks added), *agudah*—in com-
pounds *agudath*—being the Hebrew word for company or association.

The most natural opportunity for Bloom to quote himself in his
interior monologue would arise should he remember scenes in which he
himself had been one of the partners in a dialogue. Such a case presents
itself in the episode's final pages, where we find Bloom sitting in the
outdoor privy, leisurely reading a story in an old number of *Titbits*.
Much impressed that the author of this story received payment "at the
rate of one guinea a column," he dreams of trying his hand at a sketch,
based on some proverb, or by making use of the material supplied by the

rambling monologues Molly keeps up when dressing. He remembers and
quotes to himself some things she used to say (4.518–23/69.18–24).

These memories of how he used to make notes of Molly's sayings (an
allusion to Joyce's own notebooks?) take Bloom's mind completely off
the impracticable idea of a sketch or story. Instead, he relives the scene of
that morning after the fateful night of the dance where his wife danced
with Boylan, her lover-to-be:

> Morning after the bazaar dance when May's band played Ponchielli's
> dance of the hours. Explain that: morning hours, noon, then evening
> coming on, then night hours. Washing her teeth. That was the first night.
> Her head dancing. Her fansticks clicking. Is that Boylan well off? He has
> money. Why? I noticed he had a good rich smell off his breath dancing.
> No use humming then. Allude to it. Strange kind of music that last night.
> The mirror was in shadow. She rubbed her handglass briskly on her
> woollen vest against her full wagging bub. Peering into it. Lines in her
> eyes. It wouldn't pan out somehow.
>
> (4.525–33/69.27–37)

Peake speaks of a sketch, based on "The Dance of the Hours," which
Bloom thinks of writing, and which would be expressive of the fluctu-
ation in Bloom's mood demonstrated in this episode. Although there are
cases here where Bloom fluctuates, as Peake puts it, "between feeling
young and feeling old, between satisfaction and regret" (1977:183), this
scene is not one of them. Quite apart from the fact that Bloom's mind is
no longer on the idea of writing a sketch, let alone one based on some
intrinsically plotless ballet performance, the symbolism of Ponchielli's
ballet does not so much involve an abrupt movement between extremes
as rather a gradual transition from dawn, through day and twilight, to
darkness, night. The theme is elaborated later, in the night scene,
"Circe," into a ceremonial dance to the music of a pianola, while Bloom
"stands aside" (15.4030; 4061ff./575.16; 576.04ff.). This cannot but
mean that the theme has some importance for Bloom. This importance,
however, does not attach to the theme as such, but derives from the
welcome opportunity it offers him to explain to Molly what it is all about,
just as he tries to explain the meaning of "metempsychosis"
(4.339ff./64.18ff.) or the philosophy of Spinoza (11.1058/284.36).
Hence his thought, "Explain that . . ." Now, does this mean that Bloom
remembers that he really did explain the symbolism of the dance to
Molly that morning? The German translator, Wollschläger, evidently
believes it does, for he puts it like this: "Ihr den erklärt" ["explained it to
her"], die Morgenstunden, Mittag, wie dann der Abend naht, dann die
Nachtstunden" (98). But I am not convinced that this is the right
interpretation. The trouble is, of course, that these nonfinite verb forms

may signify anything. We have a comparable case in "Sirens." The scene
is the dining room of the Ormond Hotel, where Bloom and Goulding are
sharing a table. Sounds of song and piano music from the saloon reach
them by way of the public bar, adjoining the dining room. They listen to
Simon Dedalus singing a tenor air from the opera *Martha*, the door to the
bar having been set ajar by the waiter at Bloom's request. While enjoying
to the full the sound of Dedalus's still glorious voice, Bloom muses:
"Wish I could see his face, though. *Explain better*. Why the barber in
Drago's always looked my face when I spoke his face in the glass. Still
hear it better here than in the bar though farther" (11.721–23/275.12–15,
italics mine). If you look at a person's face when speaking to him, you are
in a better position to explain things to him, and he will have less
difficulty understanding: That is what Bloom wants to say. He illustrates
this general thesis by drawing upon an actual experience. His "Explain
better," therefore, does not necessarily mean that he or anybody else did
explain anything specific or was going to do so. It only implies that
people, under certain conditions and if they wanted to, *could* explain
things better, according to Bloom. Similarly, Bloom's "Explain that" in
"Calypso" might refer to a hypothetical case, meaning "one could
explain that" or "I could explain that." This, however, should then be
transposed, as Bloom is now looking back upon the event under discussion, into "I could have explained that." Bloom depicts himself as
wanting to explain, perhaps even making an abortive attempt, but Molly
does not really listen to him (no more than she does when he lectures her
on metempsychosis or Spinoza), for she is busy brushing her teeth. But is
Bloom being quite honest? Can he really have been so eager to explain
the musical symbolism? I doubt it. What he must have had in mind,
actually, was to draw Molly out on the subject of Boylan. He suspects
that Boylan must have made quite an impression on her that "first
night" she danced with him, and talking about the music might just
possibly lead up to it. Then Molly comes straight to the point; Bloom has
not forgotten their short dialogue. He himself will never once use
Boylan's name in relation to Molly. Even in conversations in which
others will bring up the subject of his wife's concert tour, he makes a
point of avoiding the hateful name. Here in "Calypso," however, he is
quoting Molly, and so there is no way of getting round it. "Is that Boylan
well off?" Molly asks, and Bloom, caught unaware, concedes, "He has
money," but, wondering what could have been her reason for asking, he
adds, "Why?" Molly's answer, going off on a tangent, may well have
perplexed him; at least there is no record of Bloom's continuing the
conversation. Now, reminiscing on his seat in the closet, he remembers
giving up the idea of humming the dance melody in order to elicit some
reaction on Molly's part, and deciding then and there to make a more

direct allusion to it by saying, quasi-offhandedly, something such as "Strange kind of music that last night," which means, of course, "That was a strange kind of music, last night, don't you think?" This construction is not at all unusual in Bloom's interior monologues, as for instance when he thinks (remembering a witty saying of Arthur Griffith's): "Ikey touch that: homerule sun rising up in the northwest" (4.103–4/57.38–39).

It should be noted that, in Bloom's thoughts, "last night" does not refer to the preceding evening (15 June), but to the night of the dance, a few weeks before; it is part of what he *might* have said to Molly the next morning.

In retrospect, we may argue that all this business of humming or making allusions cannot but support the view that Bloom has not explained anything at all. If he had really been explaining the idea behind the dance of the hours, why should he have to wait for a chance of alluding to this music in order to broach the subject? I am inclined to go even further and doubt whether Bloom did make any allusion at all. There is no explicit mention of this in the text. Bloom may have conceived this idea of alluding to the music and may even now remember the actual words of the introductory phrase he contemplated using that morning after the ball, but the question remains: Did he use it? It sounds quite implausible, to say the least. For one thing, if he did, why are we not told of Molly's response? She would surely have shown some reaction and Bloom would equally surely have remembered. Furthermore, there is a striking correspondence between the sequences "Explain that" and "Washing her teeth," on the one hand, and "Allude to it" and "The mirror was in shadow," on the other. In both cases Bloom seems to have been easily discouraged: first, brushing her teeth, Molly would not pay attention anyhow; then, it would be difficult to study her face in the mirror under these circumstances, and so, both times, he lets the moment pass. Now he is quoting from an imaginary conversation, employing words and phrases he was never going to utter, just as when he contemplated saying a few ready-made words about Dignam's funeral to Mr. O'Rourke and then seems to have changed his mind (cf. 4.118–25/ 58.13–20). Dejectedly, he has to admit that, for some reason or other, his stratagems would not work.

The next paragraph takes up the theme of Ponchielli's opera ballet again: "Evening hours, girls in grey gauze. Night hours then: black with daggers and eyemasks. Poetical idea: pink, then golden, then grey, then black. Still, true to life also. Day: then the night" (4.534–36/69.38–41). Bloom now stops looking back in a mood of despondency. He resumes his interior monologue in a fresh effort to take his mind off those disturbing thoughts about Molly and Boylan. At the same time, he seeks to compensate for his frustration at not having taken advantage of the opportunity to explain the symbolism of the dance to Molly by working it out for himself. Reassured somehow, he may go out now and face the day that lies in store for him.

As Harvey observes, "Joyce is concerned throughout *Ulysses* to emphasize 'the dance of the hours': he does so not by picturing Bloom's day in the romantic hues of Ponchielli's ballet but by referring to simple mechanical time, to watches, clocks, and church bells" (1970:106). Time does play an essential role. Not only is there the all-pervading massive stream of time on which Bloom is borne along from early morning till dead of night, and not only do we find flashbacks and reminiscences, sometimes stretching far back into Bloom's past, but there are also a great many explicit references to certain points in time, especially in contexts dealing with Bloom. Occasionally, time seems to hang heavy on his hands, as in "Lotus Eaters," but then again he seems in a hurry, as in "Cyclops." What he is constantly aware of, however, and what is preying on his mind all day, is the thought of the advancing hour of four, when the assignation will take place in his own house, the time Boylan is coming to see Molly, ostensibly to bring the program of her so-called concert tour to the north (it turns out to be one single concert, to be given in Belfast), which Boylan is managing as her impresario.

Astute readers have often wondered how Bloom could have known about the rendez-vous, a point Ellmann has already drawn attention to (1955:569). "Who was the letter from?" (4.310/63.27) Bloom had asked Molly and the only thing she told him—as far as the reader is allowed to know—was "O, Boylan. He's bringing the programme" (4.312/63.29). Yet, a few hours later, we learn that Bloom knows more than the reader. From the funeral carriage (in "Hades") he sits looking at posters announcing some theatrical and musical events in the week to come: "They went past the bleak pulpit of saint Mark's. . . . Hoardings: Eugene Stratton, Mrs Bandmann Palmer. Could I go to see *Leah* tonight, I wonder. I said I. Or the *Lily of Killarney*? . . . . Martin Cunningham could work a pass for the Gaiety. Have to stand a drink or two. As broad as it's long. He's coming in the afternoon. Her songs" (6.183–90/92.03–11). Bloom thinks of going to see *Leah*, a play that will be staged in the Gaiety Theatre, with Mrs Bandmann Palmer in the title role. His unfinished thought, "I said I," may have something to do with that performance, but the reader is left guessing: What did Bloom say, and when, and to whom? Apparently, there is also some connection with Boylan's visit, for Bloom's concluding thought is about him and Molly: "*He's* coming . . . *Her* songs." We know now that Bloom is aware of the time of Boylan's visit ("in the afternoon") but we still do not know for sure how he had got this information.

We are getting nearer the truth at the end of "Lestrygonians." Around two o'clock, Bloom spots Boylan walking toward him along Kildare Street; wanting to avoid a meeting he hurries across to reach the museum, meanwhile searching his pockets as if he were looking for something. One of the things he digs up is the Agendath leaflet he had picked up at the butcher's at breakfast time and that reminds him, presumably, of something he had heard in the bedroom that morning when he brought Molly her breakfast: "He thrust back quick Agendath. *Afternoon she said*" (8.1186–87/183.32–33, italics mine). So it must have been Molly herself who told him.

But that is not all. Nearly two hours later, Bloom is walking along Wellington Quay, trying to suppress any thoughts of Boylan's visit by concentrating on food: "Eat first. I want. Not yet. *At four, she said.* Time ever passing. Clockhands turning. On. Where eat? The Clarence, Dolphin. On" (11.187–89/260.40–42, italics mine).

Up to a point the information is complete now. Molly must have told her husband more than just "He's bringing the programme," as the reader has been given to understand. But when? Broadly speaking, there are two schools of thought.

As McBride points out (1979, 1981), Molly may very well have given Bloom every detail at once for all we know, answering his question about the letter by stating flatly: "O, Boylan. He's bringing the program in the afternoon, at four." Bloom, however, then suppresses this shattering piece of information, and it is some time coming out in the course of the day, the passage quoted above not being the only one to refer to the specific hour; compare "At four" (11.305/264.02), "At four she" (11.309/264.07), "At four" (11.392/266.12). Note that the passage "Not yet. At four she. Who said four?" (11.352), which is corrupt in the Random House edition (265.11), does not belong in this series. In the Ormond bar Boylan asks whether the results of the Gold Cup race had already come in by telegraph: "Wire in yet?" Lenehan hastens to answer and starts telling him that *she* (Miss Douce?) had said that the results would be in by four o'clock. Boylan, impatient, wants to know *who* said that—something like that. Bloom, meanwhile, is still outside on the quay. He has seen Boylan enter the bar and wonders: "What is he doing in the Ormond?"

However, Molly may have said just that: "He's bringing the programme." Later, *after breakfast,* as Kenner notes (1980:48–51), Bloom may have returned to the bedroom to take leave of Molly before setting out for the city—as well as to get the latchkey he had forgotten (and will forget once more) to shift to the black suit he is wearing now. As Kenner observes, "Knowing that the writer of the 'bold hand' will be coming by, knowing what this portends, it would be callow and un-Bloomlike to just slip out the front door" (1980:48). This critic visualizes that leavetak-

ing—a "painful scene," which Joyce left unwritten—along the lines of
Bloom asking Molly point-blank: "What time is Boylan coming?" and
Molly answering: "In the afternoon, at four." Then Bloom must have
responded by saying something that was clearly expected of him, and he
did so either on the spur of the moment or as the result of thinking things
over while eating breakfast. That must have been what he was reminded
of when he passed the theater bills that morning ("I said I"), but we still
do not know what his actual words were. In fact, we will not learn what
Bloom must have said until Molly, looking back on the day and evaluating Bloom's behavior, remembers: "because he [Bloom] has an idea
about him [Boylan] and me hes not such a fool *he said Im dining out and
going to the Gaiety*" (18.81–82/740.12–14, italics mine). This, then,
must have been the scene Bloom relives in a flash while talking to M'Coy
in the fifth episode (5.154–56/75.14–17). He had told the latter about
Molly's concert tour, avoiding Boylan's name, as usual, but he remembers vividly the address on the envelope, in Boylan's handwriting ("Mrs
Marion Bloom"). In his mind's eye he sees Molly, still in bed; she is
bored because, having finished *Ruby: the Pride of the Ring*, she has
nothing to read ("No book") and is now dealing out cards to amuse
herself, while the cat lies curled up on the bed. When Bloom brought
Molly's breakfast tray up, however, there were no cards and there was no
cat either; it is not until Bloom opened the kitchen door to go to the
outhouse (4.467–69/67.39–68.02) that the cat could have gone upstairs.
By having Bloom think "At four, she said" Joyce gave us a clue,
expecting us to reconstruct the unrecorded scene for ourselves.

When we think of it, there is indeed a blank somewhere, a stretch of
time not accounted for. The last we see of Bloom in this episode he is
coming out of the jakes, in shirt sleeves, presumably. Having gone back
inside he must have put on waistcoat and jacket, and when we see him
next he is already far from home, walking leisurely along Sir John
Rogerson's Quay south of the river. And, yes, he has not left without his
hat (5.21/71.26)—it must have been hanging on its customary peg after
all, and another mechanical gesture would have been enough to retrieve
it. There is one thing he forgot, though (in the inner turmoil of the
leavetaking scene?), and that is his key. Like Stephen that same morning,
he has set out as a "keyless citizen" (17.1019/697.30), and at the end of
the day they will find themselves together on Eccles Street as a "keyless
couple" (17.81/668.17).

According to Mason, Bloom receives a letter from his daughter "on
holiday in Mullingar" (1972:42), but Milly, for all that she may be
amusing herself in her spare time, has a regular job in a photographer's
establishment. We even learn from Bloom's thoughts while he is eating
his breakfast how much she earns: "Twelve and six a week. Not much.

Still, she might do worse" (4.425/66.32). We will learn, too, what Molly thinks about Bloom's motives for sending Milly to Mullingar. She resents her husband's leaving her alone in their big house all day long: "especially now with Milly away such an idea for him to send the girl down there to learn to take photographs . . . on account of me and Boylan thats why he did it Im certain the way he plots and plans everything out" (18.1004–9/766.10–16).

Milly's final remark about Boylan's song, coming on top of the latter's note to Molly, picked up from the hall floor that morning along with the letter from Milly, must have given Bloom a nasty jolt to judge from the fact that phrases from this song ("Those Lovely Seaside Girls") recur in his musings several times during the day. This is what Milly writes: "There is a young student comes here some evenings named Bannon his cousins or something are big swells and he sings Boylan's (I was on the pop of writing Blazes Boylan's) song about those seaside girls. Tell him silly Milly sends my best respects" (4.406–9/66.12–16). At first Bloom associates the song with his own daughter. Having read and reread her letter while finishing breakfast in the kitchen, he keeps thinking of her "with troubled affection." He is reminded of a boat trip they made and remembers her as a kind of seaside girl herself: "On the *Erin's King* that day round the Kish. Damned old tub pitching about. Not a bit funky. Her pale blue scarf loose in the wind with her hair. *All dimpled cheeks and curls, Your head it simply swirls*" (4.434–38/67.02–7). Soon, however, the memory of his daughter is superseded by the ever-present thought of Boylan. His retina still retains the image of the strip of torn envelope (Boylan's letter) he saw peeping from under Molly's pillow when he entered the bedroom with the tea tray. He remembers Boylan as a swaggering brute, posing as a coach driver on his day off, singing this popular song. He thinks of him, not without some bitterness, presumably, as a "friend of the family," which he has been, up till now anyway, since Bloom became acquainted with him in September the year before (cf. 17.2170/732.31), and he smiles inwardly at Boylan's vulgar, slightly ridiculous way of pronouncing "swirls" as "swurls," whatever the difference may be: "Seaside girls. Torn envelope. Hands stuck in his trousers' pockets, jarvey off for the day, singing. Friend of the family. *Swurls*, he says" (4.439–40/67.08–10). Milly also seems quite familiar with Hugh Boylan. She knows he is nicknamed "Blazes" but has probably been told not to call him that. This, at least, might explain her parenthetical remark. Another explanation has been suggested by Ellmann; in the index of one of his books, under the entry "Boylan, Blazes," he states: "confused with another Boylan by Milly" (1972:196), implying that there must have been a song composer of that same name. Any proof of his existence, however, has not been unearthed, as far as I know, and, the way I see it, Milly's remark is prompted either by her reflecting that a nice girl should not use bad language or by her fear of seeming to show disrespect with regard to Boylan, who is after all a friend of the family and her mother's impresario to boot. With "Boylan's song," then, Milly seems to refer to a popular hit about seaside girls, which Boylan is fond of singing.

More than once the reader is reminded that Boylan is a singer as well as a businessman. At night Molly recalls that "he was in great singing voice" (18.149/742.09) when he came to see her that afternoon as arranged, and Bloom, entering the front room, finds the music of "Love's Old Sweet Song," open at the last page, on the music rest of the piano (17.1303ff./706.21ff.), which suggests that Molly and Boylan have been singing together; they may have been rehearsing for Molly's concert. Anyway, Boylan does not appear in public, as a performer on the stage, that is, as we learn from Bloom's interior monologue in "Sirens." In the Ormond dining room, at about the same time Boylan is visiting Molly, Bloom, while listening to Simon Dedalus singing, thinks of tenors getting women "by the score." Once again, phrases from Boylan's song pass through his mind: "My head it simply. . . . *He can't sing for tall hats.* Your head it simply *swurls*" (11.687–88/274.13–15, italics mine). That is why I am doubtful of Kain's statement that Molly is "to sing with Boylan" (1959:257), presumably at the planned concert in Belfast. I believe that Boylan will go there primarily in his capacity as concert manager, although Adams also assumes that Molly is to sing "Love's Old Sweet Song" with Boylan at the concert (1962:71). Kain's assumption may be based on a false clue such as Bloom's seeming to suppress Boylan's name when asked about the artists who will be on the concert tour: "O yes, we'll have all topnobbers, J. C. Doyle and John MacCormack I hope and. The best, in fact. —And *madame*, Mr Power said smiling. Last but not least" (6.221–24/93.06–9). From the context, however, we may conclude that it is not Boylan's but Molly's name Bloom avoids mentioning this time, prompted probably by sheer modesty or by a need of privacy, unwilling to share the thought of his wife with the occupants of the funeral carriage.

Power's remark has set him thinking of Molly anew; she must be up by now, he assumes: "And *madame*. Twenty past eleven. Up. Mrs Fleming is in to clean. Doing her hair, humming. *Voglio e non vorrei.* No. *Vorrei e non.* Looking at the tips of her hairs to see if they are split. *Mi trema un poco il.* Beautiful on that *tre* her voice is: weeping tone. A thrush. A throstle. There is a word throstle that expresses that" (6.237–41/93.24–29).

However, that is not all. As in "Sirens," where the air from *Martha* plays a comparable role, Bloom is deeply involved, emotionally. He knows perfectly well that Molly is singing the duet from *Don Giovanni* with the baritone Doyle and not with Boylan: she told him so herself that morning (4.314/63.31) and that is one thing that could be checked easily if he wanted. Still, for him, as Hall pointed out long ago (1951:78ff.), the duet becomes a symbol of Molly's adultery. It may not be Boylan who will be singing Don Giovanni's part, yet it is he who will lure Zerlina away from her poor Masetto. This is something Bloom feels painfully certain of from the very moment he has picked up Boylan's letter from the hall floor.

Anyhow, Bloom will not comply, surely, with Milly's naïve request to give Boylan her best respects, any more than he will ask Boylan for a job for Corley at Stephen's request (see 16.229–34/619.13–20).

The sequence where we find Bloom scanning Milly's letter and pouring himself a cup of tea before loading Molly's breakfast tray (4.280ff./62.34ff.) gives rise to a few questions, such as: Who put the pieces of paper in the letterbox? The text ("Putting pieces of folded brown paper in the letterbox for her") has "for her," not "for herself," and yet both the French and the older German translation explicitly state that it was Milly herself who did so: "Elle *s'envoyait* des bouts de papier d'emballage pliés dans la boîte aux lettres" (Morel, 62) and "steckte *für sich* Stücke gefalteten, braunen Papiers in den Briefkasten" (Goyert, I.100), respectively (italics mine). As Milly must have been a child of four at the time, this seems rather improbable. It may have been Molly's idea, as she had tried—out of sheer boredom—to deceive herself in the same way when she was a girl in Gibraltar, something she will remember in her nocturnal soliloquy: "the days like years not a letter from a living soul except the odd few I posted to myself with bits of paper in them" (18.698–99/757.29–31).

In the beginning of this chapter I referred to a scene in which Bloom is wondering where he may have left his hat. He has stopped a moment to study the condition of the soil in his garden, and now he resumes his walk to the outhouse: "He walked on. Where is my hat, by the way? Must have put it back on the peg. Or hanging up on the floor. Funny I don't remember that. Hallstand too full. Four umbrellas, her raincloak. Picking up the letters. Drago's shopbell ringing. Queer I was just thinking that moment. Brown brillantined hair over his collar. Just had a wash and brushup. Wonder have I time for a bath this morning. Tara street. Chap in the paybox there got away James Stephens, they say. O'Brien" (4.485–91/68.20–27). This passage contains many a crux, as might be seen from the various ways translators have dealt with it. The common reader may argue that it is no concern of his to find out where Bloom had put his hat as long as he, Bloom, seems to have retrieved it, but translators are in a different position. They do have to decide, for instance, how to pass on the somewhat cryptic message conveyed by the words "Or hanging up on the floor." In some translations, Bloom thinks his hat may have fallen to the floor, in others he supposes it is hanging somewhere upstairs on the first floor, but why should he have run up the stairs to an upper story just to put away his hat, knowing he would have to go out again shortly, anyway? He even seems to shrink back a moment from climbing the stairs to the landing when feeling the need to relieve himself: "Heaviness: hot day coming. Too much trouble to fag up the stairs to the landing" (4.463–64/67.35–36). To reach the garden he has to use the back-door leading off a passage at the foot of this landing, but first, as we have seen, he rummages in the kitchen table drawer to look for something to read in the outhouse: "In the tabledrawer he found an old number of *Titbits*. He folded it under his armpit, went to the door and opened it. The cat went up in soft bounds. Ah, wanted to go upstairs, curl up in a ball on the bed" (4.467–69/67.39–68.02). From Bloom's actions and the cat's response it seems that there is another door besides the back door to the garden, a door (it has been mentioned before; cf. 4.456/67.26) that opens into the passage from which stairs lead up to hall-floor level. When all is said and done, therefore, we are left with a sense of confusion.

Another objection that might be made is the following: when leaving to go to the butcher's, Bloom takes his hat from the peg it was hanging on: So what could have prevented him from hanging it back on the same peg when reentering the house? After all, his movements can be checked easily from the moment he comes back after having done his shopping to the time he goes out into the garden. Having scooped up the letters from the floor, he hears Molly's voice calling him; he enters the bedroom straightaway, it seems. Molly having urged him to bring her her tea, he goes down to the kitchen to prepare her breakfast. Having taken up the breakfast tray to the bedroom, Bloom lingers for a few minutes, because Molly asks him to explain the meaning of "metempsychosis," a word she had stumbled upon in a book she has been reading, until a smell of burning sends him scurrying down the kitchen stairs again, leaving him no time to close the door properly. Having managed to salvage the kidney, he sits down to his own breakfast, drinking his tea and reading and rereading Milly's letter. Soon after that, he passes through the garden on his way to the outhouse, having left the house by the back door. It is then that he starts wondering about his hat. When we look back over the chain of events outlined above, it is hard to see at which point Bloom could have sneaked away—for no apparent reason—just in order to find some unusual place for his hat. He simply must have put it back on the peg, as he himself supposes he did. That would have been the natural thing to do as soon as he had entered the hallway. The text, however, is of little help, because, as Kenner observes (1980:46–47; 70),

Bloom's passing through the front door on returning from his errand to the butcher's has not been recorded explicitly.

As he always does when confronted with an unusual or intriguing phenomenon, Bloom instantly starts thinking of possible explanations. Slightly annoyed at having to admit to himself that he is unable to account for his own actions during a certain stretch of time, he tries to figure out what might have occurred and to find excuses for his seemingly irrational behavior: the hall stand is too full, for one thing, and, furthermore, he must have been stooping in order to pick up the letters: Could he have dropped his hat in doing so? He realizes very well that spotting Boylan's letter, addressed to "Mrs Marion Bloom" (a recurrent motif; cf. "Bold hand: Mrs Marion" [13.843/369.42]), has given him quite a shock. He may have been too preoccupied to notice such details as hanging up a hat, an automatic gesture at all times.

"Picking up the letters" is one of those utterances that offer no formal clue as to tense. But the reader knows one thing for sure: present tense cannot be implied for the letters have been picked up already. Why, then, does Bloom suddenly recall the moment he picked them up? This is a question that translators must have asked themselves, and the answers they gave may be guessed from the resulting translations of this phrase: "C'est en ramassant les lettres" (Morel, 67), "Hob die Briefe auf" (Goyert, I.109), and "Ich hob grad die Briefe auf" (Wollschläger, 96). Bloom is still racking his brains for a plausible explanation of his failure to visualize the whereabouts of his hat, and it is this notion that has been expressed most clearly by Morel, whose version suggests something such as, "Whatever it was, it must have happened when I was picking up the letters." This may be because he managed to avoid the trap of switching to a finite verb. Goyert's translation, while being formally correct, lacks any allusion to the function of the phrase in the context. By inserting a modal adverb, *grad* (i.e., *gerade* [just]), Wollschläger may have meant to convey the notion that we are not dealing here with a simple statement of fact, but with an attempt on Bloom's part at retrieving events that his short-term memory has failed to store. This modal adverb enables us to read more into this phrase than meets the eye.

Bloom's thoughts now switch, rather unexpectedly, to a similar case of what to him are strange coincidences: "Drago's shopbell ringing." It must have been one of those coincidences or correspondences Bloom is always keen on. Thinking about his daughter's birthday (the day before), when she was fifteen, he is struck that the date was 15 June: "Fifteen yesterday. Curious, fifteenth of the month too" (4.415/66.20). Listening to Simon Dedalus starting to sing an air from *Martha* just when he, Bloom, is going to write a letter to Martha Clifford, he reflects: "*Martha* it is. Coincidence. Just going to write" (11.713/275.03).

Such coincidences, however, should not be thought of as purely haphazard. There may always be a link somewhere. What is the link between Bloom's recalling his picking up the letters and the ringing of Drago's shop bell? To answer this question and to reconstruct Bloom's train of thought, we have to go back to the very moments preceding his finding the letters on the hall floor. Walking back home, with the kidney wrapped up in a side pocket, he had been reading a company's prospectus about purchase of land in Palestine, with visions of orange groves and melon fields. When the sky clouds over, however, his mood changes and his thoughts turn from fertile groves and lush fields to the barren landscape of the Dead Sea: "Grey horror seared his flesh. Folding the page into his pocket he turned into Eccles street, hurrying homeward" (4.230–31/61.21–22). He quickens his steps, he wants to be home already: "Be near her ample bedwarmed flesh. Yes, yes" (4.238–39/61.30–31). Entering the hallway, he must have been almost out of breath. Visions of Molly reclining in bed crowd his mind, and the first letter he looks at proves to be addressed to her, in a "bold hand," at that. No wonder his heart skips a beat: "Two letters and a card lay on the hallfloor. He stooped and gathered them. Mrs Marion Bloom. His quickened heart slowed at once. Bold hand. Mrs Marion" (4.243–45/ 61.35–37).

Aroused by the memory of this seemingly trivial detail, Bloom's thoughts turn back to another occasion when he had experienced an even more memorable coincidence. From these thoughts we may surmise that Bloom had once seen Boylan leave a barber's shop at a moment when he, Bloom, had just been thinking about him. Bloom must have been passing near there when he had heard the shop bell ringing and, on looking that way, had seen the door opening and Boylan emerging. All this must have happened some time before 16 June, before Bloomsday. It has stuck in Bloom's memory primarily because Boylan was involved, but the memory probably has been reinforced because it was accompanied by a striking coincidence.

As said before, Bloom is keen on coincidences. There is a similar case in "Hades." As the funeral carriage passes some hoardings displaying announcements of theater performances and concerts, Bloom is reminded of Boylan's impending visit to Molly. A moment later, Cunningham, from the carriage window, makes a move to salute Boylan, whom he sees coming out of the door of the Red Bank restaurant, and Bloom's mind is quick to register: "Just that moment I was thinking" (6.197/92.20).

Later that day Bloom will remember this moment, the memory of the experience again being accompanied by sexual overtones. He is sitting in a pub, having a glass of wine and a cheese sandwich. His thoughts are on food and on the problem of how people in former times found out which things were edible and which not. They may sometimes have been attracted by the smell or the look of things, he supposes, but then he thinks of a possible objection: "Yes but what about oysters. Unsightly like a clot of phlegm. Filthy shells. Devil to open them too. Who found them out? Garbage, sewage they feed on. Fizz and Red bank oysters. Effect on the sexual. Aphrodis. *He was in the Red Bank this morning.* Was he oysters old fish at table perhaps he young flesh in bed no June has no ar no oysters" (8.863–68/174.41–175.05, italics mine). In the same episode Bloom will remember that other chance view of Boylan, when he saw the latter's "brown brillantined hair," the scene he thinks of when crossing his back garden after breakfast. Walking on after his light snack at Davy Byrne's, which has made him feel decidedly better, Bloom passes a blind young man standing at the curb (a piano tuner, as will be revealed in "Sirens," on his way to the Ormond Hotel). Bloom offers to help him.

—Do you want to cross? Mr Bloom asked.
The blind stripling did not answer. His wallface frowned weakly. He moved his head uncertainly.
—You're in Dawson street, Mr Bloom said. Molesworth street is opposite. Do you want to cross? There's nothing in the way.
The cane moved out trembling to the left. Mr Bloom's eye followed its line and saw again the dyeworks' van drawn up before Drago's. *Where I saw his brillantined hair just when I was.* Horse drooping. Driver in John Long's. Slaking his drouth.

(8.1077–85/180.33–181.02, italics mine)

We learn from this passage that the barber's shop Bloom visualizes in "Calypso" is located in Dawson Street. In fact, Drago's is "a hairdresser at 17 Dawson Street in the southeastern quadrant of Dublin, approximately a mile and a half south of Bloom's home" (Gifford, 1974:58). This means, obviously, that Bloom cannot actually hear "Drago's shopbell ringing" when going out through the back door. We have to work out this phrase in the same way as we have done the one immediately preceding it, "Picking up the letters." Once again, the action is in Bloom's mind only. He remembers hearing the shop bell and seeing Boylan leave the shop just when he, Bloom, was—just doing what? Thinking of Boylan (and Molly), probably. This may have happened at any time during the past fortnight, but the event comes to mind this very moment, the memory having been set off by his "picking up the letters" (especially Boylan's letter). As usual, Bloom is quick to suppress any thought of Boylan by forcing himself to turn his attention to practical, everyday matters. In this case he reminds himself that he could do with a bath on this day that promises to be hot, as he had only had a perfunctory wash that morning. As we may infer from Molly's stream of consciousness in the final episode (18.904–5/763.19), there is no bath in the house.

Gordon (1981b) has offered an attractive hypothesis that goes far to explain a few otherwise puzzling details in Bloom's attempt at reconstructing events and impressions. We know that in the kitchen in the basement of the Blooms' house there is a row of five house bells (17.150/670.23), and, if we assume that Molly, from the bedroom, rings one of these bells just as Bloom enters or when he is picking up the letters (coincidence again!), Bloom may have associated the sound (audible in the hall, presumably) with Drago's shop bell. But why, of all the shop bells in town, just Drago's, the hairdresser's? Before Bloom entered the house, a cloud had passed from before the sun and he had noticed warm sunlight, which "came running from Berkeley road" (4.240ff./61.32ff.) like a golden-haired girl, running to meet him. Bloom may have associated this fleeting image with Milly, his daughter, whose blond hair he used to ribbon (17.896–97/694.02–3). Thinking vaguely, perhaps, of Milly's hair ("Queer I was just thinking"), he enters the house. The bell sound he then hears reinforces this association and engenders the memory of Drago's, where Bloom, more or less recently, has seen Boylan's brown brillantined hair. The moment Bloom picks up the mail he hears Molly calling him (4.246/61.38). As Gordon sees it, Molly cannot have heard Bloom come in; in fact, not realizing perhaps that he was not in the house, she may have been ringing and calling already for quite some time.

Although Gordon's hypothesis is attractive, it harbors a lot of conjecture. Molly may very well have known, for instance, that Bloom had gone out to do some shopping; after all, he had told her so (4.52–57/56.20–25). She may have lain awake, waiting for him to come home, perhaps even expecting a letter from Boylan. In short, there is always the danger of overexplaining, a tendency to be afraid of loose ends.

EPISODE FIVE
"Lotus Eaters"

*T*HE CAMERA eye now follows Bloom while he is walking along (rather aimlessly at times, as when he suddenly turns into a church for no apparent reason) and looking round him at the sights of the city of Dublin at about ten in the morning. After breakfast Bloom had been thinking of going to have a bath at the public baths in Tara Street (4.490/68.26). On his way there he changes his mind, apparently, before crossing the Liffey, deciding to go first to the Westland Row post office, where he hopes to collect a letter. In "Ithaca" it will be shown in retrospect that he winds up having his ablutions in the Turkish Baths on Leinster Street (17.337–39/676.13–15), which is more in keeping with the Oriental strain in "Lotus Eaters."

The circuitous route Bloom takes to reach the post office has been remarked upon by several critics. Bloom may not wish to encounter any friends or acquaintances, but apart from that he is troubled, naturally, by the thought of Molly and Boylan.

For all Bloom's aimless wanderings, however, he keeps track of what happens around him, always on the lookout for causes and effects, always asking why things are as they are. He likes to think of himself as being of a scientific turn of mind, but in reality for him the phenomenal world is just, as Gordon observes, "an occult network of influences and correspondences" (1981a:52).

Somehow Bloom has reached the area of the North and South Docks, near the mouth of the Liffey, with their characteristic skyline of waterside cranes. From the quays Bloom circles around to Westland Row. Having halted before a shop there, and reading, in a desultory way, the legends on packets of tea displayed in the shop window, he takes off his hat. It is one of his characteristic traits that for such gestures he always needs some justification or excuse for his own peace of mind ("Very warm morning"), in case somebody might be looking. What he wants to do, prior to entering the post office, is to take the card he will use as identification from behind the headband of his hat. It is not visible, but he knows the exact spot where to find it, having checked it that very morning (4.70/56.41). This card bears the pseudonym (Henry Flower) under which he is carrying on a clandestine correspondence: "While his eyes still read blandly he took off his hat quietly inhaling his hairoil and sent his right hand with slow grace over his brow and hair. Very warm morning. Under their dropped lids his eyes found the tiny bow of the leather headband inside his high grade ha. Just there. His right hand came down into the bowl of his hat. His fingers found quickly a card behind the headband and transferred it to his waistcoat pocket" (5.20–26/ 71.25–32).

The postmistress having handed him back his card with a letter, Bloom slips both into a side pocket (5.65/72.34–35). Ripping the letter open inside his pocket with one hand, he continues his walk, but is stopped by M'Coy, an acquaintance, whose wife is, like Molly, a singer, and who engages him in conversation, telling Bloom about an engagement *his* wife might get. Bloom, alerted, knowing of M'Coy's habit of borrowing valises for alleged concert tours without ever returning them, tries to discourage him by telling him that Molly is going to sing in Belfast on the twenty-fifth. Having got rid of him after some more talk, about Dignam's death and funeral this time, Bloom can at last have a look at his letter. "Prudent member" that he is (cf. 12.211/297.34) and always afraid of meeting acquaintances at less opportune moments, he hides the letter inside the newspaper he carries (5.221–22/77.10–11). He finds a deserted spot just round the corner, under the Westland Row station wall across from a timber yard. The only human being in sight is a child playing marbles. Slowing down in order to read the letter, Bloom avoids stepping on some chalk lines drawn on the pavement, showing the pattern of an abandoned hopscotch court.

He now starts reading Martha's letter, taking care to keep it hidden inside the folded newspaper. What the letter says, trivial as it is, will be enough to buoy him up and influence his mood at various points of the day, and all kinds of phrases from it—especially faulty ones ("before my patience are exhausted") or silly endearments ("naughty darling")—will stick in his mind. Just now, he feels quite satisfied by Martha's response to his letters so far, except for one thing; in her first letter Martha seems to have suggested that they meet one day, in church of all places, but that is something Bloom will never do. He does not want to get involved as deeply as that. He remembers what she wrote but rejects the idea promptly: "Could meet one Sunday after the rosary. Thank you: not having any" (5.270–71/78.26–27).

Walking slowly on, he scans the letter once more, "murmuring here and there a word" (5.263/78.18). Having finished, he takes it from the newspaper and puts it back into his side pocket. He continues down Cumberland Street, and, under the railway arch where the Loop Line passes overhead and where he feels sheltered and inconspicuous some-how, he takes the empty envelope from his pocket and tears it to shreds, which he then scatters in the road. Meanwhile he has reached the church of All Hallows. Stepping into the rear porch—the church front being in

Westland Row—he doffs his hat. This seems a conventional gesture of reverence, but here it serves Bloom as camouflage: he wants to transfer the card from his pocket to its accustomed place behind the headband (5.318–20/79.41–80.01). It is not even clear whether he had had in mind to enter the church at all; a whim seems to take him, or perhaps he just wants to rest his feet for awhile.

Once inside, Bloom reflects that a church must be a "nice discreet place to be next some girl," and this thought is followed immediately by the question: "Who is my neighbour?" (5.341/80.24). This echoes the lawyer's question to Christ in Luke 10:29, the answer being given in the form of the parable of the Good Samaritan. Most readers will recognize the allusion as such. The way Bloom uses the phrase, it assumes a new dimension and gains new force, thanks to the clash between the trite thought about sitting next to some girl and the biblical association it evokes. Bloom knows quite well that at the moment he has no neighbor; he has not even found a seat as yet. He is standing around, watching a group of women receiving Holy Communion at the altar rails. It is not until they have returned to their places that he sits down in a corner of a bench (5.354–55/80.40–42). English, it should be noted, does not differentiate between *neighbor* in the common or garden sense (someone living near one) and the same word in the sense intended by Jesus Christ in the Gospel story (a fellow human being), whereas some other languages do. In the French translation, for instance, one would have expected: "Et qui est mon *prochain?*" Instead, Morel uses an ordinary word, *voisin*: "Qui est donc mon voisin?" (79), missing a chance to remind the reader of the allusion involved.

Looking on while these pious people kneel at the altar rails, Bloom is reminded of Carey, that "fellow that turned queen's evidence on the invincibles." He remembers having heard that Carey was in the habit of receiving Holy Communion each morning: "And plotting that murder all the time. Those crawthumpers, now that's a good name for them, there's always something shiftylooking about them" (5.381–83/81.31–33). From Bloom's parenthetical remark, "now that's a good name for them," it is evident that for him the quaint phrase, "crawthumpers," must have some specific literal meaning apart from its general connotation, "Roman Catholics." What this meaning is might be guessed from the narrator's gossiping words in "Cyclops." He is repeating what "Pisser" Burke had told him about Bloom's behavior toward a Mrs. Riordan: "and not eating meat of a Friday because *the old one was always thumping her craw*" (12.507–8/306.03, italics mine). Thus "Crawthumpers" must be persons who are frequently seen beating their breasts *(craw* meaning *crop, stomach, throat)* in a kind of *mea culpa* gesture—or, simply, making the sign of the cross all the time.

Watching the priest's ministrations, Bloom is reminded once more of Martha's proposal, "Meet one Sunday after the rosary" (5.375/81.23). Looking round him at the women worshipping, Bloom thinks that for all he knows Martha Clifford might be there among them. He tries to convince himself, however, that this cannot be true. His thoughts dwelling on the letter, he suddenly panics, imagining perhaps that the envelope might provide a clue to his identity, but he is soon reassured: "By the way, did I tear up that envelope? Yes: under the bridge" (5.385/81.35–36).

Even though Bloom now seems quite positive, he will manifest this feeling of uncertainty once more, a little later. Having read Martha's letter again, in the bath this time, he seems to have transferred it to another pocket. This is shown in the next episode, "Hades." Sitting in the funeral carriage following Dignam's hearse, Bloom tries to remember whether he did destroy the envelope and where he then had put the letter: "I tore up the envelope? Yes. Where did I put her letter after I read it in the bath? He patted his waistcoatpocket. There all right" (6.168–69/91.27–29). Sitting on the beach in the dusk, Bloom is again reminded of Martha's letter and again feels for it in his pocket: "Where did I put the letter? Yes, all right" (13.779/368.08). The last we hear of it is when Bloom, relaxing in the front room of his house, long after midnight, puts it away in a drawer where there are already, among a curious collection of objects, three previous letters he had received from Martha: "What object did Bloom add to this collection of objects? A 4th typewritten letter received by Henry Flower (let H. F. be L. B.) from Martha Clifford (find M. C.)" (17.1840–42/722.21–23).

Elements from the scene in the church will crop up, as might be expected, in "Circe" (15.717–54/455.01–456.14). Two policemen approach Bloom and summon him to state his name and address. The card bearing the name of Henry Flower falls from inside the headband of his hat. Martha appears, veiled (as Bloom had imagined her to be when she was to meet him "one Sunday after the rosary"), a crimson halter round her neck (as worn by the women in the church, denoting membership in some sort of society), and a copy of the *Irish Times* in her hand (in this paper Bloom had put a small ad asking for a "smart lady typist," and Martha Clifford had been one of the forty-odd women who had answered it). As Miss Clifford, she cries "Henry!" and as the heroine of the opera *Martha* she cries "Lionel, thou lost one!" She also cries, inexplicably (for she is supposed to be ignorant of Bloom's real name), "Leopold! Leopold!"—reflecting, I think, Bloom's fear of having Henry Flower's identity revealed.

In Martha's letter Bloom finds a flower, pinned down, a "yellow flower with flattened petals" (5.239/77.30). Having read the letter, he makes a sentimental gesture: "He tore the flower gravely from its pinhold smelt its almost no smell and placed it in his heart pocket" (5.260–61/ 78.14–15).

In "Circe," when challenged by the policemen who have come to arrest him, and asked for an alibi, Bloom shows them the flower with the words, "This is the flower in question," and, according to the accompanying stage direction, what he then produces from his heart pocket is *"a crumpled yellow flower"* (15.738/455.24). It is surely not this pitiful remnant of a flower that Molly alludes to in a passage of her soliloquy in which she looks back (on the whole, with satisfaction) on the afternoon she spent with Boylan: "I wonder was he satisfied with me one thing I didnt like his slapping me behind going away so familiarly in the hall though I laughed Im not a horse or an ass am I suppose he was thinking of his fathers I wonder is he awake thinking of me or dreaming am I in it who gave him that flower he said he bought he smelt of some kind of drink not whisky or stout or perhaps the sweety kind of paste they stick their bills up with some liqueur" (18.121–27/741.19–26). The flower Molly is intrigued by must be the red carnation Boylan had picked up in Thornton's fruit shop earlier in the day (section V of "Wandering Rocks," 10.299–336/227.11–228.12). It is the same flower that Miss Douce, one of the barmaids in the Ormond Hotel, wonders about while pouring Boylan a sloe gin (11.366/265.26), the drink that Molly could still smell on his breath.

There is one thing Molly resents, and that is being slapped behind like a horse (see also 18.1368–69/776.20–22). Boylan, she supposes, must have been thinking of his father's horses: The man was a horse dealer and had been known to have sold the same horses twice over to the government at the time of the Boer Wars, as we learn from the narrator's words in "Cyclops" (12.997–99/319.30–32).

Coming out of the post office, Bloom meets M'Coy, who starts telling him how he first heard the news of Dignam's death. He had been in Conway's, a pub, the night before, together with Bob Doran and "Bantam" Lyons: that is how he introduces his tale. Meanwhile Bloom is gazing across the road at a little scene taking place in front of the Grosvenor Hotel, a well-dressed woman waiting to get up on an open cab (a so-called outsider), her escort searching his pockets for change, and a porter hoisting up a valise. The reader watches the scene through Bloom's eyes. We should realize, therefore, that for Bloom this scene is a configuration of very *definite* persons and objects. These persons and objects, moreover, are involved in *definite* actions, which are not only registered by Bloom but also interpreted by him. This notion of definiteness is signaled by an avalanche of definite articles: "Mr Bloom gazed across the road at the outsider drawn up before the door of the Gros-venor. The porter hoisted the valise up on the well" (5.98–99/73.32–34). Bloom is looking at not just *an* outsider, *a* porter, *a* valise, but *the* very outsider, porter, valise by which his attention is held here and now. Translators who change one or more of these articles into an *indefinite* one—it has been done—are in the wrong, neglecting to take into account the implications of Joyce's use of the *definite* article.

The text continues as follows: "She stood still, waiting, while the man, husband, brother, like her, searched his pockets for change" (5.99–101/ 73.34–35). The pronoun "she" is used here in a conspicuous way. As an anaphoric pronoun, it is assumed to refer to some noun of feminine gender that must have gone before, but in this case there is no such noun. At least, it is not there on the printed page, but the notion must have been present in Bloom's head; his "She," paired with, or in opposition to, "the man" in the same sentence, is simply equivalent to "the woman," and as such it should be stressed when the sentence is read out aloud: "*She* stood still . . . while the *man* . . . searched his pockets for change."

Bloom hopes to get a glimpse of a stockinged leg the moment the lady is going to mount the "outsider," but all the time he has to pretend to be listening to M'Coy. In the following paragraph the text reflects the complex situation in which Bloom's mind is operating; namely, on more levels than one. It is an attempt to register what M'Coy is saying about Holohan ("Hoppy") coming in and ordering a drink and how they got talking "of one thing or another." At the same time, Bloom's senses are busy taking in the details of the scene enacted across the road, these details being presented in third-person narrative, and in his interior monologue Bloom comments on what he sees, speculating meanwhile, as he so often does, on physical phenomena: "Doran Lyons in Conway's. She raised a gloved hand to her hair. In came Hoppy. Having a wet. Drawing back his head and gazing far from beneath his vailed eyelids he saw the bright fawn skin shine in the glare, the braided drums. Clearly I can see today. Moisture about gives long sight perhaps. Talking of one thing or another. Lady's hand. Which side will she get up?" (5.109–14/ 74.04–10). There is some confusion among commentators about this passage. In his concise page-by-page summary, Blamires maintains that Bloom's attention, while he is watching the stylishly dressed woman, is held "by her hand, her hair, her skin" (1966:27). The only skin, however, mentioned in the narrative part is the gleaming leather of the woman's glove, "bright fawn" (light yellowish brown), a hue no society lady in those days would dream of cultivating. Bloom can even distinguish the stripes or seams that decorate the back of such gloves (hence his tentative theory about moisture in the air promoting long sight), and that here are called "braided drums," a phrase which Gifford holds to refer to "the woman's hairdo" (1974:66). Actually, her hair and her skin will hardly be distinguishable under her hat, a wide-brimmed model, no doubt ("the laceflare of her hat in the sun"), leaving her face in shadow, and one of the last things that strike Bloom when he watches the couple drive off is her "rich gloved hand on the steel grip" (5.139/74.37). Moreover, it cannot be a coincidence that the lines about the fawn skin and the braided drums are embedded in a passage that starts with "She raised a gloved hand" and ends with "Lady's hand."

A final confirmation of the view that both "fawn skin" and "braided drums" refer to the lady's gloves and by no means to her complexion or hairdo will be found in the text itself, hundreds of pages later, in "Circe," but in order to show the connection we have to return to the paragraph beginning "Mr Bloom gazed across the road" and quote the rest of the passage. Bloom is now concentrating on the woman: "Stylish kind of coat with that roll collar, warm for a day like this, looks like blanketcloth. Careless stand of her with her hands in those patch pockets. Like that haughty creature *at the polo match*. Women all for caste till you touch the spot. Handsome is and handsome does. Reserved about to yield. *The honourable Mrs* and Brutus is an honourable man. Possess her once take the starch out of her" (5.101–6/73.35–42, italics mine). The woman's stance reminds Bloom of a lady he once saw at a polo match, and in his thoughts, mockingly, he refers to her as "The honourable Mrs." Both these elements recur in "Circe." In one of the so-called hallucinatory scenes so characteristic of that episode, Bloom is under arrest and being harassed by three society ladies who are testifying against him, accusing him of having made all kinds of "improper overtures" to them (15.1021/465.28). One of them, *the honorable* Mrs. Talboys, who reports that Bloom had seen her *on the polo ground* of the Phoenix park, comes on stage in amazon costume (15.1058ff./467.02ff.), wearing *"fawn musketeer gauntlets with braided drums."* The fawn color and the braided drums can only be associated with the sturdy riding gloves the lady is wearing, and so, in retrospect, we may conclude that what Bloom is observing in the earlier passage must also be the lady's glove, and neither her skin nor her hairdress.

In the meantime, M'Coy is still relating the events of the night before, repeating what Hoppy said to him and what he said to Hoppy (marked as quotation, in the text, by italics). On the printed page Bloom's interior monologue seems to interrupt M'Coy's tale, but both are to be thought of, naturally, as running on simultaneously, until Bloom feels obliged to make encouraging noises without losing sight of the woman. One sentence of third-person narrative is followed by a brief flash of interior

monologue ("Getting up . . ."). Then M'Coy continues his report of the
talk in the pub, interspersed with direct remarks to Bloom, not italicized
in the text. This part runs as follows:

> —And he said: *Sad thing about our poor friend Paddy! What Paddy?* I
> said. *Poor little Paddy Dignam,* he said.
>   Off to the country: Broadstone probably. High brown boots with laces
> dangling. Wellturned foot. What is he foostering over that change for?
> Sees me looking. Eye out for other fellow always. Good fallback. Two
> strings to her bow.
> —*Why?* I said. *What's wrong with him?* I said.
>   Proud: rich: silk stockings.
> —Yes, Mr Bloom said.
>   He moved a little to the side of M'Coy's talking head. Getting up in a
> minute.
> —*What's wrong with him?* he said. *He's dead,* he said. And, faith, he
> filled up. *Is it Paddy Dignam?* I said. I couldn't believe it when I heard it. I
> was with him no later than Friday last or Thursday was it in the Arch. *Yes,*
> he said. *He's gone. He died on Monday, poor fellow.*
>
> (5.115–29/74.11–26)

From the point of view of translation, there is an interesting detail in this
passage. We seem to have the same question twice: "What's wrong with
him?" The first time, M'Coy is quoting himself as having asked this
question; it has the normal stress pattern for a question of this type (i.e.,
not a yes-or-no question), the word "wrong" bearing sentence stress. In
the second occurrence, however, M'Coy is quoting Holohan, and this
time the sentence is an echo question, expressing the speaker's amaze-
ment at being asked such a question. Such echo questions are marked by a
characteristic stress pattern of their own. In this case, the word *wrong*,
while remaining decidedly emphatic, receives an almost musical, more or
less long drawn out intonation over and above the inherent sentence
stress. English has no means to mark this difference between both types
of question graphically, but there are languages, such as Dutch and
German, in which the difference may be marked in print as well, simply
by changing the word order of the sentence. It is up to the translator to
decide whether he wants the reader to profit from the legitimate possibilities offered by his own language patterns. Wollschläger, for instance, translates as follows (note the difference between "Was ist . . . los"
and "Was los ist"): "*Wieso?* frag ich. *Was ist denn los mit ihm?* frag
ich. . . . *Was los ist mit ihm?* sagt er" (103–4).

  Now Bloom's excitement is rising. The woman may get up on the cab
at any moment now, showing rich silk stockings perhaps. Just then a
tramcar passes through the street, obstructing his view. Bloom, disap-

pointed, curses the tramdriver (he will recall the incident later: 8.347–49/
160.35–38) but reflects that such things are bound to happen: "Lost it.
Curse your noisy pugnose. Feels locked out of it. Paradise and the peri.
Always happening like that. The very moment. Girl in Eustace street
hallway Monday was it settling her garter. Her friend covering the
display of. *Esprit de corps.* Well, what are you gaping at?" (5.132–35/
74.29–33).

Bloom is reminded here of a similar experience he had had a few days
before. In that case, the girl's friend had, it seems, blocked his view of
whatever he had hoped to see, thereby showing the correct spirit of
women's solidarity. The phrase *"esprit de corps,"* apart from punning,
possibly, on the double sense of *corps*, suggests that it had been a *girl*
friend, belonging to the same *body* of female human beings. What
follows, the sentence "Well, what are you gaping at?," presents a minor
problem. The phrase may be a case of quotation within interior monologue (a literary device that has been discussed before), Bloom quoting
somebody else's words in the framework of his interior monologue. He
may have been snubbed by that girl's friend, who showed such a fine
"esprit de corps"—and it still rankles to the extent that he even now
remembers the exact words she used at the time.

Alternatively, we may have here a specimen of what Prescott, listing
many instances of this stylistic device (1964:117ff.), calls Joyce's tendency to abandon narrative for drama. In other words, Bloom, in
retrospect, may have dramatized the impression he had had at the time,
imagining what the girl *might* have said in that situation.

Raleigh must be mistaken when he maintains that Bloom's father had
seen the great actress Kate Bateman play Hamlet in London in 1865
(1977b:27). Bloom's train of thought (5.194ff./76.23ff.) clearly starts
with *Leah;* Bloom would like to see Mrs. Bandmann Palmer "in that"
again, the actress who had appeared as Hamlet the night before: "Hamlet
she played last night. Male impersonator. Perhaps he was a woman.
Why Ophelia committed suicide." Perhaps Hamlet was a woman, Bloom
thinks: Is that *why Ophelia committed suicide?* Hamlet is brought in to
smooth over the transition to the suicide motif and from that to Bloom's
father (who had poisoned himself). Bloom now immediately returns to
the original subject of his musings, *Leah*, repeating the same phrase, "in
that": "How he used to talk of Kate Bateman in that." Equally, Bloom's
"And Ristori in Vienna" (mark "And"!) suggests Bloom's father talking
about Adelaide Ristori, the famous actress, acting in the same play, *Leah*
(or *Deborah*, as it was then called), in Vienna. All this, moreover, is
borne out by external evidence, such as the information we find in
Gifford (1974:68), from which we learn that Kate Bateman was "a
member of a famous English stage family, whose great success in *Leah*

was in 1863 (not 1865) at the Adelphi Theatre, 411 Strand, North Side, London, which specialized in melodramas and farces."

There has been some confusion about the identities of the characters referred to in Bloom's interior monologue: old blind Abraham, Nathan, and Nathan's (or is it Abraham's?) son. Elsewhere, I have tried to show that the main source of this confusion must be sought in the way Augustin Daly reworked Mosenthal's original play, *Deborah*, not only changing the heroine's name but also leaving out essential passages (Van Caspel, 1979b).

Tindall concludes his summary of "Lotus Eaters" by saying that "in this holy chapter Bloom has proceeded from synagogue (70) to church (78) and mosque (85)" (1959:159). The reader who takes this—no doubt slightly ironic—statement at face value, however, will look in vain for a synagogue in this episode. Tindall was probably thinking of *Bethel* (5.11/71.13), but the building of that name is not a synagogue; it is a Salvation Army Hall. Bethel, as Bloom remarks, means "House of God." A synagogue is called *Beth ha-Knesseth*, "House of Gathering." Tindall is right, of course, in having Bloom pause to enter a church, but the Turkish Baths establishment Bloom makes his way to is not a mosque; it merely reminds him of such a building by its architectural features (5.549–50/86.16–17).

The functional value of the religious notions involved has been brought out much more forcibly and explicitly by Pomeranz. Beth-El may not be a synagogue, but the name as such is Hebrew, originally, and Bloom's thoughts associate it clearly with Judaism. Similarly, the Turkish Baths building may not be a mosque, but it has definite Moslem associations. As Pomeranz observes, "Joyce uses these two pseudo-religious allusions, one near the beginning and one towards the end of a chapter containing much about religion. A considerable part of the 'Lotus Eaters' is devoted to Bloom's ideas about religion. He passes time in All Hallows Church watching the priest celebrate mass and thinking about different religious customs" (1973:344). In this way a kind of balance has been established within the structure of the episode.

In the survey of "Bloom's undatable memories of the past" which Raleigh has drawn up at the very end of his *Chronicle* (1977b:264–72), item twenty-five states that "Corny Kelleher gets a job with the undertaker, O'Neill," and to explain what this information is based on, Raleigh quotes the following lines from the episode's opening paragraph: "And past Nichols' the undertaker. At eleven it is. Time enough. Daresay Corny Kelleher bagged the job for O'Neill's. Singing with his eyes shut. Corny. Met her once in the park. In the dark. What a lark. Police tout. Her name and address she then told with my tooraloom tooraloom tay. O, surely he bagged it. Bury him cheap in a whatyoumaycall. With my tooraloom, tooraloom, tooraloom, tooraloom" (5.11–16/71.13–20). Obviously, Raleigh takes his cue from the lines "Daresay Corny Kelleher bagged the job for O'Neill's" and "O, surely he bagged it," but what he reads into them is definitely beside the point. Walking along Lombard Street East, Bloom passes by Nichols' the undertaker's, and this reminds him, quite naturally, of Dignam's funeral: "At eleven it is." As it is still early, his next thought, setting the leisurely pace for this episode, is: "Time enough." His train of thought then returns to Dignam's burial; he supposes that Kelleher (who is rumored to be a police spy on the side) will have secured "the job" (the funeral arrangements) for his own firm, H. J. O'Neill's on North Strand Road, where he is noticed by Father Conmee in the afternoon of that day, as the reader will learn from a passage in "Wandering Rocks": "Father Conmee passed H. J. O'Neill's funeral establishment where Corny Kelleher totted figures in the daybook while he chewed a blade of hay" (10.96–98/221.27–29). Bloom's thought, in short, is not a memory of the past but a speculation about the present.

A word should be said about the role of Bloom's newspaper and the misunderstanding in which it is involved, a misunderstanding whose significance will only become apparent much later. This newspaper will accompany Bloom during a long stretch of time, and we will witness him discarding it some time in the afternoon, but we never learn when and where he came to buy it. When Molly asks him in the morning what time the funeral is, Bloom replies that he thinks it will be at eleven, adding: "I didn't see the paper" (4.320/63.38). On the point of leaving the house he asks himself the same thing, echoing Molly's question: "What time is the funeral? Better find out in the paper" (4.542–43/70.07). Obviously, he has not got a paper as yet but when we see him next, an hour later perhaps, we find he has one and, indeed, the budget for his day (in "Ithaca") records that he spent one penny on a copy of the *Freeman's Journal*.

Crossing Westland Row toward the post office, he recalls the girl next-door whom he had met at the butcher's when buying kidneys for breakfast: "He turned away and sauntered across the road. How did she walk with her sausages? Like that something. As he walked he took the folded *Freeman* from his sidepocket, unfolded it, rolled it lengthwise in a baton and tapped it at each sauntering step against his trouserleg" (5.47–50/ 72.14–18). During his talk with M'Coy we see Bloom, fidgeting, wanting to move on, playing with his paper again: "He unrolled the newspaper baton idly and read idly: *What is home without / Plumtree's Potted Meat? / Incomplete. / With it an abode of bliss*"(5.143–47/74.41–75.04). Next, Bloom uses his paper to cover up Martha's letter, which he has drawn from his pocket, looking around meanwhile for a quiet spot where he can read it: "He drew the letter from his pocket and folded it into the newspaper he carried. Might just walk into her here. The lane is safer" (5.221–22/77.10–12). Even there he takes the precaution of keeping the letter inside the newspaper while reading it: "He opened the letter within the newspaper" (5.237–38/77.29). Finally, having read the letter twice, "he took it from the newspaper and put it back in his sidepocket" (5.267/78.22–23). Even in church Bloom does not let go of his paper: "He approached a bench and seated himself in its corner, nursing his hat and newspaper" (5.354–55/80.40–42).

Looking back on all these details, we cannot help feeling that there must be some design behind them and that Bloom's paper must be part of a larger pattern. Of course, the fact that Bloom—just to make sure that he will not be late for the funeral—spends a penny on a newspaper that he does not seem to read at all seriously and that he is prepared to abandon at the drop of a hat, adds something to the picture the reader makes of Bloom, but there is more to it. In the final scene of the episode, something happens that will have some bearing on the plot, with unforeseen consequences for Bloom personally. He has now entered a chemist's to order a lotion for Molly and to buy a cake of soap for himself, as he plans to go and have a bath presently. Leaving the shop, he is accosted by Bantam Lyons: "He strolled out of the shop, the newspaper baton under his armpit, the coolwrapped soap in his left hand. At his armpit Bantam Lyons' voice and hand said: —Hello, Bloom. What's the best news? Is that today's? Show us a minute" (5.517–20/85.22–26). Whether this is just a chance meeting or whether Lyons, who may have espied Bloom from a bar across the road, waylaid him, as Hart and Knuth suggest (1981:1.26), the upshot is that Lyons borrows the paper and unrolls it, turning to the sports section. He wants to see, he says, about a French horse that is running in the Gold Cup at Ascot that day, called *Maximum* II (see 16.1287–89/648.30–32). Bloom, wanting to get rid of the unappetizing fellow with his "yellow blacknailed fingers," tells him he can keep the paper, but Lyons, intent on the betting figures, presumably, does not pay attention properly, so Bloom assures him that he was just going to throw it away. At those words Lyons pricks up his ears:

> Bantam Lyons raised his eyes suddenly and leered weakly.
> —What's that? his sharp voice said.
> —I say you can keep it, Mr Bloom answered. I was going to throw it away that moment.
> Bantam Lyons doubted an instant, leering: then thrust the outspread sheets back on Mr Bloom's arms.
> —I'll risk it, he said. Here, thanks.
> He sped off towards Conway's corner. God speed scut.

Mr. Bloom folded the sheets again to a neat square and lodged the soap in it, smiling.

(5.535–44/86.01–10)

As a horseplayer, Lyons is a superstitious man. He suddenly realizes that Bloom has been talking about something he was going to *throw away*, and, noting that among the horses entered for the Gold Cup there is one called *Throwaway*, listed at the strikingly long odds of twenty to one (see 16.1280/648.23), he decides to put his money on that horse. Bloom senses something of the kind but, of course, cannot have had any precise idea of the impact of his own words.

After his bath Bloom must have put the paper back into one of his pockets, for in the funeral carriage on the way to the cemetery he offers it to Simon Dedalus in case the latter wants to have a look at Dan Dawson's speech, a topic brought up by Martin Cunningham, but he is rebuffed: "Mr Bloom took the paper from his inside pocket . . . —No, no, Mr Dedalus said quickly. Later on please" (6.154–56/91.12–14). On arrival at the cemetery, Bloom, with one hand, transfers the soap from his hip pocket to his inner handkerchief pocket and then gets off, "replacing the newspaper his other hand still held" (6.496–97/100.33), which means, presumably, that the paper wanders again into one of his pockets. Had Bloom really abandoned his paper to Lyons as he offered to do, he might have come to regret it afterward, for there are no fewer than two occasions in the course of his day where the *Freeman* copy comes in handy. First, there is the hurried service in the mortuary chapel, where Bloom uses it to protect his trousers from getting dusty; the mourners kneeling here and there in the praying desks, "Mr Bloom stood behind near the font and, when all had knelt, dropped carefully his unfolded newspaper from his pocket and knelt his right knee upon it" (6.585–87/103.15–17). Second, Bloom uses his paper to prevent Richie Goulding, who is sitting across from him, from throwing inquisitive glances at what he is writing: "Hope he's not looking, cute as a rat. He held unfurled his *Freeman*. Can't see now" (11.859–60/279.10–11). Finally, rising to go, Bloom leaves the paper on the table: "Can leave that *Freeman*" (11.1123/286.30), blissfully ignorant of the fact that *Throwaway*, a rank outsider, has just won the Gold Cup.

EPISODE SIX
"Hades"

B LOOM is no longer alone, as he was in the preceding episode; he is part of the small gathering that has turned out to bury Paddy Dignam. A shadowy figure, this Dignam: practically the only thing Bloom remembers about him is that he had a red face from drinking too much whiskey (6.307/95.24), and Molly depicts him as one of those good-for-nothings who squander the household money on their drinking companions, recalling him as "always stuck up in some pub corner" (18.1281–82/774.04). Still, Bloom has dressed in black on this hot day to attend Dignam's funeral; this tells us more about Bloom than about Dignam. It is true there is a moment when Bloom feels mildly irritated at the thought of the funeral. On his way to the chemist's, he realizes that he must have left both the recipe for the lotion he was to order for Molly and his own latchkey in his other trousers when changing into his black suit. At first he is annoyed, but then his immediate reaction is that Dignam himself can hardly be blamed: "He walked southward along Westland row. But the recipe is in the other trousers. O, and I forgot that latchkey too. Bore this funeral affair. O well, poor fellow, it's not his fault" (5.467–69/84.08–10). Bloom, then, is among the mourners at the funeral, but he is not really *with* them. There is a lot of talk but no real communication. He remains an outsider, who is always talked about behind his back. As Watt remarks, "Bloom does not belong to any one social group, but participates superficially in a great many of them" (1972:234).

Whereas in the previous episode Bloom's mood had been one of relaxation and self-satisfaction, in "Hades" his thoughts take a gloomy turn, revolving persistently around death and mortality. Toward the end, however, his common sense prevails. Looking at all those statues, crosses, and what not, proliferating all over the burial grounds, he reflects that it would be "More sensible to spend the money on some charity for the living" (6.930–31/113.05–6). When he leaves the cemetery, his will to live has clearly reasserted itself: "The gates glimmered in front: still open. Back to the world again. Enough of this place . . . Plenty to see and hear and feel yet. Feel live warm beings near you. Let them sleep in their maggoty beds. They are not going to get me this innings. Warm beds: warm fullblooded life" (6.995ff./114.39ff.).

In an episode such as this one, where Bloom finds himself in the midst

of a relatively large number of characters, the author needs a great deal of
.third-person narrative. Bloom is the only one who is allowed to have his
interior monologue recorded, and the attentive reader will often observe
and appreciate how monologue is used to relieve the continuous pattern
of narration. A case in point is: "My kneecap is hurting me. Ow. That's
better" (6.613/104.06). We had already been told how Bloom, in the
mortuary chapel, had knelt down with the others, spreading his newspaper on the floor to avoid soiling his trousers. His thought about his
kneecap transmits a much more direct experience, has a much stronger
impact, than any words that could have been used in plain third-person
narrative, such as: "Mr Bloom's kneecap was hurting him. He shifted his
knee a little and felt decidedly better."

The deeper meaning of "Unclean job" (6.20/87.23–24) seems to have
eluded translators. "Dreckige Arbeit" (Goyert, I.141), "Dreckiges Ge-
schäft" (Wollschläger, 123), "Vilain boulot" (Morel, 86), "Trabajo nada
limpio" (Valverde, I.185), and "Feina desagraïda" (Mallafrè, 92)—all
these translations amount to the same thing ("dirty or repulsive job")
and thus miss the point, for that is not at all what Bloom has in mind (the
Italian translation, using "immondo" instead of "sporco" [De Angelis,
120], may be nearer the mark). Waiting, with the others, for the carriage
to start, Bloom is musing on the way a corpse has to be handled before it
can be laid to rest, and his final thought must be a relic from his Jewish
heritage, "unclean" meaning "ceremonially impure" in Jewish law (in
the Torah, the instances of defilement all relate in some way to death).

The isolation that Bloom experiences is twofold. As Sultan remarks,
"he is cut off from those around him and he is cut off from his family
line" (1964:102), his father having committed suicide and his son, Rudy,
having died as an infant, eleven days old. In the funeral carriage, hearing
Simon Dedalus cursing Mulligan for corrupting Stephen, Bloom thinks,
"Noisy selfwilled man. Full of his son." But then he reflects: "He is
right. Something to hand on. If little Rudy had lived. See him grow up.
Hear his voice in the house. Walking beside Molly in an Eton suit. My
son" (6.74–76/89.02–5).

A few minutes later, the sight of a dogs' home reminds Bloom of his
father's dog and of the old man's suicide note, a thought that will recur
several times during the day: "Dogs' home over there. Poor old Athos!
Be good to Athos, Leopold, is my last wish. Thy will be done. We obey
them in the grave. A dying scrawl. He took it to heart, pined away. Quiet
brute. Old men's dogs usually are" (6.125–28/90.19–23).

The dog's name, Athos, might have gone unnoticed here but for
Gifford's claim that the animal was "named after a mountain at the tip of
a peninsula in eastern Greece (also called the Mountain of Monks)"
(1974:84). Bloom's father, having lived in various European countries,

might have heard in his time about this famous monastery for all we know, but why name his dog after such a mountain? In Bloom's father's lifetime, Alexandre Dumas's novel *Les Trois Mousquetaires* (1844) was already extremely popular throughout Europe, as was his no less famous novel *Le Comte de Monte-Cristo* (1845), which young Stephen Dedalus, as we are told in chapter two of *A Portrait of the Artist as a Young Man*, used to read in the evenings in "a ragged translation." I surmise, therefore, that it may well have been the first of the three musketeers, Athos, Porthos, and Aremis, and not the Greek promontory, who lent his name to old Bloom's dog.

The occupants of the carriage have been laughing freely at some funny story. Cunningham urges them to look a little more serious, but Dedalus remarks that Dignam himself would surely not have grudged them a bit of mirth. This turns their thoughts back for a few moments to "poor little Paddy" and his unexpected death. The scene is brief but eminently suited to highlight Bloom's position as an outsider. It is *his* view, not *theirs*, as Morton maintains in his summary: "He died suddenly—an easy death, they note" (1970:34), that Dignam should be envied for his sudden death. The others, of course, as Catholics, inwardly deplore the very fact that there cannot have been time for the last rites of the Church to be performed:

> Mr Power gazed at the passing houses with rueful apprehension.
> —He had a sudden death, poor fellow, he said.
> —The best death, Mr Bloom said.
> Their wideopen eyes looked at him.
> —No suffering, he said. A moment and all is over. Like dying in sleep.
> No-one spoke.
>
> (6.310–15/95.27–34)

Bloom must have felt their disapproval, but he does not show any signs of embarrassment. This is, as Ellmann says, "his first declaration of independence" (1972:49). At the same time, of course, it emphasizes his isolation.

Somehow the conversation has turned to the subject of suicide. One says that it is the greatest disgrace to have in the family; another observes that it is considered a sign of cowardice. Cunningham, deliberately avoiding Bloom's eyes, tries to steer them away from this topic, for he knows, as the others apparently do not, that Bloom's father ended his own life by taking poison; he tells Power so afterward (6.529/101.31). Bloom, while appreciating Cunningham's tactful attempts at sparing him acute embarrassment, is reminded once more of his father's death and the circumstances surrounding it, remembering even quaint little details, meaningless in themselves, such as the shape of the coroner's ears: "That afternoon of the inquest. The redlabelled bottle on the table. The room in the hotel with hunting pictures . . . The coroner's sunlit ears, big and hairy. Boots giving evidence. *Thought he was asleep first. Then saw like yellow streaks on his face. Had slipped down to the foot of the bed.* Verdict: overdose. Death by misadventure. The letter. For my son Leopold" (6.359–64/97.02–8, italics mine). Note that the italicized sentences, although incorporated in Bloom's interior monologue, are not his own thoughts in origin. Instead of being memories of things he had observed himself, they summarize what he remembers about the evidence given by boots, the hotel servant, when heard as a witness. It is another unmistakable case of quotation within interior monologue. In Bloom's monologue these sentences function as a kind of indirect speech, which might be paraphrased as follows: "Boots, giving evidence, stated that he when entering the room thought he (Bloom Senior) was asleep, but that he then saw what looked like yellow streaks on his face and that he noticed that the old man had slipped down to the foot of the bed."

It cannot have been Bloom himself who remembered entering the room and seeing the streaks on his father's face. He was not even there at the time his father was found. That very morning, in a burst of self-pity, trying to shake off the sad memories of his father's death, he had been thinking: "I'm glad I didn't go into the room to look at his face" (5.207–8/ 76.37–38).

As Cunningham had told Power, Bloom Senior at one time had owned the Queen's Hotel in Ennis, County Clare (6.529–30/101.32). The reader will find this detail confirmed in "Ithaca," where "a photocard of the Queen's Hotel, Ennis, proprietor, Rudolph Bloom" (17.1880/ 723.31–32) is mentioned among the objects in a drawer of the sideboard in Bloom's front room. It is in one of the rooms of this hotel that Bloom's father was found after he had poisoned himself. There is not any clear evidence or indication, however, that the Bloom family actually lived there at any time. On the contrary, among Rudolph Bloom's various residences enumerated in that same episode, no mention is made of Ennis. The list occurs twice, once in more or less chronological order, it seems: "Rudolf Virag (subsequently Rudolph Bloom) of Szombathély, Vienna, Budapest, Milan, London and Dublin" (17.534–36/682.09–11), and the second time in a not wholly identical, retrograde series as a "retrospective arrangement of migrations and settlements in and between Dublin, London, Florence, Milan, Vienna, Budapest, Szombathely" (17.1907–8/ 724.24–26). Moreover, among the documents in this drawer is a press cutting, a notice in which Bloom's father announces his change of name by deed poll. It is quoted in full as follows, and it shows old Bloom's Dublin address: "I, Rudolph Virag, now resident at no 52 Clanbrassil street, Dublin, formerly of Szombathely in the kingdom of Hungary, hereby give notice that I have assumed and intend henceforth upon all occasions and at all times to be known by the name of Rudolph Bloom" (17.1869–72/723.18–22).

From Leopold Bloom's reminiscences in "Oxen of the Sun," it follows that it must have been in this house in Clanbrassil Street that he grew up and lived in until the time of his marriage at the age of twenty-two. First we see him as a schoolboy: "walking on a nipping morning from the old house in Clanbrassil street to the high school, his booksatchel on him bandolierwise, and in it a goodly hunk of wheaten loaf, a mother's thought" (14.1046–48/413.07–10). A few years later, he recalls, he had already been a traveler for the family firm, who used to bring home "many a commission to the head of the firm, seated with Jacob's pipe after like labours in the paternal ingle (a meal of noodles, you may be sure, is aheating), reading through round horned spectacles some paper from the Europe of a month before" (14.1057–60/413.19–23).

We may conclude, therefore, that Rudolph Bloom owned the hotel in Ennis but did not actually live there. At the time of his death he may have been there on a chance visit, but it is safe to assume that he went there on purpose when planning to commit suicide. This is borne out by what at first sight seems a rather cryptic thought in Bloom's interior monologue in the cemetery scene. Dignam's coffin has been lowered into the grave, and the mourners, standing around, have taken off their hats. In the ensuing silence a donkey is heard braying, foretelling rain. Bloom thinks of the popular belief that asses hide when feeling that they are going to die, and he reflects that that is just what his father must have done: "Far away a donkey brayed. Rain. No such ass. Never see a dead one, they say. Shame of death. They hide. *Also poor papa went away*" (6.837–38/110.25–27, italics mine).

In trying to reconstruct what the hotel servant may have said at the inquest, we assumed that it was Rudolph Bloom's body that "had slipped down to the foot of the bed," but it is not at all certain that that is what the man told the coroner. Bernard Benstock, for instance, suggests that it is either the bottle of poison or the suicide letter that is meant (personal communication). I doubt if this could ever be decided with any degree of certainty or even probability. I would expect a more or less empty bottle to drop down to the floor from a person's fingers rather than travel or roll all the way down to the foot of the bed, and I do not see how an envelope could *slip down* either. A blanket perhaps? Yes, a blanket might easily have slipped down. After all, the month was June; it might have been a warm night. An argument in favor of the bottle theory is the circumstance that, as Bloom remembers, this bottle with its red label was standing on the coroner's table at the inquest, so boots giving evidence would naturally point to this crucial exhibit. However, we do not have a verbatim report of what he said—and even when pointing at the bottle he must have said *something*. The trouble is that what we know about the scene is only that which Bloom's memory allows us to know. So then we might wonder why his memory would suppress relatively harmless items in boots's testimony, such as the bottle (already mentioned in Bloom's own interior monologue), the letter, or, possibly, the blanket. His failure to reveal what it was that had slipped down to the foot of the bed may lead us to suspect the workings of a psychological block, a reluctance to repeat the exact terms boots had used if and when he had meant to refer to Rudolph Bloom: the body, the old gentleman, Mr. Bloom (Senior), deceased, whatever. So uncertainty remains.

There is more in this passage that is uncertain. What, for instance, happened to the letter? Could Bloom have pocketed it before the official inquiry started? If not, how could an nineteenth-century Irish coroner brush aside what was clearly a suicide note and pronounce a verdict of death by misadventure? Could he have insisted on being shown the contents of the letter? When did Bloom find the letter? The next day (28 June)? Note that the letter is *not* referred to in boots's testimony, at least not explicitly. And when was the inquest held? Not necessarily the same day, we must assume.

We have Bloom's own word for it that he did not go into the room to look at his father's face. Of course, he may have entered the room without lifting the sheet and then have found the letter addressed to him. However, that seems rather far-fetched, so how did he get hold of the letter? Was it simply handed to him by the hotel manager (if there was such a person) as soon as he (Bloom) arrived at the hotel? Somebody must have summoned him from Dublin, after all. And what was in the letter, exactly? Could its contents be pieced together from the fragments remembered by Bloom in "Ithaca" (17.1883–86/723.36–40)? What is the meaning of the opening words: "Tomorrow will be a week that I received"? What did Rudolph Bloom receive six days before? The consensus seems to have been that it was the news of his wife's death (Raleigh, 1977b:72). The mind boggles: Was old Bloom unaware, ensconced in his Ennis hotel, that his wife, in Dublin, was ill or even dying? And assuming this to be so, did he not hasten to Dublin to see to things as soon as he had been notified? He was not exactly bedridden, because he went out to buy aconite. And he did not even attend the funeral? Such incredible happenings would not have left any traces in Bloom's memories? And would not Rudolph Bloom (in a letter to his son!) have written: "Tomorrow will be a week your dear mother died" or some such phrase, rather than using this kind of business letter term, "I received"? Could, then, "business" be the key word? Is Molly's hint at a financial ruin (18.982–83/765.26–27) sufficient evidence to go by? If everything had been all right, would Bloom not have taken over the hotel business after his father's death?

There is something else. Having mentioned the letter, Blamires says: "Phrases from it linger with him" (1966:34) and then quotes: "No more pain. Wake no more. Nobody owns" (6.365/97.09). Are those phrases from his father's letter, indeed? Or rather Leopold's own thoughts plus a phrase from the doggerel that had run through his mind earlier (6.332–33/96.12–13)? Or could Blamires be right after all as to the phrase "No more pain"? Could the occurrence of "Nobody owns" in the rhyme be one of those Joycean coincidences? That is, could old Bloom have written, for instance, "Nobody owns me anything"?

Shari Benstock, in an interesting study on the printed letters in *Ulysses*, has asked similar questions (1982a:422), and Bernard Benstock, discussing the nature of evidence in *Ulysses*, has submitted that the opening phrase of the suicide note suggests that the old man may have received a foreclosure notice (1982:50). Anyhow, the text does not offer any hard and fast facts compelling us to believe that old Bloom's impulse to kill himself was triggered directly by his wife's death rather than by the thought of his impending bankruptcy.

Moreover, what Bloom remembers about his father (17.1889–92/ 724.03–7) presents a strikingly detailed picture. The situation described might have lasted for years ("increasing doses") and could hardly be thought of as covering a bare six days' period of widowerhood (during which time Leopold himself would not even have been living on Clanbrassil Street). Then, one day, Bloom Senior gets some very bad news (this is a conjecture, of course) and, having been a widower for some time, decides to go to Ennis and end it all.

Among those reminiscences of Bloom's we find "the face in death of a septuagenarian, suicide by poison." We have to assume, therefore, that Bloom did have a look at his father's face after all, perhaps not the first day, when the shock was too great (that may be meant in the passage at 5.207–8/76.37–38), but surely later, after the body had been prepared for burial.

It has been assumed (Benstock and Benstock, 1980:15) that Bloom's thought "She would marry another. Him? No" (6.548/102.12) refers to Dignam's widow. I propose a different interpretation of this passage. When we remember that Bloom in thinking of Molly, usually, and in thinking of Boylan, always, uses pronouns instead of names, and when we read the passage aloud, stressing "She," we shall see what Bloom means to say. He is posing a hypothetical case: "If I were dead, *she* (i.e., Molly) would marry another. *Him* (i.e., Boylan)? Oh, no." Bloom is quite positive about Molly's remarrying if she were left a widow (consider the verb form, "would": if Bloom were referring to Mrs. Dignam he would have used "may" or "might" or "could"), so I cannot see why translators should add a note of uncertainty, as has been done by Morel ("Elle reconvolerait *peut-être*," 100, italics mine). There is no *perhaps* in Bloom's thought.

The whole paragraph (6.544–55/102.07–20) is about widows in general (Hindu spouses, Queen Victoria) and about Bloom's own situation, not specifically or exclusively about Mrs. Dignam.

As we see, Bloom is not really distressed by the notion as such of Molly remarrying after his death, but his spontaneous response to the idea of *Boylan* marrying her is a firm "No." Immediately, however, his usual tolerant and reasonable mood takes over: "Yet who knows after?"

Leaving the chapel where the mourners have attended a brief funeral service for the late Patrick Dignam, Bloom finds himself walking beside Tom Kernan, as he had already done before, when entering the grounds. Evidently, he is not particularly eager to respond to Kernan's attempts at conversation. Bloom knows, of course, that Kernan like he himself is only nominally a Catholic. Still, he resents Kernan's insinuating ways and his attempt to remind him that the two of them have something in common when all is said and done. At least that is how I read the sequence "Beside him again . . ." that concludes the following passage:

—Sad occasions, Mr Kernan began politely.
Mr Bloom closed his eyes and sadly twice bowed his head.
—The others are putting on their hats, Mr Kernan said. I suppose we can do so too. We are the last. This cemetery is a treacherous place.
They covered their heads.
—The reverend gentleman read the service too quickly, don't you think? Mr Kernan said with reproof.
Mr Bloom nodded gravely looking in the quick bloodshot eyes. Secret eyes, secretsearching. Mason, I think: not sure. Beside him again. We are the last. In the same boat. Hope he'll say something else.

(6.654–63/105.13–24)

Bloom reflects on the fact that he is walking beside Kernan again: Had the latter sought him out on purpose, perhaps? He remembers Kernan's words, "We are the last," repeating them mockingly (quotation within interior monologue) and putting his own interpretation upon them: "we, you and I, are the only not quite genuine Catholics here, we are in the same boat, we are outsiders, both of us." That is, Bloom suspects, what Kernan intends to convey.

Having expressed his dissatisfaction with the way the service was conducted, Kernan then states that to his taste the Protestant burial service is simpler and more impressive anyway. To illustrate this he quotes the well-known words *"I am the resurrection and the life,"* adding: "That touches a man's inmost heart" (6.670/105.31). Bloom's response is as simple and as lacking in enthusiasm as could be: "It does." This should only be seen as a sample of polite conversation. Bloom is not in the mood to start a discussion on matters of ritual. That in his own inmost heart he does not hold much to the idea of resurrection is shown quite clearly by the trend of his interior monologue, a train of thought released by Kernan's remarks:

> Your heart perhaps but what price the fellow in the six feet by two with his toes to the daisies? No touching that. Seat of the affections. Broken heart. A pump after all, pumping thousands of gallons of blood every day. One fine day it gets bunged up: and there you are. Lots of them lying around here: lungs, hearts, livers. Old rusty pumps: damn the thing else. The resurrection and the life. Once you are dead you are dead. That last day idea. Knocking them all up out of their graves. Come forth, Lazarus! And he came fifth and lost the job. Get up! Last day! Then every fellow mousing around for his liver and his lights and the rest of his traps. Find damn all of himself that morning. Pennyweight of powder in a skull. Twelve grammes one pennyweight. Troy measure.
>
> (6.672–82/105.34–106.04)

Naturally, if you take Bloom's affirmative responses in this case and in similar cases at face value, you are bound to come up with totally wrong conclusions about his views in such matters. It is not the idea of resurrection but the thought of death and decay as something irrevocably final which is prominent in Bloom's mind. His interior monologue makes it perfectly clear that the idea of the dead rising from their graves does not impress him at all: "that last day idea," he calls it, and his first reaction to Kernan's remarks about the Protestant burial service is the thought: "That is all very well for you but those solemn words you quoted will not be able to touch the heart of the man in his coffin down there." The point is that Bloom is quite willing to concede that the words quoted by Kernan may touch some people's hearts—as long as *living* people are concerned. The only thing he denies, inwardly, is the possibility of such words having any significance for the dead.

The gravediggers having finished their job, the mourners drift away in the general direction of the exit, taking their time. Bloom walks alone now, "unheeded," strolling along, reading a gravestone inscription here and there. All those angels, crosses, pillars, and so forth that people put up on tombstones sometimes (features unknown in Jewish cemeteries, as Bloom may have remembered) seem an absurd waste of money to him. He is particularly irritated at the unrealistic way the inscriptions are phrased: So and so, "who passed away" or "who departed" on such and such a date—as if they did it of their own free will. Then he reflects that it would definitely be of greater interest to learn what the people buried there did in life: "More interesting if they told you what they were. So and So, wheelwright. I travelled for cork lino. I paid five shillings in the pound. Or a woman's with her saucepan. I cooked good Irish stew. Eulogy in a country churchyard it ought to be that poem of whose is it Wordsworth or Thomas Campbell" (6.937–41/113.15–19). It has not gone unnoticed that Bloom is alluding to Thomas Gray's well-known "Elegy Written in a Country Churchyard." In this connection Peake refers to Bloom's "mental habit of adapting or misquoting familiar quotations" (1977:187) without specifying, however, whether he considers Bloom's substitution of "eulogy" for "elegy" a free adaptation or a simple error of memory, an unintentional misquote. Bloom's use of this phrase, I think, implies that he is fully aware that the title of the poem he has in mind speaks of "elegy," but he thinks that "eulogy" would be a more suitable term in this case. Kreutzer calls this Bloom's "wort-spielerische Umdeutung" (1969:196), or *playful renaming*, of the original title, and Schneider uses similar terms. The latter, however, seems to contradict himself. On the one hand, he points out that Bloom's errors of speech include a great number of *unintentional misquotes*, and, on the other hand, he holds that it is a *playful impulse* that makes Bloom give the poem a new title (1970:42).

In particular, it is the phrase "it ought to be" that leads me to believe that Bloom, far from misquoting the poem's title, is consciously punning on it. Assuming this to be true, the question remains: What motive might he have had for doing so? Kreutzer and Schneider both look for the answer in Gray's poem itself; as they see it, Bloom seems to think that the title does not do justice to the poem, but this presupposes on Bloom's part a more than superficial knowledge of Gray's lines. Is this a tenable assumption? I doubt it. Discussing Bloom's attitude toward literature, Schutte points out that Bloom's "references to literature are confined to mention of such standard figures as Robinson Crusoe, Enoch Arden, and Rip Van Winkle" (1957:121). Schneider himself, for that matter, has to concede that when Bloom quotes from English literature he always picks the best-known lines, passages almost everybody is familiar with (1970:41).

As I see it, the *title* of Gray's "Elegy" seems the only thing Bloom remembers about the poem. He does not refer to anything specific in the poem at all. His thoughts are not really on the "Elegy"; they are still dwelling on the inscriptions he is reading on the tombstones. His suggestion that such inscriptions should tell us more about the deceased's lives, however, is not such an original idea as it may seem. Bloom may have been thinking of certain Jewish burial customs. In Jewish cemeteries, the gravestones—simple enough in themselves—frequently carry long-winded inscriptions, full of praise and usually mentioning the deceased's profession or function in the community. In some cases, as on the grave of the man whose task it is to perform circumcision, this function is not only mentioned in words but also indicated by a certain symbol at the head of the tombstone. A housewife might very well be praised for her good cooking and her efficient housekeeping, and that is, I believe, what Bloom is thinking of when he imagines a woman's grave adorned with a symbolic saucepan, the inscription bearing the legend "I cooked good Irish stew." A graveyard, he suggests, should be a place of *eulogy*, where the living might come to read the praise of the dead; that is how I understand his pun on *elegy* and *eulogy*.

We would expect *éloge* for *eulogy* in a French translation. This would match French *élégie*, but surprisingly enough Morel has, "Élégie dans un cimetière de campagne devrait être intitulé ce poème" (111), which means that the poem, in Bloom's opinion, ought to bear the title "Elegy in a Country Churchyard"—which it bears already! French readers with some knowledge of English literature must have been puzzled by this passage, one surmises. Needless to say, the humorous aspect of Bloom's thought has become totally obscured.

Naturally, the phrase "Or a woman's with her saucepan," which is part of Bloom's interior monologue cited above, is meant, as we have seen, to evoke the picture not of a woman but of *a woman's grave*, bearing a saucepan as a symbol of her domestic virtues. Several translators have failed to take into account the function of the case ending: "Of een vrouw met haar braadpan" (Vandenbergh, 132), "Ou une femme avec sa casserole" (Morel, 111), "O una mujer con su cacerola" (Valverde, I.219), "O una dona amb la seva cassola" (Mallafrè, 119). None of these versions catches the nuance. The only translator to have seen the point, I think, is Wollschläger: "Oder bei einer Frau ihre Bratpfanne mit drauf" (160). The same genitive construction as in "a woman's with her saucepan" is found a few lines later: "Old Dr Murren's" (6.942/113.20), but here the translators mentioned above prove to have grasped the meaning: "Hier is dat van de oude dr. Murren," "La tombe du vieux Docteur Murren," "La del viejo doctor Murren," "La del vell doctor Murren," and "Da, das vom alten Dr. Murren."

Speaking of loose ends in *Ulysses*, Adams has drawn attention to this particular grave and the elusive Dr. Murren. Does Bloom really *remember* Dr. Murren, as Adams has it (1962:235)? As we have seen before, Bloom is just strolling along, reading the texts on the tombstones from time to time. It strikes him that they abound in euphemistic phrases such as "passing away" and "departing this life," and he is reminded of a phrase used by Protestants, "entered into rest." At the same moment he happens to be passing by Dr. Murren's grave, his eyes registering the name. What follows then, about the great physician having called him home, may or may not be an inscription Bloom reads on the doctor's tombstone; it is hard to decide which. Because it is a conventional saying people often quote at a medical doctor's death, it may equally well be one of those bits of lore Bloom's memory is crowded with. Anyway, the sight of Murren's grave is just something that breaks in on Bloom's thoughts, distracting him for a fleeting moment. Walking on, Bloom picks up the thread of his initial thoughts about Protestants, remembering that they call a cemetery "God's acre," a reflection that has nothing to do with the trite phrase about the great physician or with old Dr. Murren either, unless the latter had been a Protestant. In that case, however, his grave would not have been here but in the Protestant burial ground of Mount Jerome, and Bloom, his thoughts still dwelling on these euphemisms found on tombstones, may indeed have *remembered* seeing it there. Still, this needs a lot of guesswork. Why would Bloom go and visit Murren's grave? He seems to have known him, and the doctor *may* even have attended Molly during her pregnancy (see 8.391–400/162.01–12), but that is all we can say.

In the beginning of the episode a curious little problem crops up when we try to figure out the seating arrangement in the coach in which Cunningham, Power, Dedalus Senior, and Bloom are following Dignam's hearse. As this is exactly the order in which these four men enter the carriage, the situation looks simple enough at first, and the way it is described by Hart and Knuth seems to cover the facts: "As Bloom and Dedalus are the last to enter the carriage, they are sitting on the near (left) side, so that when Simon tries to get a good look at Stephen, who is to the right of the carriage, he has to do so by 'stretching over across' the others" (1981:I.26). The reference here is to the scene where Bloom, looking out of the window, spots Stephen on his way from the tram stop on Tritonville Road, presumably (Kenner, 1980:14), to Sandymount beach (6.37–44/88.04–10). A similar situation arises when Boylan, sporting a flashy straw hat, is seen leaving the Red Bank restaurant on D'Olier Street. The time now being about a quarter past eleven, he cannot yet be "on his way to Molly," as Tindall has it (1959:159); he is not due on Eccles Street until four in the afternoon. As the coaches are traveling north, Cunningham and Power, who spotted Boylan first, salute him through the open window on the far side. Again, Dedalus has to lean over: "Mr Dedalus bent across to salute. From the door of the Red Bank the white disc of a straw hat flashed reply: spruce figure: passed" (6.198–99/92.21–22). To appreciate such situations fully the reader should consult a Dublin city plan showing public buildings, shops, offices, and so forth. Besides, all the necessary information is to be found in Hart and Knuth (1976:II, maps III and V).

So much for Mr. Dedalus. That Bloom must be sitting on the near side is confirmed by a fragment of interior monologue. The funeral procession is proceeding due north along O'Connell Street. There is a lull in the conversation after Bloom's stunning remark about a sudden death being the best death. Bloom sits staring out of the window: *"Dead side of the street this.* Dull business by day, land agents, temperance hotel, Falconer's railway guide, civil service college, Gill's, catholic club, the industrious blind. Why? Some reason. Sun or wind. At night too. Chummies and slaveys. Under the patronage of the late Father Mathew. Foundation stone for Parnell. Breakdown. Heart" (6.316–20/95.35–40, italics mine). When Bloom thinks of "this" side, he means *his* side, of course, and, as all the addresses he refers to in passing are on the left side of O'Connell Street, looking north, it must indeed be the near side where he is sitting, across from Mr. Dedalus. We cannot be sure if Bloom is facing north or south; the only thing we are reasonably sure of is that Cunningham must be seated in the opposite corner on the far side, for on one occasion we are told, "His eyes met Mr Bloom's eyes" (6.260/94.10), and again, in another scene, during the talk about suicide, Bloom's thoughts clearly show that Cunningham must be facing him: "Martin Cunningham's large eyes. Looking away now" (6.343–44/96.25–26), and: "He looked at me" (6.349/96.32), "He looked away from me. He knows" (6.358/97.01). It follows, then, that the fourth passenger, Mr. Power, is sitting beside Bloom, in the other far side corner across from Cunningham.

So far all this seems plain sailing, but there is a hitch, for on seeing Dodd, who is a notorious moneylender, Cunningham *nudges* Mr. Power (6.250/93.40). Nudging a person means pushing him slightly with one's elbow "to draw attention privately," so we are faced with the intriguing question whether you can nudge a person who is sitting across from you in an opposite corner. Tap his knee, yes, but *nudge* him? In the French translation, which is even more explicit than the original in mentioning the elbow as the means by which Cunningham tries to draw Power's attention, the question is answered in the affirmative: "Martin Cunningham poussa *du coude* M. Power" (92, italics mine), whereas the author of the modern German translation apparently intended to convey a notion similar to what the definition quoted above calls *privately* by introducing the adverbial *heimlich* (secretly): "Martin Cunningham stiess Mr. Power heimlich an" (132). Anyway, Morel's translation had better be rejected, and in order to reconcile the various bits of information gathered so far we shall have to assume that Cunningham nudged Power not with his elbow but with his knee—not too difficult a feat in the narrowly confined space of the carriage. Besides, there is a precedent in "Calypso," where we find Bloom, who is carrying Molly's breakfast tray, *nudging* the door to the bedroom open *with his knee* (4.300/63.16).

There is yet another scene in "Hades" that would be easier to understand if we could think of Power and Cunningham as sitting side by side instead of opposite each other. This scene starts with Power (inspired, no doubt, by the sight of Boylan a minute or so earlier) inquiring of Bloom about Molly's concert tour (without mentioning her name), which he knows quite well will be organized by Boylan. Bloom, reluctant to use either his wife's or, even more so, Boylan's name, starts talking at some length about the financial aspect of the tour, but he is cut short rather rudely. In answer to Power's next query, he explains that he cannot go himself, because he will have some business of his own in County Clare (this is the annual visit to his father's grave in Ennis on the anniversary of the old man's death, 27 June 1886). So far, he has been talking solely to Power, answering the latter's questions patiently. Cunningham, in an attempt perhaps to smooth over the rude way Bloom's discourse was interrupted (he manages to finish it after all), now voices his approval of the scheme and chimes in with a remark about Mary Anderson, an actress who was appearing in Belfast just then. Meanwhile, Power, seemingly missing or, anyway, disregarding Cunningham's remark, perhaps even interrupting him as he did Bloom, continues his relentless interrogation, and now Bloom is in a quandary. Polite as always, he wants to acknowledge Cunningham's observation without seeming to evade replying to Power's question. I visualize him looking first to Cunningham and observing, in response to the latter's remark about Mary Anderson, that, yes, she is being toured by Louis Werner, and then hastily turning afresh to Power in order to answer the latter's question, this fresh start being marked by Bloom's artificially enthusiastic "O yes, we'll have all topnobbers" (6.221/93.06–7). Finally, Power takes Bloom up on the sentence he did not quite finish, hinting that Mrs. Bloom ("*madame*") will be "the bright particular star," as someone will say later. The whole passage (6.211ff./92.36ff.) can only be understood in recognition of the fact that Bloom's reply consists of two parts, his initial remark being addressed to Cunningham, and his following words being directed to Power. Rattled as he may be, he has managed, again, to leave Boylan out of it.

As we know, Bloom is always loath to think of Boylan and will do anything to avoid uttering his name. Yet, on more than one occasion that day, he has to answer questions about the coming concert tour, and a few times he will be forced to confirm, with the utmost reluctance, that Boylan is the organizer. Once, asked by M'Coy in "Lotus Eaters," "Who's getting it up?" he manages to evade the issue by talking about "a committee formed" (5.163/75.24), being lucky in that M'Coy does not press the point. Again, being asked exactly the same question by Nosey

Flynn in "Lestrygonians," he tries to wriggle out of it by explaining, "Well, it's like a company idea, you see. Part shares and part profits." This time, however, the dodge does not work, and when Flynn asks him point blank: "Isn't Blazes Boylan mixed up in it?" he gives in: "—Yes, he said. He's the organiser in point of fact" (8.797/173.09). Finally, in "Cyclops," there is the following conversation, Alf Bergan and Joe Hynes having been talking about a boxing match that had been managed by Boylan:

> —He knows which side his bread is buttered, says Alf. I hear he's running a concert tour now up in the north.
> —He is, says Joe. Isn't he?
> —Who? says Bloom. Ah, yes. That's quite true. Yes, a kind of summer tour, you see. Just a holiday.
> —Mrs B. is the bright particular star, isn't she? says Joe.
> —My wife? says Bloom. She's singing, yes. I think it will be a success too. He's an excellent man to organise. Excellent.
>
> (12.988–95/319.20–27)

As noted before, the scene in the carriage would be easier to envisage if we could have Bloom face both Cunningham and Power. It would be easier then, at any rate, for the reader to imagine him looking from one to the other and addressing them in turn in quick succession. Moreover, it would be easier to understand Bloom's reaction to Power's final words: "His eyes passed lightly over Mr Power's goodlooking face. Greyish over the ears. *Madame:* smiling. I smiled back. A smile goes a long way. Only politeness perhaps. Nice fellow" (6.242–44/93.30–32). All this smiling back and forth—and, above all, having Bloom's eyes pass lightly over Power's face—it is rather a puzzling situation. If we could have Bloom and Power seated opposite each other, the whole constellation would be more natural in some respects, but there is an equally iron-clad case for a seating arrangement that calls for Bloom and Power, on the back seat, facing Dedalus and Cunningham, respectively. That this is the most likely configuration, has been argued convincingly by Brown and Knuth in a lively and well-documented study (1981).

When Bloom tries to tell an anecdote (6.262ff./94.13ff.) about Reuben J. Dodd, the moneylender they have just seen walk by on Sackville Street (now O'Connell Street), the seating arrangement in the carriage must have proved an additional drawback, apart from the fact that Bloom entangles himself in irrelevant details and bungles the whole thing. Dedalus and Cunningham, both facing Bloom, are able, from that position, to launch a frontal attack against him, thwarting his clumsy efforts at telling a good story well, the former interrupting him a few times, and the latter cutting him short, restarting in a more effective way, pretending not to hear his attempt at coming out, at least, with the point ("Yes, Mr Bloom said. But the funny part is . . ."[6.285/94.42]), and finishing the story himself. Bloom begins with a kind of introduction to the story: "That's an awfully good one that's going the rounds about Reuben J. and the son." That is as far as he gets for the time being, for he is interrupted immediately by Power, asking: "About the boatman?" This, of course, is a case of hitting below the belt, for Power's seemingly innocent question already hints at the point of the story, but Bloom, civil and patient as always, assents: "Yes. Isn't it awfully good?" Now he might have started on the story but for Dedalus, who turns out to be the only one present who has not yet heard it and who shows some impatience to be told: "What is that? Mr Dedalus asked. I didn't hear it." Encouraged, Bloom begins at last, but he immediately starts off on the wrong foot by mentioning a girl whose actual role in the case, which he fails to make clear, is not important, anyway. Moreover, his story, as Shari Benstock puts it, "meanders along a trail of ambiguous pronoun referents that eventually conflate the principal characters and leave the audience in total confusion" (1982b:708). "There was a girl in the case and he determined to send him to the isle of Man out of harm's way but when they were both," Bloom begins, but again he is checked by Dedalus, who seems a bit confused about Bloom's "he" and "him" and wants to know if he is referring to Dodd's son, that awkward youth, a "hobbledehoy" such as Bloom himself may have been at sixteen (see 15.3333/548.26–27): "—What? Mr Dedalus asked. That confirmed bloody hobbledehoy is it?" Bloom assures him that he is indeed speaking of Dodd's son and goes on with the story, the result being nothing but confusion and misunderstanding on Dedalus's part: "—Yes, Mr Bloom said. They were both on the way to the boat and he tried to drown . . . . . —Drown Barabbas! Mr Dedalus cried. I wish to Christ he did! Mr Power sent a long laugh down his shaded nostrils. No, Mr Bloom said, the son himself" (6.272ff./94.25ff.). The confusion, however, is not entirely Bloom's fault. Having made it clear—by his affirmative reply to Dedalus's question—that it is Dodd's son he is talking about, he was going to say, obviously: "he tried to drown himself by jumping over the wall into the Liffey." Dedalus, however, does not let him finish the sentence, for he is—or pretends to be—under the impression that in Bloom's story, as it develops in fits and starts, the son tried to drown the father—*not the other way round, as is sometimes thought.* Hence his cry "Drown Barabbas!" to which he adds that he would not be sorry at all if the boy *did* drown Dodd Senior. "Barabbas," of course, *is* Reuben J. Dodd. Later in the day, Ben Dollard will call him that (see 10.889–94/244.03–10 and 10.950–51/245.35–36). Bloom, in a desperate, hurried effort to clear up the muddle, tries to explain that it was a suicidal impulse on the son's part. His struggle with language results in: "No, [I mean to say that] the son [tried to drown] himself." That is the moment at which Cunningham impatiently—and rudely—decides to intervene. Incredibly, Bloom ends by applauding Cunningham's telling of the story that should have been *his* story by rights (6.290/95.06), but, then, it *is* no longer his story. In Shari Benstock's words, "we realize . . . that Bloom's story has collapsed, that he has lost his way, lost command of the appropriate language, lost sight of his narrative goal, lost touch with his audience" (1982b:712). The punch line, alluding to the florin Dodd gave the boatman for saving his son's life, is spoken by Simon Dedalus: "One and eightpence too much" (6.291/95.07).

EPISODE SEVEN
"Aeolus"

*T*HE STYLE and technique of "Aeolus," on the narrative level, seem conventional enough, no more disquieting anyway than what the reader may have got accustomed to from his experience of the preceding episodes. Internally, there is the characteristic pattern he may have come to regard as typically Joycean, constantly weaving from the outside to the inside world and back, a blend of third-person narrative, interior monologue, and occasional dialogue. Externally, however, the episode presents a new and unexpected feature, a typographical oddity, the narrative being interspersed with phrases—in capitals—that look like newspaper headlines. Is this still a novel in the conventional sense? So far, there had hardly been any need for the reader to consider this question. For the first hundred-odd pages *Ulysses* certainly looks like a novel, but from the seventh or eighth episode, or, even more conspicuously, from the eleventh episode onward, the book seems to outgrow the conventional model of the novel.

With regard to episode seven, we might say that the use of this typographical device, the insertion of these so-called headlines as an artificial element that somehow disrupts the novelistic pattern of character and event, already gives a faint indication of what will become a dominant force in later episodes.

The remark has been made that these phrases, usually referred to as "headlines," are rather "captions under imaginary illustrations, probably photographs, added by an anonymous sub-editor" (Hodgart, 1974: 129). For a great many, but surely not for all of them, this might hold true. Some headings, however, are neither headlines nor captions. What to think, for instance, of such headings as "SAD" (7.291/125.01) or "HIS NATIVE DORIC" (7.326/126.01)? Such phrases, and a few others as well, cannot be viewed as anything else but ironic comments, voiced by an anonymous onlooker, and heralding the disintegration of realistic modes of presentation in episodes to come.

In general, the function of the headlines might very well be to reflect what Herr calls "the varieties of journalistic overstatement that daily feed a dependent and largely uncritical public opinion" (1982:160). She also emphasizes the episode's implicit background of political and, particularly, religious censorship, the "censoring impulses present in Irish society" (1982:142). Why else, for instance, does the archbishop phone twice to the editor (7.62/118.02), and why is his letter taken so seriously (7.181/121.30)?

Peake is perhaps laying it on a bit thick asserting that these mildly ironic headlines "consistently exhibit the inflation, insincerity, vulgarity and ignorant lying of the journalistic corruption of rhetoric" (1977:195). We should not forget that the conversation going on in the editorial rooms is, after all, as Hayman describes it, light, witty, superficial, purely rhetorical (1971:174); the characters in this scene should not be blamed for simply seeming to be what they really are, in their social context. What matters more is how they see Bloom and Stephen and, by the same token, how Bloom and Stephen see them.

If this episode makes anything clear it is that Stephen is beginning to assert himself as the artist he is going to be, no longer brooding upon pale vampires as in "Proteus" but presenting—in the parable he tells—the paralyzed city of Dublin in ironic detail. We see Bloom, right at the beginning of the episode, in his role of advertisement canvasser, doing a spot of work—for the first time that day—in order to earn a few pounds' worth of commission (his own estimate, as will be seen from the passage at 8.1057–58/180.13, is that it will amount to two pounds eight). His interior monologues are sometimes of a quite deceptive simplicity, as may be demonstrated from two instances in the scene in which Bloom is introduced, asking for a copy of Keyes's ad, which had appeared in a past edition of the *Freeman's Journal*:

—There it is, Red Murray said. Alexander Keyes.
—Just cut it out, will you? Mr Bloom said, and I'll take it round to the *Telegraph* office.
. . . .
   Red Murray's long shears sliced out the advertisement from the newspaper in four clean strokes. Scissors and paste.
—I'll go through the printingworks, Mr Bloom said, taking the cut square.
—Of course, if he wants a par, Red Murray said earnestly, a pen behind his ear, we can do him one.
—Right, Mr Bloom said with a nod, I'll rub that in.
   We.

                                                    (7.25–37/116.27–117.08)

The final "We" echoes Murray's use of the pronoun: It is Bloom ridiculing, apparently, Murray's *pluralis majestatis*. The reader may be reminded of a similar case in the last line of the preceding episode, where Bloom, trying to shrug off the uneasy feeling of having been snubbed, inwardly ridicules Menton's haughty manner of thanking him for drawing attention to a "dinge" in his, Menton's, top hat when they were leaving the cemetery: "Thank you. How grand we are this morning!" (6.1033/115.41). The memory of this scene will stick in Bloom's mind all day. Now seeing Nannetti, the foreman in the printing works, checking a "galleypage," he reflects that you have to be sure of your spelling in this kind of job. This reminds him of Cunningham's favorite spelling conundrum, in which words such as *symmetry* and *cemetery* appear side by side, and then the memory of the scene of his humiliation—it took place in the *cemetery* and was witnessed by *Cunningham*!—crops up in an outburst of *esprit de l'escalier*: "I should have said when he clapped on his topper. Thank you. I ought to have said something about an old hat or something. No. I could have said. Looks as good as new now. See his phiz then" (7.171–73/121.18–21). This explains, by the way, why Bloom, in one of the visions in "Circe," will be hailed by the "Daughters of Erin" in their mock *ora pro nobis* litany as "Mentor of Menton" (15.1943/ 498.25).

Obviously, to the translator this simple "We" in the passage quoted above does not present any problem. This contrasts sharply with another snatch of interior monologue from the same passage, apparently no less simple: "Scissors and paste." The seemingly objective narrative voice tells us how Murray cuts out the advertisement, but the reader should be aware that Bloom is looking on meanwhile, waiting for Murray to hand him the newspaper cutting he has asked for. The descriptive term "clean" (in "four clean strokes") leads us to expect the point of view to be Bloom's. We know he is always eager to show his appreciation of any expert handling of things he may come to witness. Now the narrative merges into interior monologue: Murray's use of the shears reminds Bloom of the idiom "scissors and paste," providing another example of quotation within interior monologue. The phrase cannot refer to anything he actually observes, for Murray, while using *scissors*, is in no way engaged in fastening anything with *paste*. The phrase might be a sly hint on the author's part, alluding to the presence of what Kenner calls "the second narrator," or "the one responsible for the external world," for it is he who, in Kenner's words, "with a certain malicious eye for the malapropos, *pastes captions across the page* throughout the text of this episode" (1978:75, italics mine). What Bloom may be thinking of is the use of this idiom as a title of certain popular features—columns or even whole pages—in weeklies and other papers. Translators should acknowledge that Bloom, as so often, is using a ready-made phrase; his thought, in other words, is by way of being a quotation. To convey this idea, translators should look for an equivalent phrase without sticking to a literal translation as the easiest way out. As always, a correct interpretation is a prerequisite for an adequate and satisfactory translation.

Bloom's thought may even have a more specific background. Phelan—

quoted by Herr (1982:160)—has pointed out that it alludes to Arthur Griffith's *Scissors and Paste*, "a short-lived journal that pieced together headlines from various official newspapers to form ironic commentaries on current events while avoiding censorship."

Telephoning from the editor's office, Bloom learns that Keyes, whom he has to see about the advertisement, may be found in Dillon's auction rooms, on one of the quays, only a few blocks away. He hurries off, followed by a file of newsboys. MacHugh, standing at the window, stares after him.

—He'll get that advertisement, the professor said, staring through his blackrimmed spectacles over the crossblind. Look at the young scamps after him.
—Show. Where? Lenehan cried, running to the window.

A STREET CORTÈGE

Both smiled over the crossblind at the file of capering newsboys in Mr Bloom's wake, the last zigzagging white on the breeze a mocking kite, a tail of white bowknots.
—Look at the young guttersnipe behind him hue and cry, Lenehan said, and you'll kick. O, my rib risible! Taking off his flat spaugs and the walk. Small nines. Steal upon larks.

(7.439–49/129.26–36)

The newsboys are mocking Bloom, imitating his flatfooted walk. He himself is fully aware that he is being made fun of, as will be disclosed in a later episode ("Nausicaa"); seeing a gentleman, whom he had observed passing before, return now along the beach, and wanting vaguely to get up and turn back to town himself, Bloom thinks: "Walk after him now make him awkward like those newsboys me today" (13.1056–57/ 375.42–376.01).

The phrase "Taking off his flat spaugs and the walk" has proved a pitfall for at least one translator, although its analysis seems simple enough. As to syntax, "to take off" is a transitive verb, with "his flat spaugs and the walk" as its direct object, and the preceding phrase, "the young guttersnipe behind him," as its implied subject. As to semantics, "to take off" here means "to ridicule by imitation," and has to be distinguished as such from the intransitive verb *to take off*, which means *to depart* or *to start* (as of an airplane). Whereas the French, the Dutch, and the older German translations correctly convey the notion of imitation, the modern German translation shows some confusion on this point. It seems as though Wollschläger held Bloom himself to be the implied subject of "taking off," used in the intransitive sense. For the

syntactic pattern to make sense—in the absence of a transitive predicate—
Wollschläger had to smuggle in a preposition and finally had to treat the
nominal constituent "the walk" as a kind of independent exclamation,
marked as such in German by taking the nominative case. In short, he
translates as though Lenehan's words had been something such as, "How he
takes himself off with his flat feet—and that walk!!" The result is: "Wie er
abhaut mit seinen Plattfüssen, und dieser Gang!" (182). This translation
reads quite well as it stands, but, failing as it does to take into account the role
of the newsboys who perform their antics at Bloom's expense, it evokes a
picture that differs essentially from that which must have been intended by
the author.

The scene of Bloom's short talk with Murray, in the latter's mana-
gerial cubicle of the paper he works for, has been spread over three
sections. In the first, headed "GENTLEMEN OF THE PRESS," Bloom's business,
the matter he came to see Murray for, had actually been concluded. On
the point of leaving, he is detained by Murray, who draws his attention to
the stately figure of William Brayden, the owner of the press, who has
just entered the building and is now passing up the staircase, "steered by
an umbrella, a solemn beardframed face" (7.45–46/117.18–19). It is he
who lends his name to the heading of the second section of this sequence:
"WILLIAM BRAYDEN, ESQUIRE, OF OAKLANDS, SANDYMOUNT." In an awed whis-
per, Murray asks Bloom: "Don't you think his face is like Our Saviour?"
He is referring, of course, to the traditional image of Christ which
pictorial art has presented to Western eyes for ages. Murray's remark
releases a train of thought or, rather, of associations in Bloom's mind,
starting with a picture that he had seen somewhere and that had cropped
up in his memory once before that same morning: "Martha, Mary. I saw
that picture somewhere I forget now old master or faked for money. He is
sitting in their house, talking. Mysterious" (5.289–90/79.06–8). A Rubens
painting (oil on panel) depicting the well-known scene of Christ in the house
of Martha and Mary has been in the possession of the National Gallery of
Ireland since 1901, but, as Thornton observes (1968:81), it does not conform
with the description given by Bloom. It does not, for instance, show Martha,
jar on her head, getting the supper, as Bloom seems to remember (5.295/
79.13–14). Besides, if he had seen this painting in the gallery in Dublin, he
surely would not have been so vague about it. The assumption, however,
that Bloom is thinking of a "painting," specifically, is not founded on
anything of a factual nature in the text; the term Bloom uses is "picture."
Chances are, therefore, that he saw a reproduction of either a painting or a
drawing in some daily or weekly paper. I am stressing this seemingly
irrelevant point because there is a parallel, as I see it, with Bloom's next
associative image: the picture of Mario the tenor. The link is provided by the
word "Martha," the name of the biblical figure calling to mind Flotow's

opera of that name, and this in its turn evoking the picture of the famous tenor in his role of Lionel, singing the air "M'appari."

As Ellmann has pointed out (1972:64), Bloom's reply ("Or like Mario") reduces the impressive publisher's appearance to a slightly comic operatic figure. Murray, in an attempt to soften the blow and to suppress the implications of this comparison, insists that the resemblance he remarked upon is the primary one. Bloom, as if to say to himself, "Have it your own way," then again imagines Mario as he stands on stage with a hand on his heart and a Christ-like face. This is the passage discussed and paraphrased above in its entirety:

> —Don't you think his face is like Our Saviour? Red Murray whispered.
>
> The door of Ruttledge's office whispered: ee: cree. They always build one door opposite another for the wind to. Way in. Way out.
>
> Our Saviour: beardframed oval face: talking in the dusk. Mary, Martha. Steered by an umbrella sword to the footlights: Mario the tenor.
>
> —Or like Mario, Mr Bloom said.
>
> —Yes, Red Murray agreed. But Mario was said to be the picture of Our Saviour.
>
> Jesusmario with rougy cheeks, doublet and spindle legs. Hand on his heart. In *Martha*.
>
> > *Co-ome thou lost one,*
> > *Co-ome thou dear one!*
>
> (7.49–60/117.23–37)

Objections have been raised as to the plausibility of Bloom's having been able to hear Mario sing. Adams points out that because Mario made his last stage appearance in 1871, at Covent Garden, when Bloom was just five years old, "Bloom's remembering him in *Martha* is clearly a surface impossibility" (1962:169). Blamires speaks of "a lapse of verisimilitude" and believes that Mario retired from the stage as early as 1867 (but this may have applied to Ireland specifically), so "Bloom, who was born in 1866, could scarcely have memories of his performances" (1966:44). Anyway, the assumption by Moseley (1967:83) that Bloom remembers Mario's singing in *Martha* is certainly unwarranted. Of course, Bloom may have heard others sing the popular air; in fact, he will hear it sung by Simon Dedalus in the bar of the Ormond Hotel that very afternoon. It is evident, moreover, that Bloom knows what Mario looked like when acting Lionel's part, but nowhere does he state explicitly that he ever witnessed a live performance of the opera with Mario, or anybody else for that matter, in that famous role. What stimulates Bloom's train of thought at that moment is, in essence, a visual memory, just as in the case of the biblical scene. In both instances he is thinking of something he saw a *picture* of. We should not forget that such popular airs and songs used to appear in print quite regularly. As to this particular aria, Bloom's detailed description of Mario's appearance on the stage perfectly fits the illustration on the title page of one of these editions, reproduced in Schneider's study on quotations in *Ulysses* (1970:107). The accompanying text says, "Martha, Martha, O Return Love! The Air Sung by Signor Mario with English Words by Charles Jefferys, London." The picture shows a romantic, languishing figure, doublet and spindle legs and all, such as might well have aroused Bloom's imagination.

The third of the three sections the opening scene is divided into, the one in which Bloom finally leaves Murray's office, is headed "THE CROZIER AND THE PEN." What this means becomes clear in the text of the section itself, supplemented by what we are told under the heading "NOTED CHURCHMAN AN OCCASIONAL CONTRIBUTOR" (7.178–79/121.27–28). Murray, having failed to impress Bloom by his whispered comment on Brayden's interesting face, now announces "gravely": "His grace phoned down twice this morning." The reference is to William J. Walsh, Archbishop of Dublin (Gifford, 1974:103), whom Ellmann characterizes as "quick to put pressure on the press" (1972:64). Then, in the section "NOTED CHURCHMAN," Bloom witnesses Nannetti, the *Telegraph* foreman and proofreader, checking a "galleypage," when the latter suddenly looks up, asking one of the typesetters: "Wait. Where's the archbishop's letter? It's to be repeated in the *Telegraph*" (7.181/121.30–31). We may surmise, therefore, that the archbishop phoned in order to insist that the letter he had sent to the *Freeman's Journal* be published in the *Evening Telegraph* as well, in an attempt to make the press, as Ellmann puts it, "accommodate the Church's position" (1972:64). All this has been condensed in the heading "THE CROZIER AND THE PEN," a true journalist's phrase. A crozier being a bishop's pastoral staff, the phrase implies that His Eminence has these two weapons at his disposal in order to further the interests of the Church as he sees fit.

Watching a typesetter distribute type by hand, Bloom is duly impressed by the speed at which he works, especially because he believes, wrongly, that the man *reads* the words "backwards first." Dignam's name, for instance, so Bloom imagines, would appear as "mangiD kcirtaP" (7.206/122.19). There is no evidence that he actually *sees* anything such as that—perhaps he just tries to spell the name out, in reversed order, in his head. In reality, a typesetter works in the normal order (P-a-t-r-i-c-k), from left to right; the only difference is that the letters are put in (in the composing stick) upside down—each single type, moreover, being in reversed writing, in "mirror image."

Curiously enough, Bloom might after all be right, in a sense, for the typesetter is said to be *distributing* type, which may mean that he is putting the loose letter types back into the compartments of the letter cases. After use, the blocks of type are lifted bodily from the galley and put back into the composing stick. The typesetter then starts taking the letters out one by one to distribute them to the respective compartments; this time he is, logically, working from right to left and so, in a sense, he is *reading backwards*!

Anyway, because Hebrew *is* written and read from right to left, Bloom is somehow reminded of Seder night in his parents' home, when his father used to read the story of the Exodus, sitting with his Haggadah book and "reading backwards with his finger" to him. Under a headline that has a New Testament flavor ("AND IT WAS THE FEAST OF THE PASSOVER"), Bloom's memories revert to the Pesach home ceremony, which annually commemorates, in a spirit of rejoicing, the Exodus from Egypt as told in the Old Testament:

> Poor papa with his hagadah book, reading backwards with his finger to me. Pessach. Next year in Jerusalem. Dear, O dear! All that long business about that brought us out of the land of Egypt and into the house of bondage *alleluia. Shema Israel Adonai Elohenu*. No. that's the other. Then the twelve brothers, Jacob's sons. And then the lamb and the cat and the dog and the stick and the water and the butcher. And then the angel of death kills the butcher and he kills the ox and the dog kills the cat. Sounds a bit silly till you come to look into it well. Justice it means but it's everybody eating everyone else. That's what life is after all.
>
> (7.206–14/122.19–30)

Bloom's notion of "everybody eating everyone else" derives from what he still remembers of the folk song "Chad Gad'ya" ("One Only Kid"), a kind of cumulative chant, which is sung merrily at the end of the Seder meal and which bears little relation to the story of the Exodus.

Henke's interpretation of this passage is misleading in the extreme, because it is based on selective quotation:

> Ireland is itself a "house of bondage," spiritually bankrupt and enthralled by English domination. Bloom's theological meditation offers a scathing critique of Irish biblical rhetoric: "All that long business about that brought us out of the land of Egypt and into the house of bondage *alleluia* . . . Justice it means but it's everybody eating everyone else. That's what life is after all" (p. 122).
>
> (1978:117)

Due to the deliberate omission of a few lines of print, the meaning of the original has been distorted in an unpardonable way. Any reader who is not familiar enough with *Ulysses* to be struck immediately by the incongruity of the quotation must get the impression that Bloom's "it" in the phrase "Justice it means" here refers to "that long business." In Bloom's train of thought, however, there is no doubt but that it refers to the song about the cat and the dog and so on, chanted at the end of the meal. As to Bloom's "that long business," it refers to the lengthy, repetitive ceremonial phrases proper, to be intoned by the master of the house as he is sitting at the head of the table. Bloom is neither the first nor the last to think this particular part of the Seder rather tedious; there is a general feeling that the ceremony could do with some shortening without any detriment to its character or its meaning. Anyway, the mild, even slightly nostalgic criticism contained in Bloom's musings—hardly a serious "theological meditation"!—is not directed against any "Irish rhetoric," biblical or otherwise, as Henke maintains; it is just the outcome of one of those memories of his late father that cross Bloom's mind from time to time.

In this case, as we have seen, these memories have their origin in Bloom's mistaken belief that typesetters read the words backwards. Joly submits the possibility of another associative link. Of the scene in the case room, he says: "In *Ulysses*, Bloom is ever conscious of family origins, and nearly always from a perspective that is Jewish. Thoughts of a dead friend, Paddy Dignam, trigger memories of a deceased father" (1982:197). Joly's argument—a case of overexplaining—is rather weak. Nowhere in *Ulysses* do we get the impression that Dignam was such a close friend of Bloom's as all that. Just now he has seen Hynes handing in his press account of Dignam's funeral for the evening edition of the *Telegraph* (see 6.878ff./111.31ff. and 7.76–80/118.20). Walking on through the case room, with "the silent typesetters at their cases" (7.163/121.09), he stops to watch one of them at work (7.204/122.17)—not necessarily the same one who was going to handle Hynes's report—and, taking Dignam's name, which he has just been reminded of, as an example, he starts wondering about technical details of printing. It is these technical aspects and not any thoughts of Dignam as such which set off the memories of his father.

Having found out where he can reach Keyes, Bloom hurries off, as he wants to persuade this businessman to give a three months' renewal of the advertisement in question. Whereas Bloom, hovering on the fringes of the company gathered in the editor's office, is barely tolerated, Stephen, entering after Bloom has left, is greeted quite civilly and treated as an equal, as one whose views and opinions are valued. He has come, as he had promised he would that morning, to ask the editor to publish Mr. Deasy's letter to the press on the subject of foot-and-mouth disease, a copy of which letter he has brought with him. He stays to listen to the talk going on, occasionally taking part in it, and finally inviting those present to come and have a drink in a nearby pub. Twice he is asked to listen to striking samples of Irish oratory, quoted by O'Molloy and MacHugh, respectively.

To understand Stephen's associations in this context, we should retrace our steps to the point where he first thinks of the ghost's words in *Hamlet*, his reaction being due to O'Molloy's mentioning a case of alleged fratricide. He recalls the scene where the old king's ghost reveals to his son the truth about his death, how he had been murdered by his own brother, who had poured poison in his ear; "J. J. O'Molloy turned to Stephen and said quietly and slowly: —One of the most polished periods I think I ever listened to in my life fell from the lips of Seymour Bushe. It was in that case of fratricide, the Childs murder case. Bushe defended him. *And in the porches of mine ear did pour.* By the way how did he find that out? He died in his sleep. Or the other story, beast with two backs?" (7.746–52/139.21–28). The phrase, italicized in the text, seems to fascinate Stephen. He will use it more than once, twisting it around, manipulating it to suit his purpose, finally losing sight of the fratricide aspect altogether. He takes it up, for instance, during the discussion in the National Library (in "Scylla and Charybdis"), when putting forward his theory about Shakespeare and *Hamlet*. "List, list, O, list!" the ghost had cried to Hamlet, and Stephen, looking at his listeners, thinks: "They list. And in the porches of their ears I pour" (9.465/196.38). Still intrigued by the question how king Hamlet could have been aware of the manner of his own murder, because he died in his sleep, Stephen goes on to say: "The soul has been before stricken mortally, a poison poured in the porch of a sleeping ear. But those who are done to death in sleep cannot know the manner of their quell unless their Creator endow their souls with that knowledge in the life to come. The poisoning and the beast with two backs that urged it King Hamlet's ghost could not know of were he not endowed with knowledge by his creator" (9.466–71/196.39–197.03).

Returning to the scene in the newspaper office, we find Stephen himself in the role of the listener, listening with the others to Professor MacHugh's version of a famous speech by John F. Taylor. MacHugh, trying to outdo O'Molloy, is quoting this speech of Taylor's not so much for what it says, actually, but for what it stands for in the history of Irish orators, as a fine example of eloquence. Taylor had spoken of some hypothetical Egyptian high priest, asking the Jews why they were not willing to accept Egypt's culture, religion, and language. In doing so, Taylor was alluding to what was really at stake in his time and, specifically, in the debate he was taking part in, namely Irish independence and the revival of Gaelic. Taylor's speech was a reply, MacHugh explains, to Mr. Justice Fitzgibbon, who had spoken against the Gaelic movement, openly showing his contempt of it. "It was then a new movement. We were weak, therefore worthless," MacHugh adds (7.807–8/141.19–20).

In the ensuing silence after MacHugh's words, the bare feet of the newspaper boys are heard "rushing along the hallway and pattering up the staircase" (7.877–78/143.25–26). "That is oratory," MacHugh declares. He is referring, of course, to Taylor's speech, but Stephen reflects that such "Noble words" (7.836/142.14) may well turn out to be as ephemeral as the daily paper the boys are going out to distribute. He is thinking of Daniel O'Connell's famous Sunday-morning meetings in the 1840s and imagines the many hundreds of thousands of ears the tribune's words were poured into, this time reshaping the original quotation in a curious way: "Gone with the wind. Hosts at Mullaghmast and Tara of the kings. Miles of ears of porches. The tribune's words, howled and scattered to the four winds" (7.880–82/143.28–30).

O'Molloy, having announced that he is going to recite "one of the most polished periods" he ever heard, pauses a moment to make sure he has his listeners' attention: "Pause. J. J. O'Molloy took out his cigarette-case. False lull. Something quite ordinary. Messenger took out his matchbox thoughtfully and lit his cigar. I have often thought since on looking back over that strange time that it was that small act, trivial in itself, that striking of that match, that determined the whole aftercourse of both our lives" (7.760–65/140.02–9). In this interior monologue Stephen comments on O'Molloy's gesture: it is a "false lull," a deceptive quiet, a moment of suspense that should be followed by something unmistakably impressive; this may turn out, however, to be a banal commonplace. The situation reminds him somehow of a passage such as might be found in certain cloak-and-dagger stories. "Messenger" may even be the name of a character in such a story (otherwise, why not "*The* messenger"?). We have seen examples of quotation within interior monologue before, but this particular "stylistic intrusion," as Gifford calls it (1974:115), is rather puzzling. By now, readers must have become used to Stephen's habit of quoting freely from the works of such lofty spirits as Aristotle, Aquinas, Dante, and Shakespeare. Here, however, he is clearly parodying phrases that we only expect to encounter in a certain kind of novel, belonging to so-called trivial or pulp literature. The motive is not immediately clear. Stephen's reaction, puzzling in the sense that we would not have expected him to have read such novels at all, might be attributed, I think, to a feeling of embarrassment. Because he is conscious that O'Molloy is addressing him personally (7.746/139.21) and will be awaiting his approval or his critical opinion anyway, he probably tries to shrug off the embarrassment this causes him by inwardly ridiculing the whole situation.

When Stephen hands the editor Mr. Deasy's letter to the press, there is a slight misunderstanding, because MacHugh seems to assume that the letter is Stephen's: "—Good day, Stephen, the professor said, coming to peer over their shoulders. Foot and mouth? Are you turned . . .? Bullockbefriending bard" (7.526/132.16–18). MacHugh's reaction is something Stephen had foreseen more or less when he had promised Mr. Deasy, headmaster of the school where he is teaching, to do his best to have the letter published. More specifically, it was Mulligan he had in mind, as the latter was always giving him nicknames, such as "jejune jesuit" (1.45/4.09), "Kinch, the knifeblade" (1.55/4.21), "unclean bard" (1.475/15.40), and "toothless Kinch" (1.708/22.28). That is why Stephen, passing out through the school gate that morning, two copies of Mr. Deasy's letter in his pocket, thinks, "Mulligan will dub me a new name: the bullockbefriending bard" (2.430–31/36.02–3). Mulligan will *not*, by the way, for the simple reason that he will remain ignorant of Mr. Deasy's letter and the role Stephen plays in its publication, but Stephen himself seems mightily pleased with his *trouvaille*, repeating the phrase three times in all. The first time, in Crawford's office, we have seen above. The second time, the scene is the National Library, where Stephen is expounding his views on *Hamlet*. He has given a copy of Mr. Deasy's letter to George Russell, who is on the staff of the *Irish Homestead*—nicknamed "the pigs' paper"—asking him to pass it on to Norman, the editor (9.316–21/192.38–193.02).

Both times, so far, the phrase has cropped up in Stephen's interior monologue in direct connection with the letter. The third time, however, the phrase seems to have assumed a life of its own, being no longer associated with Stephen's efforts to help Mr. Deasy in his fight against cattle disease. Moreover, it is now no longer confined to Stephen's *thoughts*, but uttered aloud in a conversation with Frank Costello, one of those present in the Maternity Hospital: "Francis was reminding Stephen of years before when they had been at school together in Conmee's time. . . . You have spoken of the past and its phantoms, Stephen said. Why think of them? If I call them into life across the waters of Lethe will not the poor ghosts troop to my call? Who supposes it? I, Bous Stephanoumenos, bullockbefriending bard, am lord and giver of their life" (14.1110–16/414.42–415.07).

It is curious to see how Stephen retains his interest in Mr. Deasy's letter till late at night, even though he must have been in a state of utter exhaustion by then. Sitting with Bloom in the cabmen's shelter, before his "untastable apology for a cup of coffee" (16.1141/644.26), and seeing Bloom glancing through the late edition of the *Evening Telegraph* that happened to be lying on the table, the first and only thing he wants to know is whether the letter had actually been printed. Stifling a yawn, he puts his query to Bloom in a roundabout, somewhat enigmatic way: "—Is that first epistle to the Hebrews, he asked as soon as his bottom jaw would let him, in? Text: open thy mouth and put thy foot in it. —It is. Really, Mr Bloom said (though first he fancied he alluded to the archbishop till he added about foot and mouth with which there could be no possible connection) overjoyed to put his mind at rest and a bit flabbergasted at Myles Crawford's after all managing to. There" (16.1268–73/648.07–14). It appears, then, that O'Molloy's pessimistic outlook on the chances that the letter will be published had been ill-founded. Crawford, having read Mr. Deasy's letter halfway through in a cursory way (7.539ff./132.30ff.), had "crammed the sheets into a sidepocket" with the words, "That'll be all right. I'll read the rest after. That'll be all right" (7.585–86/134.12–14). Later, when following Stephen's invitation to have drinks in a pub close by, Crawford had been seen pulling the typed sheets out of his pocket again, and thereupon O'Molloy, observing the clumsy way Crawford handled them, had insinuated to Stephen that he would not be surprised if the editor bungled the whole thing: "I hope you will live to see it published" (7.907/144.21). Stephen's satisfaction at having accomplished at least one more or less self-imposed task that day is an understandable feeling, but why Bloom should be surprised, even "flabbergasted," at "Myles Crawford's after all managing to," may not immediately be clear, for Bloom had not been present when Mr. Deasy's letter was handed to the editor, so how could he have known that such a letter existed at all (let alone that it was about foot-and-mouth disease)? The answer might be that he could have heard about it in the Maternity Hospital, when he had gone there to inquire after Mrs. Purefoy (in "Oxen of the Sun"). There had indeed been some talk about a letter to the press in Bloom's hearing. It starts with Lenehan coming up "to the feet of the table to say [to Stephen, apparently] how the letter was in that night's gazette and he made a show to find it about him (for he swore with an oath that he had been at pains about it) but on Stephen's persuasion he gave over the search and was bidden to sit near by which he did mighty brisk" (14.529–33/398.10–15)—typically Lenehan's, the sponger's, way of ingratiating himself. Costello, under the impression that they are talking about something written by Stephen himself, asks whether it was poetry or a tale but is told by Lenehan that it is about diseased cattle: "Faith, no, . . . 'tis all about Kerry cows that are to be butchered along of the plague" (14.545–47/398.30–31). That is where Bloom pricks up his ears: "What, says Mr Leopold with his hands across, that was earnest to know the drift of it, will they slaughter all? I protest I saw them but this day morning going to the Liverpool boats, says he. I can scarce believe 'tis so bad, says he" (14.565–68/399.12–16). Bloom, who had once worked for a cattle salesman, supposes it must be some other, less serious disease, but Stephen protests that he has it from a reliable source that it is really a matter of foot-and-mouth disease: "Mr Stephen, a little moved but very handsomely told him no such matter and that he had dispatches from the emperor's chief tailtickler thanking him for the hospitality, that was sending over Doctor Rinderpest, the best-quoted cowcatcher in all Muscovy, with a bolus or two of physic to take the bull by the horns" (14.573–78/399.22–27). So Bloom seems to have put two and two together, having understood enough of the drunken talk to identify the letter when he sees it in the paper a few hours later.

It is clear that the sentence "A woman brought sin into the world" (7.536/132.26), which crops up in the scene where Stephen shows the editor Mr. Deasy's letter, is neither third-person narrative nor a remark made by someone in Stephen's hearing, but part of the latter's interior monologue, consisting, as so often, of snatches of quotation. Responding to the professor's salutation (quoted above), Stephen explains that the letter is Mr. Deasy's, not his. The editor chimes in with a vivid recollection of Mr. Deasy's wife, and Stephen is reminded of this phrase as used by Mr. Deasy in talking to him in his study that morning (2.390/34.39–40). Bits and pieces of some other phrases used by the headmaster pass through Stephen's mind as he listens to the editor, who is calling up an absurd picture of a soup-throwing Mrs. Deasy (7.530–38/132.20–29). Apparently, Stephen had not had the faintest idea that Mr. Deasy was married, but now he realizes that Crawford has been speaking in past tense throughout in talking about Mr. Deasy's wife. That is, I think, why he wonders: Could Mr. Deasy be a widower? At that moment, Stephen might quite well be thinking of his *father*, who is also a widower. The first time he thinks of his *mother* in this episode, and only indirectly so, occurs further down, in the section headed "LENEHAN'S LIMERICK." The limerick that Lenehan whispers in Stephen's ear, intended to mock the "ponderous pundit MacHugh," reminds Stephen of Mulligan's quip at MacHugh's expense, "In mourning for Sallust." But he is not really interested in either Lenehan or MacHugh. What still rankles him is the insult he suffered at Mulligan's hands when once he overheard the latter say to his mother: "*O, it's only Dedalus whose mother is beastly dead*" (1.198–99/8.19–20). As he explained to Mulligan, in feeling offended he was not thinking of the offense to his mother but of the offense to himself (1.218–20/8.42–9.02). Now, in the newspaper office, the egocentric young man's inner thought (quotation within interior monologue again) reveals quite clearly that it is still the offense to himself he cannot forget. As far as he is concerned, Mulligan may freely mock such pompous fools as MacHugh, but when he starts mocking or even offending Stephen himself, especially by speaking of his, Stephen's, mother in such a brutal way, the thrust goes too near the quick for comfort: "In mourning for Sallust, Mulligan says. Whose mother is beastly dead" (7.583–84/134.10–11), the mother for whom he, Stephen, is still in mourning, too.

As mentioned above, Stephen has to listen to MacHugh's quoting a speech by John F. Taylor in which the latter evokes an imaginary scene in ancient Egypt, in which a high priest is heard addressing the youthful Moses. Halfway through, MacHugh's words are interrupted or, rather, accompanied by a brief flash of interior monologue of Stephen's: "Nile. Child, man, effigy. By the Nilebank the babemaries kneel, cradle of bulrushes: a man supple in combat: stonehorned, stonebearded, heart of stone" (7.851–54/142.33–37). Obviously, "child" and "man" refer to *two* stages in Moses' life and a *third* stage is alluded to when Stephen thinks of Moses as "that stony effigy in frozen music, horned and terrible," a phrase quoted by O'Molloy a few moments before (7.768/ 140.12–13) when referring to the *Moses* by Michelangelo, the famous statue in San Pietro in Vincoli in Rome (not in the Vatican, as Joyce has O'Molloy say). In Stephen's interior monologue there is a kind of coalescence of images due to the coincidence of Moses' figuring in both quotations he listens to. In his mind he sees a process of growth, of development, an evolution: Moses growing up from the babe in the ark of bulrushes to the adult fighter, and finally turning into the cold statue with a heart of stone.

In an earlier scene, the numbers two and three had already played a role in Stephen's thoughts about rhyme. Crawford has been deploring loudly the lack of literary talent; nowadays, he claims, there are no longer any outstanding pressmen or any great pleaders at the bar. Now he is silent but his mouth keeps working nervously. Watching him, Stephen is reminded of the lines of poetry he had tried to compose that morning when strolling along the beach, having turned over in his mind such phrases as "pale vampire," "mouth to her mouth's kiss," and the like (3.397ff./48.01ff.); to write them down he had torn a bit off Mr. Deasy's letter to the press (3.404–7/48.10–15).

I do not think, though, that Stephen remembers this scene on the seashore *directly*. He does not need to, anyway, because an intermediate memory crops up in his thoughts as he hands Crawford the typed sheets of the letter and sees again the "Bit torn off" (7.519/132.08). His thoughts now reveal the definitive form his tentative phrases had been modified and condensed into: "*On swift sail flaming / From storm and south / He comes, pale vampire, / Mouth to my mouth*" (7.522–25/ 132.12–15).

Since Prescott's *Notes* (1952:152) we know that Stephen's poem is a remake of the final stanza of one of Douglas Hyde's poems in his *Love Songs of Connacht* (1895), poems translated from the Irish. There is no vampire in Hyde's stanza, but Stephen practically copied its last line, "His mouth to my mouth." Joyce has provided a clue in "Scylla and Charybdis," where he has Haines buy the *Love Songs* (9.512–14/ 198.16–19).

We now come to the rhymes. Blamires's summary, I think, is basically right: "Crawford's mouth twitches with excitement. Stephen's mind goes back to his poem, the image of the kissed mouth, then to the search for rhymes, which suddenly are concretized, men in couples, girls in threes" (1966:52). Having remembered his poem, Stephen starts speculating about a possible connection between the notions of "mouth" and "south," then switches to the feature of rhyme in general: "His [Crawford's] mouth continued to twitch unspeaking . . . Mouth, south. Is the mouth south someway? Or the south a mouth? Must be some. South, pout, out, shout, drouth. Rhymes: two men dressed the same, looking the same, two by two" (7.709–16/138.14–22). For what is, essentially, an auditory phenomenon Stephen here uses a visual metaphor: "two men dressed the same, looking the same." This may be an allusion, as Gifford points out (1974:113), to a passage in Book II of Dante's *Divina Commedia* (*Purgatorio* XXIX:134–35), although it must be remarked that the two men Dante speaks of in that context are not at all *dressed* the same: *Appresso tutto il pertrattato nodo / vidi due vecchi in abito dispari, / ma pari in atto ed onesto e sedo* (Behind this throng I have just described / I saw two old men, *unlike in raiment*, / but like in bearing and venerable and grave). In Dante's lines, moreover, there are just *two* old men, no more, whereas for Stephen the point is the *repetitive* character of rhyme: his men, any number of them, are walking in couples, *two by two*. Anyway, Stephen's interior monologue shows that he must have been thinking specifically of Dante's terza rima, the three-line stanza (*terzina*) with its typical rhyme scheme, although his selecting three *nonconsecutive* lines (*Inferno* V:92, 94, 96), cannot do justice to the structure of this schema, which is characterized by the fact that, as Reynolds puts it, "the middle verse of a terzina prepares the ear for the sound of the rhyme word to come in the next terzina" (1981:94). These fragments of lines (lines that Stephen may have quoted in full in his interior monologue) are only, as Thornton aptly remarks, "quotations illustrating rhyme" (1968:120), rhyme as repetition of identical sounds:

> . . . . *la tua pace*
> . . . . *che parlar ti piace*
> *Mentre che il vento, come fa, si tace.*

He saw them three by three, approaching girls, in green, in rose, in russet, entwining, *per l'aer perso*, in mauve, in purple, *quella pacifica oriafiamma*, gold of oriflamme, *di rimirar fè più ardenti*. But I old men, penitent, leadenfooted, underdarkneath the night: mouth south: tomb womb.

(7.717–24/138.23–30)

Stephen is conscious of the contrast with his own dull rhymes: "He [Dante] saw them [the rhymes] three by three," in groups of three, that is (the terza rima), like girls attired in garments of various hues. Is Stephen thinking of the groups of rhymes in general or is he alluding to a specific group of three girls as described by Dante somewhere? Gifford suggests that the phrase "three by three," denoting girls approaching in bands of three (1974:113), would derive from *Purgatorio* XXIX:110. Such a line, however, should be quoted in its context, and we had better first say a few words about the lines that lead up to it.

Among the groups proceeding along a kind of seven-lane highway in the divine pageant as described by Dante in Canto XXIX is a two-wheeled chariot, a triumphal car, drawn by a gryphon (lines 106–8). Then the text continues as follows (lines 109–11):

> *Esso tendeva in su l'una e l'altra ale*
> *tra la mezzana e le tre e tre liste*
> *si ch'a nulla, fendendo, facea male.*

What these lines amount to is that the gryphon, evidently walking in the middle lane, kept spreading its wings high above the *three lanes* on either side so as not to hurt anybody or anything. The car is further described in detail, and then the poet sees *three young women* approach dancing beside the right wheel, the first in blazing red, the next in bright green like emerald, and the third in white, white as freshly fallen snow (lines 121–29). To the left of the chariot Dante sees *four young women* frolicking in purple garments (lines 130–32) and the rear of this part of the pageant is brought up by the two aged men we have already referred to (lines 133–35). In short, no mention is made of girls marching in threes; there is *only one group* of just three young women.

Both Thornton and Gifford, supplementing the missing words and lines in Stephen's interior monologue, have given extensive translations of the fragments referred to, but in my opinion all that is beside the point. It is not the meaning but only the musical quality of Dante's verse which Stephen is interested in just now and which he is trying to translate into visual images. Mixing elements from the *Inferno*, the *Purgatorio*, and the *Paradiso*, Stephen is concerned solely with the way these Italian verses sound. He discerns a striking contrast between the feminine rhymes of the *terza rima* (masculine endings, which predominate in English, being extremely rare in Italian anyway) and the heavy-footed masculine rhymes he used himself (mouth:south, tomb:womb). The latter, he feels, look like old men shuffling along in pairs, dark, heavy.

In a final comment on the speech he has just been quoting, MacHugh, apparently eager to be confirmed in his opinion, turns to Stephen while following the others on their way to the pub: "—Come along, Stephen, the professor said. That is fine, isn't it? It has the prophetic vision. *Fuit Ilium!* The sack of windy Troy. Kingdoms of this world. The masters of the Mediterranean are fellaheen today" (7.909–11/144.24–27). Of Mac-Hugh's phrase "Kingdoms of this world," Thornton remarks: "This probably alludes to Christ's statement to Pilate in John 18:36: 'My kingdom is not of this world: if my kingdom were of this world, then would my servants fight, that I should not be delivered to the Jews: but now is my kingdom not from hence' " (1968:126), and Gifford offers the same view (1974:119). In this biblical passage, however, Christ speaks of a spiritual kingdom or dominion, whereas MacHugh is clearly alluding to states and nations of the past in a material sense, kingdoms once mighty and prosperous, now impoverished and ruled by foreign masters. It is much more likely that the phrase has its origin in the story told in Matthew as well as in Luke, which says that Jesus "was led by the Spirit into the wilderness to be tempted by the devil." One of the ways in which the latter tried to tempt Jesus is described in Matthew 4:8–9: "Again, the devil took him to a very high mountain, and showed him all the *kingdoms of the world* and the glory of them; and he said to him, 'All these I will give you, if you will fall down and worship me' " (italics mine). Those, I assume, are the kingdoms MacHugh's phrase alludes to. The professor's frame of reference is a historical rather than a theological one: it includes Troy but leaves no room for Jerusalem.

Starting on his "Parable of the Plums," Stephen mentions a Dublin street, Fumbally's Lane, off Blackpitts. Of all the street names he might have picked at random, this one must have some special significance for him, as may be seen from the interior monologue it is accompanied by: "—Two Dublin vestals, Stephen said, elderly and pious, have lived fifty and fiftythree years in Fumbally's lane. —Where is that? the professor asked. —Off Blackpitts, Stephen said. Damp night reeking of hungry dough. Against the wall. Face glistering tallow under her fustian shawl. Frantic hearts. Akasic records. Quicker, darlint!" (7.923–29/145.03–9).

The same intensely vivid memory had visited him once before that same day. Sitting on the rocks of Sandymount beach in the morning (a scene in "Proteus"), he had been watching a couple of gypsies, a man and a woman, picking cockles. He imagines the woman in town at night, plying her trade as he had seen a woman do in Fumbally's Lane once: "When night hides her body's flaws calling under her brown shawl from an archway where dogs have mired. . . . A shefiend's whiteness under her rancid rags. Fumbally's lane that night: the tanyard smells" (3.375–80/47.16–22). There is no consensus among critics about the exact nature of the underlying experience from which Stephen's memory derives. According to Gifford, the passage in "Aeolus" is a "recall of a street encounter with a prostitute" (1974:119), rather a vague comment, which does not answer the obvious question: What, exactly, happened in Fumbally's Lane that night? Peake is more precise. To him it is evident that among the "many disparate thoughts and experiences" that go into the making of Stephen's parable is the lane where he, Stephen, "had embraced a prostitute" (1977:196). But Blamires casts Stephen in a different role. Of the scene on the beach he says, "the woman reminds Stephen of a shawled gypsy girl he saw in the arms of a man one night in Fumbally's Lane" (1966:17) and in his summary of Stephen's parable he says that "it concerns two old ladies from Fumbally's Lane, the place whose mention brings back to Stephen's mind a memorable incident . . . when he saw a couple making love in the darkness" (1966:56).

The problem amounts to this: What is Stephen's role in this scene that seems to haunt his thoughts—actor or only spectator? Moreover, is it the mention of the place that brings back to his mind the incident, as Blamires holds (and it is not, after all, as if someone else mentioned the name of the street), or is it the other way around? Could it be the persistent memory that has determined his choice of a name?

It may seem mainly a matter of taste, but in view of the intensity of the memory as evinced by Stephen (note the "Frantic hearts") I am inclined to assign him an active part in the encounter. Besides, and this is merely a practical consideration, could (and would) Stephen have come so close as to have been able to catch the whispered words ("Quicker, darlint!") if he had only been a passer-by, watching a couple making love in the dark?

The uncertainty remains but, more on an impulse than on anything else, my vote goes to Peake. Of course, some readers may feel that this very uncertainty, this refusal on the author's part to settle the question for us, bears some relevance to the plan and scope of the book. However, it may very well have an artistic function in that it reveals the author's attitude. The character's inner thoughts are there for the reader to perceive, to take in and to digest, but beyond that the latter has nothing to hope for or to expect. The author has to leave some margin for the twilight zone of those thoughts and memories that fail to reach the surface of the character's stream of consciousness, and he should not be expected, therefore, to resolve any ambiguity that may arise in the interior monologues he presents.

EPISODE EIGHT
"Lestrygonians"

*I*N A SENSE, "Aeolus" and "Lestrygonians" are counterparts: whereas in the former, as Peake points out, "the monologues are subordinate to the dialogue" (1977:189), the latter, as Friedman puts it, "is really Bloom's *monologue intérieur* interrupted by a narrator filling in objective details and by a series of dialogues" (1974:142). A key episode, "Lestrygonians" has been called "the book's most tightly written section" (Mason, 1972:46) and "in some respects the most painful chapter" (Hart, 1968:55). It will inform the reader of all he needs to know about Bloom's deepest emotional preoccupations in order to understand the rest of the book as far as Bloom's day is concerned. It is a densely packed episode but not a particularly difficult one. Bloom's monologues reveal interesting insights into his character and his idiosyncracies, but equally important to the reader are the memories called up in those monologues, memories from Bloom's past life, especially the happy early years of his marriage as contrasted with the frustrations of his present home life. Seeing, for instance, someone he knows, Bob Doran, enter a pub in Adam Court, he remembers that on those premises there used to be a music hall, and his thoughts turn back some ten years: "I was happier then. Or was that I? Or am I now I? Twentyeight I was. She twentythree. When we left Lombard street west something changed. Could never like it again after Rudy. Can't bring back time. Like holding water in your hand. Would you go back to then? Just beginning then. Would you? Are you not happy in your home you poor little naughty boy? Wants to sew on buttons for me. I must answer. Write it in the library" (8.608–13/ 168.02–9).

Bloom here picks up the thread of earlier thoughts (they had been interrupted by his meeting with Mrs. Breen), recalling this same period: "Happy. Happier then" (8.170/155.35). From the context it is evident that in these two passages, only twelve pages apart, Bloom is thinking of the time Molly and he, with little Milly, were living on Lombard Street West. After Rudy's death (January 1984), Bloom remembers, there had been a change in his and Molly's marital sexual relations: "Could never like it again after Rudy." Here we come upon one of those not infrequent cases that leave the reader floundering about in the syntax of interior monologue, groping for an implied subject. In this respect the earlier passage, "Happy. Happier then," is not much different. *Whose* happiness is meant? In languages whose morphological rules require adjectives to conform to the gender and number of the corresponding noun, translators have to ask themselves such questions. Morel evades the issue altogether by speaking not of happy people but of happy times, happy days: "Les beaux jours. Les plus beaux" (152), and Mallafrè, in his Catalan translation, takes "Happier" to refer to a plural subject: "Més feliços llavors" (163), implying—and why not?—something such as, "We both were happier then." In the later passage, however, Bloom is more explicit: It was he himself who was happier then. But now another question might be raised: *Who* could never like it again after Rudy's death? The subject might be either Bloom or Molly—or, again, both, and in Bloom's interior monologue these subjects would have to be represented by the pronouns "I," "she," and "we," respectively. Now, if a translator decides to stick to the text as closely as possible and if the syntax of the target language allows him to retain the inherent ambiguity, he is within his rights and there is no problem. A translation such as "Hatte nie mehr richtig Spass dran, nach Rudy" (Wollschläger, 235) is not absolutely unambiguous (only a *plural* subject being excluded), but it is only a shade less ambiguous than the original. In Romance languages matters are different. When Morel decides to use "ne s'y plaisait plus" (did not like it anymore), he has already committed himself, so he may just as well add the subject ("she") he is thinking of: "Elle ne s'y plaisait plus après Rudy" (164). A first-person subject would have required "ne m'y plaisais plus." In the interpretation of the Italian translator De Angelis, it is Bloom himself who "could never like it again." In Italian the personal pronoun in nonemphatic subject position may be suppressed; the verb form (*ho* in this case) suffices to signal an implied first-person subject. In the Italian *Ulisse*, therefore, Bloom thinks something such as, "I have never taken any pleasure in it after Rudy": "Non ci ho mai preso gusto dopo Rudy" (251). Spanish has a different syntactical construction, something along the lines of "It could not please me / her / us anymore after Rudy." So, when we find Valverde translating "No le pudo gustar otra vez después de Rudy" (1.289) we may infer from the indirect object pronoun (*le*, not *me*) that he holds Molly to be the implied subject of the English sentence. As Mallafrè's translation shows, Catalan has a similar sentence structure, reflecting the same interpretation: "Ja no li va agradar mai més després del Rudy" (175). Senn had already drawn attention to the ambiguity inherent in this passage (1982b:18).

Major patterns in this episode are Bloom's obsessive preoccupation with the passing hours and the way Boylan's imminent visit to Molly constantly preys on his mind, themes already touched upon in an earlier chapter. On the whole, Bloom's wanderings and musings at lunch-hour time have not given rise to any significant problems of interpretation or to any striking disagreement among critics. Still, a few remarks, mainly on minor points, might be in order.

In the passage quoted above there is a seemingly simple phrase that proved a stumbling block to more than one translator: "Just beginning then" (8.611/168.06). Morel has: "Recommencer tout" (164), Goyert has: "Wieder anfangen" (I.271), Wollschläger, adding a question mark, translates: "Noch einmal anfangen damals?" (235), and De Angelis has: "Ricominciare daccapo" (251). In all these translations the gerund—or elliptic progressive form—has been twisted around into an infinitive and all of them convey the notion of starting all over again, starting from scratch, which is not at all what the phrase in the source language means.

In order to understand the phrase's meaning we have to remember that Bloom, as said before, is pursuing a train of thought he had started on earlier, when indulging in sentimental memories (8.155ff./ 155.17ff.). Furthermore, we should take into account that this elliptic phrase finds itself embedded between "Would you go back to then?" and the emphatic, insistent "Would you?"—quite in keeping with Bloom's way of thinking. Another sample of this type of phrasing is found in a later episode. The time is nine o'clock at night, and Bloom's thoughts run as follows: "Go home. Too late for *Leah. Lily of Killarney*. No. Might be still up" (13.1212–13/380.19–21). Here, too, the main stream of the interior monologue—in this case amounting to: "Shall I go home? No, better not. Molly might still be up"—is interrupted for a moment by a seemingly irrelevant subliminal thought: "It is too late now to go to the theatre to see either *Leah* or the *Lily of Killarney*."

In the passage under discussion there is a similar intrusion, namely the phrase "Just beginning then," and what it means will become clear when we turn back to the passage in which we find Bloom reminiscing about the period he repeatedly refers to by "then": "Milly was a kiddy then. Molly had that elephantgrey dress with the braided frogs. . . . Never put a dress on her back like it. Fitted her like a glove, shoulders and hips. *Just beginning to plump it out well*" (8.163–69/155.27–33, italics mine). As I see it, this is what Bloom means in 8.611/168.06: "Would you be willing to go back, back to that time when Molly started to put on fat? Would you now?" There is no criticism of Molly implied in this thought: Bloom does like his women plump. Thinking about Molly that morning, in the funeral carriage, he may deplore that her body is "getting a bit softy," trying to explain this phenomenon in a "scientific" way, but the result, especially the plumpness, still pleases him: "The shape is there still. Shoulders. Hips. Plump" (6.207/92.31–32). Note the same sequence in both passages: shoulders, hips, plumpness.

Still savoring his reminiscences of the happy days in Lombard Street, Bloom recalls a specific night, the windy night when he went to fetch

Molly after a concert at which old Professor Goodwin was the pianist (8.184ff./156.10ff.). The whole scene presents itself to his mind in vivid detail. Having raked up the fire on coming home, they sat there till near two o'clock, Molly "taking out her hairpins. Milly tucked up in beddyhouse. Happy. Happy. That was the night" (8.199–201/156.29–30). At this point Bloom's flow of memories is interrupted by his encounter with Mrs. Breen. To judge from his reaction (a surprised "Oh, how do you do, Mrs Breen?"), he must have been so engrossed in his thoughts that he had not seen her coming along. As a result, the reader does not learn what was so special about that night—not, that is, until he will be enlightened by Molly in a passage in her soliloquy in which she remembers Boylan admiring the shape of her foot (18.246ff./744.41ff.). She wonders what he sees in it and then, with one of those characteristic switches of hers (from "him" = Boylan in 18.262/745.17 to "him" = Bloom in 18.263/745.19), she calls up that same cozy scene in the house on Lombard Street ten years ago: "I dont like my foot so much still I made him spend once with my foot the night after Goodwins botchup of a concert so cold and windy it was well we had that rum in the house to mull and the fire wasnt black out when he asked to take off my stockings lying on the hearthrug in Lombard street west" (18.262–66/745.18–23).

This case is no exception. It is one of the functions of "Penelope" to pick up loose ends from earlier episodes in the book, a process that already starts in "Ithaca" in a more systematic way.

Obviously, Bloom still believes that he was happier "then," and the corollary of this thought is that he is less happy—or even downright unhappy—*now*. This reminds him of Martha Clifford's letter in which she asked him whether he was not happy in his home (see 5.246/77.38–39). He scoffs at the kind of happiness she might offer him but feels he should at least answer her letter.

On Grafton Street the sight of a display of petticoats and stockings in a shop window reminds him once more of his home life and of Molly's budding affair with Boylan. He realizes that there is no sense in speculating about going back in time. What has happened just had to happen. He will have to fall back on his futile correspondence with Martha after all. In her letter she had urged him to write her a long letter and tell her more (5.251ff./78.04ff.), promising to tell him all when they would meet. Well, he might tell her all, indeed, and the questions he had asked himself are now answered as follows: "Useless to go back. Had to be. Tell me all" (8.633/168.32).

This seems a plausible enough interpretation but with Joyce, as Senn says, there is always room for speculation and doubt. Instead of going back in time Bloom might have meant going back in space, back home, that is (he will feel a similar urge a few times more in the course of the day, without following it up, however). The petticoats and stockings he admires in the shop window remind him of Molly's striped petticoat and rumpled stockings, which he had seen lying about in the bedroom that morning (4.265, 322–25/62.16, 63.41, 64.02), and from there his thoughts jump once more to Boylan's planned visit to Molly in the afternoon. Bloom is now on his way to the National Library, where he wants to look up a certain advertisement in a local or regional paper, but that will not take much time. So he could easily return home after that to prevent any goings-on when Boylan arrives to bring Molly the program, but what would be the use? What will happen—if not now, then some other time—just "had to be."

From O'Connell Bridge, Bloom sees a rowboat at anchor bearing an advertisement for trousers. The idea appeals to him, as he is in the publicity business himself, and he remembers having seen posters stuck up in urinals advertising cures for venereal disease, even though posting bills in that place was explicitly prohibited:

> Good idea that. Wonder if he pays rent to the corporation. How can you own water really? It's always flowing in a stream, never the same, which in the stream of life we trace. Because life is a stream. All kinds of places are good for ads. That quack doctor for the clap used to be stuck up in all the greenhouses. Never see it now. Strictly confidential. Dr Hy Franks. Didn't cost him a red like Maginni the dancing master self advertisement. Got fellows to stick them up or stick them up himself for that matter on the q.t. running in to loosen a button. Flybynight. Just the place too. POST NO BILLS. POST IIO PILLS. Some chap with a dose burning him.
>
> (8.93–101/153.28–38)

Still looking down into the water of the Liffey, Bloom even remembers he once saw in such a place a POST NO BILLS sign somebody had tampered with, probably a chap who suffered from the disease in question himself and had pills on his mind, understandably. By scratching away the oblique down stroke of the N and the lower half of the B, partly, this unknown joker had produced the queer phrase about 110 pills.

There was not much the translators could do with this passage: the joke is virtually untranslatable. Wollschläger decided, therefore, to leave the original text as it was, just adding a translation of the first part and a kind of explanation of the second: "Ist auch genau der richtige Platz dafür. Plakatankleben verboten: POST NO BILLS! Ganz schön gerissen: Billig, pillig. POST 110 PILLS. Irgendein Kerl, den der Parterre-Schnupfen brennt" (214). Morel must have realized that a translator had better think up two entirely new phrases so as to make the second look like a passable transformation from the first. His translation presupposes a man using a pencil to change CA into TA, to add TE to BINET, and to strike out SULT, thus transforming the advertising doctor's "consulting room" into "your bum face": "La place rêvée. CABINET DE CONSULT. TA BINETTE DE CON! Quelque client à qui il en cuit" (150).

In Spanish, Valverde has come up with "CARTELES NO. CÓRTESELO" (I.271), meaning "No bills. Cut it off!" Rather drastic, to say the least. In Catalan, Mallafrè also went decidedly beyond the original: "NO HI AFIXEU CARTELLS. IIO HI PIXEU CATXETS" (161), which, I assume, means "Post here no bills. Piss here IIO pills," punning cleverly on AFIXEU and PIXEU, on the one hand, and on CARTELLS and CATXETS (*cachets*) on the other. In both cases, moreover, the "technique" of scratching away letters and adding strokes here and there seems plausible enough.

Equally untranslatable is Bloom's pun "Flybynight," coming on top of "running in to loosen a button" in the passage quoted above. A *fly-by-night*, as dictionaries tell us, is "one who makes night excursions or decamps by night" and that, indeed, is one aspect of the meaning Bloom must have in mind. It is an aspect most translators have taken into account—the only aspect, in fact, they were able to cope with. Renderings such as "Oiseau de nuit" (Morel, 150) and "Nachtschwärmer" (Wollschläger, 214) or a paraphrase such as "Laufen nachts herum" (Goyert, I.246) cannot but miss the point. Bloom, I think, is alluding to the noun *fly*, denoting that part of a man's trousers, down the front, where in his time, in the prezipper era, the buttons used to be.

If you use an idiom for Bloom's "running in to loosen a button," such as Catalan "quan entrava corrent *a fer un riu*" (161, italics mine), literally "to make a river" (a kind of baby talk), the link with the trouser fly is lost, of course, so Mallafrè in translating "Flybynight" just leaves it at "Volen de nit" (i.e., "[They] fly by night)." Valverde uses a less graphic expression: "al entrar a la carrera *para hacer aguas*" (to make water) (I.271, italics mine), and then shows he must have appreciated the pun in *fly* by translating: "Braguetazo [*fly* as part of trousers] con nocturnidad."

Passing the *Irish Times* building (8.323ff./160.07ff.), Bloom is reminded of the small ad he had put in that paper some time previously ("Wanted, smart lady typist to aid gentleman in literary work" [8.326–27/160.11–12]) and of the forty-four letters he has collected so far. We now realize that Martha Clifford, whose letter he had received that very morning, must have been one of those "lady typists" who had taken up his deceitful offer of a job. In a later episode we shall learn that Bloom had already got three letters from her before that (17.1840–42/722.21–23); as to their contents, we are left in the dark apart from a hint or two, paraphrased in Bloom's interior monologue, such as "Meet one Sunday after the rosary. Do not deny my request" (5.375/81.23). About Bloom's own letters that must have preceded the one he is going to write later in the day, we are not told anything, which leaves us wondering how in the world he had managed to work round from "literary work" to "naughty darling" and that sort of thing.

Bloom remembers another letter, from a Lizzie Twigg, and even—a surprising feat of memory—recalls her giving George Russell as a reference: "My literary efforts have had the good fortune to meet with the approval of the eminent poet A. E. (Mr Geo. Russell)" (8.331–32/160.16–18).

The sight of a squad of constables passing Trinity College reminds Bloom of the day Joseph Chamberlain visited Dublin in 1899 to receive an honorary degree at Trinity. There was a meeting of Irish nationalists that same day, protesting against British policy in South Africa. The meeting was broken up by the police, and Bloom, who had got himself swept along with a crowd of students, has a vivid memory of a mounted policeman who seemed to have had it in for him. His thoughts turn to the Irish nationalist movement in general and to its great leader Charles Stewart Parnell in particular. On Grafton Street, he suddenly spots the latter's brother, John Howard Parnell, the present city marshall, and he is struck by the coincidence: "There he is: the brother. Image of him. Haunting face. Now that's a coincidence. Course hundreds of times you think of a person and don't meet him" (8.502–4/165.04–6). John Howard, Bloom reflects, is not a merry sight: "Look at the woebegone walk of him. Eaten a bad egg. Poached eyes on ghost" (8.507–8/165.10–12). The latter phrase (punning, of course, on "poached eggs on toast") is attributed to Oliver St. John Gogarty, who said it, however, not of John Howard but, according to Lyons (1976:29), of a certain Lennox Robinson.

Walking on, Bloom is overtaken by a tall bearded figure, who is pushing a bicycle and is accompanied by a young woman. He recognizes the man: it is Russell, so here is another coincidence (Bloom's day is full of them), and on top of that there is this young woman Russell is talking to. She might be that Lizzie Twigg who had mentioned the poet in her letter: "And there *he* is too. Now that's really a coincidence: second time . . . With the approval of the eminent poet, Mr Geo. Russell. That might be Lizzie Twigg with him . . . What was he saying? . . . Something occult: symbolism . . . She's taking it all in. Not saying a word. To aid gentleman in literary work" (8.525–32/165.30–38, italics mine).

Bloom's initial reaction on remembering Lizzie Twigg's phrases had been: "No time to do her hair drinking sloppy tea with a book of poetry" (8.332–33/160.18–19). Now the sight of this young woman, whether she is or is not Lizzie Twigg, confirms his prejudice against esthetes in general: "Her stockings are loose over her ankles. I detest that: so tasteless. Those literary etherial people they are all. Dreamy, cloudy, symbolistic. Esthetes they are" (8.542–44/166.07–9).

Having entered the Burton restaurant, Bloom is repelled by the pungent smells and the sight of men wolfing their food. Although he is hungry he decides he "couldn't eat a morsel here" (8.673/169.33). Before leaving, however, he gazes round the dining hall as if looking for somebody: "Mr Bloom raised two fingers doubtfully to his lips. His eyes said: —Not here. Don't see him. Out. I hate dirty eaters. He backed towards the door. Get a light snack in Davy Byrne's. Stopgap. Keep me going. Had a good breakfast" (8.694–98/170.15–20). Sultan assumes that Bloom is looking for Boylan and, naturally, he has to admit in the same breath that this is very strange indeed: "His searching for Boylan in a place he intends to leave is unusual enough; but, as he would know in a normal frame of mind, there is absolutely no possibility that the affluent and natty rake would patronize a restaurant like the Burton" (1964: 125). Peake offers a similar interpretation of this passage, citing it as one of the moments when Bloom is tormented by thoughts of Boylan in this episode: "he looks round the Burton restaurant to ensure that Boylan is not there" (1977:202). But Morton believes—and I think he is right— that Bloom is merely "inventing a polite excuse for backing out of Burton's restaurant" (1970:43). Bloom has already decided to leave the dining hall, but he is always afraid of being conspicuous. When wanting to check the little card inside his hat that morning, for instance, he pretended that he was just taking off his hat to wipe his forehead (5.20–26/71.25–32). And when he was wondering whether a blind man, passing his fingers over a girl's hair and skin, would feel that the hair was black and the skin white and then tried to touch his own belly under his waistcoat and shirt, he first looked around ("No-one about") but still wanted to make believe that there was nothing out of the ordinary in his behavior: "Might be settling my braces" (8.1139/182.19–20). So now he needs some justification for turning round and leaving the place.

We know he will go out of his way to avoid Boylan, even refraining from mentioning his name, so why would he stand there in full view of the eaters, at the risk of meeting Boylan's gaze if he really thought it possible that Boylan might be lunching there? Bloom is just acting, not wanting to show too openly how disgusted he is; the possibility that he is either searching for Boylan, or looking around to make sure that Boylan is not there, should be ruled out. Could Bloom, then, have been looking seriously for somebody else? Before reaching the Burton, only a few blocks away, he had been thinking of a young chap he might go and have a chat with: "He crossed at Nassau street corner and stood before the window of Yeates and Son, pricing the field glasses. Or will I drop into old Harris's and have a chat with young Sinclair? Wellmannered fellow. Probably at his lunch" (8.551–54/166.17–20). So there is a fair chance that it is this "young Sinclair" Bloom expects to find at his lunch in

Burton's, a view shared by the Benstocks (1980:18). Bloom may even pretend to be looking for him so as to feel more at ease. These assumptions, however, cannot be verified, for young Sinclair (we do not even know whether this is his first name or his family name) is not heard of any more in *Ulysses*.

Sometimes the meanderings of Bloom's stream of consciousness are hard to follow. He is easily distracted and his thoughts come and go, disappearing for a time, then rising to the surface again. A case in point is the scene where we find Bloom resuming his walk, having had a glass of wine and a cheese sandwich in Davy Byrne's bar: "Mr Bloom walked towards Dawson street, his tongue brushing his teeth smooth. Something green it would have to be: spinach, say. Then with those Röntgen rays searchlight you could" (8.1028–30/179.20–23). According to Gifford, Bloom is speculating that you could clean your teeth with Röntgen rays (1974:148), but where, then, does the spinach come in? Besides, it is the tense form (it *would have to be*), in the first place, that warns the reader to look for some link with an earlier thought of Bloom's. Burgess holds that what we have here is a sequel to thoughts that Bloom must have been pursuing while in the urinal in Davy Byrne's, thoughts the reader cannot possibly be aware of for the simple reason that he is not told about them (1973b:54), but, as I see it, the thoughts we need are all in the text. We have only to go back a few pages.

Enjoying his glass of wine in the bar and staring at the tins of sardines on the shelves, Bloom had started thinking about food, especially about "All the odd things people pick up for food" (8.856/174.32–33). He thinks of curious habits and imagines strange happenings: "Chinese eating eggs fifty years old, blue and green again. Dinner of thirty courses. Each dish harmless might mix inside. Idea for a poison mystery" (8.869–71/175.06–9). At the time he did not pursue this thought but now, having left the bar, he picks up the thread of his thoughts again, still dwelling on the poison mystery: The poisoned spinach could be traced by means of Röntgen rays, he supposes. His flow of thoughts is deflected again, this time by a dog getting in his way, but walking on he sees a display of toilet seats in a plumber's shop window which must have reminded him once more of food and digestion, and he resumes his speculations on the poison mystery. The sight of the sanitary equipment, as the text states explicitly, "turned back his thoughts," his former "you could" (8.1030/179.22–23) being taken up again as "They could": "turned back his thoughts. They could: and watch it all the way down. . . . But the poor buffer would have to stand all the time with his insides entrails on show. Science" (8.1045–50/179.40–180.05). It is fairly evident, I feel, that Bloom here thinks of X-rays as a "searchlight" and not as a means of cleaning one's teeth.

The following paragraph contains a trap for readers: "At Duke lane a ravenous terrier choked up a sick knuckly cud on the cobblestones and lapped it with new zest. Surfeit. Returned with thanks having fully digested the contents. First sweet then savoury. Mr Bloom coasted warily. Ruminants. His second course. *Their upper jaw they move. Wonder if Tom Rochford will do anything with that invention of his? Wasting time explaining it to Flynn's mouth. Lean people long mouths. Ought to be a hall or a place where inventors could go in and invent free.* Course then you'd have all the cranks pestering" (8.1031–38/179.24–32, italics mine). In "Wandering Rocks" the reader will come upon a scene where Tom Rochford is showing and explaining his invention to Lenehan, M'Coy, and snuffling Nosey Flynn (10.465ff./232.04ff.), but that scene does not occur until a few hours later. As we have seen, Bloom has just left Davy Byrne's, where he had a light snack. On entering the pub, he had been hailed by Nosey Flynn, who was sitting in a corner sipping his grog, and later three other customers had come in: Paddy Leonard, Bantam Lyons, and Tom Rochford. There has not been any talk about the latter's invention in Bloom's presence, but he has heard about it, apparently; it may have been common knowledge in Dublin. Seeing Tom Rochford has reminded Bloom of this invention, and now the thought of it just crosses his mind, interrupting another chain of associations: a dog throwing up some half-digested food reminds him of ruminants and their jaw movements. This in its turn calls up the image of Nosey Flynn's ugly face: "Look at his mouth. Could whistle in his own ear. Flap ears to match" (8.768/172.21–22), which turns his thoughts for a moment to the others he saw in the bar, among them Tom Rochford. The pendulum immediately swings back to Flynn, to whom he had tried to explain how Molly's singing tour was to be organized (8.784–85/172.37–38)—a sheer waste of time, he thinks.

These alternating thoughts arrange themselves in a pattern that reads like a rhyme scheme: *a* (jaws and mouths), *b* (Rochford's invention), *a* (Flynn's mouth, lean people's mouths), *b* (hall for inventors). The reader should note that *a* rhymes with *a* and not with *b*.

Bloom's leisurely walk will have an abrupt and panicky ending. Coming from Molesworth Street—having helped a blind young man cross Dawson Street—he reaches Kildare Street: "Mr Bloom came to Kildare street. First I must. Library" (8.1167/183.11), and it is clear that he has more than one objective in that street. First he will have to consult the newspaper files in the National Library (see 8.1043–44/179.38–39), a matter of business (see 7.154–55/120.37–38). Then there was something else he wanted to see, some detail of the anatomy of goddesses (see 8.919–32/176.24–39), for which he would have to enter the National Museum near the library. Emerging into Kildare Street, however, he

spots Boylan, who is nearing from the left, skirting the library building.
Wanting to avoid him, Bloom alters his course; he veers to the right,
deciding, on the spur of the moment, to pass through the museum, which
he wanted to visit anyway: "His heart quopped softly. To the right.
Museum. Goddesses. He swerved to the right" (8.1169–70/183.14–15;
see diagram in Hart and Knuth [1976: II, map IX]). Bowen's comment that
Bloom "ducked into the library to avoid Blazes" (1975:151) is one of
those errors critics are prone to commit once in a while when dealing with
Ulysses. Anyway, Bloom reaches the museum gate, glances at his watch,
presumably ("After two" [8.1178/183.24]), and has only to cross the
forecourt now. He still forces himself not to look in Boylan's direction.
Instead, he starts going through his pockets as if looking for something
specific. One of the things he comes up with is "Agendath Netaim," the
advertisement for Zionist settlements he had picked up at the butcher's
that morning. In addition to the acutely felt presence of Boylan, this
reminds him of the bedroom scene when he brought Molly her breakfast
and the words she must have spoken come back to him: "Afternoon she
said" (8.1187/183.33).

EPISODE NINE
"Scylla and Charybdis"

*T*HE SCENE of "Scylla and Charybdis," an episode steeped in literature, is the National Library on Kildare Street, the hospitable center where "under the benign direction of Thomas W. Lyster, 'the quaker librarian,' the students and intellectuals of Dublin met to read and talk" (Kellogg, 1974:148). There is some confusion among critics as to the room in which the discussion on Shakespeare takes place. Some sources call it "the director's office" (Tindall, 1959:173; Blamires, 1966:76; Morton, 1970:43) or simply "the librarian's room" (Mason, 1972:48), whereas Kellogg informs us that the room in question is "the assistant librarian's office." The assistant librarian at the time was William Kirkpatrick Magee (Gifford, 1974:157). He was an essayist of some standing in Dublin literary circles who wrote as "John Eglinton," and it is under this name that he appears in *Ulysses*. His rank is also given as sublibrarian (Kellogg, 1974:151), a term Stanislaus Joyce uses in writing about him in his diary in 1904 (quoted by Ellmann, 1982:147). Then there is a Mr. Best, a "junior librarian of aesthetic tendencies" (Mason, 1972:48), but well on his way to becoming a scholar in the field of Irish studies, whose English translation of Jubainville's *Cycle mythologique irlandais*, the book he shows Haines in the library (9.93/186.24), had been published the year before. Lyster's subordinate, as Schutte calls him (1957:33), and assistant director, as he is listed by Gifford (1974: 160), in time he was to be Lyster's successor. His full name was Richard Irvine Best. Excellent portraits of the three officials as they were in real life have been drawn by Schutte, who devotes a whole chapter to them.

The situation that develops in this episode is an example of what Woods calls *fictionalization* of "real persons" (1974:43), as when Conan Doyle narrates that Sherlock Holmes had tea one day with Gladstone. In "Scylla and Charybdis" Joyce fictionalized Russell and the librarians and depicted them as having had a discussion with Stephen. This discussion, the whole scene in the library, is thereby established as being part of Stephen's—but not necessarily of, for instance, Russell's—life story.

All this is extraneous information. In the text, the only one to get a label indicating his official standing is Mr. Lyster. From the opening sentence on, he is consistently referred to as "the quaker librarian," and not until we have reached 9.581/200.16, when he is called away by an attendant, do we learn what his name is. He is already called away earlier, right at the beginning, but in that case it is a "noiseless attendant" (9.07/184.08), who, having set the door ajar, beckons him silently. This attendant apparently knows where to find him, but this is no absolute proof that the room is his, the director's, own office. Lyster may have dropped in on the assistant librarian from time to time to join in the discussion. As things stand, he missed most of it, for he seems in constant demand. Readers may get the feeling that he never even sits down. As the episode opens he leaves the room, having been called away for some unknown reason, lingering a moment to utter some platitudes, which Stephen, left alone with only two listeners, is promptly going to sneer at. These listeners are John Eglinton (9.18/184.20) and (George) Russell (9.46/185.11), the poet who writes under the pseudonym "A. E." Among themselves, those present refer to one another by their real names, which explains why John Eglinton apparently feels pleased and flattered when he hears Stephen quote a "Mr Magee": "nature, as Mr Magee understands her, abhors perfection. Eglintoneyes, quick with pleasure, looked up shybrightly. Gladly glancing, a merry puritan, through the twisted eglantine. Flatter. Rarely. But flatter" (9.870–74/208.17–22). Eglinton, having responded to Stephen's sneering remark by a sharp retort, mocking Stephen in his turn, looks over to Russell, who is sitting in the shadow, for some support or a sign of approval, perhaps, but there is no reaction as yet: "Glittereyed his rufous skull close to his greencapped desklamp sought the face bearded amid darkgreener shadow, an ollav, holyeyed. He laughed low: a sizar's laugh of Trinity: unanswered" (9.29–31/184.31–34).

Gifford (1974:157) explains the entire first sentence of this passage as a description of Russell, but this is only true of the latter half of the sentence ("the face bearded . . . holyeyed"). The glittering eyes and the reddish hair (see Schutte, 1957:41) belong to John Eglinton, as does the desk lamp. This lamp (note that it is "his" lamp) is mentioned again some time later: "John Eglinton looked in the tangled glowworm of his lamp" (9.225/190.17–18). His desk is also referred to twice: "Buck Mulligan rapped John Eglinton's desk sharply" (9.655/202.14) and "Suddenly happied he jumped up and reached in a stride John Eglinton's desk" (9.1054–55/213.29–30). The repeated use of the possessive pronoun and the possessive case of his name, respectively, surely lends support to the assumption that the discussion takes place in Eglinton's room. Moreover, if it were Lyster's own office, it would not have been logical for Stephen to wonder what reason the librarian could have had to join them: "Why did he come? Courtesy or an inward light?" (9.332–33/193.15–16).

Russell's next remark shows, as the Quaker librarian's opening words did, that the discussion must already have been going on for some time:"—All these questions are purely academic, Russell oracled out of

his shadow" (9.46–47/185.11–12). He goes on to talk about art as
revealing ideas and bringing the human mind "into contact with the
eternal wisdom, Plato's world of ideas," all the rest being "the speculation of schoolboys for schoolboys." Stephen takes up the challenge, and
Eglinton caps Stephen's words with a witty remark about Aristotle.
Again he utters an inviting laugh and now, at last, he is rewarded by a
smile from Russell: "—The schoolmen were schoolboys first, Stephen
said superpolitely. Aristotle was once Plato's schoolboy. —And has
remained so, one should hope, John Eglinton sedately said. One can see
him, a model schoolboy with his diploma under his arm. He laughed
again at the now smiling bearded face" (9.56–60/185.23–28). This makes
it clear that the "sizar's laugh of Trinity" in the earlier passage ("He
laughed low: a sizar's laugh of Trinity: unanswered") should be attributed to Eglinton and not to Stephen, as Gifford seems to suggest. Having
explained that a sizar is a student at Trinity College who pays reduced
fees, he continues: "A sizar's laugh is therefore the laugh of a dependent
(as Stephen has borrowed money from AE and therefore been dependent
on him)" (1974:157). The laugh is Eglinton's, so why bring in Stephen?
Or Russell?

The moment Eglinton has summoned up the picture of a model
schoolboy with his diploma under his arm, Mr. Best, young, sympathetic, bearing a bright new notebook in his hand, enters the room. He
comes forward, "towards his colleague" (9.90/186.21), whom the ensuing conversation shows to be Eglinton. So, if the latter is a librarian,
Best is too.

Meanwhile, Stephen continues the exposition of his views on *Hamlet.*
Having brought up the subject of the bard's marriage, he refutes Eglinton's contention that Shakespeare is generally thought to have made a
mistake in marrying Anne Hathaway. "A man of genius," Stephen says,
"makes no mistakes. His errors are volitional and are the *portals of
discovery*" (9.228–29/190.21–23, italics mine). At that moment the door
opens to let in Mr. Lyster. Before Eglinton's response is recorded,
Lyster's entrance is described in two lines of narrative: "*Portals of
discovery* opened to let in the quaker librarian, softcreakfooted, bald,
eared and assiduous" (9.230–31/190.24–25, italics mine). Here, then, we
have an example of what is perhaps the most characteristic feature of this
episode: The narrator keeps as close as possible to Stephen's point of
view, and in the narrative passages he often takes his cue from the
dialogue. His descriptive phrases are such as might have been used by
Stephen, had he been asked to describe the action. Such descriptions, as
Mason puts it, "take over vocabulary from an immediately preceding
utterance" (1972:48) or, as Peake characterizes the episode's technique,
"The language of the narrative frequently echoes that of the dialogue"

(1977:207). We do not have to look far to find more passages in which this phenomenon may be observed.

Russell announces that he has to leave, because he is due at the editorial office of the *Irish Homestead*. Incidentally, it was this paper, as Ellmann records (1982:163), which in August of 1904 published Joyce's "The Sisters," the first story in *Dubliners;* it earned him a pound. Joyce did not sign his own name but used the pseudonym "Stephen Daedalus."

The discussion is interrupted, and the talk around Stephen turns to local literary gossip. Lyster alludes to a forthcoming anthology of modern Anglo-Irish poetry, to be edited by Russell, and Lyster's final word, an adverb of manner, is immediately picked up in the narrative to describe the way he behaves while addressing Russell, Eglinton, and Best. The function of the point of view is made explicit by Stephen's next thought, "See this. Remember," and once more, a few lines farther down, when he thinks, "Listen," immediately followed by a long paragraph of literary tidbits. Such details, as well as the circumstance that he seems to be outside the "cone of lamplight," underline Stephen's position as an outsider, a detached observer. He feels he is going to use all this, all he sees and hears, as the raw material out of which literature must be created, so much so that some time later, going out, he foresees himself looking back on this afternoon of Shakespeare dispute and saying, or writing, "One day in the national library we had a discussion. Shakes" (9.1108/215.07). Here is the passage summarized above: "—They say we are to have a literary surprise, the quaker librarian said, friendly and earnest. Mr Russell, rumour has it, is gathering together a sheaf of our younger poets' verses. We are all looking forward *anxiously*. *Anxiously* he glanced in the cone of lamplight where three faces, lighted, shone. See this. Remember" (9.289–93/192.08–14, italics mine). More than once this device has a mildly humorous effect, which may have something to do with the common human experience that there is always something comic about an echo. A few more examples may illustrate this (italics mine in all of them).

Mulligan having entered, the librarian tries to draw him into the discussion: "—Yes, indeed, the quaker librarian said. A most instructive discussion. Mr Mulligan, I'll be bound, has his theory too of the play and of Shakespeare. *All sides of life* should be represented. He smiled *on all sides* equally" (9.503–6/198.06–10).

The talk has veered round to all kinds of brilliant or would-be-brilliant theories about Shakespeare's true or supposed identity. Mr. Best points to Oscar Wilde: "—The most *brilliant* of all is that story of Wilde's, Mr Best said, lifting his *brilliant* notebook" (9.522–23/198.29–30).

Sometimes a slight variation is worked in, as when Mr. Best puts his oar in again and the echo miraculously turns the original phrase into its opposite: "—But *Hamlet* is so personal, isn't it? Mr Best pleaded. I mean, a kind of private paper, don't you know, of his private life. I mean, I don't care a button, don't you know, who is killed or who is *guilty* . . . He rested an *innocent* book on the edge of the desk, smiling his defiance" (9.362–66/194.07–12).

What Mason and Peake have to say about the language of the narrative taking over phrases from the preceding dialogue shows only one aspect of the episode's technique. The device in question may be operated the other way round as well, in which case the vocabulary of the narrative *foreshadows* a character's immediately following utterance, as in this passage (italics mine, also in the next quotations): "The benign forehead of the quaker librarian enkindled rosily *with hope:* —I *hope* Mr Dedalus will work out his theory for the enlightenment of the public" (9.436–39/196.03–6).

What Peake does point out, however, and what might be called a variant of the device sketched above, is that very frequently the way in which things are said reflects what is being said, "as though the speakers were actors, underlining their words with exaggerated gesture and intonation" (1977:208). Again, the device may work both ways, the adverb of manner either following (echoing) or preceding (foreshadowing) the utterance. An example of the former is this passage: "—A *shrew*, John Eglinton said *shrewdly*, is not a useful portal of discovery, one should imagine. What useful discovery did Socrates learn from Xanthippe?" (9.232–34/190.26–28). The latter type may be illustrated by the following examples: "—Yes, Mr Best said *youngly*, I feel Hamlet quite *young*. The bitterness might be from the father but the passages with Ophelia are surely from the son" (9.387–89/194.36–38), and "—But Ann Hathaway? Mr Best's quiet voice said *forgetfully*. Yes, we seem to be *forgetting* her as Shakespeare himself forgot her" (9.240–41/190.35–37).

Passages such as these—and they are frequent—are especially apt to bring out the artificial character of the text. It is all very well to say that events and scenes in the library are being viewed through Stephen's eyes exclusively, but the reader may feel, nevertheless, that the author has overdone it by allowing the narrative voice (assumed to be speaking from Stephen's point of view) to anticipate what the participants in the discussion are going to say. Used in this way, the device makes the reader feel conscious of being manipulated, of having to cope with what Peake calls "an authorial vision shaping and colouring everything in the chapter" (1977:208).

A no less striking aspect of this authorial presence comes to the fore when we turn our attention to the way the characters sometimes seem to lose their individual identities. When this happens they are not called by their names but handled like puppets and described by their outward features and the roles they play in the scene. When Mr. Best looks from Russell to Eglinton and then to Lyster, after having raised the objection about their forgetting Anne Hathaway quoted above, this is narrated as follows: "His look went from brooder's beard to carper's skull, to remind, to chide them not unkindly, then to the baldpink lollard costard, guiltless though maligned" (9.242–44/190.38–40). The light of the one desk lamp leaves the greater part of the listeners' bodies in shadow: Russell, *brooding* on "formless spiritual essences" as he "oracled out of his shadow" (9.46–49/185.11–20), is recognized by his beard (9.30/184.32), and Eglinton, with his "carping voice" (9.215/190.05), by his "rufous skull" (9.29/184.31). Those two have been taking part in the discussion, and Best, by his looks, seems to rebuke them mildly for leaving Shakespeare's wife out of the picture. Then he turns to the Quaker librarian (a "lollard"; i.e., a heretic in the eyes of his mostly Catholic fellow citizens), whose head ("costard") is bald (9.12/184.14, cf. also 9.231/190.25) and glows pink in the lamplight. The final phrase, "guiltless though maligned," is rather enigmatic. Gifford has a note saying that Thomas Lyster "was subject to public suspicion about his loyalties because he was not a Roman Catholic" (1974:168). This may be true, but it seems rather far-fetched to bring it up in connection with Shakespeare. One could think of another interpretation. At first, Mr. Best, just by saying, "*we* seem to be forgetting her," appears to include Mr. Lyster among those who are guilty of forgetting Anne Hathaway, thereby "maligning" him, but then he realizes that the librarian has only just returned to the room. So *he* cannot be blamed for forgetting the bard's wife, he is "guiltless," and the look Mr. Best sends him is somewhat different from the one he sends the other two, as is made clear by the structure of the sentence. The explanation offered by Gifford has the drawback in that it raises the question: "How can the reader know this?" Of course, he cannot, not from the text itself, the way the reader knows for instance that the scene is not just any library but the National Library from the fact that Bloom is heard asking to see the files of the *Kilkenny People* for last year (9.585ff./200.20ff.), as he had told Crawford he was planning to do (see 7.974–76/146.25–27).

Stephen's thoughts in this episode are constantly commenting on what happens around him, on what the others are saying, and on what he says himself. It cannot be denied that on the printed page his flow of thoughts sometimes seems to interrupt the dialogue, but the reader should be aware that Stephen's thoughts and the utterances he listens to are often meant to be thought of as simultaneous. If, however, there is a link between those thoughts and those utterances, it is clearly a one-sided relation: Stephen hears what the others are saying, but the others are not aware of what Stephen is thinking.

When, for instance, the librarian asks, "Do you think it is only a paradox?" (9.542/199.10), he does not respond, obviously, to anything in the foregoing ten lines that transcribe Stephen's stream of consciousness. Instead, he refers to an earlier remark by Mr. Best, "Of course it's all paradox, don't you know" (9.527–28/198.36). We just have to take into account the lightning speed of Stephen's train of thought to explain the librarian's seemingly slow-witted response. Besides, there is a signal in the text: "the quaker librarian *was asking*" (italics mine). This conspicuous form, "was asking," instead of the normal "asked," may be meant to bridge the gap between Best's remark and Lyster's response. It suggests that Lyster's question had already been breaking in upon Stephen's flow of thoughts before it stopped, the words reverberating in his mind, as it were.

It has been recognized all along that behind Stephen's theorizing about *Hamlet* what he is really concerned with—not for the first time that day—is the mystery of fatherhood. As Kenner (1955:252) has pointed out, there is a certain analogy between the "modes of theological paternity" Stephen is brooding upon during his walk along the beach (in "Proteus") and the "various patterns of fatherhood" discussed or hinted at in "Scylla and Charybdis." Now it is all very well for the reader to keep these correspondences—the very thing Joyce revels in—at the back of his mind, but he should not be too rash in drawing conclusions that have no solid foundation in the text. In other words, he should beware of critics that do not hesitate to attribute to Stephen feelings and attitudes for which there is no evidence or justification in the text at all. Stephen's whole discourse is nothing but an outburst of bitterness, directed against fatherhood ("A father is a necessary evil") in a desperate attempt to renounce sonship.

EPISODE TEN
"Wandering Rocks"

A PARTICULARLY striking feature of "Wandering Rocks" is, as Peake puts it, "its division into sections, each presenting an episode in a different part of the Dublin streets, linked to each other by brief snatches of conversation or incident taken from earlier or later sections" (1977:213). The function of these brief snatches, also called intrusions, interpolations, or intercalations (French, 1976:118), more specifically heterotopic transitions (Senn, 1974b:34) or heterotopic interpolations (Knuth, 1976:135), lies in that they serve as "synchronic links between sections which are spatially remote" (Knuth, 1976:135). Briefly interrupting the narrative flow, they indicate that the action of the section the fragment has been excised from is to be thought of as more or less simultaneous with the action of the section into which this fragment has been transplanted. There is at least one clear case in which the interpolation has not been taken from any earlier or later section in this episode itself but refers to an incident in a different episode altogether. It is the passage "Two old women fresh from their whiff of the briny trudged through Irishtown along London bridge road, one with a sanded tired umbrella, one with a midwife's bag in which eleven cockles rolled" (10.818–20/242.07–10); it is found in section XIII, in which Stephen is the main character. The link with him can be traced in the preceding phrases from his stream of consciousness: "Orient and immortal wheat standing from everlasting to everlasting," which take us back to similar esoteric quotations within his interior monologue in the "Proteus" scene (3.41–44/38.06–9), associations with childbirth and navel cords triggered by the sight of the two women, one of whom swings a "midwife's bag" (3.29ff./37.33ff.).

As both Knuth (1976:121–58) and Hart (1974:181–216) have pointed out, the interpolations have not been strewn in at random. After all, within this relatively short period of time (from 2:55 to 4:00 P.M.) there must have been innumerable actions or events taking place simultaneously, so we should not be surprised, knowing Joyce's methods of economy, to discover some sort of system in the distribution of the interpolations. In short, there seem to exist what Hart calls "causal relationships between the interpolations and their contexts." Not in all the thirty-odd cases, however, have these causal relations—based on associations, mainly—been explained satisfactorily. Hart, for instance, in his complete list of interpolations (1974), puts a question mark against the following passage from section IX, in which Tom Rochford is demonstrating a certain contraption he seems to have invented (or wants to sell): "He slid it into the left slot for them . . . Lawyers of the past, haughty, pleading, beheld pass from the consolidated taxing office to Nisi Prius court Richie Goulding carrying the costbag . . . and heard rustling from the admiralty division of king's bench to the court of appeal an elderly female with false teeth smiling incredulously and a black silk skirt of great amplitude" (10.468–75/232.07–14). The only connections I can think of are the following. The numbered disks of Rochford's contraption face the onlookers with a mechanical, lifeless stare, just as the statues of famous Irish lawyers and judges in the hall of the Four Courts building with their lifeless eyes stare down upon the passers-by. Rochford's device, moreover, is supposed to show which turns are on and which turns are over in variety shows. For the elderly female, the cases heard in the courts seem to be nothing but turns in a show: she does not want to miss any of them, as will become evident from an interpolation in section X: "An elderly female . . . left the building of the courts of chancery, king's bench . . . having heard in the lord chancellor's court the case in lunacy of Potterton, in the admiralty division the summons . . ., in the court of appeal reservation of judgment in the case of Harvey versus the Ocean Accident and Guarantee Corporation" (10.625–31/236.29–36). This, however, is an exceptional case. In contrast to the more hidden "implicit cross-references, linguistic and nomenclatural ambiguities, and apparent errors," great numbers of which have been pointed out by both Hart and Knuth, the bulk of the interpolations are not hard to trace, although early critics, such as Smith (1927), may not always have been aware of them.

Critics in general have come to accept the interpolations without much protest, along with many other antinovelistic devices in *Ulysses*. The principle as such, of course, is not absolutely new, but the technique is different from the methods applied in the traditional novel, in which the author warned the reader explicitly as soon as he intended to shift the scene of action temporarily. In *Ulysses*, however, the reader suddenly finds these interpolated fragments interrupting the narrative without having been warned. There is only one case in which the notion of simultaneity has been made explicit by a specific conjunction. It occurs in section II, a brief scene in which Corny Kelleher is seen standing in the doorway of the undertaker's office, chewing a blade of hay. The case is quite exceptional insofar as the interpolation cannot boast an independent position but has been reduced to the status of a subordinate clause: "Corny Kelleher sped a silent jet of hayjuice arching from his mouth *while a generous white arm from a window in Eccles street flung*

forth a coin" (10.221–23/225.09–11, italics mine). The actions combined
in this one sentence are not only synchronous but also similar events: the
jet of hay juice and the coin (a penny, as the reader will learn later
[18.346/747.34]) each describe a parabolic path. Still, these actions are
spatially distinct, so much so that it would be physically impossible for
Kelleher to see the penny being thrown to the one-legged sailor of section
III. It is in virtue of this circumstance alone that the clause in question can
be considered an interpolation at all, for the usual concomitant
phenomenon—the interruption of the narrative flow proper—seems
lacking here, which makes the passage a highly deceptive one. Hence
Morton's erroneous statement in his summary of this section: "Corny
Kelleher works in the O'Neill funeral home. . . . He . . . steps to the
door to look out. *He sees a coin tossed to the begging sailor* (which, we
find out later, comes from Molly Bloom), and chats with the policeman
on the beat" (1970:47, italics mine).

   Walking along the North Strand Road at a leisurely pace, Father
Conmee has ample opportunity to observe his surroundings. He passes a
few shops and a public house (on his side of the road) and also, as we learn
in section I, O'Neill's funeral establishment across the road, "where
Corny Kelleher totted figures in the daybook while he chewed a blade of
hay" (10.96–98/221.27–29). Soon after, Conmee reaches Newcomen
Bridge, where he gets on a tram: "On Newcomen bridge the very
reverend John Conmee S.J. . . . stepped on to an outward bound tram"
(10.107–9/221.42–222.02). This is the scene that is found, phrased
slightly differently, as an intrusion in section II: "Father John Conmee
stepped into the Dollymount tram on Newcomen bridge" (10.213–
14/225.01–2). The question has been raised whether this passage is a true
interpolation or not. Gifford (1974:216) lists it as such, whereas Hart
(1974:203) does not. We are told in section II that Kelleher has finished
his bookkeeping chores and has come to the doorway. It is true, then, as
Knuth remarks (1976:135), that he could have noticed the priest board
the tram, had he taken the trouble to look in that direction. In view of the
data supplied in section I, supported if need be by a glance at a map of
Dublin, this cannot be considered absolutely impossible, and in that case
the use of the term "heterotopic" would be ill-founded. Still, what is
lacking in this passage is an unambiguous phrase linking Conmee with
Kelleher and identifying the sentence as part of the narrative. Knuth,
therefore, tends to believe that it is a real heterotopic interpolation, and I
think he is right. We should not forget that the narrative flow, as the
context shows, is interrupted by what is a paragraph in its own right, the
narrator being obliged to start anew with "Corny Kelleher" even though
he had been referring to him all the time so far. We see Kelleher now
standing at the door:

There he tilted his hatbrim to give shade to his eyes and leaned against the doorcase, *looking idly out.*

Father John Conmee stepped into the Dollymount tram on New-comen bridge.

Corny Kelleher locked his largefooted boots and *gazed,* his hat downtilted, chewing his blade of hay.

(10.211–16/224.37–225.04, italics mine)

I may be wrong, but phrases such as "looking idly out" and "gazed," combined with the repeated mention of the tilted hatbrim, might be meant to warn the reader that Kelleher does *not* take the trouble to look and, therefore, does *not* observe Conmee's boarding the tram. This would confirm Knuth's tentative conclusion that the Conmee passage in section II is a heterotopic interpolation in its own right.

At the end of section I we are told that Father Conmee, walking through the fields after a short tram ride, has taken out his breviary. The last we hear of him he is reading from Psalm 119, which, like many another psalm, is divided into units or paragraphs. These units, each consisting of eight lines, are arranged in alphabetical order, each unit being assigned one of the twenty-two consonants of the Hebrew alpha-bet. Now Father Conmee is interrupted a moment in his reading by a young man and a young woman coming through a gap in the hedge, both trying to hide their embarrassment, the young man by hastily raising his cap, the young woman by bending down and removing a twig that had clung to her skirt. Just before these young people emerge from the hedge, Conmee is finishing the *Resh* section of the psalm; what he is seen reading, *Principium verborum tuorum,* and so forth (10.197/ 224.22–23), is the last verse of that section. Then, after this brief scene of confusion on the young people's part, Father Conmee, bearing up quite well, even blessing them "gravely," continues his reading, and what he reads then is the very next verse, the opening verse of the *Shin* section (*Principes persecuti sunt me,* etc.). In a way, therefore, this intrusion is an interpolation, be it a homotopic one, insofar as it interrupts the narrative flow without really interrupting the action, a feature it shares with true heterotopic interpolations. Conmee's act of blessing the young man and his girl is a mechanical gesture, we may assume, a reflex movement, which takes no more time than turning a page of his breviary. The scene is a pseudo-interpolation, preparing the reader of this episode for the many genuine heterotopic interpolations still to come.

An interesting aspect of the psalm quotation that closes the section is drawn attention to by Peake. He cites Gilbert as claiming that Father Conmee "is pitted against the counter-subject of the episode, the Viceroy, as the Irish Catholic Church against British rule, Christ against Caesar" (1930:227n.1) and points out (1977:212) that Father Conmee is not presented as opposed to the Viceroy at all; on the contrary, he is said to remember with some nostalgia "oldworldish days, loyal times in joyous townlands." Conmee, the Jesuit, the representative of law and order, need not be afraid of being persecuted by princes, as it says in the psalm. In Peake's view, therefore, the psalm verse that rounds off the priest's portrait is "the crowning irony of the section."

In section III its subject, the one-legged sailor, moving on crutches, is seen on Eccles Street and heard growling his song, "For England, home and beauty," a few words at a time. He passes the Dedalus girls, Katey and Boody, on their way home from school, and thereupon the narrative is interrupted, but only briefly, by a fragment dealing with two characters (O'Molloy and Lambert) who will not appear in this episode until section VIII.

> He swung himself violently forward past Katey and Boody Dedalus, halted and growled: —*home and beauty.*
> J. J. O'Molloy's white careworn face was told that Mr Lambert was in the warehouse with a visitor.
> A stout lady stopped, took a copper coin from her purse and dropped it into the cap held out to her. The sailor grumbled thanks, glanced sourly at the unheeding windows, sank his head and swung himself forward four strides.
>
> (10.233–41/225.20–28)

For several reasons the interpolation in this passage is of special interest. In general, as we have seen, such heterotopic interpolations are "dislocated fragments which actually belong to the action of other sections" (Knuth, 1976:135). Such displaced fragments are taken bodily or in slightly varied form from their original locations and grafted on to other sections, either preceding or following. From the interpolation in this case the reader understands that O'Molloy must have told somebody in the grain merchant's office that he wanted to see Mr. Lambert, who is employed there, but turning to section VIII the reader will find that such an event is not recorded there. O'Molloy must have acted already on the information received, for at the very beginning of that section he is seen groping his way into the warehouse, a former abbey, without so much as saying to Lambert, "They told me you were here."

Then there is the question: What is the reason for the interpolation to be found just here, in this section and at this point? Hart's comment is: "Both the sailor and J. J. O'Molloy are begging. There is an ironic contrast between the sailor's song and the tales of insurrection being told in Mary's abbey" (1974:204). What Hart alludes to in his first statement is O'Molloy's desperate attempts to raise money, a point taken up by French (1976:120) as well. With Myles Crawford, that morning, O'Molloy had drawn a blank (7.996ff./147.16ff.), and now he will probably try Ned Lambert for a loan. There is a certain correspondence indeed, but there is also a contrast. The beggar is seen to be successful: a stout lady gives him something and Molly Bloom's "generous white arm" throws him a penny, but whether O'Molloy will succeed in wheedling anything out of Ned Lambert the reader will never learn, unless O'Molloy's entering Barney Kiernan's with Lambert a few hours later and ordering drinks means anything (see 12.1018/320.11).

What Hart says about the ironic contrast between the sailor's song ("*For England . . .*") and the Irish rebel tales told in the warehouse is right, of course, but the interpolation is primarily about O'Molloy's "white careworn face," and it is not O'Molloy who is telling tales of insurrection, it is Lambert. In section VIII, while the latter explains some historical details to his visitor, O'Molloy will be hovering modestly in the background. Apart from any contrast, we might think of a certain parallelism between the Dedalus girls and O'Molloy. From Bloom's thoughts about him in "Aeolus"—"Cleverest fellow at the junior bar he used to be. Decline, poor chap . . . Practice dwindling. A mighthavebeen. Losing heart. Gambling. Debts of honour" (7.292–304/125.02ff.)—we know that O'Molloy must be a lawyer who has come down in the world. And from the unnamed narrator's gossip in "Cyclops" (12.1022ff./ 320.15ff.) we may surmise that he is doing some shady law business in which Ned Lambert is involved (so the latter did help him out, after all?). The Dedalus girls also have their worries; living on charity, it seems, they do not know where their next meal may be coming from. Just now, they are hungry, as the very next section will reveal, and we can easily imagine their faces to be white and careworn, too. Besides, for all the interest that may attach to the causal relationships between the interpolations and their contexts, we should not overlook internal relations, contrasts, or parallelisms within the sections themselves. In this case, for instance, we witness the sailor growling "home and beauty," no less, within the poor girls' hearing. The reader will not be long in realizing that the Dedalus sisters have not much of a home, and as to beauty, whatever it may mean in the sailor's song ("The Death of Nelson"), there is little chance of beauty to be found in their living quarters either. This very afternoon some curtains they still had will be sold in Dillon's auction rooms for a meager five shillings (section XI). Whichever way we look at it, the sailor's words may have been contrasted deliberately with the presence of the Dedalus girls.

In section IV, Maggy Dedalus, in answer to a question from Katey, tells her and Boody that Dilly, their elder sister, had gone "to meet father" (10.289/226.38–39). A few lines before there was a brief interpolation:

"The lacquey rang his bell. —Barang!" (10.281–82/226.31–32). The words are simple enough, but the event this statement purports to refer to cannot be known to the reader at this stage. It is a forecast of a scene in section XI, and not until the reader reaches that section will he learn that the lacquey with his handbell is stationed by the door of Dillon's auction rooms (Bachelor's Walk, north of the Liffey), while Dilly is standing on the sidewalk outside the auction hall, listening to the cries of the auctioneer, who is showing a pair of curtains and inviting bids on them: "The lacquey by the door . . . shook his handbell twice again and viewed himself in the chalked mirror of the cabinet. Dilly Dedalus, loitering by the curbstone, heard the beats of the bell, the cries of the auctioneer within. Four and nine. Those lovely curtains. Five shillings. Cosy curtains. Selling new at two guineas. Any advance on five shillings? Going for five shillings" (10.643–48/237.06–13). In this passage we hear the auctioneer calling out the bids as heard by Dilly, who is standing outside, and in between we hear her regretful silent comment ("Those lovely curtains," etc.). There is no absolute proof of this, but I have always felt that the passage should be read in this way—a view shared by Shari Benstock, who points out that "the Dedaluses auction off some of their family goods" (1978:167). Are we to assume that Dilly has been hanging around there for hours? Bloom spots her outside Dillon's around one o'clock after having left the *Telegraph* office, and it strikes him that she is *still* standing there, so he must have seen her there before. We know, indeed, that he had gone there to look for Keyes, the tea merchant (cf. 7.411–13/128.28–31 and 7.430–31/129.16–18), but he must have been too preoccupied, then, to take notice of her consciously. From Bloom's thoughts we may conclude that it must have been common knowledge in Dublin that the Dedalus family had to sell some of their possessions from time to time: "Dedalus' daughter there still outside Dillon's auctionrooms. Must be selling off some old furniture" (8.28–29/151.33–34).

One gets the definitive impression, anyway, that Dilly is waiting for her father, waylaying him perhaps; the meeting may even have been prearranged (neither shows any sign of surprise), or else Dilly knows from bitter experience where to go and look for him, witness her reproachful question: "Were you in the Scotch house now?" (10.675/238.05–6). The Scotch House is a pub on Burgh Quay, south of the Liffey (Hart and Knuth, 1976: II, map VIII), but Dedalus came from around the corner of Williams's Row (unobserved by Dilly, apparently) and had been looking for money, as he tells Dilly in an attempt at being funny, "all along the gutter in O'Connell street" (10.703/238.39–40). Thus when he assures her, in answer to her question, that he had *not* been in the Scotch House just now, he may have been speaking the truth. Nonetheless, Dilly has sized him up correctly from the start, she sees and probably smells he has been drinking and concludes that he must have borrowed a few shillings from someone. Her guess that he must have gotten just *five* shillings may have been inspired by the price those curtains had fetched at the auction. The reader, by the way, knows for sure that Dedalus has been drinking: He left the newspaper office with Ned Lambert to have a drink in The Oval around noon (7.351–52/126.30–31; 7.453–56/130.04–7) and may have come from there just now, the pub in question being located in Middle Abbey Street, near O'Connell Street. Having taken leave of his daughter, Dedalus continues his walk upstream. Presently, he will be joined by Bob Cowley and Ben Dollard (section XIV), and the three of them will finally find themselves in the bar of the Ormond Hotel around four o'clock, as told in "Sirens."

The reader will remember that Bloom asks Molly in the morning if he should bring her another book now that she has finished *Ruby: the Pride of the Ring* (4.345–58/64.25–39); he puts this book into an inside pocket (4.382/65.26) and later in the day he reminds himself: "That book I must change for her" (6.154–55/91.12–13). It is, obviously, a matter of changing—that is, returning one book and renting, not buying, another, a small fee having to be paid, as may be seen from the day's budget (17.1465/711.20).

There has been some misapprehension as to the place where Bloom picks up the book. Morton, for instance, in his summary of section X, says: "Bloom's examination of the bookstalls is in search of a novel for his wife. He examines and rejects some pornographic pieces, and chooses *Sweets of Sin*." (1970:48). Obviously, pornographic pieces could not have been lying around in bookstalls in the Dublin of 1904. It is true Bloom has been rummaging among books on book carts, but that is not where he is looking for a book for Molly; it is where he is accustomed to pick up second-hand books for his own library. In section IX he is spotted by M'Coy and Lenehan as a "darkbacked figure," scanning books on a cart, and the former remembers an occasion when Bloom bought a book on astronomy from a bookstall in Liffey Street (10.525–28/233.27–36). To change the book, however, Bloom has to enter a shop, and even there such books as his wife expects him to bring home have to be fetched from a back room. Bloom rejects a few books he had brought home once before, such as *Tales of the Ghetto* and *Fair Tyrants*, and finally settles on *Sweets of Sin*. As Hart puts it, with an allusion to the Simchath Torah motif, no doubt, "In the city's sanctum, the undercover porn-shop, *Sweets of Sin* is produced from behind the curtain, like the ark of the tabernacle" (1974:187), or rather, I would say, like the scrolls of the Torah from inside the ark in the synagogue.

Simchath Torah, as we shall see in time, is the label attached to Bloom's "bookhunt along Bedford row, Merchants' Arch, Wellington

Quay" in "Ithaca" (17.2048–49/729.02–3), where it is listed among the causes of Bloom's fatigue at the end of the day. Simchath Torah, the "rejoicing in the law," which follows the Jewish feast of Sukkoth, marks "the annual completion of the synagogue reading of the Pentateuch" (Thornton, 1968:482), each Sabbath a portion of the books of Moses (the Torah) having been recited in the synagogue, the year round, after which the reading cycle is taken up anew.

But why is the book hunt referred to in "Ithaca" under this label? The correspondence might be sought in the notion of a cycle of reading starting afresh. In section x Bloom is looking for a book for Molly (10.585–641/235.18–237.05); she wants books of a certain type, preferably mildly pornographic, and she is quite prepared to read them over and over. One of those books, *Fair Tyrants*, Bloom had brought her twice, but she had not realized this, she remembers (18.493/751.41–42), until she came to page fifty. She does not complain, she just registers the fact. As far as she is concerned, the cycle of reading may very well be resumed.

As I said, Smith in his time (1927!) seems not to have been aware of the interpolations in this episode. This illustrates that critics over the years had to *learn* to read *Ulysses*—as Senn has said—and learn the hard way. In his summary of section IX, for instance, Smith says: "M'Coy and Lenehan pass Bloom at bookstall; later they pass Bloom's house" (1927; 1970:41). The explanation is, of course, that he mistook the interpolation "A card *Unfurnished Apartments* reappeared on the windowsash of number 7 Eccles street" (10.542–43/234.10–11) for a factual statement about the action of this section, without taking into account that Eccles Street and Wellington Quay, along which both men are walking at that moment (10.532/233.40–41), lie about one mile apart as the crow flies. In fact, the interpolaton carries on the action of the "source section" (i.e., section III) for a brief instant, adding new, significant information, such as the house number, which in its turn enables the reader to identify the woman whose hand throws the coin to the sailor. Later, Molly herself will pinpoint the time she threw the penny and put the card back on the window sash: "he [Boylan] must have been a bit late because it was ¼ after 3 when I saw the 2 Dedalus girls coming from school . . . when I threw the penny to that lame sailor for England home and beauty" (18.343–47/747.30–35). What might be the rationale of the place of the interpolation in section IX? The explanation offered by Hart, Lenehan's tale being about Molly and both she and he preparing to meet Boylan (1974:208), does not, I think, exhaust the possibilities. A weightier reason might be the link, not between Molly and Lenehan but between Molly and M'Coy. Lenehan has hardly started his tale when M'Coy interrupts him in an attempt to boast about his wife, the point being that

Mrs. M'Coy is Molly's hated rival as a singer: "—I know, M'Coy broke in. My missus sang there once. —Did she? Lenehan said. A card *Unfurnished Apartments . . .* Eccles street. He checked his tale a moment but broke out in a wheezy laugh" (10.540–44/234.08–13).

This interpolation, furthermore, is not the only example of an intrusion that extends beyond the action of the section it stems from or belongs to, properly speaking. I have discussed the case of an interpolation referring to an action that must have preceded, logically speaking, the events narrated in the "mother section." In section XIII, however, we have an interpolation that, just like the one in section IX, carries on the action of the main section (in this case, section I), developing it a bit further, the time interval being somewhat longer in this case. Thumbing the pages of second-hand books on a book cart, Stephen is reminded of his own school prizes, books his sisters must long since have taken to a pawnshop without ever being able to redeem them (see section IV). He won those prizes at Belvedere College, Dublin, and Father Conmee, then rector of Clongowes Wood College, Stephen's former school, had been instrumental in getting Stephen into Belvedere. Conmee is now nearing the goal of his journey: "I might find here one of my pawned school-prizes. *Stephano Dedalo, alumno optimo, palmam ferenti.* Father Conmee, having read his little hours, walked through the hamlet of Donnycarney, murmuring vespers. Binding too good probably" (10.840–44/242.31–35). As is apparent, the intrusion is triggered by Stephen's thought of the Latin inscription on the flyleaves of his school prizes. It shows the priest continuing his walk, somewhere in the country, the narrative picking up the thread some ten minutes after his encounter with the young people in section I (see the chart drawn up by Hart, 1974: facing page 210).

It is not surprising that Smith did not recognize the interpolations as such in section XII any more than he did in section IX. He has Mr. Kernan, actually the sole subject of the section, meet Simon Dedalus and talk with him about Emmet's death and burial. As to the supposed encounter with Dedalus, Smith must have been misled by the little scene interpolated at 10.740–41/239.39–240.01, a fragment that forecasts the opening lines of section XIV (10.882–83/243.33–34). His error about Emmet, the Irish rebel (10.764–72/240.27–33), may have been due to an additional difficulty. The first nine episodes of *Ulysses* have conditioned the reader sufficiently to enable him to recognize and appreciate the device of interior monologue, but so far the subject of the stream of consciousness had been either Stephen or Bloom. Now, in section XII, we have to deal with the lengthy, rather smug interior monologue of a minor character, Mr. Kernan, agent for a firm of tea importers, a monologue that spreads over two pages, with no more than a bare ten sentences of straight narrative, and this unusual situation may have proved an unexpected obstacle.

Smith neither spotted the interpolations nor was able to tell interior monologue from dialogue, but Stanzel, although aware of the device and its function, mistakes for interpolation what is, actually, interior monologue in the following paragraph: "Mr Kernan glanced in farewell at his image. High colour, of course. Grizzled moustache. Returned Indian officer. Bravely he bore his stumpy body forward on spatted feet, squaring his shoulders. Is that Ned Lambert's brother over the way, Sam? What? Yes. He's as like it as damn it. No. The windscreen of that motorcar in the sun there. Just a flash like that. Damn like him" (10.755–60/240.17–23). In his comment on this passage, Stanzel assumes that the question about Lambert's brother is part of a dialogue between two unknown partners, but whereas Smith believed this "dialogue" to be part of the narrative, Stanzel thinks the monologue he mistakes for a dialogue is of the nature of a heterotopic interpolation. He is wrong, of course. Apart from the fact that interpolations in this episode (with one exception, as we have seen) are typographically marked as such by appearing in paragraphs of their own, dialogues being marked by the use of dashes, an interpolation is supposed to possess a "mother section" of its own. If this were a conversation, therefore, and not something existing in Kernan's mind only, it should be possible to trace the fragment in one form or another in one of the other sections, but nowhere else in this episode—or, for that matter, in the rest of the book—do we find any mention of this elusive figure, Sam Lambert.

One wishes that Fischer-Seidel, who reprinted Stanzel's text (dating from 1955) in her collection of German essays on *Ulysses* (1977:255–79), would at least have added a critical note.

There is another point in this section where Stanzel makes things more complicated than they really are. Right from the start the reader moves freely in Mr. Kernan's consciousness. Walking down James Street, Kernan relives the scene of the successful sales talk he had with Mr. Crimmins, publican, repeating in his interior monologue what was being said, chiefly quoting to himself his own ingratiating phrases (10.720–37/239.16–36). Halting before the mirror in a hairdresser's shop window, he admires his stylish appearance, reflecting: "Aham! Must dress the character for those fellows. Knight of the road. Gentleman. And now, Mr Crimmins, may we have the honour of your custom again, sir. The cup that cheers but not inebriates, as the old saying has it" (10.748–51/240.10–13). The opening paragraph of this section has dealt with the preliminaries. There is some talk about the weather, Mr. Crimmins serves Kernan a drink, then they turn to the news, the topic of the day being the explosion aboard the *General Slocum* in the New York harbor, and Kernan, sensing the lie of the land, winds up with some impressive remarks about corruption in the States. Now, standing before the mirror, Kernan remembers with some satisfaction, quoting himself *in extenso*, how he finally got down to brass tacks and managed to book an order for his firm. As suggested before, Stanzel's ideas on this section are not very clear. He quotes the opening scene and then continues: "Es folgt *ein kurzes Stück Dialog*, in welchem die Worte der zwei Sprecher einmal sogar in einem Satz zusammengefasst werden: 'And now, Mr Crimmins' (Sprecher Mr. Kernan), 'may we have the honour of your custom again, sir' (Sprecher Mr. Crimmins)" (1955:141, italics mine).

It is not clear what Stanzel may have meant by this "brief fragment of dialogue." From the interpolation onward (10.740–41/239.39–240.01) there is no dialogue at all. Anyway, there is no doubt in my mind that the entire sentence Stanzel quotes, "And now, Mr Crimmins, may we have the honour of your custom again, sir," far from having to be assigned to two different speakers, must be thought of as having been uttered by Kernan, the commercial traveler, who is proud of the skill he shows in handling Mr. Crimmins, his customer, and who is now citing himself in his interior monologue. I stress this view of the situation because, even in recent summaries, a certain vagueness about the actual state of affairs has prevailed. Morton depicts Kernan as "applauding the success of his recent deal with Pulbrook Robertson" (1970:49), and Blamires likewise explains that Kernan is "looking back with pleasure on the deal he has just done with the firm of Pulbrook Robertson through a Mr Crimmins" (1966:101).

What happens, however, is this: Mr. Kernan, agent for Pulbrook, Robertson and Co. (see 17.1980–81/726.35 and 17.2075–76/729.33), has not done any business *with* this firm but *for* and *on behalf of* them, and the man he has closed the deal with is the publican, Mr. Crimmins, a regular customer, it seems, whom he has persuaded to renew the order for tea ("the cup that cheers") to be supplied by the firm for whom he travels.

In spite of his dressy appearance, Kernan remains the true commercial traveler, who has to be careful, not to say obsequious, in talking to his potential customers. It is evident, for instance, that he never forgets to call his present customer either "Mr Crimmins" or "sir"—a social nicety the publican, on his part, need not bother with. Stanzel may have thought that Crimmins urged Kernan to have another drink, but this does not seem probable. The mistake of attributing the phrase "may we have the honour of your custom again, sir" to Mr. Crimmins might have been avoided, anyway, had Stanzel borne in mind that the publican would certainly not go "sirring" a mere commercial traveler.

EPISODE ELEVEN
"Sirens"

*A*T THE naturalistic level, Bloom's story in "Sirens" is not too hard to follow. Within the general framework, Bloom's own actions hardly deserve that name. He is an observer, a spectator rather than an actor, he is an onlooker and a listener, whose vantage point—he is sitting in the Ormond Hotel's dining room—does not allow him to see and hear quite everything that is going on in the adjacent bar and in the saloon adjoining it. The sounds of music and song from the saloon, however, do reach him and after the door to the bar has been set ajar at his request—the better to hear Simon Dedalus's singing—he has even a limited view of the bar, in particular of that section of the counter that is being served by Miss Douce. The impact of all this on Bloom's mind is reflected, as usual, in his stream of consciousness. His interior monologue reveals the extent to which he is engulfed by the emotions aroused by the songs he listens to, his mind being flooded by memories of the happy early years of his courtship and marriage.

Basically, and leaving aside, for a moment, the so-called overture, the pattern of this episode cannot be said to deviate from that which the reader has got to know in the preceding episode: third-person narrative, interspersed with interior monologue and dialogue, but the narrative and the monologue seem to have lost their more or less inconspicuous, matter-of-fact character. The reader now finds himself in front of a transparent screen behind which the outlines of an initially vague authorial presence become more and more visible. The author twists the interior monologue around at will, taking possession of a character's consciousness and intruding in the most bizarre and often, one feels, deliberately misleading ways into the narrative, using stylistic techniques—such as repetition, variation, and imitation—suited to the eminently musical nature of the episode. Its opening sentence, for instance, "Bronze by gold, Miss Douce's head by Miss Kennedy's head, over the crossblind of the Ormond bar heard the viceregal hoofs go by, ringing steel" (11.64–65/257.26–28), returns in a playful variation on a theme as "Yes, bronze from anear, by gold from afar, heard steel from anear, hoofs ring from afar, and heard steelhoofs ringhoof ringsteel" (11.112–13/258.37–39), and Miss Kennedy's questions, "Who? Where?" (11.71/257.35), are echoed—and answered, in a sense—in the narrator's report: "Bloowho went by by Moulang's pipes" (11.86/258.09), the transformation of "Bloom" into "Bloowho" reminding the reader, somehow, of grace notes in a musical score. This answer, however, is a question as well, a question asked by an impatient reader-listener who was under the impression that he was going to hear a story about two barmaids but suddenly finds the narrator interrupting his own story and turning to Bloom: "Bloom went by." At the very first word the reader, surprised, asks: "Who?"—blending the words into "Bloowho?"—and the narrator confirms that it is indeed "Bloom" (11.102/258.26) who is walking past all those shops, but at the same time he keeps talking about the barmaids. The reader, or listener, insists: "But Bloom?" (11.133/259.19), and the narrator, taking his cue from the barmaids' talk about "his goggle eye" and "your other eye," obliges by describing another stage in Bloom's progress along the quays. Yes, yes, he seems to say, it was *Bloom whose* eye took in the names: "Bloowhose dark eye read Aaron Figatner's name" (11.149/259.37).

Still, in spite of all such quasi-musical effects, the episode remains a literary text, pursuing its aims, whatever they may be, by means of literary devices, however unorthodox perhaps. What matters, in the last analysis, is the functional value of any such devices as the author may see fit to use; in this case they do serve the story by heightening the reader's awareness of the tensions involved and by transmitting Bloom's troubled feelings of despondence and strain. The state of turmoil he is in is intensified, if anything, by the impact of the songs he hears, their words—as much as their music—acting as catalysts. At the narrative level, readers may encounter occasional difficulties due to the way polyphonic structures have been simulated. Ranking foremost, therefore, in what follows will be such questions as what happens, and where it happens, linked with problems of interpretation and, sometimes, translation.

Since the thirties, critical tradition has had it that the opening pages of "Sirens" are, in themselves, devoid of meaning but should be compared, as far as their function is concerned, to an opera overture.

Peake has argued that the episode's opening should be taken not as an overture but as a kind of prelude to the narrative proper, a prelude in which distorted fragments from the episode serve as verbal equivalents to musical chords, the specific meanings and denotations of the words and phrases having been wiped out or "muffled" deliberately; frequently such phrases may even suggest a wrong meaning (1977:225ff.). In general, though, we should not be too rash in assuming that the fragments of the prelude, or overture, lack unity or are utterly unrelated. Closer inspection may reveal an inner coherence not much less strong than that of the episode itself. Of course, the paradox remains that is inherent, *mutatis mutandis*, in every opera overture as well: The prelude could only have been written after the episode had been composed, and it can only be fully understood or appreciated after the episode has been read.

Speaking about the interpolations in "Wandering Rocks," Hodgart remarks: "One interpolation is not drawn from the other sections but from a later chapter: the 'bronze and gold' Sirens watch the Viceregal procession in the next chapter" (1978:98). He refers, no doubt, to the passage in section xv where the narrator interrupts his report on Cunningham's mission of charity (he is collecting donations for Dignam's widow) to present to the reader, for the first time in the book, the Ormond barmaids, Miss Kennedy and Miss Douce. We hear Cunningham, who seems to have had a cab at his disposal by the authorities, speaking to Power, referring to the Dignam boy (see 10.01–5/219.01–7):

—The youngster will be all right, Martin Cunningham said, as they passed out of the Castleyard gate.

The policeman touched his forehead.

—God bless you, Martin Cunningham said, cheerily.

He signed to the waiting jarvey who chucked at the reins and set on towards Lord Edward street.

Bronze by gold, Miss Kennedy's head by Miss Douce's head, appeared above the crossblind of the Ormond hotel.

—Yes, Martin Cunningham said, fingering his beard. I wrote to Father Conmee and laid the whole case before him.

(10.956–65/246.01–10, italics mine)

Cunningham must have arranged with the cab driver for the latter to wait for them elsewhere; around 5 P.M., as we learn from "Cyclops" (12.1588ff./ 336.15ff.), they are going to pick up Bloom at Barney Kiernan's pub, thence to proceed to the Dignams' home at Sandymount, but for the time being they set out on foot. As the empty car drives off, the accompanying sounds of the horse's hoofs may be thought of as having triggered the association with the scene where the barmaids are watching the viceregal cavalcade rolling by, for it is the approaching sound of hoof irons by which they have been lured away, from their stations behind the counter, to the window. On a deeper or let us say more abstract level, the reader might feel there is another link hidden in the text, a link that becomes apparent when we consider the nature of the missions both men, Cunningham and the Viceroy, are engaged in. Like the former, the Viceroy has embarked on a mission of charity, for he is "on his way to inaugurate the Mirus bazaar in aid of funds for Mercer's hospital" (10.1268–69/ 254.31–32), an event Bloom had seen announced on a poster earlier in the day (8.1162–64/183:05–7). He even recalls having read or heard that the proceeds of the first performance of Handel's oratorio *The Messiah* were donated to this same hospital; this concert, which Handel himself conducted, actually took place in Dublin on April 13, 1742 (Gifford, 1974:150–51).

What Hodgart says about the strange occurrence of Miss Douce and Miss Kennedy in an interpolation in "Wandering Rocks" is true insofar as the barmaids do not have a section of their own in that episode. Still, they are mentioned in section XIX among the citizens that witness the viceregal procession: "Above the crossblind of the Ormond hotel, gold by bronze, Miss Kennedy's head by Miss Douce's head watched and admired" (10.1197–99/252.29–31). It is not until "Sirens," however, that they start taking part in the action. They even head the episode, opening both the prelude ("Bronze by gold heard the hoofirons") and the narrative proper: "Bronze by gold, miss Douce's head by miss Kennedy's head, over the crossblind of the Ormond bar heard the viceregal hoofs go by, ringing steel" (11.64–65/257.26–28).

Chiming in with the "musical" or even "fugal" nature of the episode, the order in which the barmaids' heads appear in the text has been reversed. This need not mean that Miss Douce and Miss Kennedy are presented as having changed places. The point is—assuming that the picture they offer the onlooker is read from left to right in both cases— that in section XIX of "Wandering Rocks" they are seen from the outside, the reader, in a sense, sharing the Viceroy's point of view, whereas in "Sirens" the narrator presents the scene as viewed from the interior of the bar, where the action is. Moreover, there has been a shift from sight to sound, from optics to acoustics: In section XIX of the preceding episode the barmaids *watch* and admire the cavalcade; in this episode they are said to *hear* the steely sounds of the hoofs.

The barmaids soon return to their places behind the bar, where they sit down on upturned crates, waiting for their tea to draw so as to enjoy their tea break. The time is about 3:30 P.M. (afternoon closing hours for pubs such as we have now seem not to have been in force in 1904).

Miss Douce, freshly back from her holiday, which she appears to have spent at a seaside resort, shows Miss Kennedy her sunburned neck. The ladies start discussing remedies for sunburn, and Miss Douce mentions an assistant in a chemist's shop whom she had asked for a skin lotion, referring to him as "that old fogey in Boyd's" (11.124–25/259.10). It turns out that Miss Kennedy knows him well, both ladies having met him in a concert hall one night, and she even uses a somewhat stronger term, calling him a "hideous old wretch" (11.138/259.24). They start giggling and finally break out in hysterical laughter when they imagine being married to that old fogey with his "bit of beard" and his "greasy nose" (11.169ff./260.19ff.).

Throughout this scene, in fact right from the beginning, the implied narrator has been throwing in various hints and references meant to remind the reader of Bloom, who is just now, during the barmaids' hilarious chatter, walking west along Wellington Quay on the right (southern) bank of the Liffey. Immediately upon his description of the barmaids' final outburst of laughter, the whimsical narrator interjects what looks like an ironic comment on his own narrative: "Married to Bloom, to greaseabloom" (11.180/260.31). All this has given rise to the curious misunderstanding that Miss Douce and Miss Kennedy are actually ridiculing Bloom, exploding into mirth at the thought of being married to him—an error of long standing, as it happens. Obviously, Bloom must still have been walking along on the other side of the river when the barmaids were looking out over the crossblind, and, besides, there is no indication at all that either recognizes him, later, when he leaves the bar and passes them.

Meanwhile, Miss Douce moved over to the end of the bar to show a customer a shell she had brought back from her holiday, thus getting within Bloom's range of vision. Through the open bar door Bloom gets a glimpse of the scene (11.934–44/281.16–28). Miss Douce's tan reminds him of Boylan's song about the seaside girls and of the lotion he ordered for Molly, but that is all there is to it: never any sign of recognition, neither from him nor from her, for that matter. The latter might have been expected, after all, if Bloom were really identical with that "old fogey in Boyd's," for, as Blamires puts it in his paraphrase, "Bloom watches Lydia Douce and knows that, though looking away, she is conscious of his gaze" (1976:118). Finally, when the ballad sung by Ben Dollard is nearing its climactic end, Bloom decides he had better leave before the others start pouring out of the music room into the bar: "Time to be shoving. Looked enough" (11.1073/285.13–14). On arriving, Bloom and Goulding had entered the Ormond dining room directly, using the quayside entrance. Now, on leaving, alone, Bloom passes out of the dining room doorway so as to have a last look at Miss Douce, wondering, in a fleeting moment, whether she might be the Martha Clifford he had just been writing to: "Pass by her. Can leave that *Freeman*. Letter I have. Suppose she were the?" (11.1123/286.30–31). There is an ironic slant to this scene insofar as Boylan has preempted any success Bloom might hope to have with Miss Douce. Passing deaf Pat, the waiter, in the doorway, Bloom leaves the Ormond by way of the bar, even saluting the barmaids (11.1135/287.02). Neither one, however, shows any sign of recognition, and surely, if the thought of being married to Bloom had ever crossed their minds, they would hardly have been able to refrain from sniggering and whispering behind his back with renewed gusto.

As French remarks, there are three styles in the episode: the dialogue, Bloom's interior monologue, and the narrational comment, styles that are surely distinguishable but at the same time constantly merging (1976:128ff.). From the passages she quotes to illustrate the episode's highly complex texture, the impression might be gained that this merging is achieved mainly at the levels of the interior monologue (which is exclusively Bloom's) and the narrational style. We should not forget, however, that echoes of the dialogue, too, may be audible in the language of the narrative, lending it that rhapsodic (or, as French puts it, "lyrical") quality without which the overall technique would not be intrinsically different from that of earlier episodes such as "Lotus Eaters" or "Lestrygonians." The transition from one style to another is sometimes accompanied, or rather conditioned, by the narrator's moving from one vantage point to another, spatially speaking, and, just as there are three different, yet somehow anastomotic styles, there are three separate yet mutually accessible locations, the episode's three main sites of action: the bar, the saloon, and the dining room, all of which are felt to be present in the following passage: "On the smooth jutting beerpull laid Lydia hand, lightly, plumply, leave it to my hands. All lost in pity for croppy. Fro, to: to, fro: over the polished knob (she knows his eyes, my eyes, her eyes) her thumb and finger passed in pity: passed, reposed and, gently touching, then slid so smoothly, slowly down, a cool firm white enamel baton protruding through their sliding ring" (11.1112–17/286.18–24). The narrator here describes the scene in the *bar*, where Miss Douce ("Lydia"), mildly flirting with Mr. Lidwell, a customer ("his eyes"), and meanwhile caressing the beerpull, listens to Ben Dollard singing the ballad "The Croppy Boy" ("croppy"), the sounds of which come from the *saloon*. At the same time these sounds reach Bloom in the *dining room*, and he is even able, the door to the bar having been set ajar, to catch sight of Miss Douce behind the counter, suspecting that she is fully aware of his gaze ("my eyes") in spite of her listening pose.

What strikes the reader in this passage, and throughout the episode, is that the narrative style, as compared to earlier episodes, makes use of a highly artificial kind of prose, closely akin to poetry. There are such formal characteristics as alliteration (laid Lydia . . . lightly / passed . . . pity / slid so smoothly, slowly), inversion (laid Lydia), and even meter: The passage starts with a string of four anapaests, if we allow for a caesura in the middle of a compound (béér / pull) and pronounce "Lydia" as a two-syllable word, and it closes with a sequence of four iambs:

pro-trú- / ding thróugh / their slí- / ding ríng.

In between, moreover, the reader may find several such groups consisting of four iambs, such as:

then slíd / so smóóth- / ly, slów- / ly dówn.

A further striking feature in the first sentence is the transition from more or less conservative, albeit rather lyrical, third-person narrative to a strange outburst of playful comment: "leave it to my hands." Instead of continuing his description of the scene, the narrator seems to pull himself up short, as if to remind the reader that he should not take the characters in this episode too seriously. The phrase is a quotation, echoing Miss Douce's words spoken in answer to Miss Kennedy's advice as to trying a certain concoction (borax with cherry laurel water) for her sunburned skin: "And leave it to my hands, she said" (11.121/259.06). A possible meaning of her remark might be that she fears such a lotion might leave stains on her hands or might stick to them somehow, which would explain why Miss Kennedy then recommends adding glycerine or, perhaps, using glycerine instead of cherry laurel water: "Try it with the glycerine, miss Kennedy advised" (11.122/259.07). For Miss Douce's words to be understood in this sense, as an objection (chiming in with her next rather skeptical reply to her colleague's additional advice: "Those things only bring out a rash"), the verb form "leave" as spoken by her should be construed not as an imperative but as an infinitive.

It is evident that this seemingly simple phrase must have posed a problem to anyone who had to translate the text. Whatever meaning the translators might want to attach to the phrase in question, there is one bare fact they will have to recognize, which is that the author—whom we assume to have known what he was doing—saw fit to quote Miss Douce's remark some thirty pages farther down as part of his narrator's comment, employing exactly the same words. So what are they to do? Senn says that "translators ought to be as consistent as the author himself" (1970:521). If we accept this as a valid criterion, and I see no reason why we should not, we shall find that of the translators mentioned earlier Wollschläger, at any rate, passes the test: "An den glatten vorstehenden Bierzapfhahn legte Lydia leicht die Hand, scheulos, *lass ihn meinen Händen*" (396, italics mine). In her talk with Miss Kennedy, Miss Douce had uttered the same words in this German translation ("Und lass ihn meinen Händen"), but whereas readers might have wondered what she could have meant by "ihn" in that passage, now, as the noun *Bierzapfhahn* is of masculine gender, there is no doubt that the pronoun is supposed to refer to the "smooth jutting beerpull." The sexual overtones in this scene are unmistakable, so much so that the passage has come in for some adverse criticism. Adams, for example, comments that "such touches as Lydia's fondling of the beer-pull are, I fear, no better than adolescent pseudo-Freudianism" (1966:149). We should not forget, however, that Bloom's interior monologue, soon to rise to the surface ("she knows his eyes, my eyes, her eyes"), is already creeping in on the narrator's comment: The voice may be the narrator's but the point of view is Bloom's. Throughout Ben Dollard's singing of the ballad, Bloom has steadily been observing Miss Douce's pose, his thoughts returning constantly to Molly and Boylan, and there is no denying that his mind really is a bit adolescent at times: Any sexual significance that might be read into Miss Douce's gestures ("leave it to my hands") is not likely to be lost on him. In Wollschläger's translation the unashamedly erotic nature of Miss Douce's stroking of the beerpull is hinted at by the adverb *scheulos*—that is, *unafraid*, which stands for the original *plumply*. The others took this as an adjectival phrase, descriptive of Lydia's hand (rounded, full), but Wollschläger may well be right, seeing that the word is on a par with that other adverb, "lightly."

Neither Goyert nor Morel tried to achieve consistency: The way they translate Miss Douce's words in the earlier passage differs radically from the way they reproduce the phrase in the beerpull scene (italics mine): "—*Und dann sieh mal meine Hände*, sagte sie. —Versuch mal Glyzerin, riet Miss Kennedy" (I.420). "Auf den glatten, vorspringenden Zapfhahn legte Lydia leicht die Hand, rundlich, *lass ihn meinen Händen*" (I.466–67). "—*Et ce que j'en ai sur les mains!* dit-elle. —Essayez de la glycérine, conseille Miss Kennedy" (252). "Sur le manche lisse de la pompe à bière posait légère la main de Lydia, potelée, *laissez-moi faire*" (280). Nowhere is there any echo of the former passage, which amounts to saying that the reader cannot fully appreciate the phrase for what it is—namely, a quotation introduced by the narrator as an ironic aside. What else? The point of view seems to be Bloom's, but he cannot have heard Miss Douce saying, "And leave it to my hands." He had not even reached the Ormond when she spoke those words.

There are more cases of this type in the episode. Bloom, one supposes, cannot have heard Lenehan asking Boylan in the bar, "Got the horn or what?" (11.432/267.15), and he could not have heard or seen Miss Douce doing her *Sonnez la cloche* act (11.404ff./266.25ff.). Now, it is not surprising that these phrases become motifs associated with Boylan's progress toward Eccles Street, marking, for instance, the horse's trot: "Horn. Have you the? Horn. Have you the? Haw haw horn" (11.526–27/ 270.01–2), and again: "Atrot, in heat, heatseated. *Cloche. Sonnez la. Cloche. Sonnez la.* Slower the mare went up the hill by the Rotunda, Rutland Square" (11.763–65/276.20–22). What *is* surprising, however, is that these verbal motifs should recur in what, again, seems to be Bloom's interior monologue:

> Instruments. A blade of grass, shell of her hands, then blow. Even comb and tissuepaper you can knock a tune out of. Molly in her shift in Lombard street west, hair down. I suppose each kind of trade made its

own, don't you see? Hunter with a horn. Haw. Have you the? *Cloche.*
Sonnez la. Shepherd his pipe. Pwee little wee. Policeman a whistle. Locks
and keys! Sweep! Four o'clock's all's well! Sleep! All is lost now. Drum?
Pompedy. Wait. I know. Towncrier, bumbailiff. Long John. Waken the
dead. Pom. Dignam. Poor little *nominedomine.* Pom. It is music. I mean
of course it's all pom pom pom very much what they call *da capo.* Still you
can hear. As we march, we march along, march along. Pom.

                                            (11.1237–46/289.31–42)

Blamires, summarizing Bloom's thoughts in this passage, includes "barmaid with chiming garter," but the phrase "Haw. Have you the?" is
passed over. Skipping the locksmith and the chimneysweep, too, he does
mention the night watchman, whose cry ("all's well"), he says, leads to
"All is lost now." Besides, I assume, the notions of night and sleep may
also have called up the image of sleepwalking Amina in *La Sonnambula*
and the memory of the tenor aria mentioned by Goulding. The words, by
the way, seem to have lost their tragic overtones in this context. But the
enigma remains with regard to the presence of the "horn" and the
"cloche," verbal motifs that have no right to be found in Bloom's interior
monologue. There is nothing for it but to postulate, once again, the hand
of some commentator who speaks in an aside to the audience, an
"arranger" who makes his interfering presence felt in this way.

The same arranger must have been at work in the scene where Bloom
meets this woman: "A frowsy whore with black straw sailor hat askew
came glazily in the day along the quay towards Mr Bloom. When first he
saw that form endearing? Yes, it is. I feel so lonely. Wet night in the lane.
Horn. Who had the? Heehaw shesaw. Off her beat here" (11.1252–55/
290.07–11). With this "When first he saw . . ."—an allusion to the aria
sung by Simon Dedalus—the commentator is already deriding Bloom,
inflating the latter's startled reaction (a prosaic thought of "Haven't I
seen this woman before?") into a mock-poetical phrase, but when Bloom
remembers the night he was accosted by this woman in a lane, the
arranging commentator, like an actor in a Pirandello play, really gets into
his stride, mocking Bloom mercilessly: "Oh, really? And who had the
horn then, and who has the horn now—he, she, Boylan, Molly?" The
sequence stands out as a *corpus alienum* in this paragraph, which has an

otherwise matter-of-fact tone we recognize as typically Bloom's, leaving the reader wondering whose voice it is he hears.

Among the shops Bloom passes on his walk along Wellington Quay is Bassi's, the statue and picture-frame maker's. Through Bloom's erroneous interpretation of an article of Catholic dogma, the Virgin Mary statues he sees displayed in the window remind him of the Greek or Roman goddesses in the museum ("Those today"): "By Bassi's blessed virgins Bloom's dark eyes went by. Bluerobéd, white under, come to me. God they believe she is: or goddess. Those today. I could not see. That fellow spoke. A student. After with Dedalus' son. He might be Mulligan" (11.151–54/259.39–260.02). Out of context it is probably impossible to grasp the full meaning of such an elliptical phrase as "Those today," or even of a semielliptical one as "I could not see." Although the transition from narrative to monologue in this passage is all but imperceptible, these phrases must belong to Bloom's interior monologue—so much is clear at any rate. In fact, their origin may be traced back to a chain of associations that passed through his mind earlier in the day when he was having a light snack in Davy Byrne's, as told in "Lestrygonians." His eyes following the pattern of the veins in the oak counter slab, he starts musing about the relation between curves and beauty, about "shapely goddesses" such as may be admired in the museum, about the kind of food and drink gods and goddesses were supposed to ingest—a diet of nectar and ambrosia—and about the process of human digestion, rather disgusting in contrast. A queer thought crossed his mind: What about a rectum? Would such a marble goddess have a visible hole behind? As he had to visit the library anyway, Bloom decided to pass through the museum, which is a kind of companion building to the library, separated from it by a lawn, in order to scrutinize those anatomical details he is especially interested in (8.925–32/176.31–39), but he was thwarted in his purpose. A student passed through the museum at the same time, interrupting him or perhaps even preventing him at all from inspecting the statues at close range. Later, on leaving the library, as told in "Scylla and Charybdis," Bloom passes Stephen Dedalus talking to this same student and he guesses, rightly, that this must be Mulligan, for he remembers that Mr. Dedalus, on being told that morning in the funeral carriage that they had just passed Stephen, had asked: "Was that Mulligan cad with him? His *fidus Achates!*" (6.49/88.15). Why, one wonders, does it take Mulligan, who reports having seen Bloom in the museum (9.609–10/201.03), so long to show up in Eglinton's office, later on, especially if he and Haines had arranged to meet in the library? And why did not Haines wait for him instead of hurrying off to the city to buy a book recommended by one of the librarians? And were bookshops open on a Thursday afternoon in 1904?

Anyway, the visit to the museum must have been a frustrating experience for Bloom, and the thought of the nude goddesses keeps pestering him. Looking at Miss Douce's virginal face in the Ormond bar scene, he reflects that men might use women as musical instruments, and the image of holes in a flute reminds him of the one hole he failed to see: "Body of white woman, a flute alive. Blow gentle. Loud. Three holes, all women. Goddess I didn't see" (11.1088–90/285.33–34).

In the saloon, Ben Dollard is reminding Bob Cowley and Simon Dedalus of the night he had to sing at a concert but "had no wedding garment" (11.473/268.22–23). The three had repaired to the saloon to make music. Ben Dollard sits down at the piano and starts playing a few chords. Dedalus, it seems, recognizes the music as the accompaniment to a well-known duet in which Ben Dollard used to sing the bass part: "*Love and War*, Ben, Mr Dedalus said. God be with old times" (11.459/268.04–5). Apparently, these words are intended as an allusion to a specific occasion, for Bob Cowley immediately chimes in with, "Poor old Goodwin was the pianist that night" (11.466/268.14), and Mr. Dedalus describes old Goodwin as "a crotchety old fellow in the primary stage of drink" (11.471/268.19–20). It is then that Ben Dollard recalls to memory the lack, sadly felt at the time, of a "wedding garment," without which he could not present himself on the stage, apparently. His remark causes them to laugh uproariously. As most people will know, the phrase is one of those so-called biblical expressions, but that is not the point. As an idiom, "wedding garment" denotes a qualification for participating in something, as when a concert singer needs a dress suit, and even if there were any specific reference to the story in Matthew 22, which I doubt, this would not explain the men's outburst of laughter. As I see it, the point is that it is Ben Dollard, a confirmed bachelor, who reminds them that he had no wedding garment.

The reminiscing continues, and the reader learns that it was Father Cowley who saved the situation that night of the concert. He knew that the Blooms in those days were hard up but used to have a lot of opera cloaks and the like (Molly may have needed the things for her concerts), and he thought that Ben might perhaps borrow a suit from them. It took some time to root the Blooms out, as the only clue he had was that they were living on Holles Street, but, having located them, Ben was lent a dress suit, for which Bloom did not even want to take any money and of which he now remembers in particular the tight trousers. After some more of this desultory talk, Dollard finally starts singing, accompanying himself on the piano. "Love and War" is a duet (Gifford, 1974:239) for tenor (the "Lover") and bass (the "Warrior"), and Ben Dollard is supposed, of course, as a bass-baritone, to sing the warrior's part. His mind, however, is still on Cowley's landlord, the Reverend Hugh C.

Love, whom they had been talking about that very afternoon in connection with the trouble Cowley has with his creditors (as narrated in
section XIV of "Wandering Rocks"), so he gets the text wrong, singing
"When *love* absorbs my ardent soul" instead of "When *war* absorbs my
ardent soul," whereupon he is interrupted by Cowley: "—War! War!
cried Father Cowley. You're the warrior. —So I am, Ben Warrior
laughed. I was thinking of your landlord. Love or money" (11.532–34/
270.08–10).

The characters in this scene are pitilessly held up to derision: There is
nothing of the warrior in poor old Ben, and there is nothing heroic in the
others either, social misfits, both of them, as much as he is, pathetic in
their attempts to drown their misery in song and music. Bloom's mood,
however, might be characterized as one of "resigned understanding"
(Knight, 1952): His impulse to follow Boylan has died down ignominiously.

For all that Bloom clearly suffers under the thought of Molly's
infidelity, nowhere is he reported to have dropped his affair—for what it
is worth—with Martha Clifford. It is true that if he can help it the whole
thing will never get beyond the stage of a strictly epistolary affair.
However, at the end of the day we find him carefully putting away
Martha's typewritten letter (17.1840–42/722.21–23), the one he had
received that morning, and we learn that among the miscellaneous
objects in the drawer of the sideboard, which he adds it to, there are
already three previous letters from her (17.1796–98/721.11–13). In the
course of the day Bloom's thoughts revert to Martha's latest letter
several times. First he plans to answer it in the National Library, where
he is going to consult newspaper files: "I must answer. Write it in the
library" (8.613/168.08–9). Again, passing the post office on Molesworth
Street, he reminds himself, not too enthusiastically, that he has to
answer Martha's letter. There is even a shop nearby where he could buy
some notepaper, but he puts it off, wanting to think it over or simply
shrinking from the task: "Postoffice. Must answer. Fag today. Send her
a postal order two shillings, half a crown. Accept my little present.
Stationer's just here too. Wait. Think over it" (8.1132–34/182.11–13). It
is not revealed why Bloom fails to write his letter in the library, but, a few
hours later, we find him nearing Upper Ormond Quay, where there is
also a post office, and once more there is a convenient shop, a tobac-
conist's this time, where notepaper is sold, right at the corner. He still
feels he simply has to reply to Martha's little note: "To Martha I must
write. Buy paper. Daly's. Girl there civil" (11.229–30/262.01). Then,
having bought notepaper and envelopes, he is sidetracked into the
Ormond Hotel and, once there, decides to write the letter right there in
the dining room: "Better write it here. Quills in the postoffice chewed
and twisted" (11.821/278.05–6). He asks the waiter for pen and ink and a

blotting pad, and, pretending to Richie Goulding that he is answering an ad, he manages to finish his letter at last (11.895–901/280.12–19), right under Goulding's eyes, behind the newspaper he has prudently put up as a screen. Having addressed the envelope, Bloom has some misgivings about the P.S. he had added ("I feel so sad today. So lonely"), which might be too poetical, but after all he is glad he has finished the job that has been on his mind all day. Relieved, he will now proceed along the quay to the nearby post office: "Done anyhow. Postal order, stamp. Postoffice lower down" (11.909/280.28).

In contrast to Martha's letter to Bloom (5.241ff./77–78), Bloom's reply to her is never shown to the reader in its definitive draft. Fragmented parts are scattered throughout the text, and the reader, as Shari Benstock observes, "is carried through the writing process, which is woven into the narration (itself determined by the musical motifs of the chapter) as well as in Bloom's internal monologue" (1982a:419). So, if the reader wishes to try his hand at a reconstruction of a more or less final draft of Bloom's letter, he will never be sure to have found all the answers. Of course, it is obvious that a pattern such as "It is utterl imposs. Underline *imposs.* To write today" (11.862/279.13–14) means that Bloom is writing something like "It is utterly impossible to write today," with the word "impossible" underlined, but what about "Ask her no answ" (11.866/279.18)? What, if anything, does Bloom mean to ask Martha? And is the elliptic phrase "Write me a long" (11.868/279.21) really to be incorporated into Bloom's letter as something like "Write me a long letter," or does it belong, as I believe it does, to his interior monologue only, a reminiscence of Martha's "Please write me a long letter and tell me more" (5.251/78.04)?

As most readers will know, phrases from Martha's letter tend to crop up in Bloom's mind throughout the day anyway. Here, as so often, the reader would do well to distinguish between Bloom's primary, "autochthonic," thoughts and those that fall under the category of "quotation within interior monologue." To give an example, Boone (1982:84n.9) quotes "I have such a bad headache today" (13.778–79/368.07–8), claiming that this "associative leap" of Bloom's thoughts in "Nausicaa" "reveals his unconscious identification with female bodily cycles," as Bloom has guessed from Edy Boardman's behavior that she is "near her monthlies." Boone does not make it sufficiently clear, however, that the "I" in this quotation is not at all identical with Bloom's ego. The sentence is a straight quote from Martha Clifford's letter, as Bloom very well knows, witness his immediately following thought, "Where did I put the letter? Yes, all right." It simply means that at the time he read the letter, Bloom already suspected that Martha, when writing it, suffered from the same female complaint.

A similar ambiguity as presented by the phrase "Write me a long" is found in a passage preceding the actual writing of the letter, a passage in which Bloom's reply to Martha is, in a sense, prefigured. Bloom suddenly realizes that the air Dedalus is singing is from the opera *Martha*, and his interior monologue at this point runs as follows: "*Martha* it is. Coincidence. Just going to write. Lionel's song. Lovely name you have. Can't write. Accept my little pres. Play on her heartstrings pursestrings too. She's a. I called you naughty boy. Still the name: Martha. How strange! Today" (11.713–16/275.03–6). Obviously, "Can't write . . . today" is something Bloom is planning to put into his letter in one form or another, and the same holds for "Accept my little pres(ent)." What follows ("Play . . .") is Bloom's own comment on the way he is handling the affair. The intriguing fragment "She's a" seems an unfinished thought: Some less flattering qualification may have been intended, but Bloom cannot think offhand of a term strong enough to characterize a woman who is able to write such silly things as "I called you naughty boy," a direct quote from Martha's letter this time. Less clear, however, is the status of "Lovely name you have." The coincidence of the names, Martha and *Martha*, may have reminded Bloom of what Martha said in her letter, "I often think of the beautiful name you have" (5.248/ 77.40–78.01), prompting him to return the compliment. In that case the phrase would be part of the rough draft, the letter Bloom is already composing in his head. There is, however, no confirmation of this, because the phrase does not appear among the bits and pieces that, for the reader, constitute the final version, a fact that would speak for another interpretation. Musing over the names, Bloom may have been harking back to what Martha said about his (assumed) name, Henry Flower. His memory being at fault somewhat, Martha's "beautiful name you have" is turned into "lovely name you have," but this need not mean that Bloom was going to use the phrase in his letter. Instead, it would mean, again, a case of quotation—misquotation, rather—within interior monologue. And what to make of "So excited" in the final draft (11.869/ 279.22)? It may be argued that this is part of Bloom's interior monologue, but we have just been told that Bloom is utterly bored (11.863/ 279.15), so where does the excitement come in all of a sudden? I think that this is an instance of make believe; it is just part of Bloom's game. By an act of pretending, by asking her to believe that he is getting excited when thinking of her, he hopes to impress Martha or even to excite her in earnest. I submit, therefore, that the words "So excited" must have found a place somewhere in Bloom's letter, the same as "it will excite me" (11.888/280.03–4).

Bloom, as we have seen (11.822–23/278.07–8), has asked the waiter, bald Pat, to bring him pen and ink and a blotting pad. When Morton, in his summary, claims that Bloom "gets some notepaper from Pat" (1970:51), he contradicts his own correct statement in the preceding paragraph, "Meanwhile, Bloom is buying paper for his letter to Martha." Bloom knew that he would find pen and ink in the post office, but he would have to buy his own notepaper, of course. This is not such a trivial detail as it might appear on the face of it. On the contrary, it is an essential element in the plot: If Bloom had not stopped in Daly's to purchase his notepaper and envelopes he might not have spotted Boylan and might not have entered the Ormond at all.

Throughout the episode Pat is characterized by two specific features; he is *bald* and *bothered*: "came bald Pat, came bothered Pat" (11.287/ 263.22), "he whispered, bald and bothered" (11.318/264.17–18), "Bald Pat, bothered waiter" (11.444/267.27). Peake, however, refers to him as being "bald, bothered and hard of hearing" (1977:220) and once more, toward the end of his section on "Sirens," he calls him "deaf and bothered" (1977:233). This reflects the confusion we find in the early translations of *Ulysses*. Both Morel and Goyert took "bothered" to mean "troubled" or "worried," although they might have learned in Patrick Weston Joyce's glossary of Anglo-Irish phrases (1910:221) that "bothered" (from Irish *bodhar* [deaf]) is said in Ireland of a person who is hard of hearing. Besides, James Joyce himself has taken care to provide enough clues in the text and to spell it out for the reader in such passages as "Bald Pat who is bothered mitred the napkins. Pat is a waiter hard of his hearing" (11.915/280.37–38), or, in the scene in which Bloom and Goulding want to enjoy Simon Dedalus's singing: "Bloom signed to Pat, bald Pat is a waiter hard of hearing, to set ajar the door of the bar. The door of the bar. So. That will do" (11.669–71/ 273.35–36). In this passage we can formally see and hear Bloom mouthing the words when he repeats "The door of the bar" in an attempt to make the waiter understand what he asks him to do. A similar situation develops later when Bloom, wanting to settle his bill before leaving, signals the waiter and apparently mouthes the words, "How much": "Much? He seehears lip-speech. One and nine. Penny for yourself. Here. Give him twopence tip. Deaf, bothered" (11.1001–3/283.10–12). This is the only passage in which "deaf" and "bothered" appear together, but note that they are not linked by a conjunction, as in "bald and bothered." Hence Wollschläger's modern German translation, "Taub, schwerhörig," must be deemed correct. Bloom's thought may be paraphrased as "The man is deaf, or, as they say here, bothered." Bloom does not leave at once but stays a while to listen to Ben Dollard's song, and deaf Pat listens too: "Listen. Bloom listened. Richie Goulding listened. And by the door deaf Pat, bald Pat, tipped Pat, listened" (11.1028–29/283.41–42), and when Bloom leaves at last, by way of the bar, Pat is still standing there: "By deaf Pat in the doorway straining ear Bloom passed" (11.1130/286.38).

Somehow, Pat has understood what Bloom wants now. He brings pen, ink, pad, and clears the table: "Bald deaf Pat brought quite flat pad ink. Pat set with ink pen quite flat pad. Pat took plate dish knife fork. Pat went" (11.847–48/278.36–37). As Peake points out, alluding to 11.842/ 278.30, "When Pat brings the materials, Bloom has been thinking of girls practising 'scales up and down,' and the delivery is made in three evenly-accented octaves of monosyllables" (1977:221). In reading aloud, I might add, the three octaves in this passage should really be sung, not spoken, the first and second rising, the third falling, for instance.

From the point of view of the episode's *musical motifs*, the second instalment of Bloom's letter (11.888–94/280.03–11) is especially interesting. In the saloon Bob Cowley, having accompanied Simon Dedalus, has now started playing a voluntary (11.799/277.20), and Bloom, musing on the arithmetical basis of music, has been aware of the sounds coming from the piano all the time: "Instance he's playing now. Improvising" (11.838/278.25). Again, having signed his letter and pausing a moment to ponder on some postscript he might add, it strikes him that Cowley has changed the tune: "What is he playing now? Improvising. Intermezzo" (11.889–90/280.05). Starting on his postscript, he feels his mental processes clearly undergoing the influence of the measure of the piece of music Cowley is playing. While still thinking about a suitable P.S., he is humming, or perhaps he is "tambourining" with his fingers on the table (cf. 11.863–64/279.15–16), beating time: "P.S. The *rum tum tum*" (11.890/280.06, italics mine), and then, while writing "How will you punish me?" he mentally stretches these six syllables into two units of four syllables each in which the *"rum* tum *tum"* beat is easily recognizable: how-*will*-you-*pun* / you-*pun*-ish-*me*. The notion of punishment, combined with or even reinforced by the potent meter of Cowley's music, now recalls to Bloom's mind the image of the next-door maid servant in Eccles Street: "Crooked skirt swinging, whack by" (11.891/280.07). It is an image once removed, reminding the reader of the mental picture Bloom had when standing next to this maid servant in the butcher's shop that morning, remembering how she uses to beat the carpets in the back yard: "Strong pair of arms. Whacking a carpet on the clothesline. She does whack it, by George. The way her crooked skirt swings at each whack" (4.150–51/59.09–11), and again, his eyes still resting on the girl's hips: "The crooked skirt swinging, whack by whack by whack" (4.164/59.26–27). The image fades away, and the music (la *la* la *ree*) "trailing off" in minor, Bloom feels like adding another postscript, a post-postscript, and a sad one at that, a P.P.S. in minor. This will be written down as "I feel so sad today. So lonely" (11.894/280.10–11), but in Bloom's inner ear it will still conform to the same persistent beat: la-*la*-la-*ree* / I-*feel*-so-*sad* / to-*day*-la-*ree* / so-*lone*-ly-*dee*, which is the way this passage should be read. Even Bloom's initial movements after finishing his letter seem to remain under the spell of the meter: He-*blot*-ted-*quick* / on-*pad*-of-*Pat* (11.895/280.12), but this mood wears off as soon as he gets busy with the envelope and the *Freeman*, making a great show—for Richie Goulding's benefit—of copying an address out of the newspaper, in fact just selecting the first two names from the alphabetical list of death notices (11.857/279.07; cf. also 6.157–59/91.15–17).

Martha Clifford's address as written down by Bloom ("c/o P. O. Dolphin's Barn Lane") is followed by a brief passage (11.901–3/280.19–22) that is a tightly packed cluster of associations, associations with, on the one hand, Molly and, on the other, Mrs. Breen, whom Bloom had already known as young Josie Powell (cf. 8.273–74/158.31–32), a certain Luke Doyle's residence in Dolphin's Barn being the place of his first meeting with both Molly and Josie. Molly still remembers Bloom's kissing her heart "at Dolphins barn" (18.330/747.15), and in "Nausicaa" Bloom remembers the charades they played at Dolphin's Barn "in Luke Doyle's house" (13.1106/377.16), but when Bloom recalls Molly's kisses: "She kissed me" (13.1102/377.11), he is thinking of another place and another time altogether. This phrase harks back to his train of thought in the preceding paragraph, in which he is looking over to the Hill of Howth, recalling his lovemaking to Molly under the rhododendrons or the ferns there. That is where *she* kissed *him*.

Bloom's associations follow an intricate pattern. He starts by blotting the words of the *address* he has just written, *over* the still more or less discernible traces of the *letter* on the blotting pad, so as to prevent Goulding from reading either the text of the letter or the name and address on the envelope. Looking at the result, he reflects that this might be an excellent idea for a story, one of those stories they publish in *Titbits*. This very morning, sitting at stool, he had been reading such a story: "Our prize titbit: *Matcham's Masterstroke*. Written by Mr Philip Beaufoy, Playgoers' Club, London. Payment at the rate of one guinea a column has been made" (4.502–4/68.39–41). And further: "He read on . . . Neat certainly. *Matcham often thinks of the masterstroke by which he won the laughing witch who now.* Begins and ends morally. *Hand in hand.* Smart" (4.512–15/69.11–14). In Bloom's interior monologue this quotation from *Titbits* is now drastically abridged; in a flash, his memory skips a few phrases but supplies two salient details: "Matcham often thinks" and "the laughing witch" (11.903/280.21). Translators must have thought that there is something wrong with this sentence, if we may call it that, for most of them have hastened to add what they apparently suspected to be a missing preposition. Morel has, "Matcham pense fréquemment à la rieuse magicienne" (274) and Wollschläger,

"Matcham denkt noch oft an die lachende Hexe" (388). Valverde's Spanish and Mallafrè's Catalan translations also insert a preposition: "Matcham piensa a menudo en la risueña brujita" (I.435), and "Matcham pensa sovint en l'enriolada fetillera" (293). The Dutch translator, Vandenbergh, resisted the urge to try and correct Joyce's text, for he reproduces Bloom's thought faithfully: "Matcham denkt vaak de lachende feeks" (326). In my view, he is right. Bloom cannot have forgotten the happy ending of the *Titbits* story that impressed him so much with its professional touch ("neat" and "smart" were his own words for the story), and the title of the story cannot have slipped his mind. There is no need for this Matcham character to remind himself of the "laughing witch": After all, he married her, so what he often thinks of is not his bride but the masterstroke by which he won her. The author's name, Beaufoy, will crop up in Bloom's mind several times in the course of the day. In fact, it provides the link with the following snatch of interior monologue: "Poor Mrs Purefoy" (11.903/280.22). In order to understand how such an association might have come about, the reader should turn back to the scene where Bloom meets Mrs. Breen (8.202ff./156.31ff.). In the course of the conversation, wanting to change the subject, Bloom asks for news of Mrs. Purefoy, who is expecting a baby; that is, he wants to do so, but in a slip of the tongue he speaks of Mrs. *Beaufoy*, realizing immediately that he must have been thinking of the author of "Matcham's Masterstroke" (8.275–79/158.33–39). Now, in the Ormond, it is not so much the address, Dolphin's Barn, as his own remembered *Fehlleistung* that turns his thoughts back to his meeting with Mrs. Breen. Anyway, Mrs. Purefoy, so he is told, has been in the lying-in hospital on Holles Street for three days already, having "a very stiff birth." Bloom is very sorry to hear that and decides to call at the hospital later. Each time he thinks of Mrs. Purefoy the slip of the tongue returns. Sitting on the beach in the dusk, he reminds himself that he wanted to go and ask at the hospital whether Mrs. Purefoy's baby has yet arrived: "Mrs Beaufoy, Purefoy. Must call to the hospital" (13.959/373.11–12). As Bloom himself will realize, later that day, his encounter with Mrs. Breen is of the utmost importance—from the reader's point of view it is even a major functional element in the plot—because his meeting Stephen at last will depend on it. In "Circe," while running after Stephen, Bloom wonders: "What am I following him for? Still, he's the best of that lot. If I hadn't heard about Mrs Beaufoy Purefoy I wouldn't have gone and wouldn't have met" (15.639–41/452.10–13).

Finally, Bloom's stream of consciousness comes to a stop when he remembers what else Mrs. Breen had told him, a sad tale about her crazy husband, Dennis. She shows him a postcard the latter had received that morning, with the cryptic message "U.P." (8.255–64/158.09–19), which she pronounces "up." After Bloom's comment, "Poor Mrs Purefoy," this final thought of his, "U.P.: up" (11.903/280.22), is expressive of a similar feeling of pity, compassion with the lot of women in general and of poor Mrs. Breen in particular.

There has been some confusion among critics about songs and singers in this episode. Strong is right when he says that Cowley sings a phrase or two from the tenor romance from *Martha*, but when he adds, "Richie Goulding says it is the most beautiful tenor air ever written" (1949:34), he is wrong. Goulding refers to an air from *La Sonnambula*, a Bellini opera; the text leaves no doubt on this issue. After their performance of the duet—and it is not Simon Dedalus whom we hear singing of "love and war," as Cope has it (1974:219), but Dollard and Cowley—the latter two have joined forces to get Dedalus to sing Lionel's air from the opera *Martha*. He seems rather reluctant at first, but they keep going on at him: "—Go on, blast you! Ben Dollard growled, Get it out in bits. —M'appari, Simon, Father Cowley said" (11.586–87/271.24–25). To encourage him, presumably, Cowley then sings the opening lines himself, in Italian and unaccompanied (11.594–95/271.33–34), turning his face toward a print (*A Last Farewell*) on one of the walls, until he is interrupted by Dollard. Cope is mistaken again when he assumes that it is Simon Dedalus who is singing "to a dusty seascape" (1974:237). At last, Dedalus gives in (he may have been putting on a show, after all), sits down at the piano, and starts the prelude. Cowley stops him, first telling him: "Play it in the original. One flat" (Lionel's air is in the key of B flat, as Gifford [1974:246] points out), and then offering to accompany him (11.602–5/271.41–272.04).

It is at this point that confusion sometimes sets in, mainly because there are two separate scenes of action. The narrator, using a kind of semi-indirect discourse, as if Bloom were chewing on Goulding's words together with his food, now switches from the saloon to the dining room, where Bloom and Goulding are having dinner. Bloom is not "mashing his steak, kidney, liver, gravy and potato into one 'mashed mashed' mess," as Gordon says (1981a:70); at one point he is only mashing his mashed potatoes in the liver gravy (11.553/270.31). The order Pat takes is: liver and bacon for Bloom, steak and kidney pie for Goulding (11.499/269.11), and those are the dishes he then serves (11.519–22/269.33–37). Sounds of song and music must have reached the diners on and off, and Goulding, who may have heard Cowley's voice, starts telling Bloom what he thinks is the finest tenor air ever composed: "Most beautiful tenor air ever written, Richie said: *Sonnambula*. He heard Joe Maas sing that one night" (11.610–11/272.09–10). Goulding is always talking in superlatives; his later remark to Bloom, "Grandest number in the whole

opera" (11.828/278.14), seems to be one of his stock phrases, as Stephen
Dedalus, a nephew of his, remembers: "He drones bars of Ferrando's *aria
di sortita*. The grandest number, Stephen, in the whole opera. Listen. His
tuneful whistle sounds again, finely shaded, with rushes of the air, his
fists bigdrumming on his padded knees" (3.100–103/39.28–31).

Meanwhile, Bloom is studying Goulding's sickly face (the man suffers
from Bright's disease) and not listening too attentively to his words:
"Tenderly Bloom over liverless bacon saw the tightened features strain"
(11.614/272.13–14). A little later, while Goulding is still talking about
this air from Bellini's opera, we see Bloom again glancing at Goulding's
face, remembering the jolly fellow Richie once was: "Bloom askance over
liverless saw. Face of the all is lost. Rollicking Richie once" (11.646–
47/273.09–10). The repeated "over liverless (bacon) saw" seems to
suggest that it is the same face Bloom is looking at in both passages.
There is no need to install a wall mirror not mentioned before and to
assume that Bloom is looking at his own face, as Blamires does in his
summary of this scene: "Bloom catches sight of his own dejected face in
the wall mirror" (1966:113). The harping on "liverless" may signify
that Bloom does not eat his bacon (not kosher?). Anyway, when Bloom
gets around to asking Goulding: "Which air is that?" the answer he gets
is, "*All is lost now*" (11.629/272.32). This aria, I would like to stress, is
mentioned only, it is not being sung. It is obvious that the words as such
(in the original: Tutto è sciolto, title of one of the poems in Joyce's *Pomes
Penyeach*) have a special significance for Bloom, who cannot help being
conscious that just now Boylan is on his way to Molly and that the course
of events cannot be stopped: All is lost now.

Just as Stephen remembers uncle Richie whistling this *aria di sortita*
from Verdi's *Il Trovatore* (an *entry* not an *exit* song, as Gifford [1974:35]
has it), so Goulding now whistles the tune from Bellini's *La Sonnambula*, so
as to make Bloom understand which air he is referring to. Having listened a
little while, his mind still lingering on a few details from the opera's plot
which he now remembers, Bloom concedes that it is a beautiful tune: "A
beautiful air, said Bloom lost Leopold. I know it well" (11.642/273.05), a
remark that would have been pointless if the air were already being sung at
that very moment.

Cowley finishes the prelude. The moment Dedalus breaks into song,
Richie Goulding recognizes his still beautiful voice, and at a sign from
Bloom the waiter sets the door to the bar ajar (11.663–72/273.28–38).
Bloom will be intensely moved by Dedalus's singing of Lionel's air; the
voice, he thinks, is a lamentation (11.793/277.13), it reminds him of the
night "when first he saw" Molly and love was born. Noon quotes
"Glorious tone he has still," holding that this is what Bloom says to

Goulding (1972:80), but in my view those words are not spoken aloud. The whole paragraph (11.695–700/274.23–29) is unmistakably interior monologue.

In his summary of this scene, Blamires has Bloom's fingers winding and unwinding "an elastic band in his pocket" (1966:113). In the text, however, there is no mention of a *pocket;* there is, instead, a *packet,* the one that contains the two sheets of notepaper and the two envelopes Bloom has just bought in Daly's (11.295/263.32), held together by a catgut band. It follows that Bloom, later, will not be "extracting the notepaper from his pocket," as Blamires phrases it (1966:115); he will simply take out one sheet and one envelope from his packet, as is apparent from the interior monologue that accompanies his more or less absent-minded conversation with Goulding (11.824–27/278.09–13), specifically from his thought "Take out sheet notepaper, envelope: unconcerned."

Moreover, the order of the winding and unwinding process is different from that suggested in Blamires's paraphrase. Bloom starts by *unwinding* the band: "Bloom unwound slowly the elastic band of his packet" (11.681–82/274.06–7). He then begins *winding* and generally playing with it: "Bloom wound a skein round four forkfingers, stretched it, relaxed, and wound it round his troubled double, fourfold, in octave, gyved them fast" (11.682–84/274.08–10). If this means that Bloom is winding the band, more than once, round eight fingers, four on each hand—and I think it means just that—it is obvious that this is a feat he could not have managed in his pocket, with one hand.

There is more to these seemingly trivial errors than meets the eye. In Blamires's summary the reader loses track of the catgut band altogether, but in the text the way it suffers at Bloom's hands plays an important role, acting as it does as a kind of safety valve for Bloom's emotions and his mounting tension while he is listening to the aria from *Martha*, or, anyway, as a signal to be interpreted as such by the sensitive reader.

Bloom, indeed, does not stop manipulating the catgut band: "Bloom looped, unlooped, noded, disnoded" (11.704/274.34), but, in the silence following Simon Dedalus's last soaring notes and the ensuing applause, his tension slowly ebbs away (note his "slack fingers"): "Bloom ungyved his crisscrossed hands and with slack fingers plucked the slender catgut thong. He drew and plucked. It buzz, it twanged" (11.795–96/277.15–17). Still, musing on the song's theme, the "lost one," and in general on the more cruel aspects of human life, on separation and sudden death, Bloom feels his tension rising again: "Yet more Bloom stretched his string" (11.802–3/277.23–24), reaching a climax when he applies these themes to his own situation. Dedalus, who was present at Dignam's funeral that very morning, is now singing lustily; likewise, Bloom will soon be forgotten after his death and then, who knows, Molly might even marry Boylan, but that bounder will tire of her and leave her and then *she* will suffer: "Gone. They sing. Forgotten. I too. And one day she with. Leave her: get tired. Suffer then" (11.806–8/277.28–30). At least, that is how I read this passage, but, as so often in *Ulysses*, there is room for another interpretation. French concludes from Bloom's interior monologue that he *is angry with Molly* (1976:165), but whereas I quote lines 806–8/ 28–30, her quotation comprises lines 807–9/29–31 (beginning with "Leave her: get tired"), and thus the meaning of the preceding phrases, "Forgotten, etc.," is left unexplained. French's alternative interpretation seems to imply that it will not be Boylan but rather Bloom himself who might decide to leave Molly some day. But, then, what is he waiting for? He knows quite well—in fact, he tells himself all the time—that Molly's affair with Boylan is already in full swing, so the notion of Bloom waiting till "one day she with" before leaving her does not make sense.

Anyway, whether Bloom is angry with Molly or, instead, is pitying her for the unhappiness that may be in store for her, the rational thought that too much happiness might be boring is not convincing enough to appease the turmoil in his mind. On the contrary, it reminds him of the question Martha Clifford asked him in her latest letter (5.246/77.38), and this breaks the spell: "Yet too much happy bores. He stretched more, more. Are you not happy in your? Twang. It snapped" (11.810–11/277.32–33). As signaled by the snapping of the band, the tension is released in the same moment when Boylan is nearing Eccles Street, where Molly is waiting for him: "Jingle into Dorset street" (11.812/ 277.34). Bloom's thoughts switch from Molly to Martha. Remembering that he owes her an answer: "Better write it here" (11.821/278.05), he gets ready for his task while thinking of what he is going to reply and making noncommittal remarks to Goulding all at once; the crisis having passed, he can now tear or crumble to pieces the remains of the elastic band that had provided an outlet for the uproar of his emotions: "Yes, Mr Bloom said, teasing the curling catgut line. It certainly is. Few lines will do. My present. All that Italian florid music is. Who is this wrote? Know the name you know better. Take out sheet notepaper, envelope: unconcerned. It's so characteristic" (11.824–27/278.09–13).

Dedalus's performance is followed by a pause in which there is some talking and drinking, and in which Bloom writes his letter to Martha. He decides to leave but is arrested by renewed sounds from the music room, where "Bob Cowley's outstretched talons griped the black deepsounding chords" (11.998–99/283.06–7). Ben Dollard has been prevailed upon to sing a popular sentimental ballad, "The Croppy Boy," and the episode's last vocal number is going to be heard. Bloom stays to listen to the end, taking care, however, to get out before singers and listeners come crowding into the bar.

When Bloom has his doubts about the possibly too poetical tone of the postscript he has added to his letter, he is quick to attribute this impulse, this fancy that took him, to the influence of the music he has been exposed to: "Too poetical that about the sad. Music did that. Music hath charms. Shakespeare said. Quotations every day in the year. To be or not to be. Wisdom while you wait" (11.904–6/280.23–25). The phrase that Bloom ascribes to Shakespeare, erroneously, sticks in his mind and is transformed into a pun a few pages later. Listening to Ben Dollard's singing of the ballad of the young rebel, and conscious that all around him staff as well as customers are listening too, Bloom starts wondering what people may think when they hear music (11.1049ff./284.25ff.). He remembers a night at the theater when he looked down from a box upon the orchestra, and he also remembers the associations he had at the time, as when the concert piano, its flap having been raised, reminded him of a yawning crocodile's mouth, and the *charms* music is said to have (note the archaic "hath"!) turn into *jaws* in his interior monologue: "Semigrand open crocodile music hath jaws" (11.1054–55/284.31–32).

The "music hath charms" passage quoted above is followed by a brief, puzzling paragraph that looks curiously out of place here: "In Gerard's rosery of Fetter lane he walks, greyedauburn. One life is all. One body. Do. But do" (11.907–8/280.26–27). These lines echo, with slight variations, a passage in Stephen Dedalus's interior monologue in the library episode in which he imagines Shakespeare walking in a certain London neighborhood: "Do and do. Thing done. In a rosery of Fetter lane of Gerard, herbalist, he walks, greyedauburn . . . One life is all. One body. Do. But do" (9.651–53/202.09–12). After this passage Bloom's interior monologue continues as if there had not been any interruption at all. And, of course, there has not, not in Bloom's thoughts at any rate.

Neither Thornton nor Gifford was in a position to explain how Stephen—or rather Joyce—could have known about Shakespeare's connection with Gerard. Since then, Ellmann has discovered that among the books Joyce had in his flat in Trieste there was a small volume called *A Day with William Shakespeare*, which must have been Joyce's source. It was written by a "Maurice Clare," which was, as Ellmann informs us, "the pseudonym of a prolific writer of the period named May Byron" (1977:59), and it had been published in 1913. As Ellmann points out, it is this Maurice Clare who speaks of the fine garden Gerard had in Fetter Lane and who has Shakespeare call on him.

Critics, as might be expected, have been mystified by this strange, unexplained authorial intrusion, based, it seems, on a conspiracy between author and reader, who are the only ones to know of the earlier event the passage alludes to. We should consider that Stephen's original statement had been reshaped before it was transplanted. Having undergone a process of alienation, it can no longer be called Stephen's thought as soon as it finds itself interpolated in Bloom's interior monologue—without being part of it, properly speaking—in an episode in which Stephen is not present at all, apart from being referred to briefly by Lenehan (11.253ff./262.26ff.). As I see it, the passage is an ironic aside on the author's part, directed at Stephen as the latter has appeared in the library scene. Bloom has been thinking of Shakespeare as a useful supplier of quotations ("Wisdom while you wait"), and the author takes time off to interrupt Bloom's thoughts in order to mock Stephen, warning the reader that the younger man in his role of Shakespeare exegete should not be taken any more seriously than Bloom, who knows Shakespeare mainly or perhaps exclusively through quotations. The irony of the situation is enhanced by Bloom's next thought, "Done anyhow" (11.909/280.28): Whether Stephen will give heed to his (or Shakespeare's) injunctions, "Do and do" or "Do. But do," remains to be seen, but Bloom cannot be accused of shirking what he considers his duty; he does not need Shakespeare's wisdom to tell him what to do.

Groden also rejects the view that the "Fetter lane" passage might be meant to reside in Bloom's mind. He thinks it more likely that "it represents another announcement by the narrator of his own power to make connections between elements in the book." This passage, as he sees it, does not link Bloom and Stephen, but Bloom and Shakespeare, cuckolded men both of them, and he concludes: "It is an assertion of the narrator's independence, his freedom to use any material already part of the book and to make any connections or juxtapositions he chooses" (1977:42). And, I might add, it certainly offers enough scope for us to assert the critic's independence in this respect.

EPISODE TWELVE
"Cyclops"

DUE TO its unusual narrative structure, "Cyclops" confronts the reader with specific interpretative problems. There seem to be two radically different narrative instances or "alternating voices," as Topia (1976:363) puts it. On the one hand, we have a first-person narrative, an eyewitness report by what may well turn out to be an unreliable witness; on the other, we find blocks of text of a heterogeneous nature and varying length interrupting the narrative flow from time to time.

Basically, Sultan discerns a similar dichotomy (1964:232ff.), but, apart from the I-narrative proper, he bundles the dialogues and the comments to the listener into a subcategory of their own. Together with the interpolations, he thus comes near to distinguishing three planes of utterance: first-person narrative; dialogue and comment; and interpolations.

In Hayman's view as well the episode develops on three levels (1971:176). On the first we witness the events (including dialogue) that take place in the pub, as reported by the anonymous narrator; on the second there are the same narrator's cynical comments; and on the third we find the thirty-odd violently contrasting interpolations that must be attributed to a stage manager or "manipulator."

All this may be relevant in some ways, but it would certainly simplify and at the same time clarify matters if we just viewed this episode as consisting of two different kinds of text: a *spoken* eyewitness account (faithfully taken down in writing) and a series of interpolations which are parodies of *written* texts.

Whatever term we may apply to these interpolations, it is obvious that their language is wholly different from that of the narrative background and that among themselves they are not homogeneous either; Senn calls them "heteroglossic parodistic passages" (1974b:34). Although these passages intrude upon the narrative, they cannot be said to appear out of the blue. There is always some link with the narrative or dialogue immediately preceding the insertion. The action in the pub then seems to be told all over again in the parodied styles of Irish legend, medieval romance, scientific proceedings, or newspaper accounts; elsewhere a chance remark gives rise to an absurdistic report of a spiritualistic séance; and when the Citizen—an anti-British fanatic—takes out his handkerchief, there follows a florid description (12.1438–64/331.39–332.28) of a "muchtreasured and intricately embroidered ancient Irish facecloth."

As Staples observes, this episode is "a dramatic representation of xenophobic Fenianism" (1976:393). In a discussion of the opening paragraphs, he demonstrates that the names of streets and buildings mentioned there cannot have been taken at random: "Joyce furnishes the reader with the precise denotative names of persons and places; the range of connotative resonances thus embedded in the texture of his work is limited only by the reader's knowledge of the city of Dublin and . . . of the chronicle of Irish martyrdom" (1976:398–99).

The opening word of the episode ("I"), occurring as it does outside dialogue or interior monologue, already implies the fictional presence of a narrator, and the reader may well ask: "Who is this figure that is telling the story, and to whom is he telling it?" and: "When is he doing so and where?" We shall find, however, that the teller's identity is not going to be disclosed: He will remain nameless (nobody addresses him by his name, as he himself addresses Joe Hynes and Alf Bergan by theirs) and so will the silent listener. Appearing, phantomlike, at Bloom's trial in "Circe," the narrator is still "a Nameless One" with a "featureless face" (15.1143/470.03–4). He gives himself away as being identical with the "Cyclops" narrator by using such phrases as "Gob, he organised her," harking back to his sardonic comments on Molly Bloom's affair with Boylan (12.996–1002/319.28–36).

There are a few bits of information, though, which the reader may have access to. From the narrator's own words we know that he is a "collector of bad and doubtful debts," and from his behavior it is obvious that he is a pub-crawler, constantly expecting other customers to offer him drinks without ever reciprocating the courtesy. Most important, however, is his apparent knack of picking up any bit of gossip to be heard in Dublin, and the eagerness with which he passes the information on to anybody who may be induced to buy him a drink. The reader should be warned, though, not to take what the narrator says at face value, because, as Ellmann points out, "Much of what he claims to know is false, as his evident relish in every malicious tidbit implies" (1972:110).

In telling his story of what happened in the pub, the narrator has to quote what the customers said in his presence, and he does so quite extensively sometimes. This type of quotation may be considered a relict of what Glowinski calls "the standard novelistic model, where dialogue ceases to be only a natural phenomenon, but also becomes one of the indicators of the novelistic world, a certain novelistic signal" (1977:109). The listener—and there has to be a listener—is not in a position to check the facts; he has to accept the narrator as a kind of omniscient author and to stop marveling at the teller's prodigious memory.

Attempts have been made to identify the nameless one. Raleigh (1977b:144) thinks he must be the "longnosed chap" Molly refers to in her soliloquy: "that longnosed chap I dont know who he is with that other beauty Burke out of the City Arms hotel was there spying around as usual" (18.964–65/765.05–7), but obviously that is not much to go on. Garvin (1976) and Schoenberg (1976) have tried to show that the anonymous narrator is none other than Simon Dedalus. Objections, of course, immediately come to mind. In this episode, the narrator is drinking nothing but beer, whether bitter or porter. This does not seem in character with Dedalus, somehow, but it might be explained away as a matter of the gift horse. Anyway, in "Sirens," when he has to pay for his own drink, he orders a whiskey. Another thing that bothers me is the conspicuous absence of the narrator's highly characteristic expletives, "gob" and "begob," in any of Simon's utterances elsewhere in the book. Both words are strictly confined to "Cyclops" (apart from the one passage in "Circe" referred to above), "gob" occurring as many as twenty-six and "begob" no fewer than fifteen times. Besides, in "Sirens" there is no sign of Dedalus being in a hurry to leave the Ormond, and, as Benstock pointed out to me, there is a marked difference between the nameless narrator's low Dublin idiom and Dedalus's wit and relatively cultured tone. I think, moreover, that Dedalus would consider it far beneath himself to try to make a living as a debt collector.

As to the when and where of the scene, both men are sitting in some pub, presumably, perhaps a few hours after the events described in the episode have taken place. The narrator has lost count of the drinks he has managed to cadge since entering Barney Kiernan's: "two pints off of Joe and one in Slattery's off" (12.1564–65/335.28), he muses while urinating side by side with the listener in the backyard of the unnamed pub, a scene Hayman refers to as the "famous gonorrheal micturition" (1974:264). Incidentally, Joe Hynes has treated the narrator not to two but to three pints in all, as far as I can see: 12.145/295.39, 12.755–57/312.42, and 12.1411/331.10.

In referring to the same passage, Sultan speaks of the narrator's "vomiting" (1964:236). In view of the circumstance that the narrator seems to be talking steadily while making water this sounds rather implausible; he is a hardened drinker no doubt, and, though he may be spitting ("hoik! phthook!"), I do not think he is vomiting. Anyway, he checks himself before revealing the name of the man who stood him a drink in Slattery's, a pub on Suffolk Street, south of the Liffey. Having finished, he remarks in an aside, commenting on his output with some pride and his customary share of exaggeration: "gob, must have done about a gallon."

Meanwhile, word has got round (Lenehan being the source of the rumor) that Bloom must have had a substantial bet on *Throwaway*, the horse that surprised insiders by winning the Gold Cup race, and that he has now gone to collect his winnings. The first reaction comes from the narrator himself, who is reminded by Lenehan's remarks of a story he was told by Andrew ("Pisser") Burke about a mean trick played by Bloom in the days when the Blooms were staying at the City Arms Hotel. The passage, in which two parallel or identical but nonsimultaneous activities are interwoven in an ingenious way, runs as follows:

> So I just went round the back of the yard to pumpship and begob (hundred shillings to five) while I was letting off my (*Throwaway* twenty to) letting off my load gob says I to myself I knew he was uneasy in his (two pints off of Joe and one in Slattery's off) in his mind to get off the mark to (hundred shillings is five quid) and when they were in the (dark horse) pisser Burke was telling me card party and letting on the child was sick (gob, must have done about a gallon) flabbyarse of a wife speaking down the tube *she's better* or *she's* (ow!) all a plan so he could vamoose with the pool if he won or (Jesus, full up I was) trading without a licence (ow!) Ireland my nation says he (hoik! phthook!) never be up to those bloody (there's the last of it) Jerusalem (ah!) cuckoos.
>
> (12.1561–72/335.24–37)

In her discussion of this episode, Henke has dealt with this particular scene in the following terms:

> In the midst of J. J. O'Molloy's account of Congolese atrocities, Lenehan first accuses Bloom: "I know where he's gone . . . He had a few bob on *Throwaway* and he's gone to gather in the shekels" (p. 335). Within a few moments, the Dubliners indict their victim on charges of conspiracy and avarice. They judge him on "circumstantial" evidence, having already condemned him in their minds. In the pub watercloset, the narrator ponders the case between asides on urination. He concludes that Bloom's actions must have been slyly calculated, "all of a plan so he could vamoose with the pool if he won" (p. 335).
>
> (1978:148)

Apparently, Henke has been confused by the extent to which information has been condensed in this passage, mixing up the present scene in the pub with Bloom's alleged plan to slink away with his winnings, if any, in a card party of some ten years before. The narrator's words, "when they were in the" (taken in conjunction with his "pisser Burke was telling me"), are supposed to remind the reader of earlier passages such as "Time they were stopping up in the *City Arms* pisser Burke told me" (12.504/305.40–41), in which Burke, a fellow guest of the Blooms, it seems (cf. 18.965/765.06), has been established as the narrator's informant, a rich source of gossip. The scene called up by the narrator's dark hints shows us Molly speaking to Bloom from an upstairs room by means of some intercom device, while he was taking part in a game of cards. The Blooms having announced beforehand that Milly, "a kiddy then" (8.163/155.27), was ill, Bloom could then pretend that Molly had just told him that the child was better or that she was worse (the latter word in the narrator's tale being drowned in a smothered exclamation of pain), depending on whether he was losing or winning. Henke's misinterpretation is due to her failure to appreciate the intricate way in which a certain hierarchy of reminiscences is being built up in this passage.

In the speaker-listener situation, signaled by such phrases as "Didn't I tell you?" (12.1362/329.33), there are occasional passages that may illustrate what Hayman calls "the phenomenon of dual time" (1974:264) so characteristic of this episode.

An instance is the passage in which the narrator appears to take a swig from a pint right before him while reliving the gratifying experience of Joe Hynes's offering him his first drink of that afternoon: "Ah! Ow! Don't be talking! I was blue mouldy for the want of that pint. Declare to God I could hear it hit the pit of my stomach with a click" (12.242–43/298.27–29). What the narrator is trying to express in this passage is, we may take it, his satisfaction in imbibing the actual drink in his hand while impressing on his listener the identical feeling of satisfaction he found in his first drink of the afternoon a few hours before. That situations such as these may easily be misjudged is shown by the way the passage has been translated into French and German. Morel switches from past to present tense in the middle of the passage: "Ah! Ouf! Dites plus rien! J'en étais tout je sais pas quoi tant ça me faisait défaut, c'te pinte. Dieu du ciel! ça fait du bien par où ça passe" (292). Disregarding the inherent ambiguity, the phenomenon of double vision, he seems to assume that the narrator is solely talking about the present drink in his hand, the drink he has just been offered by the listener, presumably. This view must have been shared, it seems, by Wollschläger. His translation may in many respects be an improvement upon the older one (Goyert, 1930), but in this particular case he has failed to grasp the intricate problem of the changing perspective: "Ah! Oh! Nicht lange gefackelt! Ich bin schon richtig verdorrt und ausgetrocknet, so nötig hab ich die Pinte. Also ernstlich, ich erklärs bei Gott, wie das Zeug mir in den Magen runtergeht, da hör ichs direkt zischen" (413). As we see, he transposes the entire paragraph into the present tense, thereby ruling out the assumption that there must be two parallel activities, one of which should be seen in retrospect. Obviously, his translation does not make sense, any more than Morel's does, if only because the narrator at that late hour could hardly be said to have to swallow his drink on an empty stomach.

One of the minor characters in this episode is unhappy Bob Doran. In Joyce's *Dubliners* he figures as the protagonist in the story "The Boarding House," a young man who is trapped into marriage, having been seduced by his landlady's daughter, Polly Mooney. Giving in to the pressure brought to bear upon him by his environment, he conforms to the basic pattern underlying most of the stories in *Dubliners* (Schutte, 1957:136). His shotgun marriage must have been common knowledge in town. The narrator seems to know all about him anyway, introducing him at an early stage as "sitting up there in the corner." As Barney Kiernan's is situated on Little Britain Street, this is quite a distance for Bob Doran to have walked there all the way from Grafton Street, where he was seen last (cf. 10.984–85/246.33–35 and 10.1150–52/251.15–17), especially in the state he must have been in. The narrator spots him the moment Alf Bergan comes in: "Little Alf Bergan popped in round the door and hid behind Barney's snug, squeezed up with the laughing. And who was sitting up there in the corner that I hadn't seen snoring drunk blind to the world only Bob Doran" (12.249–51/298.35–38). What with Alf's laughing (at Breen, a notorious idiot, who is passing outside) and the Citizen's dog's growling, Bob Doran wakes up. He recognizes Alf's voice and, clearly bad-tempered, keeps asking what it is all about, without getting any response. Meanwhile, the Citizen has espied Bloom ("that bloody freemason") walking up and down in front of the pub. In answer to the narrator's inquiry after one Willy Murray, Alf Bergan mentions to those present that he "saw him just now in Capel street with Paddy Dignam" (12.314/300.28). Understandably, this statement causes some consternation because all are aware that the said Paddy Dignam was buried that very morning. Told about this, Bergan keeps muttering, "Good Christ!" (12.327/300.42) and, once more, "Good Christ!" (12.336/301.11), as he was really under the impression of having just seen Dignam alive and well not five minutes before. As the narrator comments, "he was what you might call flabbergasted" (12.337/301.12). This is followed by a comic interpolation of some length, parodying the account of a spiritualist séance (in keeping with Joe Hynes's remark that Bergan must have seen Dignam's *ghost*), in the course of which Dignam's spirit is called up from beyond the grave. The action goes on, the Citizen pointing out that Bloom is still to be seen outside. Alf Bergan does not pay any attention to what is going on; he is absolutely stunned, as he could have sworn it was Dignam he saw. Bob Doran, still rather disgruntled, chimes in with a piece of blasphemy. This scene runs as follows:

—There he is again, says the citizen, staring out.
—Who? says I.
—Bloom, says he. He's on point duty up and down there for the last ten minutes.

And, begob, I saw his physog do a peep in and then slidder off again.
Little Alf was knocked bawways. Faith, he was.
—Good Christ! says he. I could have sworn it was him.
And says Bob Doran, with the hat on the back of his poll, lowest
blackguard in Dublin when he's under the influence:
—Who said Christ is good?

(12.377–86/302.18–28)

Having been warned off by the barman, Bob Doran stops blaming
Christ—what he means to say, of course, is that Christ cannot be good
because he has taken away poor Paddy Dignam—and starts weeping,
drunkenly lamenting Dignam's death. His behavior gives rise to a
sneering commentary by the narrator: "The tear is bloody near your
eye. Talking through his bloody hat. Fitter for him go home to the little
sleepwalking bitch he married, Mooney, the bumbailiff's daughter,
mother kept a kip in Hardwicke street, that used to be stravaging about
the landings Bantam Lyons told me that was stopping there at two in the
morning without a stitch on her, exposing her person, open to all comers,
fair field and no favour" (12.397–402/303.01–7).

In various respects this passage has proved to be a stumbling block to
translators. As pointed out before, a translation depends largely on
interpretation, and this in its turn will often have to rely on background
information, which may be of a quite concrete, factual nature. A few
examples: Cambon (1963:44), referring to Stephen's "Parable of the
Plums" (7.923ff./145.03ff.), should have known that Dublin does not—
and did not in 1904 either—boast a Newton's obelisk in the city center
("obelisco di Newton"), and in the German translation of his book
(1970:46) this error should have been recognized as such and silently
corrected (meant is, of course, *Nelson's* Column). Iser does not seem to
have had any clear ideas about the layout of the Martello Tower, seeing
he had Mulligan—on the first page of *Ulysses*—raise his shaving bowl *in
an attic*: "Mulligan, der Medizinstudent, hebt seine Rasierschüssel in
feierlicher Gebärde hoch und intoniert *im Dachzimmer* des Martel-
loturms einen Messgesang" (1972:311, italics mine). In this case, however, the author himself, in the English edition of his book, corrected the
error: "Mulligan, the medical student, holds his shaving-bowl aloft at
the top of the Martello tower, and intones: *Introibo ad altare Dei*"
(1974:204).

To understand the narrator's allusions in the passage quoted above, we
need some information that is available in "The Boarding House," a
story from *Dubliners* mentioned before. As Halper says, we should be
careful about applying to *Ulysses* what was written at another time and
in a different text, but *Ulysses* is after all a book about Dubliners, too, and

whereas readers may or may not care to profit from the inside information contained in Joyce's earlier work, no translator, I believe, can afford to miss any relevant detail that may add to our store of knowledge about characters and situations in *Ulysses*. Halper is right when he concludes that what we are told in *Ulysses* about Bob Doran's case history has been implied already in "The Boarding House." Looking back, we understand that the frustration the young man in the story falls a victim to, may, over the years, have turned him into what he is now, a chronic alcoholic. As to certain details revealed by the narrator, we should do well to realize that exaggeration comes natural to him. In "Cyclops," according to Halper (1969:74–79), we have an account of Polly (the "bumbailiff's daughter") naked on the landings. However, this account is based on hearsay and may have been embellished by the narrator. Although Polly's habit of "glancing upwards when she spoke with anyone" may have made her look "like a little perverse madonna," as the story in *Dubliners* tells us, there is no need to degrade her by calling her "an obscene madonna," as Brandabur does (1971:54). What the narrator says is not so much exaggeration, strictly speaking—not, that is to say, hyperbole as a figure of speech—but a particularly bitter, sneering way of speaking that the narrator affects, as when he refers to Bloom's wife as "The fat heap he married" (12.503/305.38). True, Molly is "None of your lean kine" (14.1475–76/425.19), and Bloom himself remembers her "Just beginning to plump it out well" (8.168/155.33) when she was ten years younger, although this may allude to Molly's progressing pregnancy at the time, little Rudy being on the way. It is also true that Molly wears "a pair of outsize ladies' drawers of India mull, cut on generous lines" (17.2093/730.17–18), and it may have some significance that Joyce himself, in the schema for *Ulysses* he gave Linati—reproduced in Ellmann's *"Ulysses" on the Liffey* (1972)—put down "Fat" as the "organ" for Molly's own episode, "Penelope." But thinking about his wife in the funeral carriage that morning, Bloom concludes with some pride and satisfaction that she still has a good figure: "But the shape is there. The shape is there still" (6.206–7/92.31).

As said before, translators have had their problems with this passage. Some failed to understand—to mention just this one point—that it must have been Polly Mooney herself (why else is she called a little *sleepwalking* bitch?) and not her mother who used to roam about the landings in her nightdress. I think the narrator's "mother kept a kip in Hardwicke street" is just an aside he puts in for the listener's benefit; with "that used to be stravaging, etc." he picks up the thread again, for his story is, primarily, about Polly, Mooney the bumbailiff's daughter.

In the opening paragraph of the episode, the nameless narrator tells his equally unnamed listener about a chimney sweep who passed him in the street while he stood talking to an acquaintance: "he near drove his gear into my eye," are his words. Similarly, he asks Hynes, who just then comes along, "Did you see that bloody chimneysweep near shove my eye out with his brush?" In both cases he uses the singular, "eye," an allusion no doubt to the Homeric Cyclops's single eye. In answer to the narrator's complaint about the chimney sweep's careless behavior Joe Hynes remarks, "Soot's luck" (12.08/292.09). Gifford considers this to be a genitive construction, and he explains the phrase as "the luck of a chimney sweep, bad luck" (1974:258). This does not make sense, because the remark is clearly meant as a (stereotyped) ironic consolation offered to people to whom something untoward has happened, as when they have been hit, for instance, by a bird's droppings. Moreover, in more than one country, seeing a chimney sweep is considered a good omen and touching one is believed to bring good luck. I think, therefore, that the phrase should be interpreted as "Soot is luck" and I find myself in agreement with Morel: "La suie, ça porte bonheur" (285), Wollschläger: "Russ bringt Glück" (404), Valverde: "El hollín da suerte" (I.451), Mallafrè: "El sutge porta sort" (305), and De Angelis: "La fuliggine porta bene" (399).

Talking about the job he is now on, the narrator happens to mention a Moses Herzog, a Jewish merchant. Joe Hynes's comment is, "Circumcised?" and the narrator confirms, "Ay. A bit off the top" (12.20/292.23). In both Thornton (1968:256) and Gifford (1974:258–59) the reader is given extensive information about a music hall song, whose chorus included this very phrase, "a little bit off the top," and Gifford explains, besides, that it is a slang expression for "some of the best," which does not make sense in this case, anyway. The one-sided reference to a popular song equally misses the point: The allusion is plainly to circumcision, as is suggested unmistakably by the context. In the background is the concept or notion of "cutting," as when a customer tells the barber: "Just a little off the top and shape the back." The expression may very well have had its origin in an allusion to a song, but the way it is used here shows that it has become an idiom in its own right, without, however, having lost its quotation character, the feature that turns it into the witticism it is.

The first interpolation in the episode, "For nonperishable goods" (12.33–51/292.37–293.16), is an expansion of what the narrator has told Joe Hynes about the conflict between Herzog and Geraghty. It is a passage in a kind of legal jargon ("legalese") which, as Hayman puts it, "inflates the significance of the Herzog-Geraghty affair while giving us names and other details missing from the narrator's irreverent account" (1974:268). It is, he says, one of the episode's "informative asides," showing that Geraghty bought the goods (tea and sugar) from Herzog, promising to pay for them in instalments of three shillings a week. He subsequently seems to have refused to meet his obligations, but one cannot say that he *stole* the stuff. I think, therefore, that the way the case is presented by Blamires does not cover the facts: "Geraghty stole tea and sugar from Herzog's, was charged and ordered to pay three shillings a week" (1966:122). Geraghty cannot have been charged and ordered to pay, for the simple reason that the case did not come up in court at all.

The interpolation, couched as it is in terms of a legal document, a contract of sale, throws some light on another detail as well. It may seem a minor detail, yet a translator, for instance, will have to take a decision one way or another, when the narrator calls this Geraghty "an old plumber" (12.20/292.23). As Gifford points out, *Thom's Dublin Directory* for 1904 "does not list a Geraghty as a plumber though it does list an M. E. Geraghty at 29 Arbour Hill" (1974:259). The latter is the address mentioned in the contract, but, whereas Herzog is explicitly referred to as "merchant," Geraghty is called "gentleman," no mention being made of any trade or profession. Gifford may be right, therefore, in surmising that the narrator uses "plumber" as a slang expression for "a clumsy, brutal person," although this may seem too specific. Perhaps we have to think of a more general kind of meaning, something like "old rascal" or "old robber." In this sense, anyway, the term was rendered by Goyert: "ein alter Gauner" (I.476) and Wollschläger: "ein alter Gannef" (404). On the face of it, Morel's phrase, "un vieux plombier" (286), is a literal translation, but because the verb "plomber" means, amongst other things, "infect with syphilis" (note "the face on him all pockmarks," 12.26/292.29), the possibility of an intended innuendo should not be ruled out.

Goldman observes that this interpolation should not be called a parody: "Strictly this is not 'parody'; it is the thing itself, an invoice. No one reads it out; it is in the hands of the character who narrates the events in the pub. In a manner similar to *collage*, Joyce interrupts the flow of his narrative to give it to us" (1966:92). The latter, of course, might be said of the other interpolations as well, but their parodistic nature (one aspect being that the events are inflated to gigantic proportions) is not always evident in the sense that it may not be clear in each case what exactly it is that is supposed to be parodied. But for the funny names (we recognize Senhor Enrique Flor presiding at the organ as Mr. Henry Flower, Bloom's alias as a lover), the Tree Wedding as an account of a society wedding (12.1266–95/327.01–36) might really have been taken from a newspaper, for instance. That there is more to the names than meets the eye has been shown in some detail by Senn in a highly diverting note (1982c:166–71). It should be pointed out that there are just thirty-two women in this ceremony, including the bride, and that there are also

thirty-two insertions in this episode if we take 12.374–76/302.14–17 and
12.405–6/303.10–11 together as one, a lament for the death of a hero
(Paddy Dignam!), and, yes, we may remember that there are thirty-two
interpolations in "Wandering Rocks" if—with Knuth (1976:135)—we
take 10.213/225.01 to be a genuine heterotopic one.

The contract or invoice referred to above might have existed; the debt
collector may even have shown it to Joe, but such a niche cannot be
allotted to other interpolations such as the Tree Wedding (an outflow of
Nolan's remark that Ireland stands in need of being reafforested) or the
mock-credo, the blasphemous Apostles' Creed, a clear case of parody,
triggered by a remark, made by the Citizen, on the cruel discipline
enforced in the British navy (12.1354–59/329.23–29).

The interpolations in this episode are autonomous texts, inserted by
the implied manipulator (Hayman's "arranger") and not to be thought of
as interrupting the story told by the unnamed narrator. After his
comment on Bloom's way of talking about natural phenomena, the
narrator immediately goes on with his account of the happenings in the
pub, the intervening parody in which Bloom is projected as "The
distinguished scientist Herr Professor Luitpold Blumenduft" (12.468/
304.39) being nonexistent from his point of view: "So of course the
citizen was only waiting for the wink of the word and he starts gassing
out of him about the invincibles and the old guard and the men of
sixtyseven and who fears to speak of ninetyeight and Joe with him about
all the fellows that were hanged, drawn and transported for the cause by
drumhead courtmartial and a new Ireland and new this, that and the
other" (12.479–84/305.10–16).

What is this cue the Citizen was waiting for? To answer this question
we have to go back to the moment just before Bloom cuts into the
conversation with his scientific explanation. The talk has been about
hanging and its effect on the victim's sex organ: "—God's truth, says
Alf. I heard that from the head warder that was in Kilmainham when
they hanged Joe Brady, the invincible. He told me when they cut him
down after the drop it was standing up in their faces like a poker"
(12.459–62/304.29–32). The Citizen, impatient with Bloom's explanations, and a fanatical patriot anyway, seizes eagerly on the phrase "Joe
Brady, the invincible" in order to start boasting of the past glory of Irish
rebellions. In the ensuing argument the name of Robert Emmet (a patriot
who was done to death in 1803), crops up, as well as that of Sara Curran,
who was secretly engaged to him. As Gifford points out (1974:274, 275),
Emmet was captured when he went to bid his fiancée goodbye, before
trying to flee into exile. It is his execution (actually only a series of
preparations for it) that is described in the then following parody on a

newspaper report of such an event (12.525–678/306.24–310.38), witness the appearance of "the blushing bride elect" (12.636/309.30).

Right from the start the prevailing attitude toward Bloom has been overtly antagonistic. A climax is reached, however, after Lenehan has begun spreading the rumor that Bloom must have backed the winner, a rank outsider, in the Gold Cup race that day at the odds of twenty to one (12.1548ff./335.10ff.).

Meanwhile, Cunningham, seeing that there is trouble brewing, tries to get Bloom out of the pub as quickly as possible. Fortunately, he has a cab waiting outside: "And he got them out as quick as he could, Jack Power and Crofton or whatever you call him and him in the middle of them letting on to be all at sea and up with them on the bloody jaunting car" (12.1768–70/341.23–26).

Thus Bloom is led out in safety in between these three companions, Cunningham, Power, and Crofton, who try to shield him from the Citizen's violence, just as Odysseus chose thick-fleeced rams, taking them *in threes* and lashing them together, to bear his men when escaping from the Cyclops's cave. As he himself tells it in book IX of the *Odyssey*, "each of my men thus had three sheep to bear him" (Rieu's translation, 1952). Another Homeric correspondence lies behind the phrase "letting on to be all at sea." On the narrative level this means that the narrator is convinced that Bloom is only pretending to fail to understand the Citizen's hints. At the same time, it ties in with the notion of Odysseus's getting on board and setting out to sea, and it explains the following interpolation about the ship cleaving the waves, surrounded by sporting nymphs, mirroring the car steering its way between "all the ragamuffins and sluts of the nation round the door" (12.1796/342.14). In Gifford's *Notes*, this interpolation is called "parody of late-nineteenth-century romantic versions of medieval legend" (1974:308). In my opinion, however, it is rather a downright pastiche of Homeric style, rich as it is in metaphor and simile, such as when the swimming nymphs are compared to the spokes of a wheel. In general, the interpolations deserve careful study, not only as literary samples in their own right but also with regard to their position in the context. As the above example shows, all the talk about different levels should not blind us to the existence of definite links, hidden or otherwise, between the interpolations themselves and the narrative parts, either preceding or following.

It has come to a point that the whole pub now turns against Bloom. In his absence—he has gone to the nearby courthouse to look for Cunningham—he is accused on any score the customers can think of. One of the things he is held in contempt for is that he, as they see it, lacks manliness. Ned Lambert relates how Bloom was seen one day buying a

tin of baby food six weeks before his son was born, and the others pounce
upon the subject, eager to give vent to their doubts about Bloom's sexual
potency, as the following conversation shows: "—Do you call that a
man? says the citizen. —I wonder did he ever put it out of sight, says Joe.
—Well, there were two children born anyhow, says Jack Power. —And
who does he suspect? says the citizen" (12.1654–57/338.10–14). Note
the racy, graphic expression used by Joe to hint that Bloom may never
have been able to have sexual intercourse! The logical objection to that,
voiced by Power, that Bloom's wife after all bore him two children (one of
whom died, as we know), is overruled immediately by the Citizen, who
comes up with what, even then, must already have been a stale joke. All
this seems straightforward enough, but in this pub scene the reader
should constantly keep alert for phrases such as those used here by Joe. If
not, one runs the risk of committing appalling errors, as has been the case
with at least one critic, French. In her discussion of this scene she states
about Bloom: "Almost in one breath he is accused of being unduly
lecherous: . . . 'I wonder did he ever put it out of sight,' and of being
impotent: 'And who does he suspect?' " (1976:147). In Joe's biting
remark there is no hint at lechery on Bloom's part at all. On the contrary,
it holds a downright accusation of impotence, a blunt suggestion that
Bloom, as Henke phrases it, "lacks the phallic force to do a man's job." In
addition to the passage quoted above, Henke quotes the narrator's
scornful comment: "Gob . . . One of those mixed middlings he is.
Lying up in the hotel Pisser was telling me once a month with headache
like a totty with her courses. Do you know what I'm telling you? It'd be
an act of God to take a hold of a fellow the like of that and throw him in
the bloody sea. Justifiable homicide, so it would. Then sloping off with
his five quid without putting up a pint of stuff like a man"
(12.1658–63/338.15–22). She winds up by fairly spelling it out for
obtuse readers ("old lardyface" is what the narrator has called Bloom
some time earlier [12.1476–77/333.04], and the phrase "new womanly
man" is an allusion to Dr. Dixon's medical testimony on Bloom's behalf
in "Circe" [15.1798–99/493.30]): "The Dubliners suggest that 'old
lardyface' is too sheepish to prove his manhood by treating drinks or by
putting his male organ 'out of sight' and into a woman. The 'new
womanly man' is a 'mixed middling' who ought to be crucified for the
common good" (1978:149).

It is interesting to see what translators have done with Joe's witty
phrase. Dealing with the issue of literary translation, Adams once
remarked that in *Ulysses* "there are a surprising number of instances
where acquaintance with the translation gives a lead toward an understanding of the original" (1973:139). In our context this remark is highly
appropriate, as may be seen from the way Joe's quip has been translated

by Goyert, Morel, and Wollschläger, respectively: "Ich möcht wohl wissen, ob er ihn je weggesteckt hat" (I.554), "A-t-il seulement pu trouver où que ça se met?" (331), "Ich möcht doch direkt wissen, ob er sein Ding überhaupt jemals irgendwo reingekriegt hat" (469). It is obvious that these translators have made conscious efforts to phrase Joe's insinuating remark as unambiguously as in the original, Wollschläger's version being perhaps the most outspoken. There are subtle variations in the way Jack Power's words have been rendered; Morel, to mention just one example, hints at Bloom's possible role in the matter more overtly than is warranted by the original ("Pourtant il a réussi à avoir deux enfants"), but on the whole it is pretty clear that the translations may very well be adduced to show that French was wrong in her interpretation of Joe's allegation.

In contrast, Cronin was not slow in perceiving that Joe Hynes is expressing grave doubts as to Bloom's sexual powers, but the context in which Cronin makes use of Joe's remark shows a line of reasoning that has a curious and—let us face it—somewhat irritating twist to it.

Speaking about Bloom's positive qualities, Cronin points out that Bloom is quite able at times "to assert vital truths in the teeth of the opposition." He then quotes the passage from the pub scene where Bloom, having spoken with some heat—and bitterness—about persecution and injustice, defends the cause of love in human relationships: "—But it's no use, says he. Force, hatred, history, all that. That's not life for men and women, insult and hatred. And everybody knows that it's the very opposite of that that is really life. —What? says Alf. —Love, says Bloom. I mean the opposite of hatred" (12.1481–85/333.09–14). Commenting on this passage, Cronin continues: "And he pays for this, and for similar pronouncements, in more ways than one. *It is typical of Joyce's method* that it is the enunciation of this simple and terrible truth that brings down upon him Hynes's cruel and brilliant sneer about his own abilities as a lover—'I wonder did he ever put it out of sight' " (1974:97, italics mine). This is an example of that misleading way critics have sometimes of trying to make a point by manipulating their quotations or, as in this particular case, by foreshortening the perspective. As the situation is presented here, the reader might easily get the impression that Joe Hynes's contemptuous words are an immediate response to what Bloom says about the role of love in society, but that is certainly not the case. There must have been an appreciable lapse of time between the two events, spanning no fewer than five pages: Bloom has left the pub in search of Cunningham; the Citizen has read aloud a newspaper report on a Zulu chief's visit to England; there has been talk about conditions in the Congo; Lenehan has hinted that Bloom must have made quite a bit of money at the races; there has been some gossip about Griffith and the

Sinn Fein movement, and about Bloom's alleged role behind the scene of its organization; Cunningham, Power, and Crofton have entered the pub; and the talk has turned again to Bloom (and his father) and to Jews in general, Ned Lambert recounting his anecdote (12.1650–52/338.05–8) about how he met Bloom one day buying a tin of baby food six weeks before his wife was delivered of a son—it is then and not till then that the Citizen and Hynes start, in Henke's words, "casting aspersions on Bloom's sexual prowess" and the conversation quoted above ensues. Hynes's reaction is clearly triggered by the Citizen's rhetorical question ("Do you call that a man?") and has no relation whatever to Bloom's utterance, long forgotten by now, about love being the opposite of hatred.

What is particularly annoying about Cronin's statement is the pretense of knowing all about "Joyce's method." Leaving out page numbers, he starts by distorting the facts so as to create a certain picture and then has the reader believe that what he sees in that picture has to be accepted—on Cronin's authority—as being "typical of Joyce's method." The result is, of course, that the real issue is obscured: Bloom's buying baby food at such an early stage—an endearing gesture after all—is not appreciated in this markedly male company; on the contrary, it is considered unmistakable proof of his effeminate nature.

EPISODE THIRTEEN
"Nausicaa"

*I*N "NAUSICAA," in Senn's words, "we enter, for the first time, a predominantly female world" (1974:281). This is reflected in the style of the first half of the episode, comprising some twenty pages devoted to Gerty MacDowell, twenty-one years old and a virgin, presumably. In these pages the reader witnesses what Burgess calls a "total takeover of woman's magazine style" (1973b:94). They are, as French puts it, "pervaded by the worst stereotypes of femaleness" (1976:157); in short, they are a perfect imitation of what has come to be called *Trivialliteratur* (popular literature). We should avoid, however, speaking too condescendingly about this type of writing. Granted that Joyce was somehow fascinated by this feminine type of prose, there is no need to condemn the novelette style bluntly, without any qualifications whatever, as a form of "bad writing" (Adams, 1966:152). Moreover, we should not wax moralistic over readers of such "sub-literature" (Goldman, 1966:94); they are seeking a road of escape, a flight from the oppressive reality of their environment, but that may be true with regard to other forms of literature as well. As Senn puts it: "To afford illusory gratifications is one of the legitimate functions of fiction, of higher literature no less than of Gerty's favourite reading matter" (1974:280).

Particularly persistent has proved the term *cheap*, whatever that may mean. It seems to come to mind readily whenever critics try to define the type of writing upon which the style of Gerty's thoughts has been modeled. It is generally agreed, in other words, that Gerty's reading matter must have been a kind of "pulp fiction" (Henke, 1978:153) or may have been found in the "cheap women's magazines of the day" (Hodgart, 1978:108). Her appreciative thoughts about "Madame Vera Verity, directress of the Woman Beautiful page of the Princess Novelette" (13.109–10/349.04–5), who seems to have given her valuable advice on make-up problems, show that the term *novelette* may have more than one meaning. It may stand for "cheap short novel," but this *Princess Novelette* (Homer's Nausicaa was a princess, after all) must have been one of those Victorian or Edwardian women's magazines so popular at the time. From advertisements of the period we know that such magazines were published weekly at what seems to have been the standard rate of one penny. It is hard to say whether this would have been considered inexpensive by ordinary people in 1904. A shopgirl such as Eveline, in the story of that name in *Dubliners*, who earned, as Gifford reminds us (1974:58), seven shillings a week, might have thought twice before spending a penny on what was, after all, a luxury. However, such girls might have been badly in need of just this kind of fiction in order to survive, mentally and emotionally, in their drab surroundings.

As we have seen, there is complete agreement among critics as to the *sources* of the style Joyce applied in the first part of the episode. There is considerably less agreement with regard to the *technique* used in elaborating the basic material, especially as to the question whether the style should be called "parody" or "pastiche."

French holds that the technique in the first part "parodies by imitation," but she has to concede that the style is markedly different from that of the parodies in "Cyclops" with their extremely high degree of exaggeration. "The parody occurs as a result of the simple accumulation of details" (1976:157), she says, which is more or less what Solmecke means to say when he maintains that Joyce forces the trivial prototype to parody itself (1969:148). According to Peake (1977:243), the style is neither parody nor pastiche, but having digested the lengthy exposition of what it is in *his* view, the reader may feel inclined to ask: If this is not pastiche, whatever *is?* Anyway, it fits Burgess's definition of pastiche: "an imitation of an existing artistic style, so close and skilful as to be indistinguishable from the original" (1973b:93). This "borrowed style," Burgess says elsewhere, is "cliché-ridden and euphemistic rather than inflated," and its language is "apt for a plebeian virgin, brought up on religion and niceness, who is eager to engage life" (1973b:102ff.). The language may be Gerty's, but the first half of the episode is nonetheless third-person narrative. The point is that this narrative is imbued with just those clichés and colloquialisms that Gerty herself might have used had she been articulate enough to use them. "Nausicaa" is one of those episodes in which, according to Henke, "we become increasingly aware of a narrative voice independent of the characters—a fictional persona whose role in the novel approximates that of the traditional omniscient author" (1978:114). It was Edmund Wilson who at an early stage (1931) remarked that in the later episodes of the novel the reader would find himself wondering "at the introduction of voices which seem to belong neither to the characters nor to the author" (1974:57). The reader, however, would do well not to start wondering or worrying too much about fictional personae or mysterious voices independent of the characters. What matters to the reader is that the resulting style is one with the easy flow of free indirect speech, without the author's pretending (as in interior monologue) to reproduce the character's intimate thoughts and feelings and that, on the contrary, the reader gets the definite feeling that this style is colored by the character's very essence, the author remaining invisible, or, as Burgess words it: "The idiom has entered Gerty's very soul and is the medium of all her musings: we stand midway between an interior monologue and a *genre* narrative" (1973b:103).

This notion of "voices" has been taken up again by Kenner. Discussing the opening sentence of "The Dead," a story in *Dubliners* ("Lily, the caretaker's daughter, was literally run off her feet"), he shows that this idiom reflects what Lily herself would say ("I'm literally run off my feet"), concluding: "So that first sentence was written, as it were, from Lily's point of view, and though it looks like 'objective' narration it is tinged with her idiom. It is Lily, not the austere author, whose habit it is to say 'literally' when 'figuratively' is meant, and the author is less recounting the front-hall doings than paraphrasing a recounting of hers" (1978:16). What happens here, long before *Ulysses*, is that we find, as Kenner says, "the normally neutral narrative vocabulary pervaded by a little cloud of idioms which a character might use if he were managing the narrative" (1978:17). Hence, Kenner adds, the manifold styles of *Ulysses*, and having asked, rhetorically: "What is the first half of 'Nausicaa,' for instance, but Gerty MacDowell's very self and voice, caught up into the narrative machinery?" he formulates the underlying principle as: *"the narrative idiom need not be the narrator's"* (1978:18).

This principle may indeed be perceived to be active in such unobtrusive phrases as "It would be like heaven" (13.214/352.01), which is Gertyese for "It would be heaven," and in this episode Kenner might even have found an instance similar to the line he quotes from *Dubliners*. In the scene where Gerty sits eying Bloom (she "could see without looking that he never took his eyes off of her" [13.495–96/360.02–3]) the narrative has: "His dark eyes fixed themselves on her again, drinking in her every contour, *literally* worshipping at her shrine" (13.563–64/361.41–42, italics mine). Here we note the same illiterate, illogical use of the term *literally* where *figuratively* or just *as it were* would be expected, and even "her every contour" sounds dubious, as if Gerty might not have been too sure of the exact meaning of the noun.

In these passages, the reader knows some definite characters (Lily, Gerty), who may be blamed, so to speak, for the somewhat anomalous use of this term, but such is not always the case. In an anonymous account such as the interpolation in "Cyclops" in which the Citizen's throwing of the biscuit tin is described as a devastating earthquake hitting the center of Dublin (12.1858–96/344.03–345.06), the idiom is just part of the narrator's, in this case the reporter's, own vocabulary. But when the reporter writes that the courthouse, totally demolished, "is literally a mass of ruins" (12.1867–68/344.14), his "literally" does *not* mean "figuratively"; it has practically no meaning at all, it only lends some emphasis to the statement.

Curiously enough, similar cases may be found in modern usage. A
White House social secretary, reminiscing about the day Charles, Prince
of Wales, called on President Reagan, told a reporter from the *New York
Times* (29 October 1982) that there had been some confusion because
nobody seemed to know for sure at which entrance the visitor was
expected. "By this time," she is quoted as telling the reporter, *"it was
literally two minutes before the Prince's arrival.* I ran down to the
Diplomatic Reception Room entrance. The rug was rolled up, two men
were mopping the floor and *the Prince's car was literally coming up the
driveway"* (italics mine).

Several critics have remarked on the counterpoint effect Joyce achieves
in this scene, establishing a parallel between the worship of the Virgin
going on in the nearby church and Bloom's "worship" of virginal Gerty
on the beach. In her detailed analysis of this passage, French, not without
a certain aplomb, says that "Gerty is and remains a virgin; the shrine
Bloom worships is her genitals" (1976:167); however, what Bloom is,
not *worshipping,* but *worshipping at,* is Gerty's drawers. For him, they
are the shrine that holds the blessed sacrament, and it is their sight that
arouses and excites him enough to make him masturbate secretly. In
"Circe," the apparition of Bloom's grandfather mentions this predilection of his. Lynch, Stephen's companion, had lifted up a side of the
slip of one of the prostitutes, and the apparition, addressing Bloom,
comments in a matter-of-fact way: "Inadvertently her backview revealed the fact that she is not wearing those rather intimate garments of
which you are a particular devotee" (15.2314–16/511.32). From Molly's
soliloquy, moreover, we learn that she is fully aware of the fascination
drawers hold for her husband: "of course hes mad on the subject of
drawers thats plain to be seen" (18.289/746.08–9), and again: "drawers
drawers the whole blessed time" (18.305/746.27). At the end, when
Gerty has left the beach and Bloom is dozing off, his confused thoughts
still circle round her underwear: "O sweety all your little girlwhite up I
saw . . . made me do love sticky . . swoony lovey showed me her next
year in drawers . . . her next" (13.1279–85/382.13–19).

The moment Gerty gets up to leave and then limps away "with care
and very slowly" Bloom realizes that she is lame; the shock he experiences marks the return to his characteristic brand of interior monologue,
which the reader must have become familiar with by now (13.771ff./
367.41ff.). Still, there are a few passages in the remaining pages of the
episode by which critics have been puzzled or, in at least one case,
confused. Such passages are found in the final pages, where Bloom
deeply feels how tired he is and where the snatches of his interior
monologue tend to become shorter and shorter. Looking over toward the
Howth Hill peninsula, he remembers the day, sixteen years ago, when he

lay there with Molly among the rhododendrons: "She kissed me. Never again. My youth. Only once it comes. Or hers. Take the train there tomorrow. No. Returning not the same. Like kids your second visit to a house" (13.1102–4/377.11–14). In his interpretation of this passage, Maddox seems to relate the phrase "Or hers" to Bloom's daughter, Milly, for he explains that Bloom "totally shies away from the possibility of a return to the happy days, or even *the possibility of taking the train to see his daughter*" (1978:83, italics mine). In fact, Milly does not come in at all. The entire scene, of which these are the opening sentences, is about Molly in the first place. The memory of their youthful lovemaking, a recurrent motif in the book up to its final lines, represents a unique and simply unforgettable experience in Bloom's life. He reflects, with regret but also with a certain amount of resignation, that neither his nor Molly's youth will ever come again. His next thought is that he (perhaps even both of them?) might go and revisit the place where they were happy once. It is a journey Molly remembers, too; it is one of those numerous memories that crop up in her soliloquy: "that was an exceptional man that common workman that left us alone in the carriage that day going to Howth" (18.369–71/748.20–22). It does not take Bloom long, however, to realize the futility of such an attempt at retrieving what is, essentially, irretrievable. Tired, resigned, Bloom now feels it is no use trying to recover the past. What he wants is something new, such as this pitiable romance with Martha Clifford. He is reminded of the letter he had been writing in the Ormond, and the address he wrote on the envelope, "c/o P. O. Dolphin's Barn Lane" (11.898–99/280.16–17), and the pointed question Martha had asked him in *her* letter about his not being happy in his home (5.246/77.38–39). This complex, the address and the question, is not a topic he cares to pursue in his present mood, so his thoughts switch to the days when he *was* happy, and he recalls the games they used to play with other young people, before their marriage, "in Luke Doyle's house" (13.1106/377.16), the association being reinforced by the coincidence of the addresses, as the Doyles' residence was situated in the same neighborhood, Dolphin's Barn. As Bloom himself realizes, his efforts at escaping (Martha, Gerty) have not been very effective; he always comes back to Molly somehow: "So it returns. Think you're escaping and run into yourself. Longest way round is the shortest way home" (13.1109–11/377.20–22).

Bloom's abortive attempt at leaving a message for Gerty—he picks up a bit of a stick and starts writing in the sand but does not get any further than "I AM A"—has had critics guessing and speculating for years, but none of them has discovered the failing noun (assuming, that is, that "A" is to be read as the indefinite article). Bloom does not finish his message, trumping up all kinds of excuses: people may walk on it; the incoming tide will wash it away; there is no room anymore in that particular spot—in short, he gives up ("No room. Let it go") and effaces the letters slowly with his boot. There is one excuse, however, that stands out as being of a different order altogether; it is followed immediately by a few phrases (more or less scrambled) that Bloom remembers from Martha's letter: "Besides they don't know. What is the meaning of that other world. I called you naughty boy because I do not like" (13.1262–63/ 381.35–37). What Martha wrote, actually, typing "world" instead of "word," was: "I called you naughty boy because I do not like that other world. Please tell me what is the real meaning of that word?" (5.244–46/ 77.36–38). The reader never learns what the word was that Martha neither liked nor understood; in his reply, written in the Ormond dining room, Bloom does not explain, as far as we can make out. This is very regrettable, because it might have provided a clue as to the message Bloom was going to write in the sand. He may well have intended to print here the same word he had used in an earlier letter to Martha, in the context of which it may have referred to himself also, because Martha wants to substitute another phrase for it, "naughty boy." Then, however, Bloom checks himself, reflecting: "Besides they don't know." Now who are "they"? In Bloom's stream of consciousness "they" usually are *women* in general; we find the pronoun with this connotation ten times within the space of about one page (13.790–830/368.22–369.25). So, the experience with Martha has led him to suppose that if she failed to grasp the meaning of "that word" (voyeur? masochist?), other women were not likely to understand such words either. That is, most probably, why he lets it go.

Having flung away the stick, Bloom sits down on the beach, presumably leaning back against one of the rocks. Before he dozes off, his thoughts revolve around Molly's upcoming concert tour to Belfast (he himself has to go to Ennis for the anniversary of his father's death), on which tour she will be accompanied by Boylan: "Short snooze now if I had. Must be near nine. Liverpool boat long gone. Not even the smoke. And she can do the other. Did too. And Belfast. I won't go. Race there, race back to Ennis. Let him. Just close my eyes a moment. Won't sleep, though. Half dream. It never comes the same. Bat again. No harm in him. Just a few" (13.1274–78/382.07–12). Most readers, no doubt, will infer from this passage that Bloom has more or less come to accept Molly's affair with Boylan. In Maddox's words, "nowhere else in the book does Bloom's mood of acceptance pass over so completely into a shrug of surrender" (1978:77). Yet there is disagreement as to the exact meaning of some of the snatches from Bloom's interior monologue. Blamires, switching from summary and commentary to interpretation, says that "Bloom's apprehension gives place to acceptance, even forgiveness ('Let him' . . . 'No harm in him'), which reinforces the view that Bloom's writing in the sand carries overtones of Christ's act when He was asked to condemn the woman taken in adultery" (1966:150–51). The inexperienced reader, for whom the text must be difficult enough as it is, should not be overly concerned about any hypothetical overtones (after all, Bloom, unlike Christ, is concerned with the adultery committed by his *own* wife). Aside from that, such a reader might easily be influenced unfairly by Blamires's careless way of quoting. By lumping together the two phrases, "Let him" and "No harm in him," which do not occupy adjoining places in the text, Blamires leads readers to believe that the pronoun "him" refers to Boylan both times. Actually, it might be argued that Bloom's thought "No harm in him" refers to the bat that keeps flitting about above his head. He had noticed the animal before (hence "Bat again"), and the shape his thoughts take (note the pronouns!) shows that he conceives of it as a male being:

> Ba. What is that flying about? Swallow? Bat probably. Thinks I'm a tree, so blind. . . . There he goes. Funny little beggar. Wonder where he lives. Belfry up there. Very likely. Hanging by his heels in the odour of sanctity. Bell scared him out, I suppose. . . . Ba. Again. Wonder why they come out at night like mice. . . . What frightens them, light or noise? Better sit still. . . . Like a little man in a cloak he is with tiny hands.
>
> (13.1117–31/377.29–378.04)

Bloom may have been just a little bit scared of the bat ("Better sit still"), but, in the last conscious or semiconscious moments before he drops off to sleep, his common sense—or simply his drowsiness—takes over: He closes his eyes, reassuring himself that the bat will not do him any harm. As Kenner puts it, "he dismisses the bat ('no harm in him') as casually as he has just dismissed Boylan" (1955:204).

Bloom may have resigned himself to the fact that Boylan will most probably share Molly's bed on the concert tour to Belfast ("Let him"), but, if there is forgiveness on his part, it will be Molly he is willing to forgive, and surely not the man he considers, as we know from his thoughts in the funeral carriage, to be the "Worst man in Dublin" (6.202/92.25).

"Nausicaa" is, as Maddox phrases it, "a stopping place in the book, a place for summing up" (1978:76), but the same passage in which we find Bloom looking back on the tiring day he has had also provides an explicit link between this episode and the next, "Oxen of the Sun." Sitting on the beach in the dusk, Bloom reflects that it is too late now to go to a theater to see either *Leah* or *Lily of Killarney*. He briefly considers going home, but decides not to, because the idea that Molly might still be up does not appeal to him. He remembers Mrs. Breen telling him (a functional meeting from the point of view of plot: in the hospital, at last, Bloom will meet Stephen) that Mrs. Purefoy, a mutual acquaintance, is still in the lying-in hospital on Holles Street, having lain in labor for three days (8.276ff./158.34ff.). Molly must have paid a visit, on more than one occasion, to the Purefoys' home, where the children were milling around, as we learn from her silent soliloquy: "the last time I was there a squad of them falling over one another and bawling you couldnt hear your ears" (18.163–65/742.27–29). Later, Bloom's thoughts by some association return to the subject of "Poor Mrs Purefoy," conjuring up the image of the latter's husband, and, remembering that the couple has a baby practically every year, he reflects: "Hardy annuals he presents her with" (8.362–63/161.11). In her comment on the maternity scene, Henke has spoiled the effect of Bloom's witticism; without indicating the source of the quotation, which, moreover, turns out to be a misquote, she says: "Theodore Purefoy, by presenting Mina with 'hearty [sic] annuals,' has reduced her to perpetual broodmare" (1978:176). Thus, the allusion to Bloom's witty thought in an earlier episode has gone overboard.

Before looking back, briefly, on the long day he has had, Bloom decides to pay a call to the clinic to inquire after Mrs. Purefoy:

> Better not stick here all night like a limpet. This weather makes you dull. Must be getting on for nine by the light. Go home. Too late for *Leah*. *Lily of Killarney* [Joyce's italics]. No. Might still be up. Call to the hospital to see. Hope she's over. *Long day I've had. Martha, the bath, funeral, house of Keyes, museum with those goddesses, Dedalus' song. Then that bawler in Barney Kiernan's. Got my own back there. . . . what I said about his God made him wince. . . . But Dignam's put the boots on it. Houses of mourning so depressing . . .*
>
> (13.1211–26/380.18–36, italics mine)

In a discussion of patterns in *Ulysses*, Senn (1982a) lists the final lines of this passage as the first of what he calls the three "major synoptic abridgments," occurring in "Nausicaa," "Circe," and "Ithaca," respectively. We recognize these lines for what they are—a very brief summary, a psychologically determined selection of the day's events so far. Out of the nine preceding episodes ("Calypso" through "Cyclops") Bloom touches only on six: "Lotus Eaters" (Martha, the bath), "Hades" (funeral), "Aeolus" (house of Keyes), "Scylla and Charybdis" (museum with those goddesses), "Sirens" (Dedalus's song), and "Cyclops" ("Then that bawler . . ."), a list notable for events remembered by the reader but left out from Bloom's recall (e.g., the breakfast scene), as well as for events recollected by Bloom but not recorded explicitly in the novel (e.g., Bloom's visit to the Dignam family).

EPISODE FOURTEEN
"Oxen of the Sun"

*B*LOOM returns to the city, most likely by tram, and in "Oxen of the Sun" he is seen entering the Maternity Hospital at about 10 P.M. in the guise of an anonymous weary wayfarer, described in an amusing imitation of Anglo-Saxon idiom: "Some man that wayfaring was stood by housedoor at night's oncoming. Of Israel's folk was that man that on earth wandering far had fared. Stark ruth of man his errand that him lone led till that house" (14.71–73/385.03–6).

There are two nurses on duty: "Watchers tway there walk, white sisters in ward sleepless" (14.76–77/385.09–10). When one opens the door to Bloom there is a flash of lightning foreboding the oncoming rainstorm. The nurse crosses herself and draws him quickly inside (Horne is one of the directors of the hospital): "Christ's rood made she on breastbone and him drew that he would rathe infare under her thatch. That man her will wotting worthful went in Horne's house" (14.83–85/385.18–21). She turns out to be Nurse Callan (see Raleigh, 1977b:164), in whose tenement on Holles Street the Blooms had lived nine years earlier: "Loth to irk in Horne's hall hat holding the seeker stood. On her stow he ere was living with dear wife and lovesome daughter that then over land and seafloor nine years had long out-wandered" (14.86–88/385.22–25). In this way the story goes on, the idiom of the narrative—and with it that of the dialogues—changing from time to time, thus spanning, in more or less chronological order, several ages of English literature.

What happens in this episode is quite simple: There is a small gathering of medical students and other young men (Stephen Dedalus among them), who sit eating and, above all, drinking, and generally carousing, in a staff room or a refectory ("the commons' hall" [14.1301/420.18–19]) of the clinic. Young Dr. Dixon, who had treated Bloom for a bee sting a few weeks before, when still employed at the Mater Misericordiae Hospital on Eccles Street, recognizes him, presumably, and invites him in to join them. Bloom starts by demurring a bit but finally accepts, feeling he could do with some rest: "And the traveller Leopold went into the castle for to rest him for a space being sore of limb after many marches environing in divers lands and sometime venery" (14.138–40/386.41–387.02).

Readers may wonder at this scene, which seems incompatible with the subdued atmosphere one expects to find in a hospital, but Lyons, a Dublin medical doctor himself, assures us that such "rowdy parties are in the tradition of Dublin Maternity hospitals" (1973:71) and that "Joyce drew on personal recollections of similar carousals when writing the Oxen of. the Sun episode."

The company Bloom finds gathered round a table includes Dixon, Lynch, Madden, Lenehan, Crotthers (a Scotsman), Stephen Dedalus, and Costello. They will be joined later by Mulligan and Bannon. The latter, "new got to town from Mullingar," is the "young student" mentioned by Milly Bloom in her letter to her father (4.406–7/66.12–14). He refers to Milly as "a skittish heifer, big of her age and beef to the heel" (14.502–3/397.20–21). How Lenehan, a sports journalist, has come to be admitted into this professional society is not clear, but the reader may remember from the story "Two Gallants" in *Dubliners* that Lenehan has developed a knack of always being present when there is a chance of free drinks to be had. In this case we may take it that he knew about Mr. Deasy's letter to the press and about Stephen's role in the matter, having been present in the editor's office when Stephen brought along the letter. So he may have pretended he just put in an appearance to reassure Stephen (but how did he know where to find him?) that the letter, thanks to him, had got into the evening edition all right: "With this came up Lenehan to the feet of the table to say how the letter was in that night's gazette and he made a show to find it about him (for he swore with an oath that he had been at pains about it) but on Stephen's persuasion he gave over the search and was bidden to sit near by which he did mighty brisk" (14.529–33/398.10–15).

Amidst the drunken discussions and ribald talk, Bloom manages to remain sober till the end. The birth of Mrs. Purefoy's baby is announced at last, and soon after, near closing time, the revelers, led by Stephen, leave the building and proceed to Burke's, a pub across the street from the hospital, where the drinking continues, at Stephen's expense, presumably. Bannon, having realized that the gentleman in the black suit is Milly's father ("Photo's papli" [14.1535/427.05]), persuades Mulligan to slip away together. The text continues: "Where's the buck and Namby Amby? Skunked?" (14.1537/427.07). These, I assume, are Stephen's words. He may be drunk but he is aware, apparently, that Mulligan ("Buck") has run out on him. Alec Bannon's name may have been too difficult for his drunken tongue, so he renders it, approximating its sound, as "Namby Amby." This nickname cannot refer to Haines, as Peake believes (1977:260), because Haines is not one of the company at all; he was to meet Mulligan later. Or was Stephen so far gone that he had not even noticed Haines's absence? Anyway, it is Haines who looks in upon Mulligan at George Moore's literary soirée (cf. 9.305–6/

192.26–27) for a moment and then leaves with the words "Meet me at Westland Row station at ten past eleven" (14.1027/412.26). Stephen resigns himself to the situation: "Aweel, ye maun e'en gang yer gates." The party breaks up in great confusion; there seems to have occurred a "very unpleasant scene at Westland Row terminus when it was perfectly evident that the other two, Mulligan, that is, and that English tourist friend of his . . . were patently trying . . . to give Stephen the slip in the confusion" (that is how Bloom remembers it, 16.263–67/620.11–16), and, finally, Stephen invites Lynch to accompany him to the brothels. Bloom is worried about Stephen, who seems very drunk by now; he feels obliged to keep an eye on him and follows both young men at a distance.

In a much-quoted letter to Frank Budgen—reproduced in Atherton (1974:314–15) and in Peake (1977:249), for instance—Joyce himself sketched the lines along which he intended to shape this episode. According to that scheme, as Atherton points out, "there are at least five processes going on in addition to the customary development of plot and portrayal of characters one expects in a novel: a series of imitations showing the development of English, a continuation of Joyce's Homeric parallels, a treatment of the growth of the human foetus, an outline of 'faunal evolution,' and a linking with earlier parts of *Ulysses*."

From the beginning, and on various grounds, the scheme has been severely censured by critics. Wilson thought that the parodies of English prose styles spoiled the story (1931), and Goldberg criticized the author for basing the episode on a "mechanical conception of literary history" (1961:140).

Critics now tend to agree that, in a sense, these parodies—or, as some prefer to call them, pastiches or imitations—*are* the story. Peake, preferring the term *parodies* to that of *pastiches* because, as he says, "they exaggerate, rather than merely imitate, the manners of other writers," does not consider them "critical" parodies in any sense: "They celebrate earlier successful adaptations of language to literary purposes as stages in the evolutionary process which has helped form the modern literary artist" (1977:261–62).

It may be true that in this episode literary expression is demonstrated to be "incapable of rendering ultimate reality," as French has it (1976: 169), but that is hardly the point. What this episode shows is that events can be narrated in any style, any kind of language, any type of literary expression, as when "the students' elaborate verbal clowning," in Hayman's phrase (1967:283), is used here to develop such serious themes as sexual experience, contraception, and masturbation. We should not forget, however, that the treatment of all these intrinsically serious themes, including the first verbal contact between Bloom and Stephen, has resulted in one of the most hilarious episodes of the book. Moreover, due to the clever display of prose styles, the reader is able to keep up his interest in a scene, trivial and inconsequential enough in itself, each new style lighting up a different aspect of that scene, reflecting changing human attitudes at the same time.

In other words, the inexperienced reader should perhaps do well to concentrate on the story as mirrored in the various styles, even if he cannot always pin down, unerringly, the authors alluded to. He need not bother about matters of biological evolution, for even experienced critics admit that they find it impossible "to reduce Joyce's details to a consistent pattern" (Atherton, 1974:320), and declare, "after prolonged search, and despite the efforts of the commentators," that they "cannot find more than a few scattered allusions to embryonic development and faunal evolution" (Peake, 1977:251). More recently, however, an attempt has been made to show the progession of months in the episode's nine-month structure and the relationships among the processes of human gestation, artistic creation, and the development of English prose style (Janusko, 1983). As to the linking with earlier episodes, the reader will have little difficulty in observing that all kinds of amusing little details, loose ends, unexpectedly fall into place in this episode, such as the connection between Milly Bloom and Alec Bannon, or the revelation that Lynch, as we learn from his own mouth (14.1153–61/416.10–19), was the "flushed young man" who, with his girl, came from a gap in a hedge and was blessed by Father Conmee earlier in the day (10.199–205/224.25–32).

Most critics and commentators have been interested, primarily, in what we might call the theoretical aspect of the episode. From the practical point of view, there are only a few readings I want to take exception to, for the simple reason that they have given rise to misinterpretation.

Having reminded the reader of the Homeric analogue—Odysseus's crew killing the sun god Helios's cattle, which is considered a crime or sin against fertility—Tindall points out that the hilarious revelers sin against fertility by cracking jokes on the subjects of pregnancy, childbirth, and contraception, which is their way of killing cows, and he adds: " '*Mort aux vaches*,' says jesting Lenehan" (1959:198). In my view, however, it is not Lenehan who uses this phrase but Costello.

It is true that Lenehan uses French or mock-French phrases from time to time, such as "*Pardon, monsieur*" (7.417/129.01), "*Thanky vous*" (7.468/130.24), and "*Entrez, mes enfants!*" (7.507/131.33). Ellmann even calls him "the parasite who speaks French" (1959:376; 1982:365), but others also do so. In "Scylla and Charybdis" French phrases are bandied about by Richard Best, John Eglinton, and Stephen himself. Anyway, even Costello's short-lived apparition in "Circe," "*A hob-*

goblin in the image of Punch Costello" (15.2150/506.13), utters a few
French exclamations, such as *"Il vient! C'est moi! L'homme qui rit!
L'homme primigène!"* (15.2159–60/506.23).

It is equally true that Lenehan does come into the picture here, but so
does Costello; it is just a matter of disentangling the situation. As
previously mentioned, Lenehan brings up the subject of a certain letter to
the press (14.529ff./398.10ff.). The narrative voice, borrowing Defoe's
style, devotes some lines to a succinct description of Lenehan's character
and way of life and then goes on to report that Costello wants to know
what this letter is about. Lenehan, addressing him by his given name,
Frank (see 14.841/407.10, and note that Vincent Lynch is addressed by
Lenehan with equal familiarity in 14.1122/415.14), explains that it is
about foot-and-mouth disease, but he himself, he adds, is not interested
in cattle at all. In fact, the reason why he had moved up "to the feet of the
table" was that he had spotted a tin of fish ("salty sprats") he wished to
partake of. It is in response to Lenehan's remark about "Kerry cows" that
Frank Costello comes up with his war cry, *"Mort aux vaches,"* and, in
case the reader starts wondering why this young man speaks French, the
narrator explains that he had been apprenticed to a brandy importer once
and might even have been stationed in Bordeaux at the time. Besides, he
seems to have been a jack-of-all-trades. What we learn of his past
(14.556–65/398.40–399.12) does not very well fit in with what we know
about Lenehan—whom, by the way, we find being referred to as "T.
Lenehan" (14.506/397.25). To return to our cows, the passage in question reads as follows:

> The other, Costello, that is, hearing this talk asked was it poetry or a tale.
> Faith, no, he says, Frank (that was his name), 'tis all about Kerry cows that
> are to be butchered along of the plague. But they can go hang, says he with
> a wink, for me with their bully beef, a pox on it. There's as good fish in
> this tin as ever came out of it and very friendly he offered to take of some
> salty sprats that stood by which he had eyed wishly in the meantime and
> found the place which was indeed the chief design of his embassy as he was
> sharpset. *Mort aux vaches,* says Frank then in the French language that
> had been indentured to a brandyshipper that has a winelodge in Bordeaux
> and he spoke French like a gentleman too.
>
> (14.544–54/398.28–40)

There is one more point to be clarified. When we turn to Gifford for
information about the French phrase used by Costello, we are told that it
means "Death to cows" (1974:348). In a similar case, Stephen reflecting
that Shakespeare "left the *femme de trente ans*" (9.1135/215.38),
Gifford at least admits that the phrase has a figurative meaning ("a
woman of experience") as well. In neither case, however, does the

annotation explain why a *French* phrase was used at all. Costello could have said "Death to cows," if that is what it means, and Stephen might just as well have been reminding himself that Shakespeare left behind a thirty-year-old woman when he went to London. The point is that in both cases the expressions used are ready-made phrases, in a word, *quotations*. It is true, of course, that the episode, in Tindall's words, is not lacking in cows, but Costello would not have employed this French phrase if he had not seen it scrawled on walls in France, where passers-by would understand its real meaning: "Down with the cops!" So, in a brilliant reversal, Joyce makes use of a quotation, a figurative expression, to convey a meaning that, on a literal level, is highly appropriate in the context. Thornton does not translate the phrase but says that "this clearly recalls the killing of the oxen of the sun in book XII of the *Odyssey*" (1968:336). Again, this may be true, but it does not explain why the allusion should have to be in French. In Stephen's case, Gifford should have given the additional information that Stephen, far from translating, quite arbitrarily, what he means to say into French before saying it, just quotes the title of a Balzac novel, *La femme de trente ans*, which happens to fit conveniently into the trend his thoughts are taking at that moment.

To wind up with Frank Costello, why is he called "Punch" Costello from time to time? Gordon surmises that Costello owes this nickname to his abnormally large head (1981a:98). It is, however, only as a hallucinatory phenomenon in "Circe" that Costello is depicted as hydrocephalic. When we meet him in such passages as 14.853ff./407.24ff., as a real character who takes part in the action in "Oxen of the Sun" (and even here things should not be taken too literally!), he is not exactly a thing of beauty either, and his skull—which may have been deformed at birth—may remind Bloom of Darwin's "missing link" (cf. "Mr Ape Swillale," 14.468/396.21), but nothing specific is said about the *size* of Costello's head. We should not forget that in this passage we see Costello through Bloom's eyes as "the wretch *that seemed to him* a cropeared creature of a misshapen gibbosity, born out of wedlock and thrust like a crookback toothed and feet first into the world, which the dint of the surgeon's pliers in his skull lent indeed a colour to, so as to put him in thought of that missing link of creation's chain desiderated by the late ingenious Mr Darwin" (14.854–59/407.25–31, italics mine). Bloom's view, we should note, is strongly biased because of Costello's rude language, which even shocks the medical students, some of whom "were for ejecting the low soaker without more ado" (14.836–37/407.04).

The grotesque, somersaulting little monster in "Circe" may remind the reader of the funny fellow in the traditional Punch and Judy show or of the title figure of the famous London weekly, but *Ulysses* itself forces us to adopt another explanation for Costello's nickname than that offered by Gordon. When Bloom ("sir Leopold") has been invited in by Dixon, he finds the following company gathered round the table in the common room (14.187–201/388.17–35): On the one hand, there are the medical men, Dixon, Lynch, and Madden (Mulligan, who had promised to come to the party [14.195–96/388.28], has not yet arrived by this time); on the other hand, there are some nonmedical revelers, Lenehan ("that was older than any of the tother" [14.173/388.01]), the Scottish student Crotthers, Stephen Dedalus, and Costello, whose status is not very clear. The Benstocks list him among the medical students in their *Directory* (1980:31;71). I have my doubts but feel defeated by the presence of a "Dr Punch Costello" among the doctors called upon to give medical testimony on Bloom's behalf (15.1795/493.26). Anyway, he is introduced in the text as Costello, "that men clepen Punch Costello all long of a mastery of him erewhile gested" (14.193/388.24–25), which may be rendered as "Costello whom people call Punch Costello because of a masterly skill he formerly showed." In plain English this may mean one of two things: Costello must have been good at preparing a nice bowl of punch, or, more plausibly, he used to be good at boxing, dealing his adversaries many a punch on the head in his time. That which Bloom suspects are traumata, deformations, suffered at birth (the misshapen ears, the dint in the forehead), may very well be explained as stigmata, plainly visible signs, of a boxing career.

In the final pages of the episode much remains obscure, even to experienced readers, as commentators and translators are assumed to be, so beginners should not expect them to provide all the answers. Annotations, it should be stressed, are supposed to give information of a relevant nature. Readers need not be told that a *rest* is a bed or couch, or that an *anker* is eight-and-a-half imperial gallons (Gifford, 1974:363). Such things are not important in the context: Dixon, having referred already to Molly Bloom's dark eyes ("Got a prime pair of mincepies, no kid"), now alludes to other parts of her anatomy when he says: "And her take me to rests and her anker of rum. Must be seen to be believed" (14.1478–79/425.22–23). This is a case of rhyming slang—already signaled by Weiss (1956)—which implies that Dixon is thinking of Mrs. Bloom's "breasts" and "bum," respectively.

There has been some confusion about a short paragraph (14.1356–78/422.01–28) believed to have been conceived in the style of Walter Pater's descriptions of Renaissance paintings. Others (Solmecke [1969:116], Gifford [1974:360]) suggest it may remind readers of Pater's imaginary childhood portrait in his *The Child in the House.* In that story a man named Florian Deleal is reminded of his own childhood by listening to an old man's tale. Solmecke holds that there are several features these childhood scenes have in common, one of them being that both Deleal and Bloom are reminded of their respective childhood days by an external stimulus. In Bloom's case there is such a stimulus indeed, but the scene evoked in his mind does not show us Bloom himself as a child, but Stephen. The confusion may be due to the fact that neither name is mentioned in this passage. To understand what is happening, we have to move back a few paragraphs. A debate is going on in which Bloom, Mulligan, Crotthers, Lynch, and Stephen all take part, and which is reported in a long paragraph (14.1223ff./418.09ff.) in a kind of pseudo-scientific jargon. Stephen concludes the chaotic discussion with some cynical remarks about maternity, directed at Bloom: "once a woman has let the cat into the bag . . . she must let it out again or give it life . . . to save her own" (14.1304–7/420.22–26). Bloom, strongly objecting to Stephen's professed views, makes a simple but sharp retort, as the narrative reveals: "At the risk of her own, was the telling rejoinder of his interlocutor, none the less effective for the moderate and measured tone in which it was delivered" (14.1307–9/420.26–29).

Stephen is silenced. Bloom's "chance word" (14.1348/421.34) has conjured up before him a vision such as has been haunting him more than once since his mother died, a vision of his mother appearing to him in a dream, "mute, *reproachful*" (1.105/5.35, italics mine). Now the vision returns, the reproach having been softened, perhaps, "shrouded in the piteous vesture of the past, silent, *remote, reproachful*" (14.1354–55/421.41–42, italics mine).

We have now reached the paragraph referred to above, beginning "The stranger still regarded on the face before him a slow recession of that false calm. . . ." This is Bloom looking at Stephen; his memory being stirred by the frown he observes on the latter's face, he remembers having seen him as a little boy, years ago, at a garden party. This must have been the party where Menton got irritated at Bloom over a game of bowls, an incident still remembered by both men (6.701/106.23 and 6.1010–11/115.16–17, respectively). Stephen was standing on an urn surrounded by the host's daughters and their "darker friend" (Molly), and Bloom had noticed that the child was looking over toward his mother from time to time. The scene evoked in Bloom's memory is described as follows:

A shaven space of lawn one soft May evening, the wellremembered grove of lilacs at Roundtown, purple and white, fragrant slender spectators of the game but with much real interest in the pellets as they run slowly forward over the sward or collide and stop, one by its fellow, with a brief alert shock. And yonder about that grey urn . . . you saw another as fragrant sisterhood, Floey, Atty, Tiny and their darker friend with I know not what of arresting in her pose then, Our Lady of the Cherries, a comely brace of them pendent from an ear, bringing out the foreign warmth of the skin so daintily against the cool ardent fruit. A lad of four or five in linseywoolsey . . . is standing on the urn secured by that circle of girlish fond hands. He frowns a little just as this young man does now with a perhaps too conscious enjoyment of the danger but must needs glance at whiles towards where his mother watches from the *piazzetta* giving upon the flowerclose with a faint shadow of remoteness or of reproach . . . in her glad look.

(14.1362–78/422.08–28)

Blamires's paraphrase of this scene bears witness to the harm that may be done by a seemingly innocent summary: "Molly, wearing ear-rings ('Our Lady of the Cherries'), Floey, Atty, and Tiny were gathered round a little boy of four or five, standing on the urn. The child kept looking at his mother with a look of remoteness and reproach" (1966:163). It is not so much the erroneous view that Molly was wearing ear-rings (I, for one, imagine her wearing a pair—"a comely brace"—of real cherries, with joined stems, dangling from one ear) as, rather, the suggestion that the "remoteness" and the "reproach" were in young Stephen's eyes (instead of in his mother's) to which we must object. As it is, this suggestion spoils the effect of the curious overlapping of Stephen's subjective impressions and Bloom's objective ones, which is one of the significant features of the scene.

It is only after eleven o'clock that time on the clock seems to become less important to Bloom. Whereas in the daytime, especially around noon, references to Boylan and the time of day keep cropping up in Bloom's thoughts, around midnight his mind will mainly be beset by "evil memories which are hidden away by man in the darkest places of the heart" (14.1344–45/421.30–31). At another level, any thoughts about his own worries will recede before his growing concern for Stephen Dedalus.

EPISODE FIFTEEN
"Circe"

*T*HROUGH the continuously shifting scene of real and imagined figures which the reader is exposed to in "Circe," it might be possible, if only just, to discern a narrative line and to recover what Kenner calls "the chain of bare happenings" (1974:351).

After some altercation at the Westland Row station, where Mulligan and Haines were to meet at ten past eleven (cf. 14.1027/412.26), Stephen and Lynch are on their way—rather the worse for drink and fatigue—to the brothel district. Moved by vague protective or paternal feelings toward Stephen, Bloom decides to follow them. Clumsy as always, he manages to lose them, but Zoe, a prostitute standing at the door, having perceived that he is in black, just as Stephen, shows him that they are inside, at Bella Cohen's, and urges him to come in too. So he joins them, takes charge of Stephen's money when he sees that the young man is going to be cheated, and pays the madame according to the tariff. There is a lot of drunken talk and some frenzied dancing. Suddenly, Stephen is scared out of his wits by his dead mother's ghostly apparition. He swings his stick, damaging the lampshade in the process, and dashes out of the house. In the street he gets into a brawl with a couple of drunken soldiers, with the result that he is knocked down by one of them. Bloom watches over him till he recovers consciousness and then proceeds to take him home with him. Lynch seems to have slipped away quietly: "And that one was Judas" (16.98/615.33).

A bare outline such as this is of a deceptive simplicity, of course. It is not clear, for instance, what happened, exactly, at the station. For one thing, what reason could Stephen have had to seek out Mulligan and Haines and pick a fight with them, if that is what he did? They were there to board a train for Sandycove, but Stephen surely had not gone back on his decision not to sleep in the tower that night? He and Lynch had walked to the station to take a train in the opposite direction, presumably, a Loop Line train to Amiens Street Station, the starting point for the red-light district. This follows from Stephen's words on leaving Burke's in the preceding episode (Denzille Lane, turning off from Holles Street, leads, via Denzille Street, to Westland Row): "Lynch! Hey? Sign on long o'me. Denzille lane this way. Change here for Bawdyhouse" (14.1572–73/428.05–6). Bloom, who must have witnessed the scuffle or whatever it was, is rather vague about it. Following in Stephen's tracks, hopefully, he is muttering: "Wildgoose chase this. Disorderly houses. Lord knows where they are gone. Drunks cover distance double quick. Nice mixup. *Scene at Westland row*" (15.635–36/452.05–7, italics mine). Later, walking Stephen to the cabman's shelter for some food and a cup of coffee prior to taking him home to Eccles Street, Bloom thinks of that scene once more. Realizing that Stephen has no place to sleep that night, Bloom urges him to go back to his father's house: "You could go back perhaps, he hasarded, still thinking of *the very unpleasant scene at Westland Row terminus* when it was perfectly evident that the other two, Mulligan, that is, and that English tourist friend of his, who eventually euchred their third companion, were patently trying as if the whole bally station belonged to them to give Stephen the slip in the confusion, which they did" (16.262–67/620.09–16, italics mine).

Some critics (Hayman, Kenner), pointing to Stephen's muttered remark, "Hurt my hand somewhere" (15.3720/563.19), hold that Stephen must have hurt his hand while slugging Mulligan in Westland Row Station, although the term "very unpleasant scene" does not necessarily imply a fistfight. Such a fight would not be in keeping with Stephen's nature, anyway (or with his physical condition). He is not even going to put up a defense against Private Carr's onslaught later (15.4745ff./601.12ff.), but, again, he did not have much of a chance in that case. Still, Mulligan may have been involved in some way: He may have tried to push Stephen away, thereby causing him to fall down and hurt his hand, for instance.

There is another school of thought (Bernard Benstock, Gordon), advocating a totally different view of this matter of Stephen's hand. The controversy between the two schools extends to another point as well, the sticky problem of Stephen's glasses. The two problems turn out to be related. In the Hayman-Kenner school of thought, it is maintained that Stephen has gone without his glasses all day, having broken them the day before, 15 June. This assumption is founded, among other things, on such remarks of his as "my sight is somewhat troubled" (15.3546/556.27) or, when he is trying to light a cigarette, "Must get glasses. Broke them yesterday" (15.3628/560.02–3). But why, then, does Stephen add, "Sixteen years ago"? Besides, a moment later the cigarette slips from his fingers (15.3641/560.18), so his failure to light it may have less to do with his defective or temporarily impaired eyesight than with the fact that he is simply dead drunk, and what we witness here, as Shari Benstock points out (1976), may well be an instance of the phenomenon known as "déjà vu." The Benstock-Gordon school, therefore, holds that the hurt hand and the broken glasses are figments of Stephen's memory; his imagination being stimulated by certain physical details of the situation, such as his failure to focus on the flame, he relives in a flash the humiliating punishment he suffered, as a six-year-old pupil at Clongowes Wood College, at the hands of Father Dolan, a well-known scene in the *Portrait* (it was not so much the pain that smarted as the crass injustice of the thing). Zoe offers to read Stephen's hand (15.3656ff./ 561.03ff.), but first she starts counting the wrinkles in his forehead: "Two, three, Mars, that's courage." He shakes his head, but Zoe persists in her fanciful assessment of Stephen's character, adding: "I see it in your face. The eye, like that," and showing what she means by frowning *"with lowered head."* Lynch, picking up her words, shouts: "Like that. Pandybat," and slaps Kitty behind twice. To Stephen, all this conjures up the apparition of Father Dolan, accusing him of shirking his homework on the excuse of having broken his glasses the day before: "Any boy want flogging? Broke his glasses? Lazy idle little schemer. See it in your eye." Zoe now starts tracing lines on Stephen's palm (15.3687/562.10). When he hears Bloom mentioning a weal on his (Bloom's) palm due to an accident he had twenty-two years ago, when he was sixteen, Stephen awakes from his trance, struck by the similarity in the numbers: "See? Moves to one great goal [Mr. Deasy's words; see 2.380/34.27]. I am twentytwo. Sixteen years ago he was twentytwo too. Sixteen years ago I twentytwo tumbled. Twentytwo years ago he sixteen fell off his hobbyhorse. (*he winces*) Hurt my hand somewhere" (15.3718–21/563.17–19). Gordon explains the sequence as follows: "His mind on Dolan and his attention focused on his hand by the fortune-telling, Stephen becomes aware of a tingling in his palm, similar to the sensation from the pandying of sixteen years ago, from the time about twenty minutes ago when he smacked the lamp post with his ashplant" (1981a:102). The reference is to the episode's opening scene, where Stephen, accompanied by Lynch, enters "nighttown," *flourishing his ashplant* (15.73/431.10) like a priest wielding his aspergillum, the holy-water sprinkler (Schneider, 1970:98)—a left-handed priest it would have to be. Again, a few moments later, Stephen is seen brandishing his walking stick: "*He flourishes his ashplant, shivering the lamp image, shattering light over the world*" (15.99–100/432.11–12). In Gordon's view this means that "Stephen impetuously whacked a cast-iron lamp with enough force to make the gaslight flicker" (1981a:187n.51). There is no indication in the text that Stephen had shifted the stick to his other hand in that short lapse of time, so, if we take Gordon's assumption to be correct, the tingling Stephen experienced must have been in the palm of his *left* hand. This, in its turn, would then fit in with the palmistry scene: It stands to reason that palmists have a predilection for the left hand when exercising their art.

In the next episode, "Eumaeus," Stephen's hand is alluded to once more, when he responds to a remark of Bloom's in a rather absentminded

way: "Who? the other, whose hand by the way was hurt, said" (16.1296/
648.41). Are we to take it that Stephen, well after midnight, still has this
tingling sensation in his left hand, caused, presumably, by his hitting the
lamppost with his stick? Or had he really and truly hurt his hand at last
when he was knocked down by Private Carr? And, one wonders, how
could Stephen's glasses—*if* he were wearing glasses—have got through
that scuffle unscathed? There always remains a margin of uncertainty.

Outwardly, "Circe" looks like a play in that it conforms to the
conventional rules for representing theatrical plays in print, complete
with stage directions. On closer inspection the reader will find that there
is only a small number of "real" characters in this play, among them the
familiar figures of Bloom, Stephen, and Lynch. For the greater part,
however, the characters turn out to be apparitions, ranging from persons
long dead, such as Bloom's grandfather, to persons who were seen in
Dublin that very day, such as professor Maginni, the dancing master;
they even include disembodied voices.

In the stage directions these apparitions loom large, acting out elaborate costume plays or pantomimes, full of "clowning," as Hayman calls it
(1967), in which Bloom, undergoing numerous magical transformations
and playing various roles, takes active part. At the same time, and on a
different level, these stage directions serve to carry along the action of the
narrative, the fantasies being "usually readily distinguishable from the
action from which they arise" (Mason, 1972:55). Not much insight is
needed to evaluate a stage direction such as "*Kitty unpins her hat and
sets it down calmly, patting her henna hair*" (15.2586–87/521.05–6),
Kitty being one of the whores in Bella Cohen's brothel, which is the main
scene of the episode: The action belongs to the realistic narrative level,
the plane of incident, whereas a stage direction such as "*Virag unscrews
his head in a trice and holds it under his arm*" (15.2636/523.05–6),
describing one of the antics of the apparition of Bloom's grandfather,
clearly belongs to the level of phantasmagoric happenings.

Gordon, running through the whole episode without confining himself to the major fantasies, tries to explain the hallucinations to a certain
extent by concentrating on "the events and sensational or psychological
processes which act together to generate them" (1981a:93–108). That his
list will provide the answers to all the riddles of this episode is too much to
expect. Such lists never do. Explanations sometimes add to the confusion, as when Gordon describes the scene evoked by the stage direction
of 15.2150–59/506.13–23 as follows: "Costello becomes, in the gathering darkness, a whirling, shrieking misbirth born through his own legs"
(1981a:98). The latter part of the paraphrase, hard to visualize as it is, is a
puzzling detail, which lacks, moreover, any solid foundation in the text.
What the stage direction suggests, as I see it, is that the revolting

hunchback bends forward and then looks back while thrusting his head
between his legs. Gordon may have been thinking of the scene in "Oxen
of the Sun" (14.854/407.24ff.) where Bloom sees Costello in real life as
"a cropeared creature of a misshapen gibbosity," who at his birth came
"feet first into the world"—but that is something quite different. It
means that the baby's breech position may have necessitated a forceps
delivery. At least, that is what Bloom, noticing "the dint of the surgeon's
pliers in his skull" (14.856–57/407.28–29), suspects must have happened
to Costello (for an alternative explanation, see the preceding chapter).

One could continue in this manner, but there would be no end to the
explaining of the myriads of puzzling details. Consider Theodore Purefoy. Even though Bloom goes out of his way to inquire after the latter's
wife, Purefoy is found among Bloom's accusers in the messiah scene
(15.1355ff./478–491). His apparition—too short-lived to be included in
such surveys as Gordon's list—is called to the stage to speak just one
clause: "He employs a mechanical device to frustrate the sacred ends of
nature" (15.1741–42/491.24–25). Of this passage, Sultan says that
Purefoy accuses Bloom of "using a masturbating device" (1964:319). It
should be evident, however, that the allusion is to the use of a condom.
Molly knows that her husband has one, as is apparent from a passage in
her soliloquy: "or Ill see if he has *that French letter* still in his pocketbook
I suppose he thinks I dont know" (18.1235–36/772.33–34, italics mine).
As has become clear in the beach scene in "Nausicaa," Bloom does not
need a mechanical device—whatever that might be—when masturbating. Obviously, Theodore Purefoy is just the man to testify against
Bloom, because he himself is far from trying to frustrate the sacred ends
of nature: The baby his wife has been delivered of just now is her ninth to
live. But why does the stage direction depict Purefoy as wearing *a fishing
cap and an oilskin jacket*? Here is another link with the preceding
episode, where we were told that Theodore Purefoy "is to be seen any fair
sabbath with a pair of his boys off Bullock harbour dapping on the sound
with a heavybraked reel or in a punt he has trailing for flounder and
pollock and catches a fine bag" (14.518–21/397.40–398.01), and we may
feel reasonably sure that Bloom *knows* this.

The fantasy scenes, queer and exuberant as they are, just have to be
accepted, to be swallowed whole, their logic being the logic of dreams.
This does not mean that the events and actions that belong to reality are
always perfectly clear and readily understandable. The reader might
want to know, for instance, what exactly Stephen is doing when he is
talking about gesture as a universal language (15.105ff./432.18ff.) and
what exactly he means by whatever he is doing. What is this movement
that "illustrates the loaf and jug of bread or wine in Omar" (15.117/
433.03), described—in seemingly precise but actually rather elusive

details—in the stage directions of 15.124–27/433.10–13? Obviously, the literary allusion is to one of the famous quatrains (*Rubaiyat*, i.e., "four-liners") of Omar Khayyám, but on the face of it that knowledge is no great help. We feel vaguely that the passage is a magic cauldron, but what it is that is brewing inside eludes us. In an audacious attempt to lift the lid of the cauldron, Brown has shown that there is much more to Stephen's stance and his words than could be expressed in the image of a priest extending his hands to consecrate the bread and wine of the Eucharist. Her hypothesis is that Stephen, Joyce's ego-projection, was familiar with a then-popular song cycle, *In A Persian Garden* (on texts from the *Rubaiyat*), and may have watched the soprano and the tenor gesticulating while singing the bread-and-wine stanza, the tenor, at several occasions, being Joyce's "rival," John McCormack, who was a splendid singer but a bad actor (1984).

Gifford quotes Khayyám's stanza in Fitzgerald's final version, but he lacks an ear attuned to poetry or to its technical aspect (meter), because in his quotation the first line is one syllable short. "Verse" should read "Verses" to restore the balance of the limping line, thus: "A Book of Verses underneath the Bough, / A Jug of Wine, a Loaf of Bread—and Thou / Beside me singing in the Wilderness— / Oh, Wilderness were Paradise enow," each line consisting of five iambs. Actually, according to Arthur J. Arberry, who edited a new version based on recent discoveries, there is no such thing as a book of verses in Khayyám's quatrain. He gives the following literal translation of the Persian text: "If hand should give (= if there should be at hand) of the pith of wheat a loaf, / and of wine a two-maunder (= a jug), of a sheep a thigh, / with a little sweetheart seated in a desolation, / a pleasure it is that is not the attainment of any sultan." Fitzgerald may have thought the meal too substantial, too wholesome, and above all too prosaic, so he substituted a book of poetry for the leg of mutton and reduced the "little sweetheart" (a boy, most probably) to an indeterminate "thou."

Stephen's first words in this episode are also accompanied by gestures: He is flourishing his stick (15.73/431.10) and perhaps even whacking a lamppost with it (15.99/432.11) while chanting phrases from the anti-phon used with Asperges (the ceremony of sprinkling the altar) during Paschal time (Gifford, 1974: 373), which, as Gifford remarks, is not identical with the Introit mentioned in the stage direction (15.74/431.11). In the Introit there is a threefold Alleluia, intoned by the priest each time on a higher note, as Schneider has pointed out (1970:98). Stephen shows his awareness of this liturgical detail, according to Schneider, by continuing, after "*Vidi aquam egredientem de templo a latere dextro. Alleluia*" (15.77/431.15), on a higher tone level, "*altius aliquantulum*," as the stage direction says (15.84/431.22). This means indeed "on a

somewhat higher note" and not "with considerable profundity," as
Gifford has it—not the only bloomer in this context. Gifford also makes a
hash of the following phrase chanted by Stephen; he translates *"Et
omnes ad quos pervenit aqua ista"* as "And all among them came to that
water," failing to see that this, apart from playing havoc among Latin
cases, will not make sense, because it is the water welling forth from the
right of the temple that comes to the people and not the other way round.
What we have here is a relative clause; it will be followed by the predicate
of the main clause, chanted triumphantly, *"Salvi facti sunt"* (15.98/
432.10), the meaning of the whole now being clear: "And all to whom
that water came were saved (or healed)," a glorification of the healing
power of water, which we would expect from "waterlover" Bloom (17.183/
671.26) rather than from Stephen, self-styled "hydrophobe" (17.237/
673.06).

Stephen's reaction, his bursting into liturgical chant, may have been
triggered by the appearance of the two soldiers, Private Compton and
Private Carr, who call him "parson," whether in jest or in earnest, there
is no telling (15.64–67/431.01–4). As Gordon points out, Stephen is
called thus because of his black suit and Paris hat; add to this that water
may still have been running through the gutters (there had been a cloud
burst an hour or so earlier), and we may be prepared to give credence to
Gordon's assumption that it is "in response to the label ["parson"] and
the rain-covered streets" that Stephen chants *"Vidi aquam,"* and so
forth (1981a:94). This may seem rather far-fetched, but, in order to
support his claim, Gordon might have quoted a strikingly similar passage
in the preceding episode: "Jay, look at the drunken minister coming out
of the maternity hospal! *Benedicat vos omnipotens Deus, Pater et
Filius"* (14.1444–46/424.24–26). It is the scene where the students and
their hangers-on are rushing out of the clinic for a final drink at Burke's,
attracting quite some attention. The evolving pattern is the same as in the
passage from "Circe": one of the bystanders calls Stephen a clergyman, a
"minister" (again, because of his black suit, presumably), and Stephen,
not slow to take the cue, immediately responds by starting to act as one.

Dialogues share in the transitions from one sphere to the other, from
outer to inner world, as they shift from the actual words spoken by
Bloom and the others in the brothel or in the street to the surreal talk in
the fantasy scenes. On the whole, however, the reader should not expect
too much psychological realism or plausibility. One example: In the
crowd that gathers in the street around the two British soldiers and
Stephen, when the latter has got into an altercation with Private Carr, we
hear two of the bystanders, bearing the ominous names of Biddy the Clap
and Cunty Kate, carrying on the following conversation, referring to
Stephen: "Did you hear what the professor said? He's a professor out of

the college." "I did. I heard that." "He expresses himself with much marked refinement of phraseology." "Indeed, yes. And at the same time with such apposite trenchancy" (15.4438–45/590.01–11). We might suggest that what these people are trying to say has been transmuted, magically, by the intellectual aura exuding somehow from Stephen, but, of course, such a suggestion does not really explain anything. It will not convince us that such characters as are presented here would be able to talk like this. Apart from these two types of dialogue, there is, on Bloom's part, quite a lot of interior monologue in this episode—comparable to the asides in drama—as when Bloom pauses in his pursuit of Stephen and Lynch to reflect: "Wildgoose chase this . . . Lord knows where they are gone" (15.635ff./452.05ff.). Passages such as this appear in print as representations of words spoken by Bloom, but the reader will easily recognize the familiar tone of Bloom's interior monologue. However, there are passages that look like actual dialogue but have no support in reality at all, as when Bloom is challenged to state his name and address by two raincaped policemen (15.717ff./455.01ff.). In this case, readers will not have any trouble in evaluating the scene—which will eventually lead to Bloom's humiliation—as one of Bloom's fantasies, expressive of hidden feelings of guilt, although the murmuring watch, passing without taking any notice of him, may have been real. As Gordon points out (1981a:94–95), Bloom's feelings of guilt may have their origin in the memory of Bridie Kelly, the girl who gave him his first sexual experience, presumably. He had been reminded of her earlier that evening (14.1063ff./413.27ff.), and now, the circumstances being more or less the same (the dark corner he is in; the wet night; the whole atmosphere of the red-light district; the suppressed fear, after all those years, that the watch whose tread they then heard might have caught him in the act), a strong sense of being on trial is aroused in Bloom.

Since Gilbert disclosed both the Homeric background and the elaborate schema Joyce had relied upon in giving *Ulysses* its structure, critics, when referring to Bloom's and Stephen's fantasies in "Circe," have tended to cling to the admittedly not wholly satisfactory term *hallucinations,* a term applied in Joyce's own schema to the "technic" of the episode. Still, as Peake points out (1977:265), although the apparitions may be presented in the manner of hallucinations, Bloom for one cannot be said to be in a really hallucinated state. The only one to be effectively scared by a hallucination in this episode—which, for the rest, is predominantly Bloom's episode—is Stephen. As has been made abundantly clear by Kenner (1974:351–52) and by Peake (1977:273), all other hallucinatory scenes seem to pass unnoticed (e.g., people go right on talking), but, when Stephen has this horrifying vision of his dead mother (15.4157ff./579.25ff.), the way the others respond to his behavior shows that they must have realized that something is seriously amiss. During this dialogue with his mother's ghostly corpse, then, it is obvious that Stephen is not aware either of his surroundings or of his own actions, but even this scene cannot be called a one hundred percent pure hallucination, because, before Stephen imagines his mother's ghost addressing him, Buck Mulligan arises as an apparition confronting another apparition.

> (*From the top of a tower Buck Mulligan, in particoloured jester's dress of puce and yellow and clown's cap with curling bell, stands gaping at her, a smoking buttered split scone in his hand.*)

BUCK MULLIGAN

She's beastly dead. The pity of it! Mulligan meets the afflicted mother. (*he upturns his eyes*) Mercurial Malachi!

(15.4166–71/580.04–10)

As Stephen told Mulligan on the top of the tower that morning, he remembers quite well the latter's reply when his, Mulligan's, mother asked him who it was in his room one day (this must have happened not long after Stephen's mother's death): "*O, it's only Dedalus whose mother is beastly dead*" (1.198–99/8.19–20). We may safely assume that this phrase has stuck in Stephen's memory ever since, and it is this very phrase he alludes to in the following passage from his dreamlike dialogue with his mother's ghost:

STEPHEN

(*choking with fright, remorse and horror*) They say I killed you, mother. He offended your memory. Cancer did it, not I. Destiny.

(15.4185–87/580.26–29)

Readers may be willing to accept the fiction that Stephen does experience a hallucination featuring his mother's threatening ghost, a vision that arises from his own suppressed feelings, no doubt, and they will find it perfectly understandable that Mulligan's cynical phrase has left its imprint on Stephen's subconscious mind, but they cannot be expected to believe that Stephen's imagination could have created all those picturesque details of Mulligan's dress. Moreover, Stephen was not even present in the D. B. C. tearoom that afternoon, when Mulligan "slit a steaming scone in two and plastered butter over its smoking pith" (10.1087–88/249.23–24). What, then, might be the relevance of this detail, the justification of its presence in the text?

For one thing, the reader is supposed to remember the scene in the tearoom, and, for another, the author expects him to be aware that Stephen did not take part in it. This means that the author must have put in this little touch of the buttered scone to force the reader to recognize Mulligan's apparition for what it is, not a genuine hallucination at all, but a fantasy or, as French (1976:189) prefers to call such insets, a dramatization. It is obvious that Joyce, as Hart points out, does not aim at creating "an accurate naturalistic rendering of what might have been in the minds of his characters in these particular circumstances" (1968:70–71). What Joyce does is to translate Stephen's nagging resentment with regard to Mulligan, and, of course, other feelings of his and Bloom's, into images for the benefit of the reader. These images do have nightmarish qualities sometimes, but on the whole they do not lack a certain bizarre humor. The episode is far too grotesque to be called "a nightmare that happens to the reader" (French, 1976:194).

The hallucinations or fantasies form more or less extensive clusters, but it is not always clear where one fantasy merges into another. We shall have to think of them as interrupting the action without actually intruding upon it; as long as they last or seem to last, time has come to a standstill.

It has not gone unnoticed that the fantasies frequently contain elements that cannot possibly be known to the characters themselves. The appearance of Mulligan's buttered scone in Stephen's fantasy is a case in point. An even stranger phenomenon is the emergence in Bloom's fantasies, occasionally, of material derived from Stephen's sphere of thought and action, and the other way round.

A much-quoted instance is the incantation "Nebrakada! Femininum!" which crops up twice in Bloom's fantasies (15.319/440.02 and [reduced to "Nebrakada!"] 15.3463/553.21), but which is a magical formula read by Stephen in a book on a huckster's cart (in section XIII of "Wandering Rocks"). There, too, the formula occurs twice (10.849/242.41 and 10.861/243.13). In this case the apparent anomaly could be explained away when we take the hint from Stephen's own thoughts; while turning over the pages of the book in question, Stephen ponders: "Thumbed pages: read and read. Who has passed here before me?" (10.845–46/242.37). The answer to Stephen's query might well be: "Bloom has," because Bloom, as the reader knows, is fond of browsing among second-hand books. That very afternoon, as we learn in section IX of the same episode, he was seen by Lenehan and M'Coy while scanning books on a hawker's cart (10.520ff./233.27ff.). The evidence is not very strong, but the possibility that Bloom also may have seen this charm that held Stephen's eye cannot be excluded altogether. On the whole, however, such cases of mental osmosis are too numerous to be shrugged off as lapses or mere coincidences; they must have been deliberate on the author's part. The reader will do well, therefore, to heed

Kenner's warning words: "This is an expressionist, not a psychological chapter, and we should beware of determining too definitely which thoughts belong to whom" (1974:357).

Whatever the source of the material used in the dramatization of Bloom's every association and memory, these fantasies' overall effect (and, we may assume, their main purpose) will be to reveal large sections of Bloom's inner life: his frustrations, suppressed desires and fears, hidden impulses, secret feelings of guilt. Not everything that is brought to light, however, should be taken literally. In quite a few of the hallucinatory scenes Bloom's emotional states, for instance, show markedly masochistic traits, but, as Maddox puts it, "Bloom's masochism is a tendency, not a definition of his whole self" (1978:123). Nor should the reader believe unreservedly all the depraved, perverse, and shameful things Bloom is accused of in the trial scene. Still, they point to certain tendencies in his nature: He may not really have written indecent letters to society ladies, but he may very well have felt vague yearnings to do so (cf. his thoughts about the lady waiting to get up on the outsider in front of the Grosvenor Hotel, 5.98ff./73.32ff.). There are two types of material in the fantasies: traceable and nontraceable. When Bloom is confronted with the apparition of Mrs. Breen, dressed in a *"man's frieze overcoat with loose bellows pockets"* (15.386–87/442.21–22) or wearing, a few moments later, a *"onepiece evening frock executed in moonlight blue"* (15.471/445.26), it is obvious that this fantasy harks back to their meeting earlier in the day (8.202ff./156.31ff.), when Bloom was struck by her shabby dress. When Bloom starts flirting with her, the reader may remember that Bloom had known her before her (and his) marriage: "Josie Powell that was" (8.273/158.31). In Molly's soliloquy in the final episode, we will learn that Molly considered her a rival at the time: "I suppose it was meeting Josie Powell . . . set him off . . . I know they were spooning a bit when I came on the scene" (18.168–71/742.34–37). This, then, is what we may call traceable material: It has a basis in Bloom's reality insofar as this can be reconstructed from data supplied by the novel itself. Similarly, when Stephen sits down at the piano in the brothel parlor and attempts to strike a few chords, he must have remembered dimly what Almidano Artifoni told him that afternoon, for at the same moment the latter's apparition rises up, holding out a roll of music, and says to him, *"Ci rifletta. Lei rovina tutto"* (15.2504/518.09). According to Gifford's *Notes*, this is supposed to mean: "Think about it. Your complete ruin" (1974:407), but this does not make sense; *"rovina"* is a verb rather than a noun here, and the meaning of Artifoni's words is, quite simply: "Think it over. You spoil everything." Artifoni had warned Stephen (in section VI of "Wandering Rocks") that he would ruin his life by not making a career for himself in singing. Significantly,

Florry, one of the whores, immediately responds to the sound of Stephen's tentative chords by encouraging him to sing something: "Sing us something. Love's old sweet song" (15.2506/518.11), but Stephen answers: "No voice. I am a most finished artist" (15.2508/518.13). Subconsciously, of course, this is his reply to Artifoni at the same time.

When THE SINS OF THE PAST rise up against Bloom and accuse him of telephoning, mentally, unspeakable messages to a Miss Dunn at an address on d'Olier Street while exposing himself indecently to the instrument in the callbox (15.3029–31/537.21–23), this need not mean that Bloom ever did such a thing, as it finds no support elsewhere in the text. It comes under the heading of untraceable material, a category that calls for extreme caution, as has been pointed out by more than one critic. Bernard Benstock, for instance, discussing the pitfalls inherent in trying to determine the precise nature of evidence in *Ulysses*, warns against "simplistic attempts to separate finitely that which is reality from someone's presumed hallucination," concluding that "it becomes necessary to suspect anything taking place in Circe that cannot be retrospectively proven" (1982:58).

In "Oxen of the Sun," the clowning was of a verbal nature: The actors in the scene seem to be sitting round the table until Stephen whips them into action by his cry of "Burke's!" Now, in "Circe," to adopt Hayman's words, "the comic is elaborated in terms of physical as opposed to verbal gesture" (1967:283). There is movement, action: The episode is not only *printed* as a drama, it *is* a drama, a "five-act drama, with a prologue and epilogue," according to Hodgart (1978:115). Whatever we call it, a "nightmare that happens to the reader" (French, 1976:194), "the dream of James Joyce" (Goldman, 1966:96), "a comic explosion" (Hayman, 1967:276), or simply "the climax of *Ulysses*" (Levin, 1944:97), an episode in which the protagonists find themselves confronted with their own dilemmas, to paraphrase Link's words (1970), one thing must be clear in the end: Gestures and clowning have not solved anything. Neither Stephen's striking or smashing the so-called chandelier nor Bloom's efforts to get Stephen safely home with him will bring about any essential change in their lives.

In a sense, Bloom's day has come to an end. His adventures so far, told in the episodes from "Calypso" through "Circe," have been summed up by the Daughters of Erin (based, of course, on the Daughters of Jerusalem, addressed by Christ in one of the Stations of the Cross). Christ's words are alluded to in Bloom's admonition: "Weep not for me, O daughters of Erin" (15.1936/498.17). Kneeling down, the Daughters of Erin then recite or chant in his honor a litany patterned on the Litany of the Blessed Virgin: "Kidney of Bloom, pray for us" and so forth (15.1940–52/498.22–499.03), twelve entries, one "for each chapter, in

the right order, and each entry characteristic and representative," as
Senn points out in a fascinating little essay in which the elusive patterns
to be discerned in this litany are expertly dissected (1982a:53–57). There
are strange overtones, semantic, rhythmic, acoustic ("Flower of the
Bath" corresponding to "Tower of Ivory," presumably, and so on), and
we should reflect that what we call a "Mystical Rose" by any other
name—such as "Wandering Soap"—would smell as sweet.

And so Bloom is going home, even though his place in Molly's bed has
been usurped by somebody else, as he very well knows or at least
suspects. When he asked his wife that morning whom the letter
was from, she answered: "O, Boylan. He's bringing the programme"
(4.312/63.29). Now, in one of his minor fantasies, his brief encounter
with Mrs. Breen, Bloom pretends to have been to the theater to see *Leah*,
adding: "Unfortunately threw away the programme" (15.497/446.26).
This sums up the situation more neatly than any exegesis could have
done.

EPISODE SIXTEEN
"Eumaeus"

*H*AVING rescued Stephen from the dangers of nighttown, Bloom guides him to a primitive nonalcoholic café near Butt Bridge, a railway bridge over the Liffey, for a cup of coffee and a bun. The customers in this cabman's shelter are, as its name denotes, mostly *jarvies* (cabdrivers, coachmen).

We seem to have outgrown the notion, popular in early criticism, that this episode's language and style were meant to reflect the weariness of the characters. Nowadays, critics such as Peake (1977) and Raleigh (1981) hold that Bloom is not tired at all. Stephen, of course, is. He is also dead drunk. As Raleigh says in his exhaustive monograph, Bloom is very much alive physically and mentally: "Above all he is overflowingly verbal, having become at last that protean talker that his wife, Nameless, and others say he is" (1981:71). There is, indeed, a kind of overenergetic, breathless quality to the episode. Bloom's words are simply gushing out of him; he has Stephen to himself at last and he intends to make the most of it. The reader should not be deceived about the outcome, though. There is a perceptible undercurrent of failure, a feeling of swimming upstream, for, actually, Stephen's and Bloom's interests do not coincide at all.

Too much, perhaps, has been made of Bloom in the role of a father in search of a son, as when Sultan sees Bloom as trying to enter into "a quasi-paternal relationship" with Stephen (1964:363). Such interpretations should be counterbalanced by a more realistic approach. True, Bloom wants to help Stephen, who, he feels, is wasting his talents, but that may very well be, as Bruns says, "because he recognizes in the young man not human but market value" (1974:382). Stephen, slowly coming to his senses, must have realized what he is in for, but all he has to offer is a kind of passive resistance to the pressure to which he is exposed.

Apart from one of the cabdrivers who reminds Bloom of Henry Campbell, the townclerk, there are two characters who stand out more clearly, more as individual human beings among the down-at-heel "jarvies or stevedores or whatever they were" (16.335–36/622.08–9). They are Skin-the-Goat, the keeper of the shanty, and Murphy, the redbearded sailor, "a man of mystery" (Raleigh, 1981:14). The former is associated with the Phoenix Park murders of 1882 in that he is rumored to be "the legendary 'Skin-the-Goat' Fitzharris, who drove the decoy cab for the getaway of the assassins from Phoenix Park and was sentenced to life imprisonment, but was released in 1902" (Raleigh, 1981:36). This rumor is alluded to in one of the scenes in which the inmates of the shelter are listening to Murphy spinning his yarns (16.576–600/ 628.33–629.19). Among them is one who is evidently not acquainted with the rumor in question, whereas Bloom and Stephen are; if the latter did not know it already, Bloom told him before entering the shelter, at any rate (16.320–25/621.33–39). So when this man makes a remark about the assassins of 1882, who had used stilettos, like the killer in Murphy's tale, both exchange meaning glances, looking over in the direction of the keeper just to see how he will react, but Skin-the-Goat does not let on that he is interested in their talk at all.

Translators have responded differently to the keeper's nickname. Wollschläger leaves it untranslated, which is perhaps for the best; to hear the Irish patriot being referred to as "Desuellacabras" (Valverde, II.239)—a literal translation—certainly sounds strange, and the French translator seems not to have grasped the structure of the compound, for he renders it as "Peau-de-Bouc" (Morel, 554), which actually means "Goatskin."

Throughout this episode there is an atmosphere of dark hints and bewildering statements, as when Corley tells Stephen that he had seen Bloom a few times in some pub on Camden Street with Boylan (16.198–99/ 618.18–20)—Corley just *might* be right, and, if he is, the reader may have discovered, as Hannay argues, "a crucial clue to Bloom's character" (1984:351)—or when the sailor tells his audience in the shelter that he had seen Simon Dedalus in Stockholm in Hengler's Royal Circus, some ten years ago, doing his act in which he shot "two eggs off two bottles at fifty yards over his shoulder": "The lefthand dead shot" (16.390/ 623.27), or when Bloom himself tells Stephen that he had met his father that day and that he gathered "in the course of conversation" that he, Simon Dedalus, had moved to a new address (16.254–57/ 620.01–4)—not to speak of outright errors cropping up in Bloom's thoughts, as when he refers to the park murders as having occurred "early in the eighties, eightyone to be correct" (16.607–8/629.28). In this atmosphere of mystification Murphy, the sailor and storyteller, is quite at home. He has his role in the plot, of course, evoking, as an adventurous voyager, Homeric associations, as well as stimulating Bloom's mind, setting off whole trains of thought, but critics have always wanted to know who or what Murphy *is*. The scene in which the sailor exhibits the tattoo on his chest is interpreted by Maddox as suggesting that Murphy is not only the Ancient Mariner, Shakespeare, and Proust, but also Joyce himself: "In essence, Murphy is a witty portrait of the artist as James Joyce" (1978:160). He gives off, as Maddox points out, "an air of fakery, but he seems the sort of fake capable of throwing off his lowly disguise and revealing a surprisingly grander true identity" (1978:160). In a sense, therefore, it is Murphy and not Bloom who "is" Ulysses in this episode. Raleigh has similar ideas about Murphy's identity. "There is massive evidence," he says, "that Murphy is a persona for Joyce himself" (1981:102), and, elaborating his thesis, he distinguishes two categories of Joyce-Murphy analogues, some relating to time and place and, besides, quite a few personal Joycean touches or details (1981:104–6).

All these, of course, are no more than hints or clues, some of which may be false. Joyce, as usual, is not going to give away anything. The reader is not even absolutely sure about the sailor's real name. There is a scene in which Murphy takes out of his inside pocket a picture post card, which he says was sent by a friend, and shows it around (16.470ff./625.35ff.). Bloom picks it up, turns it over to have a look at the address, and, finding that the card is addressed to one A. Boudin, wonders: Is this man Murphy "sailing under false colours" (16.496/626.24)?

Gordon, considering sailor Murphy "a window on an autobiographical, extra-textual story" (1981a:114), a story so large that he devotes a whole chapter of his book to it (1981a:135–55), looks for clues in the early life history of Joyce's wife, Nora Barnacle, with special reference to her Galway boyfriends or lovers, Willie Mulvey and his predecessor, Michael Bodkin, all of which points to an artistic process by which Mulvey-Bodkin and Murphy-Boudin have been fused into one character.

It must be obvious from the start that the vocabulary of this episode is marked by various types of what Raleigh calls "linguistic deadwood," such as unnecessary or irrelevant tags from foreign languages. Mostly, however, the material out of which the episode has been built up consists of circumlocutions and clichés, a really wonderful and eminently humorous collection, among which we find four instances of that paradoxical use of "literally" already discussed in the "Nausicaa" chapter, the point being that in such cases the term is followed by a phrase that is used *figuratively*. In other words, "literally" then loses its literal meaning; it becomes more or less equivalent to "what you may call" and only serves to highlight the following expression, usually a metaphorical one.

In the first example, Bloom has been listening to the talk—mainly about Parnell—that had sprung up in the shelter after the general interest in the tall tales dished up by Murphy had died down somewhat. Bloom himself has not taken part in the conversation but comments in an aside to Stephen on some of the remarks he overhears, following the drift of his own thoughts, and reflecting upon "the historic story which had aroused extraordinary interest at the time" (16.1361–62/650.34–35).

"Reflect" is the characteristic term the "Eumaeus" narrator uses to describe the workings of Bloom's mind; it usually introduces a kind of paraphrase of Bloom's thoughts (or Bloom's *words*: it is not always easy to distinguish what he thinks from what he actually says), a paraphrase not unlike free indirect discourse, but totally different from Bloom's interior monologue, which we had become used to in the book's earlier part. The figures are eloquent: Out of a total of thirteen occurrences of "reflected" listed in Hanley's *Word Index*, eight belong to this episode alone, not to speak of "reflection," with five out of fifteen.

Bloom remembers the famous divorce trial and the sensation among the public in the courtroom "when a thrill went through the packed court *literally electrifying everybody* in the shape of witnesses" (16.1373–75/651.06–7, italics mine). The discussion about Parnell and the Irish cause had started with a long harangue by Skin-the-Goat (16.985ff./640.13ff.), winding up in the narrator's paraphrase as follows: "His advice to every Irishman was: stay in the land of your birth and work for Ireland and live for Ireland. Ireland, Parnell said, could not spare a single one of her sons" (16.1006–9/640.39–42). The sailor having made a disparaging remark, a lively discussion ensues, in which one of the participants is a cabdriver, here referred to as "the cabby like Campbell, facial blemishes apart" (16.1019–20/641.10–11). This character had been introduced at an earlier stage as "one hearer who, by the way, seen from the side, bore a distant resemblance to Henry Campbell, the townclerk, away from the carking cares of office, unwashed of course and in a seedy getup and a strong suspicion of nosepaint about the nasal appendage" (16.660–63/631.05–9). When we next hear of him he is called "the jarvey who had really quite a look of Henry Campbell" (16.908/638.06–7); then, as we have seen, "the cabby like Campbell," and finally "the *soi-disant* townclerk Henry Campbell" (16.1354/650.25–26). In itself, any likeness (distant, at that) of some cabdriver with a certain townclerk seems quite irrelevant, but the fact alone that the cabby's tag is repeated so insistently cannot but suggest that somehow the name Campbell is of specific significance in the context. In a case such as this, it is not enough when an annotator simply confirms that Campbell was indeed, in 1904, the Dublin townclerk. What is relevant is that Campbell had been an Irish M.P. in the Parnell days and was the Chief's private secretary, who remained at his side till the end. As Raleigh puts it, "Joyce-Bloom's periodic reminders in the text that this broken-down cabbie looks like Henry Campbell function, as do the Skin-the-Goat recurrences, to keep, however grotesquely, Parnell and, above all, his fall, in mind throughout the episode" (1981:37).

It is interesting to see how the story of Bloom and Stephen develops against the background of the heated discussion between Skin-the-Goat and Murphy the sailor, in Bloom's "words": "the scene between the pair of them, the licensee of the place rumoured to be or have been Fitzharris, the famous invincible, and the other, obviously bogus" (16.1043–45/641.39–42). Bloom's long train of thought, commenting on the keeper's loud assertion that "a day of reckoning . . . was in store for mighty England" (16.997–99/640.28–30), ends with "as for the other he had heard not so long before the same identical lingo as he told Stephen how he simply but effectually silenced the offender" (16.1078–80/642.39–41). From the way this sentence is phrased we might infer that the foregoing rambling discourse is not a paraphrase of what Bloom was *thinking* but of what he was *telling* Stephen, or anyway the gist of it, as we might well doubt whether Bloom would actually use such phrases as "criminal propensities" or "legal luminary." Bloom having started to tell Stephen about his experience with the fanatic patriot in Barney Kiernan's that afternoon, the narrator continues in dialogue, retaining, however, the pompous, cliché-ridden style of the paraphrases, as in "He took umbrage at something or other, *that muchinjured but on the whole eventempered person declared* [instead of just "Bloom said"], I let slip" (16.1081–82/642.42–43, italics mine). From that personal experience, Bloom goes on to expound his utopian ideas about a future society of tolerance and nonviolence, winding up with what *he* calls patriotism: "*Ubi patria . . . vita bene.* Where you can live well, the sense is, if you work" (16.1138–40/644.23–25).

Stephen has been listening to this "synopsis of things in general" without much enthusiasm or any apparent interest, but at the words "if you work" pricks up his ears and reacts immediately by remarking, "Count me out" (16.1148/644.34). Bloom, surprised, points out that literary work is also of essential value: The peasant and the intellectual are equally important, as "both belong to Ireland." Stephen's retort is that in his eyes Ireland must be important because it belongs to him. Bloom is stumped and, pretending he did not quite catch Stephen's words, asks him to repeat what he said. Stephen complies but, "patently crosstempered," adds: "We can't change the country. Let us change the subject" (16.1171/645.18). Bloom feels rebuked and seeks refuge in a long sequence of thought, reported in the usual rambling style. Having just thought of trying his hand at an original sketch, such as *My Experiences in a Cabman's Shelter,* he spots the evening edition of the *Telegraph* on the table, "beside his elbow" (16.1232ff./647.08ff.). So he starts looking through the paper, confining himself to the captions until he comes upon Hynes's news item about Dignam's funeral. Piqued by finding his name misspelled as *L. Boom* but amused at the alleged presence among the mourners of C. P. M'Coy and Stephen Dedalus B.A., who had been "conspicuous, needless to say, by their total absence" (16.1264–65/648.03), Bloom points out the errors to Stephen. The latter, suddenly remembering Mr. Deasy's letter to the press about foot-and-mouth disease, wants to know whether the editor had seen fit to put it in, but the peculiar way he phrases this query, stifling a yawn at the same time, has Bloom think at first that he was referring to the archbishop's letter Bloom had heard the foreman in the *Telegraph* printing works mention that morning (see 7.181/121.30), but then he points it out to him: "—Is that first epistle to the Hebrews, he asked as soon as his bottom jaw would let him, in? Text: open thy mouth and put thy foot in it. —It is. Really, Mr Bloom said (though first he fancied he alluded to the archbishop till he added about foot and mouth with which there could be no possible connection) overjoyed to set his mind at rest . . . There" (16.1268–73/648.07–14).

While Stephen, sitting to Bloom's left, is reading Deasy's letter on page two, Bloom pores over the account of the races at Ascot on page three. He does not seem particularly impressed by the totally unexpected victory of *Throwaway*, the horse a lot of Dubliners were sure he had had his money on, he only notes that the French horse, *Maximum II*, which Bantam Lyons had seemed so keen on backing (see 5.526ff./85.34ff.), had come in last. He pities Lyons, not so much for having lost money, presumably, but rather for being such an idiot as to gamble at all: "as the event turned out the poor fool hadn't much reason to congratulate himself on his pick, the forlorn hope" (16.1291–93/648.35–37). Obviously, Bloom is unaware that Lyons had twice changed his mind: he may have intended, at the outset, to back that French horse, but, when he heard Bloom saying something about going to *throw away* the newspaper (5.537/86.03–4), he thought this a tip too good to be overlooked. So he said, "I'll risk it," and hastened to a betting office to put his money on *Throwaway*. Later, he boasts about this hunch of his in the company of Paddy Leonard and Tom Rochford while they are having drinks in Davy Byrne's, without actually telling the name of the horse he is "going to plunge five bob on," disclosing, though, that it was Bloom who gave him the tip (8.1016–23/179.07–15). It must have taken Lyons some time to reach the betting office (he may have had to borrow the money first), for a few hours later, Lenehan, who had popped into Lynam's, the bookmaker's ("to see Sceptre's starting price"), meets him there. Lenehan tells M'Coy, who was waiting for him outside: "I knocked against Bantam Lyons in there going to back a bloody horse someone gave him that hasn't an earthly" (10.517–19/233.24–26). Lenehan does not say so explicitly, but he must have talked Lyons out of backing *Throwaway*, advising him, as he did Boylan, to put his money on *Sceptre* instead, a "dead certainty." He is considerably put out, therefore, when, around 11:00 P.M., having come out of Holles Street Hospital with the medical students, he spots Lyons, who is trying to drown his misery in drink, apparently. Lenehan, feeling guilty ("Had the winner today till I tipped him a dead cert"), tries to slink away ("All in if he spots me") before Lyons gets a chance to make trouble (14.1507–14/426.13–21).

Having lost interest in the paper's stale news, Bloom becomes aware that the talk in the shelter has drifted, as he fully expected it would, to the story of Parnell's downfall and death. He points this out to Stephen, who, however, does not understand what he is talking about: "—There was every indication they would arrive at that, he, Bloom, said. —Who? the other, whose hand by the way was hurt, said" (16.1295–96/648.39–41). Bloom does not answer Stephen's irrelevant question; he listens to the voices around him of customers rehashing the old rumors about Parnell's not being dead at all, repeated again and again by people who do not really believe them. In the cemetery that morning Power, walking past Parnell's grave, had said to Hynes, voicing that popular myth: "Some say he is not in that grave at all. That the coffin was filled with stones. That one day he will come again" (6.923–24/112.40–41). So now here in the shelter: "One morning you would open the paper, the cabman affirmed, and read: *Return of Parnell*. He bet them what they liked . . . And so forth and so on" (16.1297–306/648.42–649.10). As the text speaks of *the* cabman, this must still be the same jarvey that looked like Henry Campbell, just as *the* cabby in "The cabby read out of the paper" (16.1662/659.07) turns out to be "the sympathetic personage like the townclerk" (16.1674/659.21–22). Bloom's comments (16.1307ff./ 649.11ff.), showing that he is skeptical of this idea of return, are again presented in the manner we have become accustomed to by now, the final sentence (16.1349–51/650.19–22) revealing that Bloom must have been talking all the time. There is still not much response from Stephen, though. Again, there is some dialogue between the keeper and the cabby, the latter alluding to Kitty O'Shea's charms, and this leads up to Bloom's reflections on the Parnell story, which contain that phrase, "literally electrifying everybody," I have singled out above. Once more, the passage ends in such a way as to imply that the foregoing was a paraphrase, more or less, of what Bloom was telling Stephen: "however, it was just the wellknown case of hot passion, pure and simple . . . and *just bore out the very thing he was saying* as she also was Spanish or half so, types that wouldn't do things by halves, passionate abandon of the south, casting every shred of decency to the winds" (16.1406–10/ 652.03–8). Still, the phrase "as she also was Spanish or half so," referring as it does to Molly, must have been part of what Bloom *thinks* at that moment. What he really *says* to Stephen then follows in the form of dialogue: "—*Just bears out what I was saying*, he, with glowing bosom said to Stephen, about blood and the sun. And, if I don't greatly mistake she was Spanish too" (16.1411–13/652.09–11, italics mine). Here Bloom is talking of Kitty O'Shea (whose only connection with Spain was that she went to live there for some time with her husband's relatives). It is clear what Bloom has been doing: trying to find excuses for Kitty O'Shea's adulterous conduct with Parnell, building her up into a southern, passionate type who cannot be held responsible for her actions. All this is just his pathetic attempt to absolve Molly of *her* sin of adultery. He even seeks some kind of corroboration from an outsider, taking out his pocketbook and showing Stephen a photograph of Molly: "—Do you consider, by the by, he said, thoughtfully selecting a faded photo which he laid on the table, that a Spanish type?" (16.1425–26/652.23–24).

Another instance of the idiosyncratic use of "literally" is: "Literally astounded at this piece of intelligence Bloom reflected" (16.1578/656.33). Actually, Bloom is not what you might call *stunned* at all: His brain is more active than ever, developing schemes for Stephen's future career, in which he himself, of course, is to play a prominent part. Just now, however, Stephen's problem, as Bloom sees it, seems to be where to spend the night, so Bloom's idea is to take the young man home with him. On Eccles Street he then could offer him "a cup of Epps's cocoa and a shakedown for the night" (16.1621–22/657.43). Stephen will have no choice, it seems. So Bloom gets up and pays the shelter keeper for the coffee and the bun, putting down the amount of fourpence "in four coppers, *literally the last of the Mohicans*" (16.1697–98/660.05, italics mine). This is another case of the paradoxical use of "literally" referred to above, no less extreme than the last, even more absurd, instance found in this episode. It occurs in the paraphrase of Bloom's effusion on the theme of music, in the course of which he imparts his views to Stephen (still "a bit weak on his pins") while walking with him in the direction of Eccles Street: "So they turned on to chatting about music, a form of art for which Bloom, as a pure amateur, possessed the greatest love, as they made tracks arm in arm across Beresford place. Wagnerian music, though confessedly grand in its way, was a bit too heavy for Bloom . . . but . . . Mozart's *Twelfth Mass* he simply revelled in, the *Gloria* in that being, to his mind, the acme of first class music as such, *literally knocking everything else into a cocked hat*" (16.1733–40/661.03–12, italics mine).

The mood has changed. As Raleigh points out, "when Bloom and Dedalus leave the shelter, they also leave behind the basic themes of the greater part of the episode: quarrels, violence, fraud, mystery, politics, insanity, and so on" (1981:58). Irish politics—especially the disasters of the Phoenix Park murders of 1882 and the fall of Parnell eight years later—may be considered the chief thematic concern of the episode (1981:24). It is no wonder, therefore, that "Eumaeus" is "full of disputes, public and private, actual, impending, or remembered," because that was—in historic reality—"what the Parnell story had entailed: ruptures and quarrels; violence; and finally disaster or shipwreck for all concerned" (1981:41). The result of Parnell's fall had been the same for all: *shipwreck*, and that, as Raleigh remarks, is reflected in the text: several actual shipwrecks are mentioned in this episode, and, apart from that, there are the human wrecks such as Corley, Gumley, and others. Now, however, Bloom and Stephen have left the miserable derelicts of the cabman's shelter behind them, and "all is now soft and benign in the mild early morning as the two companions, strolling arm in arm, talk of music, with Bloom thinking of it, and, hearing his companion sing, imagining the great success in store for one Stephen Dedalus, Irish tenor" (Raleigh, 1981:58).

Somewhat recovered, apparently, Stephen is singing an old German ballad, "Von der Sirenen Listigkeit." The end of this ballad is given in the text as "*Und alle Schiffe brücken*" (16.1884/665.17). Most commentators are at a loss when called upon to explain the meaning of this line. They suggest sometimes that there must be a link between *brücken*, which seems to be a verb, and the noun *Brücke* (bridge) but the significance of that hypothetical link remains in the dark. The notion of "shipwreck," introduced by Raleigh, might be of help here. After all, the words of the song's opening bars are: *Von der Sirenen Listigkeit / Tun die Poeten dichten*, and the text says explicitly that it is a song "about the clear sea and the voices of sirens, sweet murderers of men" (16.1813/663.15–16). With Senn (1975:450), we had better think of a link with German *Schiffbruch* (shipwreck) or, we might add, with *schiffbrüchig werden* (to be shipwrecked), and understand the final line as alluding to the disastrous effects of the cunning sirens' malicious doings, with, as a tentative translation: "And all the ships are wrecked."

The early morning is mild and soft, but sirens are waiting round every corner and icebergs are looming beyond the horizon. Still, as long as there is music, all is not lost. As Empson once remarked about *Ulysses:* "Music is one of the few positive arts in the curious world of the book; everybody takes singing extremely seriously" (1956:31). In "Sirens" Bloom got rid of his depressed mood by listening to Lionel's air from *Martha.* In the next episode, "Cyclops," he stood his ground when he had to face a blustering Irish patriot—we can see that in retrospect. What Stephen's singing about sirens may or may not do for Bloom is something Bloom does not know himself, and we, the readers, have no clue either.

EPISODE SEVENTEEN
"Ithaca"

WHEN readers, after the seemingly unassuming narrative flow of the preceding episode, start on "Ithaca," their first impression may well be that they will have to sit up and pay attention in earnest, for an unknown voice seems, quite unexpectedly, to be barking questions at them. This impersonal voice wants to know, for a start, which route Bloom and Stephen took when they walked together toward Bloom's house on Eccles Street and, besides, what they talked about while walking home. There is, moreover, something strange in these seemingly trivial questions: first, the reader finds that he will not have to provide the answers himself; second, he discovers that both questions and answers use a kind of scientific terminology, wrapping up simple statements of facts and events in a texture of pedantic polysyllables. Instead of asking, for instance, "What did the two men talk about on the way home?" the voice says, "Of what did the duumvirate deliberate during their itinerary?" (17.11/666.13). Similarly, instead of asking, "What did Stephen hear [when Bloom chanted the opening lines of the *Hatikvah*]?" the voice queries, "What was Stephen's auditive sensation?" (17.776/ 689.21). Yet, on second thoughts, the answer ("He heard in a profound ancient male unfamiliar melody the accumulation of the past") shows that the phrase "auditive sensation" is amazingly appropriate, much more so than "What did Stephen hear?" would have been, for, as Kenner points out (1980:142), the melody chanted by Bloom is not profound and ancient at all: What Stephen, under the spell of intoned Hebrew, *thinks* he hears, he hears in his mind, not in his ears.

Meanwhile, things are happening, as they have been happening in the preceding episodes. But this time the story is told in questions and answers—but who is asking the questions and who is giving the answers? As Hodgart says: "In a Catholic catechism it is the priest as instructor who asks the questions, the person under instruction who replies; and that is also true of formal and informal examinations. But throughout most of the process of education it is the pupil who asks, the teacher who answers, and that would seem to be the case in 'Ithaca,' although sometimes the questioner seems to be setting problems" (1978:125). We may feel, at first, that it is the reader—who has become sufficiently interested in Bloom and Stephen by now to want to learn what is going to happen when they have met at last—who is asking the questions and the narrator who is supplying the answers, but the questions frequently betray too much foreknowledge of the answers to have sprung from a blank, ignorant mind. Take this famous passage—much quoted or referred to by critics—about the characteristic features of water, summed up in answer to the question: "What in water did Bloom, waterlover, drawer of water, watercarrier, returning to the range, admire?" (17.183–84/671.26–27). This is not a genuine question insofar as it presupposes things the reader could not have known about; in other words, it prejudges the issue of whether Bloom did *admire* anything at all. The reader—if it is he who asks the questions—might have asked: "What were Bloom's thoughts or feelings while tapping water and, a moment later, returning to the range with the half-filled kettle?" And instead of replying, simply, that Bloom's mind, always keen on notions of science and technology, dwelt for a moment on the thought that a modern water supply system is a very fine thing, indeed, the narrator, elaborating the subject, might then have told the reader-questioner that Bloom, if he had had time, would certainly have pondered the many admirable qualities and properties of water, such as . . . and so forth— not very convincing, perhaps. So what about switching roles? The narrator as the questioner and the reader answering his questions as best he can? This would evoke an even less convincing picture. We have to assume, I think, that "Ithaca" poses as a printed catechism with prear- ranged questions and answers; the person under instruction, whoever he is supposed to be, has had to memorize the answers first.

All this is just metaphor and does not pretend to explain anything. Much as I am fascinated by this episode, I have a feeling that calling it a brilliant piece of prose, as is so often done, or pronouncing it *"probably the greatest chapter in the novel,"* as French does (1976:221, italics mine), will not get us very far. We might as well admit that it is simply too enigmatic in many respects, too difficult for words—just how dif- ficult may be demonstrated by turning to the passage where Stephen comments on the anti-Semitic ballad he has sung to cap, in a sense, the opening lines of the Zionist anthem chanted by Bloom.

Condense Stephen's commentary.

One of all, the least of all, is the victim predestined. Once by inadvertence, twice by design he challenges his destiny. It comes when he is abandoned and challenges him reluctant and, as an apparition of hope and youth, holds him unresisting. It leads him to a strange habitation, to a secret infidel apartment, and there, implacable, immolates him, consenting.

(17.832–37/692.01–7)

According to Sultan, Stephen comments on this *ballad of Little Harry Hughes* in terms that identify himself as the Christian child. This little boy, we might add, is the victim of what could be interpreted as ritual murder rationalized as (rather excessive) punishment for breaking someone's windows. In Sultan's words (Stephen's dream, which he alludes to, is mentioned in the passages 3.365–69/47.04–9 and 9.1206–8/217.31–34): "He [i.e., Stephen] was 'predestined' to be 'immolated' (consecrated to God), 'consenting,' by a Jew in that Jew's house, for the deliverance articulated by his dream was precisely that event; and he 'challenged' that 'destiny,' 'by inadvertence' when Bloom crossed his path and invoked the dream at the library entrance, and 'by design' first when he spurned Bloom in nighttown and struck at God and then when he rejected the coffee and bun Bloom offered him" (1964:389–90).

In French's view, the "victim predestined" is Bloom: "Stephen sings his offensive parallel to Bloom's anthem and in exegesis of it unknowingly recapitulates Bloom's day." French quotes the passage in question and adds the following interpretation: "The challenge 'by inadvertence' is the tip on the Gold Cup; the challenges 'by design' are the argument in Cyclops and the masturbation in Nausikaa, Bloom's two overt acts of defiance of convention; the 'destiny' that comes as 'an apparition of hope and youth' is Stephen; the 'secret infidel apartment' is the brothel" (1976:228).

As these quotations show, critics sometimes have it all pat; everything is in the bag and the bag is neatly sewn up—although the reader would have liked to know, for instance, just when and where and by whom Bloom was "abandoned." However, we know how Stephen was abandoned by Mulligan and Haines and later by Lynch—just as the little boy in the ballad was abandoned by his schoolfellows.

Stephen, however, is commenting on the ballad he has just sung, not on his or Bloom's situation. The "victim," Stephen explains, is led to "a secret infidel apartment," that of the host, who is a "secret infidel" (17.843/692.13), a Jew. Now, this "strange habitation" to which Stephen has been led, the kitchen at 7 Eccles Street, was a place "where none could hear them talk" (17.797/690.12), as Bloom had reassured Stephen, just as the room the Christian boy in the ballad was led to was a place "Where none could hear him call" (17.824/691.20). In Stephen's commentary (note that it has been condensed, which makes it all the more difficult to understand), the victim cannot be anybody else but the Christian boy. He challenges his destiny once inadvertently, by driving his ball over the garden wall, and twice on purpose, first by breaking the Jew's windows, and then by letting himself be lured into a secluded spot by the Jew's daughter.

The Eccles Street host, however, is not only a "secret infidel" but also a "victim predestined": All attempts to manipulate the scenario of the ballad so as to fit what happens in Bloom's kitchen must break down. Bloom is just what Eglinton, in the library scene, says of Shakespeare: "He is the ghost and the prince. He is all in all" (9.1018–19/212.28–29). There is no telling who is the victim and who is the infidel; Bloom and Stephen do not even know themselves. This is, in "Circe," what we are told to believe happens when they look into a mirror: *"Stephen and Bloom gaze in the mirror. The face of William Shakespeare, beardless, appears there, rigid in facial paralysis, crowned by the reflection of the reindeer antlered hatrack in the hall"* (15.3821–24/567.17–20). There is no recognition, as yet.

As said before, things are happening. "Ithaca" is the last episode in the novel in which things happen at all, for in the next, final episode, "Penelope," we are only *told* about things, mostly things, events, or actions that happened in Bloom's and Molly's past, or might happen in their future. In "Eumaeus," often considered an episode of utter fatigue, Bloom has already overcome the fatigue he felt and showed in "Oxen of the Sun." Actually, as has been pointed out in the preceding chapter, he is *dynamic,* he takes charge, he keeps up a patter of small talk, he conducts a lively though one-sided conversation. In contrast, "Ithaca" is a *static* episode. As Senn points out, it is a chapter that "reminds us more of things than of processes" and "yields more inert data than verbs" (1982b:22). In "Eumaeus" Bloom and Stephen walk right across town; in "Ithaca" they sit down, drink cocoa, and talk. Still, before they can relax and sip their cocoa, Bloom has had to display some lively action because he had forgotten to transfer his latchkey to the trousers of the dark suit he had put on for the funeral that morning. He is, rightly, "doubly irritated": "Because he had forgotten and because he remembered that he had reminded himself twice not to forget" (17.78–79/668.13–15). Not wanting to knock at the door so as to wake up Molly, Bloom solves the problem by climbing over the area railings, for a start, and dropping down on to the area pavement.

Having landed safely, Bloom raises the latch of the side door in the area (apparently unlocked), thus reaching his kitchen through the scullery. Trivial details? Yes, but if you do not get them right you might draw the wrong conclusions, as when Cambon has both Stephen and Bloom, guest and host ("Gast und Gastgeber"), climb a nonexistent, at least unmentioned, garden wall to enter the house through the kitchen window: "Bloom lässt seinen Hausschlüssel aus Versehen beim Umziehen in einer Hosentasche stecken, *und so sind Gast und Gastgeber . . . dazu gezwungen, über die Gartenmauer zu hangeln und durch das Küchenfenster in das Haus einzusteigen"* (1970:31, italics mine). We know, of course, that Stephen would not dream of performing such athletic feats. "Reclined against the area railings" (17.109ff./ 669.15ff.), he waits patiently until Bloom appears in the open front door, winking at him, silently inviting him in. On entering the kitchen, Bloom had already lit the gaslight, and a candle besides. Having taken off his boots, so as not to disturb Molly, presumably, and put on some kind of slippers, he picks up the lighted candle, mounts the kitchen stairs, and opens the hall door to Stephen. Incidentally, Bloom must have put his boots back on at some later moment, perhaps before accompanying Stephen into the garden (17.1021ff./697.33ff.), for we find him removing them "for the second time" (17.1484/711.42) when he is alone, relaxing in his front room. In following Bloom along the hallway, after the door has been closed and chained, Stephen notes in passing "a lighted crevice of doorway on the left" (17.121/669.29–30): It is the doorway that leads to the bedroom, where Molly has a paraffin oil lamp burning all night, and it is this "visible luminous sign" that Bloom draws Stephen's attention to later, when both are standing in the back garden, looking up at the house (17.1171ff./702.17ff., cf. also 18.912–13/ 763.28–30). When they have passed the bedroom door, Bloom, carrying his lighted candle, precedes Stephen down the staircase to the kitchen. The passage in question presents a curious mixture of quasi-scientific objectivity and personal, subjective point of view, Stephen's point of view: "Did Stephen obey his sign?" "Yes, entering softly, he helped to close and chain the door and followed softly along the hallway the man's back and listed feet and lighted candle past a lighted crevice of doorway on the left and carefully down a turning staircase of more than five steps into the kitchen of Bloom's house" (17.118–22/669.26–31). For Bloom, there would not have been any need to walk "carefully"—he is on home ground—and for him the staircase would not have been *a* but *the* turning staircase, and, of course, the kitchen would not have been "the kitchen of Bloom's house" but just "the kitchen." But why is the staircase said to consist of "more than five steps"? What Stephen experiences, I think, is just this: When you walk down an unknown staircase, you involuntarily start counting the steps, a kind of reflex accompaniment to your own footsteps, but, having reached the count of four or five without having hit the bottom, you just lose interest and stop counting.

Bloom gets busy, he draws out chairs and lights a fire, using resin-tipped sticks and bits of paper and, of course, coal, "irregular polygons (*polyhedrons*, surely?) of best Abram coal." Stephen is reminded of similar occasions in the past when somebody had kindled a fire for him. Bloom draws water from the tap, sets the kettle on the burning coals, and washes his hands, something that Stephen, declining Bloom's offer, refuses to do. When the water is at the boil, Bloom opens the kitchen dresser to get out "a packet of Epps's soluble cocoa" (17.307/675.16). The various items now exposed on the shelves inside are described in great detail: the usual plates, cups, and saucers, but also a phial of aromatic comfits (used by Molly when anticipating Boylan's visit, as we learn later: "I hope my breath was sweet after those kissing comfits" [18.1140–41/770.03–4]), two onions, one Spanish, the other Irish—the symbolic implications of which have not yet been probed, so far as I know—and so on. The bulk of those articles must have been all too familiar to Bloom, but the empty pot of potted meat, the wicker basket containing one pear, and the half-empty bottle of white port, remnants of what Boylan had ordered to be delivered at the house that afternoon (10.299ff./227.11ff.), cannot but have been new to him. Yet there is no sign of any surprise on Bloom's part, and he does not wonder silently or explicitly about the provenience of those torn betting tickets he finds on the apron of the dresser. We know, and Bloom must have guessed, that they were Boylan's and that it was he who tore them up. The scene—Boylan having gone out around 9 P.M. to buy the pink edition of the *Evening Telegraph* (cf. 13.1169–75/379.10–16 and 16.1232ff./ 647.08ff.) to look up the results of the Gold Cup races and having come back in a great rage—will be depicted graphically by Molly in her nocturnal recording of the events of the afternoon: "he was like a perfect devil for a few minutes after he came back with the stoppress tearing up the tickets and swearing blazes because he lost 20 quid he said he lost over that outsider that won and half he put on for me on account of Lenehans tip cursing him to the lowest pits" (18.423–26/749.42–750.03).

Suppressing, as usual, any thoughts of Boylan, Bloom, frowning, starts thinking about strange coincidences. Having studied—for want of anything better to do—the racing results in the paper he had found in the cabman's shelter, he knows by now that *Throwaway* had been the winning horse. In the light of that knowledge, he now looks back on the occasions when he had heard people talking about the Ascot races and, in particular, on those situations in which the words *throw* and *away* seemed to have had some mysterious significance (17.327ff./676.01ff.). He remembers the "sombre Y.M.C.A. young man" (8.05/151.06)—not a gloomy-looking man, but a black one, "a dark man," as we now learn—who had handed him a *throwaway* earlier in the day, and Bantam Lyons, who had borrowed his copy of the *Freeman's Journal* for a moment and had run off to a bookmaker's posthaste when Bloom remarked that he could keep the paper as he was going to *throw it away* anyway (5.517–48/85.22–86.15). At the time, of course, Bloom had had no inkling that Lyons, who said he just wanted to see about a French horse that was running that day, had spotted that other horse's name, *Throwaway*, in the very moment Bloom had told him, twice, that he was about to *throw away* the newspaper. Even now, Bloom still labors under the misapprehension that Lyons had placed his bet on that French horse, *Maximum II*. After the encounter with Lyons, Bloom, having refolded his paper, had directed his steps toward the Turkish Baths, walking, as we are told in retrospect, "with the light of inspiration shining in his countenance and bearing in his arms the secret of the race, graven in the language of prediction" (17.339–41/676.15–17), like Moses in Taylor's speech as quoted by MacHugh, Moses who came down from the mountain "with the light of inspiration shining in his countenance and bearing in his arms the tables of the law, graven in the language of the outlaw" (7.867–69/143.14–16). The punning parody in "Ithaca" is a strictly reader-oriented passage (Bloom, after all, was not present in the editor's office when those words were quoted), and how, incidentally, "a correspondence with the Annunciation" could have been intended in the racing tip Bloom unwittingly gives Lyons, as Blamires declares (1966:228), is anybody's guess. It is not clear, besides, how Bloom can have believed "To have brought a positive gain to others" (17.352–53/676.29–30). Bloom, as we have seen, could not know that Lyons was planning to place a bet on *Throwaway*, and he was unaware that Lyons had been dissuaded from doing so and had, under Lenehan's influence, put his money on *Sceptre*.

While sipping the cocoa Bloom has prepared for Stephen and himself, he assumes, looking at his silent guest, that the latter is engaged in composing poetry. This reminds him of his own attempts at writing verse, and suddenly the thought strikes him that there are four respects in which Stephen and he himself are essentially different: "Name, age, race, creed" (17.403/678.11). All four of these are then elaborated in the ensuing pages, and their temperaments, finally, are defined as scientific (Bloom) and artistic (Stephen). The passage that deals with the relation between their ages (17.446–61/679.21–39) illustrates what McCarthy calls the episode's central problem: "its tendency to set up a surface of straightforward factuality and to trick us into trusting a narrative point of view which at times turns out to be not altogether reliable" (1984:606). The figures in that passage are wrong, of course, but, once we realize that the catechist is clearly unreliable, we need not feel unduly worried by other equally improbable items, such as the famous list of Molly's so-called lovers (17.2133–42/731.25–36).

By a queer coincidence Bloom is reminded of the scene of his father's suicide, which he then reconstructs mentally (17.622ff./684.33ff.). As Schneider once pointed out (James Joyce Paris Symposium, 1975): "In Bloom's 'construction' [the text speaks of a scene being *reconstructed*] of the scene of his father's death the data of time and place couldn't be more precise. It is told in the typical mode of 'Ithaca' and we are spared no details. But we soon find out that in spite of all this effort to achieve scientific objectivity as many questions are left unanswered as in Stephen's sketch [about a young man and a young woman in a solitary hotel called Queen's Hotel]. There is, for example, no explanation for the puzzling question why Bloom's father bought a new hat on the day he committed suicide."

Hannay has tried to answer this question as follows: "His father's purchase of a 'new boater straw hat, extra smart' immediately prior to taking poison may have been meant to deceive the insurance company into thinking that death was accidental in order to ensure payment of the death benefits, or it may reflect Rudolph Bloom's ambivalence toward his action" (1983:144). The use, side by side, of "construction" and "reconstruction" is no mere play on words; the difference between the scenes as depicted by Stephen and Bloom is indicative of what Hannay calls "the direction in which Stephen's mind and art must grow," for, as he points out, "Bloom's scene was 'reconstructed' from memories, whereas Stephen's was 'constructed' from Bloom's advertising image" (1983:144).

After a protracted silence during which Bloom's memories revert to Milly's infancy, he musters up his courage and finally suggests that Stephen should doss down on an improvised bed in the front room. To Bloom's dismay, the invitation is declined and all those "counterproposals" (17.960ff./696.01ff.), or "pathetic alternatives" as Madtes calls them (1983:98), will come to nothing, as Bloom himself undoubtedly realizes (17.973ff./696.17ff.). There is nothing more to say, it seems, and so, rather abruptly, both men get up and leave the kitchen to go into the garden, and the catechist asks: "In what order of precedence, with what attendant ceremony was the exodus from the house of bondage to the wilderness of inhabitation effected?" (17.1021–22/697.33–35). The scene that follows, with its unmistakable echoes from Dante, has been analyzed by both Reynolds and Litz in terms of *Divina Commedia* imagery. In Litz's words: "As Dante and Vergil emerge from Hell at the end of the *Inferno* they are once more able to see the stars . . . just as Stephen and Bloom emerge from the house to confront 'The heaventree of stars hung with humid nightblue fruit' " (1974b:400). Since then, Day has added fascinating new insights to expand this basic conception, demonstrating that "in the dark garden Father Bloom and Deacon Dedalus are celebrating, in comic-symbolic mode, the Vigil of Easter" (1982:158), a liturgical ceremony during which the deacon sings the Exultet, a hymn of praise to the paschal candle. The serious overtones of all this are relieved somewhat by the deadpan question: "For what creature was the door of egress a door of ingress?" with its answer: "For a cat" (17.1034–35/698.12–13). Having left the kitchen temporarily, Bloom's cat now returns. Will his daughter, Milly, in some respects similar to a cat, return as well (17.886–92/ 693.27–34)?

At first sight the image of the "heaventree of stars" seems a bit out of joint, not exactly suited to the dry, scientific mode of the episode, but it may have been something Stephen just murmured when looking up at the sky, for Bloom, preferring a more scientific, matter-of-fact view of the celestial constellations, later rejects the poetic phrase, concluding "That it was not a heaventree" (17.1139/701.18).

The meeting draws to an end. Stephen and Bloom urinate together, after having gazed a few moments at the light of the lamp in the bedroom, and Bloom unlocks the garden door for Stephen. Standing at the open door, they shake hands while the bells in the nearby church of Saint George chime the half hour, the time now being 2:30 A.M., presumably. No mention is made of any words being spoken, not even a word of thanks on Stephen's part. It must be near dawn, for Bloom considers remaining in the garden to witness sunrise: "What prospect of what phenomena inclined him to remain?" "The disparition of three final stars, the diffusion of daybreak, the apparition of a new solar disk" (17.1256–58/705.04–6). As so often in matters of Jewish traditional lore, Bloom is wrong. There is indeed some kind of rule involving three stars, but it works the other way round: It is not about final but about initial stars, for it is not about the beginning but about the ending of a day. It says that when you can see three stars *together* in the sky it is a sign that Sabbath is over. Anyway, Bloom does not remain outside, after all; he takes up the lighted candle he had left inside the door (17.1033/698.10), but on entering the front room he hurts his head on some piece of furniture. Once inside, he discovers that Molly (with Boylan's help?) must have moved the furniture around in his absence. He registers the changes but does not seem to be unduly puzzled or surprised. A look around assures him that the familiar objects are there, only the position of some having been altered. Meanwhile, he calmly lights a cone of incense, partly as a routine act, partly in particular to fumigate the house after Boylan's visit. What irks him is that his books have been improperly arranged, or rearranged, in the course of the proceedings, some of them even having been put in upside down. He makes himself more comfortable by removing his collar and unbuttoning his waistcoat, trousers, and shirt, and then proceeds to "Compile the budget for 16 June 1904" (17.1455/711.09). According to Hodgart, Bloom's accounts for the day "are set out to the last penny" (1978:121), and at first sight his bookkeeping may impress the reader as quite precise and efficient, but a closer look may reveal several discrepancies. For one thing, anything Bloom spent in Bella Cohen's brothel has been edited out. That may be understandable, but how would he explain to Molly the expenditure of a postal order and a stamp? Then, one shilling as the renewal fee for a lending library book seems a bit steep if you look at other prices, such as those for meat. As to the latter, there not everything is clear either. The pig's foot (crubeen) and sheep's trotter Bloom bought at Olhausen's (15.155–61/434.11–18) figure in the budget as having cost fourpence and threepence, respectively. Now, when he finally decided to let a dog have all that meat, he first dumps the crubeen and then feels the trotter, remarking, "Sizeable for threepence" (15.669/453.12), but letting the trotter slide too, he mutters, "Two and six," which is just what the apparition of his father told him, reproachfully: "Second halfcrown waste money today" (15.253/437.18). If this would be the second, where would we have to look for the first halfcrown Bloom is supposed to have wasted? The postal order of two and six he sent Martha Clifford? But why would he think of that now? Besides, it would not explain how threepence and fourpence could add up to half a crown.

Sensing some persistent ache in his soles, Bloom takes off his boots and, relaxing, starts dreaming about "a thatched bungalowshaped 2 storey dwellinghouse" he might purchase one day (17.1497ff./ 712.16ff.), the detailed description of which is, as Madtes points out, "infallibly sustained, infinitely touching, and increasingly funny" (1983:102).

Having imagined in detail his possible future life in this "Bloom Cottage. Saint Leopold's. Flowerville" (17.1580/714.32), Bloom starts meditating, as he liked to do "habitually before retiring for the night" (cf. 17.1755–58/720.01–5), on schemes of making money on a really big scale, schemes that would enable him to buy this ideal country residence in cash without having to bother with complicated matters of mortgage (cf. 17.1657–71/717.06–24). It may strike the reader that Molly's role in this utopian state of affairs remains obscure, to say the least. The nearest Bloom comes to assigning her a place in his schemes is when he fancies their being mentioned in some society column: "Mr and Mrs Leopold Bloom have left Kingstown for England" (17.1614–15/715.35–36)–will "Mrs Marion Bloom" have to give up her singing career?

All these fantastic schemes seem to have crowded out any plans or hopes Bloom may have cherished with regard to Stephen's possible role in the domestic life of the Blooms. Having shut the garden door behind Stephen—without asking him where, at 2:30 A.M., he thought he was going—Bloom seems to have forgotten him completely. The first we hear of him, briefly, is when Molly, having woken up, asks her husband what he had done that day and Stephen emerges as "the salient point" of Bloom's narration (17.2269/735.32). Even so, Bloom may have put up his meeting with Stephen as a smokescreen to hide from Molly the

happenings in nighttown and not as something he really believed in
himself.

After Bloom's meditations, there seems a gap in the catechism. We
would have expected something on the lines of "What did Bloom do
next?" followed by the answer "He started to unlock the drawers of the
table he was sitting at." Instead, without any preamble, the questioner
asks, "What did the first drawer unlocked contain?" (17.1774/720.24),
and the answer omits nothing and leaves nothing unspecified. Among
the miscellaneous objects the drawer contains are three typewritten
letters from Martha Clifford, to which Bloom now adds her fourth letter,
the one he had received that very day: So much for the assumption that
this day would mark a drastic change in Bloom's life. The contents of the
second drawer—of which it is not stated if it had to be unlocked first—are
decidedly more interesting: an endowment policy, a bank passbook, and a
certificate of the possession of scrip (£900, Canadian 4% government
stock) warrant the conclusion that Bloom is a wealthy man according to
Dublin standards. Bloom has also kept an old "local press cutting
concerning change of name by deedpoll" (17.1866–67/723.15), from
which we learn that Bloom's father, Rudolph Virag, had, at some
unspecified date, changed the family name to Bloom. The text of this
note, a matter-of-fact document, is given in full, suggesting that Bloom
picks it up and reads it, for the nth time, presumably, from beginning to
end, this in sharp contrast to his father's suicide note, which he also keeps
in this drawer. He does not peruse the letter itself, he only looks at the
envelope addressed *"To My Dear Son Leopold,"* and those five words
trigger more or less confused, partially blocked memories, bringing to his
mind not whole sentences but only fragments of phrases: "Tomorrow
will be a week that I received . . . . it is no use Leopold to be . . . . with
your dear mother . . . that is not more to stand . . . to her . . . all for me
is out . . . be kind to Athos, Leopold . . . . my dear son . . . always . . .
of me . . . *das Herz . . . Gott . . . dein* . . . " (817.1883–86/723.36–40).

For reasons probably even unknown to himself, Bloom fails to en-
lighten us as to the exact wording of the letter; we just have to keep
guessing. As Raleigh remarks (1977a:595), Rudolph Bloom must have
been bankrupt at the time of his death, and Bernard Benstock, endorsing
this view, holds that the opening phrase, as remembered by Bloom,
strongly suggests a foreclosure notice (1982:50). Any thought of a direct
link between Rudolph Bloom's suicide and his wife's death must be
rejected. For one thing, there is no evidence in Leopold's memories of
both deaths all but coinciding, and, furthermore, he remembers his
father as "suffering from progressive melancholia," as "An old man,
widower, unkempt of hair, in bed, with head covered, sighing," who used

to take increasing doses of aconite (a monkshood extract) to alleviate his pains (17.1887–92/724.01–7). This sounds very much like the description of a state that might have lasted for months or even years. In "Circe" we have a curious passage that sounds like Bloom's enacting his father's role ("I am ruined" might pass for a paraphrase of old Bloom's words "all for me is out," or might even be a literal quote, after all, from the old man's letter). Here is Bloom, whispering, presumably: "Life's dream is o'er. End it peacefully. They can live on. (*he gazes far away mournfully*) I am ruined. A few pastilles of aconite. The blinds drawn. A letter. Then lie back to rest. (*he breathes softly*) No more. I have lived. Fare. Farewell" (15.1965–68/499.17–21).

Shari Benstock has commented on the suicide note from various angles. She points out that Rudolph Bloom's presence through the language of his written message contrasts markedly with his appearance in "Circe," where he speaks pidgin English with a heavy Yiddish intonation. She has a high opinion of old Bloom's mastery of English, in spite of the scarcity of data (we have only fractions of phrases, after all): "The syntax and speech patterns of the note reveal a highly articulate and perfectly proper English (which is Rudolph Bloom's third language, with German his second and Hungarian his first)" (1982a:422). As I see it, however, or listen to it, German is breaking through Rudolph Bloom's English in at least two places: "that is not more to stand" (*das ist nicht mehr zu ertragen* or *das ist nicht länger auszustehen*) and "all for me is out" (*es ist alles aus mit mir*).

Bloom's father "had been converted from the Israelitic faith and communion in 1865 by the Society for promoting Christianity among the jews" (17.1637–39/716.25–27) but, of course, such a conversion, only skin-deep, no doubt, did not mean that from then on he simply gave up all his old "beliefs and practices" (17.1895/724.10). There need not have been any real "inconsistency" here, as Blamires maintains, and the old man's idiosyncrasies should not be attributed to "the influence of drugs" (1966:242). The questioner (17.1921ff./725.03ff.) holds these idiosyncrasies to be "concomitant products of amnesia," but I think they are just symptoms of a process of regression; for instance, eating "without having previously removed his hat" is a practice—quite usual in an Orthodox, or at least traditional, Jewish environment—that Bloom Senior must have followed for years before he ever thought of adopting the Christian faith. Among the habits he had clung to was also his reading from the Haggadah at Pesach, as Bloom remembers (cf. 7.206ff./122.19ff.).

Bloom decides to go to bed, at last; to do so he does not have to go upstairs (Hodgart, 1978:121). He is sitting at the table in the front room, at the same level as the bedroom (we remember the "lighted crevice of doorway on the left," don't we?), and so we find him "walking" (17.2071/729.29) down the hallway to join Molly in bed.

Before rising, however, he silently recapitulates the events of the day—some of them at least—which he considers the causes of his "accumulated fatigue." The list that follows (17.2044–58/ 728.35–729.13) is, in Senn's words, "Bloom's last and most complete résumé, combined with what looks like one more fully fledged, schematic groundplan [the former recalls: 1. 13.1214–26/380.21–36, and 2. 15.1941–52/498.23–499.03]. It is not necessarily, or even probably, a verbatim transcription of Bloom's thoughts. The mode of the chapter, as usual, takes over and here substitutes its own pedantic regularity" (1982a:57). It is a puzzling list in many respects, and not only because of the parenthetical headings, those biblical labels (mostly from the Old Testament) that were among Joyce's last-minute additions to the page proofs of *Ulysses*. One wonders, for instance, about the validity of the overall term "causes of fatigue." What was so tiring about Bloom's breakfast? And his bath must even have been refreshing: "Glad I took that bath. Feel my feet quite clean" (6.105–6/89.38–39). "The prolonged delivery of Mrs Mina Purefoy" may have tired *her* out, but Bloom himself, having been invited by Dixon to join the company of revelers, takes a good rest while waiting for the baby to be born: "And the traveller Leopold went into the castle for to rest him for a space being sore of limb after many marches environing in divers lands" (14.138–40/ 386.41–387.02). As to the biblical appellations, readers will be tempted, of course, to look for links that might tie these headings—in a convincing, unambiguous way, preferably—to the events or episodes referred to. They will soon find that, as Senn points out, "not all entries make immediate sense" (1982a:59)—which some may consider an understatement. That is another point: Do we have to relate the parenthetical tags to specific events or to whole episodes? Any attempt at being all too systematic in this respect will be thwarted from the outset when we realize that there are fifteen items in the list, whereas the number of episodes up to "Ithaca" in which Bloom plays a role is thirteen, "Calypso" having been allotted two entries to start with ("burnt offering" and "holy of holies"). Then there is such an entry as "the bath (rite of John)," which refers, presumably, to "Lotus Eaters" but can only be tied directly to the final paragraph of that episode (5.567–72/86.36–42), and even that is not the recording of some event but only something "foreseen" by Bloom. Even more striking is the entry of "a blank period of time including a cardrive, a visit to a house of mourning, a leavetaking (wilderness)," which does not correspond to any separate episode at all. The allusion is to the Old Testament Book of Numbers, the Hebrew name of which is *Be'midbar* ("In the Wilderness"), and in the list this reference to a nonexisting episode is wedged in between "Cyclops" and "Nausicaa." It is tempting, indeed, to think of Bloom-Moses as having to wander through the "wilderness" before getting a glimpse of the promised land on Sandymount beach: "the eroticism produced by feminine exhibitionism." Numbers, incidentally, is also the book that contains a much more extensive list of "causes of fatigue": It records the stages of the march of the Israelites through the wilderness (chapter 33), a rather monotonous enumeration.

To the question whether we should try to relate the biblical phrases of the list to entire episodes or to any one particular event within an episode, there does not seem to be any satisfactory answer. In a sense, it is a paradoxical question: When Bloom looks back on his day, he does not think in terms of episodes, of course. In *Ulysses* there is no episode or chapter for the "blank period of time," but in Bloom's memory there must be a drive in a car, a visit to a house of mourning, and a leavetaking, and for him, generally speaking, the day must have been one long chain of events. This bias is especially apparent in those episodes in which he remains very much in the background or is seen moving on the fringes of whatever happens. When speaking of Bloom's retrospective view, we cannot, in other words, equate 'Sirens" with "Wandering Rocks," as is done, implicitly, by Senn when he writes: "While 'Shira Shirim' translates into Song of Songs and so roughly fits 'Sirens,' it is not at all obvious why 'Simchath Torah' ('rejoicing of the Law') should stand for 'Wandering Rocks' " (1982a:60). What Bloom remembers as one of those experiences that contributed to his growing fatigue is, specifically, "the bookhunt along Bedford Row, Merchants' Arch, Wellington Quay," and, although we do not know how long this book hunt may have taken Bloom, in "Wandering Rocks" it is only a tiny fragment, which cannot even boast a section of its own. It is Lenehan who identifies Bloom while the latter is browsing among a hawker's books. Lenehan tells M'Coy that he just met Bantam Lyons (in the betting office), who was "going to back a bloody horse someone gave him that hasn't an earthly" (10.518–19/233.25–26), and, when, under Merchants' Arch, they spot a darkbacked figure scanning books on a cart, Lenehan points him out to M'Coy as the "someone" who gave Lyons that strange tip: "There he is, Lenehan said" (10.522/233.29). In retrospect, the reader realizes that in one of the heterotopic interpolations he should already have recognized Bloom in the "darkbacked" figure, busy scanning books at the very moment Boylan was ordering fruit to be sent to Molly (cf. 10.315–16/227.27–28). Bloom's book hunt reaches its final climax and then gets a section of its own, when he borrows a book for Molly from a kind of lending library, an unsavory bookshop. In the chapter that deals with "Wandering Rocks," I have tried to show that here, at a pinch, we might find a connection of sorts with the Simchath Torah motif.

In a similar way, "the advertisement of Alexander Keyes" represents only a minor detail within the turbulent episode of "Aeolus," but it is a detail of some importance for Bloom's self-esteem, because it is a matter of success or failure. In fact, it is the first thing to come to mind when Bloom draws up another survey, an account, this time, of "imperfections in a perfect day" (*perfect* day?). The "provisional failure to obtain renewal of an advertisement" (17.2074/729.31) still irks him, apparently. But why, we keep asking, the allusion to Urim and Thummim in this connection? Urim (used in short for Urim-and-Thummim in Num. 27:21) is, as Sturdy explains in his commentary on the Book of Numbers, "A sacred lot, by which the will of God can be learnt, kept in a pocket of the breastplate which is part of the robes of the high priest. . . . It may possibly have been two stones of different colour, one for 'yes' and one for 'no': the high priest would feel in the pocket and bring one out, and the question put would be answered by the chance of which came out" (1976:197–98). Similarly, for Bloom the question remains: Will he get the advertisement, as MacHugh predicts (7.439/129.26), YES or NO?

As Senn has pointed out, the "Ithaca" synopsis reveals as much by what it leaves out (no explicit reference is made, for instance, to either Boylan or Stephen) as by what it includes. In this respect it resembles the account Bloom gives of his day when replying (with "modifications") to Molly's "catechetical interrogation" (17.2249/735.08), omitting events that happened and mentioning events that did *not* happen. As the final episode will show, Molly wisely takes his narration with some grains of salt.

The catechismal form of this episode seems to imply that there is really no more to tell, that we now know everything about Bloom and Stephen worth knowing, and that we must draw our own conclusions. As Hannay remarks, "the question-and-answer style of the 'Ithaca' episode . . . exaggerates a paradox inherent in the realistic novel, pretending to be not fiction at all but an objective inquiry into fact" (1983:141). We soon realize, however, that this is a misleading notion. It is a commonplace in contemporary critical literature that "Ithaca" tells us everything "except, very often, what we most want to know," leaving unanswered "the questions which the rest of the book so pressingly puts forward— questions involving the future lives of all three major characters" (Maddox, 1978:188; 201), but, then, the message that the episode has to offer may simply be that complex human relationships (interrelations, interactions) cannot be fathomed, however hard we try, by empirical, mathematical, or generally scientific methods. We should do wise, therefore, not to speculate about the possible consequences of Bloom's meeting Stephen—or Stephen's meeting Bloom, which is not the same thing.

It may very well be, as Kenner says, that the meeting is "neither a success nor a failure" (1980:139), but we cannot maintain that this meeting means nothing at all. Both men will certainly remember it in later years, and for Bloom in particular it must have been full of significance of some kind. Still, if Stephen fails to turn up on Eccles Street to take up singing lessons with Molly and all that, he will recede into the background soon enough. Bloom will have other problems on his hands: There is Molly, and there is Milly. So far, this mood of equanimity, of resignation and acceptance, is clearly that of "a man satisfied only to have survived," as Maddox puts it (1978:201), and that is what Shari Benstock means when she speaks of the "evasion principle" on which Bloom's psychic survival seems to depend. We have only to compare the behavior of Bloom with that of Stephen, she points out, to get a clear idea of "the difference between evasion as a survival system and escape as a self-destructive stance" (1978:161).

Bloom's report of his day's activities seems to end in an indistinct murmur (17.2322ff./737.17ff). Did he really ask for "breakfast in bed with a couple of eggs" (18.02/738.02)? There is no record of such a request in "Ithaca," but the reader is left with the definite impression that Bloom will survive, with or without eggs in the morning, whatever Molly may have in store for him.

EPISODE EIGHTEEN
"Penelope"

*T*O THE reader who has weathered "Ithaca," with its scientific or pseudo-scientific circumlocutions, the final episode, relating Molly's innermost, down-to-earth night thoughts and memories comes as a relief. Because Molly is in bed all the time—except for a brief spell during which she is sitting on the chamber pot or looking in the cupboard for a sanitary napkin—there is no action to speak of (in this respect, "Penelope," the third episode of the *Nostos*, is a true counterpart to "Proteus," the third episode of the *Telemachia*). Nor is there any dialogue, Bloom having gone to sleep after giving Molly a slightly modified account of his activities that day, as we were already given to understand in the preceding episode (17.2250–66/735.09–29). Details of what Bloom must have told her will crop up in Molly's flow of thoughts from time to time, accompanied by her critical notes. It has long been recognized that this flow of thoughts, as Hardy puts it, "is anything but random in its processes" (1975:253). Outwardly, there is a formal structure in that the typographical layout, devoid of punctuation, apart from the final full stop, clearly indicates that the text consists of eight paragraphs, or "sentences" as Joyce himself called them in a letter to Frank Budgen. Harking back to Stephen's thoughts about the "moon-drawn" tidal movements of the sea in "Proteus" (3.393/47.37), Molly's thoughts rise and fall as far as her attitude toward and, specifically, her appreciation of, her husband and her lover are concerned. The two men are now foremost in her consciousness. We used to speak of her soliloquy as a "flow," and it is fitting, therefore, that there is no full stop or comma anywhere in the text, not even between the so-called sentences. At most, there is a kind of slowing down when Molly lets herself be sidetracked, or when she resumes a topic she had not explored fully in the preceding sentence.

In the *first sentence* several men are reviewed; Bloom, of course, and Boylan, but also Father Corrigan, and Purefoy, ending up with Breen, who, according to his wife, sometimes "used to go to bed with his muddy boots on" (18.222–23/744.13). Bloom, Molly thinks, is lucky to have got her for his wife: "of course hed never find another woman like me to put up with him the way I do" (18.232–33/744.25–26). There are women who would not shrink back from murdering their husbands, like that Mrs. Maybrick, who poisoned her husband and who "must have been madly in love with the other fellow" to run this terrible risk, but "if that was her nature what could she do besides *theyre* not brutes enough to go and hang a woman surely are *they*" (18.242–45/744.37–40, italics mine).

This thought of men in general leads smoothly over to the *second sentence*, again about men: "*theyre* all so different" (18.246/744.41, italics mine). At the end of this sentence we hear about a Mr. Cuffe who had fired Bloom. Molly had gone to see him to try to make him change his mind, putting on all her charms: "I could see him looking very hard at *my chest* when he stood up to open the door for me" (18.529–30/752.42–43, italics mine). It did not work out, though: "I just half smiled I know *my chest* was out that way at the door when he said Im extremely sorry and Im sure you were" (18.532–34/753.04–6, italics mine).

This memory steers her thoughts back, in the *third sentence*, to Boylan's lovemaking and the way he had sucked *her breasts*: "yes I think he made them a bit firmer sucking them like that . . . yes *this one anyhow*" (18.535–36/753.07–9, italics mine). She keeps feeling her breasts and comparing them through all kinds of digressions, concluding: "*this one not so much* theres the mark of his teeth still where he tried to bite the nipple" (18.568–69/754.04–6, italics mine), and "*yes and its so much smoother the skin* much an hour he was at them" (18.580–81/754.19–20, italics mine).

Her thoughts about the exciting afternoon she spent with Boylan are interrupted by the long drawn-out whistling of a train in the distance, marking the beginning of the *fourth sentence*. The sound reminds her of "Loves old sweeeetsonnnng" (18.598/754.40–41), which she had been singing with Boylan, while the thought of the train drivers "in those roasting engines" reminds her of the oppressively hot day it was. The thunderstorm that woke her up was a relief: "that rain was lovely and refreshing just after my beauty sleep I thought it was going to get like Gibraltar my goodness the heat there before the levanter came on" (18.605–8/755.06–9). There follows a long digression full of reminiscences of her years in Gibraltar, where she became bored in the end, especially after the Stanhopes had left: "the days like years not a letter from a living soul" (18.698/757.29–30). It was "as bad as now with the hands hanging off me looking out of the window" (18.702–3/757.34–35), life being terribly dull on Eccles Street: "no visitors or post ever" (18.715/758.07), which causes her to sigh, "I wish somebody would *write me a loveletter*" (18.734–35/758.30, italics mine).

This provides the cue for the transition to the *fifth sentence*. Cohn says that the "he" of the midpages of this episode is "the explicitly introduced 'Mulvey was the first,' who will return only pronominally to fuse with Bloom at the very end" (1978:230). It is true that this sentence is mainly about Mulvey ("he was the first man kissed me under the Moorish wall" [18.769–70/759.29–30]), but its opening words hark back to Molly's thoughts about love letters: "*Mulveys* [i.e., Mulvey's letter] *was the first* when I was in bed that morning and Mrs Rubio brought it in with the coffee" (18.748–49/759.04–5, italics mine). Once more, a train's far-off whistling reminds Molly of her songs, and she speculates about technical details she has to keep in mind when performing a song such as "Love's Old Sweet Song," which she hopes to sing when she gets "in front of the footlights again" (18.877–78/762.29). She feels she has to break wind and, turning round, lets go to the accompaniment of the dying sounds of the train: "yes hold them like that a bit on my side piano quietly sweeeee theres that train far away pianissimo eeeee one more tsong" (18.907–8/763.21–23).

Her response constitutes the opening of the *sixth sentence:* "that was a relief wherever you be let your wind go free" (18.909/763.24). Molly's thoughts turn to Bloom, his coming home at such a late hour, his unwonted request for breakfast in bed, and all his oddities, then to the problems she has with Milly. Her thoughts are interrupted by the onset of her period (18.1104ff./769.03ff.). She gets the chamber pot out from under the bed, as she had to use it anyway.

Her last menstruation, she remembers, was only about three weeks ago, so in the *seventh sentence* she starts wondering whether there is something wrong with her. This reminds her of a visit she once paid to a gynecologist. Her thoughts then switch to Bloom in the days of their courtship, the queer things he did and said, then and also later, when they were married, but also the good qualities she admits he has, as compared with other men she knows, such as Dennis Breen, Tom Kernan, Martin Cunningham, Charlie M'Coy, Jack Power, and Simon Dedalus. She starts wondering about the latter's son, Stephen, a poet and a future professor of Italian, whom Bloom had brought home with him: Couldn't she seduce this young man, take him for a lover (18.1358ff./776.09ff.)? But, she reflects, what about Boylan in that case?

As we learn from the opening phrases of the *eighth sentence,* Boylan is an uncivilized brute anyway: "no thats no way for him has he no manners nor no refinement nor no nothing in his nature slapping us behind like that on my bottom because I didnt call him Hugh" (18.1368–70/776.20–22)—something Molly had complained of before: "one thing I didnt like his slapping me behind going away" (18.122–23/741.20–21). Her thoughts once more turn around the nature of women and around men in general and then come back to Stephen: "I wonder why he wouldnt stay the night" (18.1451–52/778.35–36), and "what a pity he didnt stay Im sure the poor fellow was dead tired and wanted a good sleep badly I could have brought him in his breakfast in bed with a bit of toast" (18.1477–79/779.24–27). As Stephen will not be there, however, Bloom may get his breakfast in bed after all. Molly's memories go back, finally, to their lovemaking on the Hill of Howth, sixteen years ago, where Bloom seduced her—or she him—and this sentence, which had started with a "no" to Boylan, now ends with a thrice-repeated "yes" to Bloom: "and his heart was going like mad and yes I said yes I will Yes" (18.1608–9/783.13–14).

In order to distinguish Molly's monologue from Bloom's and Stephen's interior monologues, which are mostly associated with action or dialogue, critics use an equivalent Latin term and call this episode Molly's *soliloquy*. When we start on this soliloquy, with its "Yes because he never did a thing like that before" (18.01/738.01), it is clear that we are plunging in the middle of Molly's stream of thought, which means that she must have lain awake for some time now. Of course, it is impossible to pin down the exact time things happen in the final episodes since Bloom and Stephen left Burke's at 11:00 P.M., but, as there has been some confusion about Molly's notion of time, let us consider whether critics who find her lacking in "sense of time" are right and whether Molly's thoughts might not hide some useful clues as to the chronology of that night. Fischer holds that in Molly's stream of consciousness any distinction between different time levels or temporal grades (*Zeitstufen*) has become blurred, and she adds: "Ueberpersonal valide erscheint ihre Selbsteinschätzung 'I never know the time' " (1973:169), which means, presumably, that when Molly says that she never knows what time it is, the reader may take this to be the objective truth. The same view is found in Cohn's study on narrative modes; speaking about Molly's soliloquy, she says: "Molly's sense of time being what it is ('I never know the time,' 747), the exact length of her insomnia cannot be known" (1978:220). I fail to see why we should attach an almost metaphysical significance to a matter-of-fact statement. We just have to see it in its context. Molly remembers waiting for Boylan (he was to show up at 4:00 P.M.) and getting nervous, fearing he was to going to stand her up—until she hears his knock at the door. She now starts to reckon back: She had gone to the window to throw a penny to "that lame sailor" she had heard singing, and, when she saw Katey and Boody Dedalus coming from school (a scene described in "Wandering Rocks," 10.228–56/225.15–226.06), she knew it must be 3:15 P.M. (she may have heard the bells of Saint George's tolling the quarter hour). So now she reconstructs the scene: "he must have been a bit late . . . home and beauty" (18.343–47/747.30–35). Molly is right, of course, about Boylan being a bit late; from "Sirens" we know that it was already 4:00 P.M. when he, in a hurry, left the Ormond bar. Incidentally, what happened to Lenehan? Boylan was not going to take him with him on his ride to Eccles Street, surely? Then why did he urge him to finish his drink and come with him on leaving the bar? Anyway, it appears that Molly must have estimated the lapse of time between 3:15 and 4:00 P.M. correctly, so there cannot have been anything essentially wrong with her sense of time. What she means to say is simply that there is no reliable timepiece in the house: she cannot trust her watch and the one clock they have (on the mantelpiece in the front room) is not much good either since it has "stopped at the hour of 4.46 a.m. on the 21 March 1896" (17.1335–36/707.22–23). To her remark on Molly's sense of time, Cohn adds the following note: "Since we gather from the time scheme of "Ithaca" (and from the schemata) that Bloom joins Molly in bed around 2 A.M., '3 quarters the hour wait 2 oclock' (772) thirty-four pages into 'Penelope' must be inaccurate counting on Molly's part (unless Joyce is being inconsistent). Two pages before the end it is 'a quarter after what an unearthly hour' (781) which is not much help; but we are also told that 'the nuns ringing the angelus' and 'the alarmclock next door at cockshout' still lie in the future" (311n.11). Yes, but this future might well be very near, for the text has "well *soon* have the nuns ringing the angelus" (18.1541–42/781.18, italics mine). Since the Angelus will be rung at sunrise, which, in mid-June, might be expected around 3:30 A.M., Molly's thought, "a quarter after"—on hearing the church bells chime the quarter hour, presumably—could very well refer to 3:15 A.M. This is where I disagree with the time scheme drawn up by Hart and Knuth, especially with their conclusion that "*Ulysses* ends shortly after 2:15 a.m., which Molly hears chiming at 781.16" (1981:I.35). They assume that Bloom and Stephen part company as Saint George's Church chimes 1:30 A.M. (17.1224–27/704.03–7), but the chiming clock only indicates an unspecified half hour, and, when we consider all that must have happened since Bloom went in search of Stephen after closing time, we might be nearer the truth if we think of Stephen's leavetaking as occurring at 2:30 A.M. instead. So, allowing Bloom half an hour for pottering around and undressing, he may have been in bed by about 3:00 A.M. When Molly claims Bloom did not wake her up (18.927–28/764.04), she probably refers to the time, around 2:00 A.M., that Bloom had entered the house and had gone down into the kitchen with Stephen. As we have seen in "Ithaca," he managed to do everything so quietly that he did not disturb her sleep, but she must have woken up when he joined her in bed. In answer to Molly's "catechetical interrogation" (17.2249/735.08), Bloom then starts recounting his day's adventures (even admitting that he had had to climb down into the area to gain entrance to the house through the scullery), after which he must have fallen asleep, tired after all his exertions. Molly, however, seems wide awake ("goodbye to my sleep for this night" [18.925/763.43–764.01]). Her thoughts constitute a running commentary on what Bloom had told her, interspersed with reminiscences from the past (the result being a family chronicle in a nutshell) and with memories of the afternoon spent with Boylan. Bloom must have mentioned his visit to the maternity clinic, for about halfway into her soliloquy she thinks: "anyhow I hope hes not going to get in with those medicals leading him astray to imagine hes young again coming in at 4 in the morning it must be if not more still he had the manners not to wake me" (18.925–28/ 764.01–4). Molly must have known that Bloom had not come in as late as 4:00 A.M., so I submit we have to read this passage as follows: "I hope he won't make a habit of staying out late, he's too old for that kind of thing, just imagine, coming in at . . . what did he tell me? (here her thoughts trail off, she feels that she has lain awake quite some time and wonders what time it is *now*), four in the morning it must be (if she were thinking of the time Bloom came home, she would have used "must have been"), but at least, whenever he did come home, he didn't wake me up, I grant him that." Still later, a long passage (beginning at 18.1175/771.03), in which Molly lists all kinds of oddities and shortcomings of Bloom's, is interrupted by the church bells chiming the hour. Molly does not register which hour it is, she just listens to the chimes and the strokes, suppressing any mention of the quarter and the half hour as well, but the bells remind her once more of what Bloom told her about his homecoming, and she plans to speak to him sternly the next day: "wait theres Georges church bells wait 3 quarters the hour 1 wait [pause in which she counts the strokes; finding that it is now 3:00 A.M., presumably, she vents once more her indignation at Bloom's behavior—coming home at 2:00 A.M., as he must have told her himself:] 2 oclock well thats a nice hour of the night for him to be coming home at to anybody climbing down into the area if anybody saw him Ill knock him off that little habit tomorrow" (18.1231–34/772.28–32). When, shortly afterward, Molly next hears the church bells chiming: "a quarter after what an unearthly hour" (18.1540/781.16), the time must now be 3:15 A.M., which, as has been pointed out, would fit in nicely with her thought that the nuns would *soon* be ringing the Angelus.

Some twenty years ago, Sultan wrote that Molly's soliloquy was "very simple reading except for one characteristic. As unconcentrated thought late at night well might be, Molly's is easily deflected from a particular subject, to return to it only after having explored the diversionary tangent" (1964:418). We may add that from the beginning the reader is not left in any doubt about this outstanding characteristic. The first page of the episode provides a striking instance of the way Molly's thoughts keep returning to certain topics, prominent among which are Bloom and his request for "breakfast in bed with a couple of eggs"—an instance, strange to say, overlooked or rather totally misjudged by Sultan himself. As said before, the reader catches Molly's train of thought when it is already well under way. Bloom's request for a substantial breakfast in bed must have come, one surmises, at the end of the recital of his adventures. Molly, wisely, has not swallowed everything he dished out; much of it, she suspects, is just a "pack of lies" (18.37/739.02) to hide the fact that he has had a woman. That is where the reader picks up the thread of Molly's thoughts: "Yes because he never did a thing like that before as ask to get his breakfast in bed with a couple of eggs since the City Arms hotel" (18.01-2/738.01-3). This thought sets off a whole train of memories, until she comes back, rather abruptly, to Bloom and his breakfast: "yes he came somewhere Im sure by his appetite anyway love its not or hed be off his feed thinking of her" (18.34-36/738.41-43). Sultan interprets Molly's reasoning as follows: "She thinks that he has had normal sexual relations with a woman and her jealousy is roused. She decides that he is not in love . . . and her perception of 'his appetite' for her (738.41-42) seems to reassure her (that she should recognize this desire for her in the present context is important)" (1964:429). Of course, this is beside the point. Molly cannot get over Bloom's unusual request for breakfast in bed, and she can think of only one reason: Bloom must be hungry, and "his appetite" can only have one cause: "he came somewhere." She does not mind as long as it is not love, and it cannot be love, because in that case he would not show any appetite at all—on the contrary, he would be "off his feed." The reader will find out soon enough that with Molly "yes" (18.34/738.41) or "yes because" (18.01/ 738.01; 18.46/739.12-13) is a typical signal that after a more or less lengthy digression she resumes the thread of her thoughts about a subject she had broached before. This may be characteristic of Molly's stream of consciousness; it is not the only feature to cause problems of interpretation. What the reader has to keep in mind when trying to follow Molly's rambling thoughts is that these thoughts are constantly switching from one male person to another, which means that the pronouns "he" and "him" may refer to Bloom as well as to Mulvey, to Boylan as well as to Stephen, not to mention Menton, Lenehan, Breen, and others.

Time and again readers have been puzzled and even confused by this frequent occurrence of the pronouns "he," "him," and "his" in Molly's soliloquy. In Benstock and Benstock (1980:229-33), they will now find a useful tool, an appendix listing references to the various indications of Molly's masculine pronouns. The authors may be trusted, of course, as far as the bulk of these references is concerned, but there will always remain cases where one or another of their readers may wish to disagree with their suggestions. Such a case is a passage on the third page of the episode (18.78ff./740.9ff.). Molly remembers the night that she, Bloom, and Boylan were walking along by the Tolka, she and Boylan holding hands and singing, and she thinks: "because he [Bloom] has an idea about him [Boylan] and me hes [Bloom is] not such a fool he [Bloom] said Im dining out and going to the Gaiety though Im not going to give him [?] the satisfaction in any case God knows hes [Boylan is] a change in a way" (18.81–83/740.12–15). The passage is plain sailing till we come to the second occurrence of "him," the one I singled out by a question mark. In the Benstock list this pronoun is marked down as referring to Bloom, but in that case one wonders what is this satisfaction Molly is *not* planning to give him? In her mind it must be something definite, not just "satisfaction" or "any satisfaction," but "*the* satisfaction." I could think of the following tentative interpretation: The first part of the passage, as far as "to the Gaiety," deals with Bloom and his attitude of silent consent where her affair with Boylan is concerned. He had let her know that he would be staying out late, so that was that, he would not come barging in on them at least. Molly then switches to Boylan: He must be satisfied with what he has got, he need not expect an extra bonus, she is not going to give him, Boylan, *the satisfaction of knowing* that Bloom is aware of their affair without being able to do anything about it.

This passage is relatively simple, as compared with a longer one in the seventh sentence, in which the problem of the referential identity of the pronouns is interwoven with the ambiguities inherent in the characteristic pattern of Molly's soliloquy, the way she digresses and then suddenly picks up the thread, the end of her various digressions being marked, as we have seen, by "yes," "yes because," or simply "and" in some cases. The sequence that leads to the passage in question starts when Molly, sensing that she is going to have her period ("that thing" [18.1105/769.03], "this bloody pest of a thing" [18.1534/781.08]), slips out of bed and makes herself more or less comfortable on the chamber pot (18.1136ff./769.41ff.). Wondering whether there is anything wrong with her, as it is only about three weeks since she had her last period, she remembers the time, years ago, she consulted a gynecologist, Dr. Collins (18.1153/770.19). She is reminded of the questions he asked her and the queer terms he used: "*asking me* if what I did had an offensive odour" (18.1160/770.27–28), "*and* could you pass it easily" (18.1163/770.31), "*and asking me* had I frequent omissions" (18.1169–70/770.39, all italics mine). There follows a digression in which we see Dr. Collins writing out a prescription and Molly chiding herself for lying to him (?), her conclusion being: "he [Dr. Collins?] was clever enough to spot that" (18.1175/771.02–3). What did Molly lie about? Her "emissions" (a word she either misunderstood or now misremembers)? And what did the doctor spot nonetheless? Her habit of masturbating? Well, she thinks, that was not her fault: "of course that was all thinking of him [with emphasis, meaning Bloom, naturally] and his mad crazy letters . . . that he had me always at myself [that he, Bloom, always excited me so, whenever I thought of him, that I simply had to masturbate] 4 or 5 times a day sometimes" (18.1175–79/771.03–8). In between the two parts of this one thought Molly remembers and quotes an instance of the things Bloom used to write in those "mad crazy letters" of his: "my Precious one everything connected with your glorious Body everything under-lined that comes from it is a thing of beauty and of joy for ever," immediately followed by her comment, showing that she knows or suspects that he had cribbed part of those phrases out of a book: "something he got out of some nonsensical book." Morel must have failed to see the logical connection between "that was all thinking of him" and "that he had me always at myself," because he construes "that he had" as a relative clause, with "some nonsensical book" as the antecedent: "une absurdité qu'il avait trouvée *dans un livre qu'il avait*" (697, italics mine). He then had to transform the remaining, now verbless fragment, "me always at myself," into a new main clause: "moi je me faisais ça à chaque instant." An objection that immediately comes to mind is that, from the formal point of view, "some nonsensical book that he had" is not at all what we would expect in Molly's language. In her specific idiolect this could not have been anything else but "some . . . book he had." The same clumsy analysis must have lain at the base of Wollschläger's translation: "hat er aus irgendeinem albernen Buch abgeschrieben *was er hatte*." He, too, is thus forced to start a new sentence after that: "ich habs mir ja immer selber gemacht" (995, italics mine).

After this digression, not leaving any loose ends, Molly resumes her account of the talk she had with Dr. Collins. The last question he asked her was whether she had "frequent omissions," and now we are told what her answer was (note "and" as a signal that the digression has come to an end): "and I said I hadnt" (18.1179–80/771.08). The doctor was not quite satisfied with that answer, apparently, for Molly remembers that he asked her, "are you sure," and that she then repeated her answer with such emphasis that he stopped pressing her for further information: "O yes I said I am quite sure in a way that shut him up" (18.1180/771.09).

A famous case of mistaken identity, dating from the early days of Joyce criticism, had its roots in a passage on the last page of the episode, where readers often failed to see that "he" and "him" in the following passage do not denote the same person: "and how *he* kissed me under the Moorish wall and I thought well as well *him* as another" (18.1603–5/783.08–10, italics mine). In his summary of the final pages of *Ulysses*, Humphrey reasons as follows: "Molly thinks about 'atheists' further: she thinks that 'they might as well try to stop the sun from rising'; this reminds her of Leopold's comment that 'the sun shines for you,' which he said during their courtship; she contemplates this event further and is reminded of details of the days she lived *in Gibraltar where the courtship occurred*; finally, she returns to Leopold's conquest (all amid flowers) and the monologue ends: ' . . . and how he kissed me under the Moorish wall and I thought well as well him as another . . .' '' (1954:46, italics mine). Since then, we have come to understand that Bloom never was in Gibraltar—or have we? Lyman, speaking about the song "In Old Madrid," alluded to at 18.1595/782.41, still declares that "Molly Bloom associates Old Madrid with *Gibraltar, where she and Leopold first fell in love*" (1983:198, italics mine).

We are nearing the end of Molly's soliloquy and, having come so far, should be able to follow the trend of her seemingly rambling flow of thoughts, although in this case there is a particularly intricate pattern we have to unravel. Before falling asleep, Molly goes back in time, she regresses, as Bernard Benstock puts it, "to romantic recollections of the past, blending first kisses with Mulvey under Moorish walls in Gibraltar with the first seduction by Bloom on the Hill of Howth" (1972:113), and it is this blending of memories that has sometimes led readers astray. Actually, the situation is perfectly clear; the thoughts that crowd Molly's mind are memories of memories, in Hardy's words: "What passes through her mind is what passed through it sixteen years ago when Bloom proposed to her. As she remembers his proposal we are suspended for a page while she tells her memory of all those memories that delayed her answer" (1975:253). To give the reader a specific, concrete foothold apart from such general considerations, we might point to the places in the text where the dovetailing of the memories begins and ends.

Molly has been thinking about atheists; they are just stupid, "they might as well try to stop the sun from rising tomorrow." This reminds her (one point on which Humphrey was right, of course) of Bloom's words "the sun shines for you," which he said "the day we were lying among the rhododendrons on Howth head" (18.1572–73/782.12–13). Other details keep flooding her memory, how he called her "a flower of the mountain" and, again, how he said, "the sun shines for you today," and, finally, how he proposed to her: "till he asked me to say yes" (18.1576–81/782.17–23). She remembers she did not answer at first because she was thinking of all she had experienced during those years in Gibraltar, all the things Bloom had had no part in and did not know of; she thought of her youthful lover, Lieutenant Mulvey, and of the romantic, Oriental sights of the town she had walked around in as a girl. All these recollections make for a long digression, but actually it is one long sentence of the polysyndeton type. It starts with "I was thinking of so many things he [Bloom] didnt know of" (18.1582/782.25)—the first and most fundamental of these things being her love affair with Mulvey, short-lived as it was—and it finishes with "and how he [Mulvey] kissed me under the Moorish wall" (18.1603–4/783.08–9). This ends the "memory within memory," making way for the resurgence of the single memory of the lovemaking with Bloom on the Hill of Howth: "and I thought well as well him [Bloom] as another" (18.1604–5/783.09ff.). This seems rather a cynical thought for an eighteen-year-old girl, and, of course, we have to take Molly's word for it that that was really what she was thinking at the time and not what she now, as a thirty-three-year-old woman, projects into this reminiscence. However, she may have been such a hard-boiled young woman already then. We have her own testimony, after all; thinking, with some disdain, of certain "Irish homemade beauties" she knows, she boasts: "I knew more about men and life when I was 15 than theyll all know at 50" (18.886–87/762.39–40). And yes, the way she almost seduced Bloom shows that these were no idle words.

The abundance of masculine pronouns in this episode should not blind us to the fact that there are instances where we have quite homogeneous bodies of text in which Molly's mind keeps concentrating on one particular person and where the pronouns, as a result, do refer to that one person throughout. There is an interesting case of this type in the first "sentence," about half-way down. Molly is remembering times when she used to go to confession, how she told Father Corrigan once that a man had touched her and how the priest then had wanted to know where:

> and I said on the canal bank like a fool but whereabouts on your person my child on the leg behind high up was it yes rather high up was it where you sit down yes O Lord couldnt he say bottom right out and have done with it what has that got to do with it and did you whatever way he put it I forget no father and I always think of the real father what did he want to know for when I already confessed it to God he had a nice fat hand the palm moist always I wouldnt mind feeling it neither would he Id say by the bullneck in his horsecollar I wonder did he know me in the box I could see his face he couldnt see mine of course hed never turn or let on still his eyes were red when his father died theyre lost for a woman of course must be terrible when a man cries let alone them Id like to be embraced by one in his vestments
>
> (18.108–19/741.03–16)

Adams, pointing out what he considers an oddity of Molly's history, quotes a single line from this passage. There is some evidence, he shows, that Molly was still in Spain in May 1886, and yet, he says, "it seems that she was in Ireland living in Rehoboth Terrace, Dolphin's Barn (p. 756), and acquainted with Bloom when his father committed suicide (June 27,

1886), for she thinks 'still his eyes were red when his father died' (p. 726). This is not precisely a contradiction, but it does crowd Molly's personal history remarkably in the spring of 1886" (1962:189). It must be evident, however, that Molly's thoughts, in the passage quoted above, are not concerned with Bloom at all, but solely with the world of priests. First she is thinking about one priest in particular, her confessor, and then her thoughts drift to priests in general. The former, Father Corrigan, would never "turn or let on," she thinks; that is to say he would never turn his head to see who was in the confession box and, even if he guessed or somehow knew, would never betray the fact. Yet, though outwardly unmoved, he cannot have been devoid of feeling, she reflects, for, looking at him surreptitiously, as she sometimes did ("I could see his face"), she had once noticed that he had been crying "when his father died" (this incident has not been mentioned before but, then, Molly's soliloquy is full of allusions to persons and events unknown to the reader), and she thinks that it must be a terrible thing when a man cries, let alone a priest. In short, all the masculine pronouns in this passage refer to priests, at first specifically to Father Corrigan, and later, starting with "Id like to be embraced by one in his vestments," to priests in general. There is more, however. Bloom's father committed suicide in June 1886 (17.622–32/684.33–685.08), but Bloom did not meet Molly until May 1887. This happened at what must have been a garden party given by Alderman Matthew Dillon, an event alluded to several times in the book. It follows that the problem posed by Adams does not exist. Molly was not yet acquainted with Bloom at the time his father killed himself by taking poison. Naturally, she will have heard the story in later years, either from Bloom's own mouth or from others; she may even have read Rudolph Bloom's suicide note, which Bloom kept in a drawer of the sideboard, in an envelope addressed "To My Dear Son Leopold" (17.1881–86/723.32–40). Anyway, Molly had practically a whole year between her affair with Mulvey in Spain and her meeting with Bloom in Dublin, a period during which she could have arrived in Ireland at any time.

Commenting on this passage, Hayman holds that "in a parallel development Bloom is subtly identified with the priest through the title 'father' which reminds Molly 'of the real father' and generates the aside, 'still [Poldy's] eyes were red when his father died' " (1982:119), but this does not impress me as being the last word on the passage under discussion. As I see it, in the sequence "no father and I always think of the real father" there is no association in Molly's mind with Bloom whatsoever. What she means to convey is just that, in the confessional, whenever she pronounced the word "father," in such phrases as "he touched me father," "yes father," "no father," she was unable to dissociate this word from its meaning in everyday life, feeling as if she were speaking, for instance, to her own father. Bloom as a father is not so very "real" to her, at that; note the way she speaks about his failure to give her a son: "its a poor case that those that have a fine son like that theyre not satisfied and I none was he not able to make one it wasnt my fault" (18.1444–46/778.26–29).

Suddenly switching from Father Corrigan to Boylan, Molly will have occasion to think about someone's father once more: "I wonder was he [Boylan] satisfied with me one thing I didnt like his slapping me behind going away . . . *Im not a horse* or an ass am I I suppose he was thinking of *his fathers* [i.e., his father's horses] I wonder is he awake thinking of me or dreaming am I in it who gave him that flower he said he bought he smelt of some kind of drink not whisky or stout or perhaps the sweety kind of paste they stick their bills up with some liqueur" (18.121–27/ 741.19–26, italics mine). In this case, of course, she refers to Boylan; slapping her as he did was something he must have learned from his father, who seems to have been a horse dealer, if we are to believe the narrator in "Cyclops" (cf. 12.998–99/319.30–32). Kain was on the wrong track when he had Molly suppose that it was Bloom who was thinking of his father (1959:255); the entire passage is about Boylan and no one else. Is Boylan, Molly wonders, now lying awake, thinking of her, or is he perhaps dreaming of her? And so, her thought about "that flower he said he bought" must refer to Boylan's flower, the red carnation he had picked up in Thornton's that afternoon (see 10.327–28/228.02) and not, as Kain assumed (1959:258), to Martha Clifford's "crumpled yellow flower" Bloom had in his pocket (see 15.738/455.24). Molly asks herself the same question the barmaids in the Ormond had asked themselves (cf. 11.366/265.26 and 11.380/265.40): Who (i.e., which woman, of course) gave him that flower? That we are dealing with Boylan is proved beyond all doubt by Molly's next reminiscence, "he smelt of some kind of drink . . . some liqueur." The reader may remember that in the Ormond bar Boylan had gulped down a sloe gin, so Molly is right, although for a moment she associated the smell with a kind of paste used for sticking up bills, but that may have been her imagination. She knows, of course, that Boylan runs a publicity agency and has people working for him, sticking up bills, for instance. Corley calls him "Boylan, the billsticker" (16.199/618.19–20).

Kain's book was first published as long ago as 1947, but that such erroneous readings as pointed out above are sometimes slow in dying is demonstrated in a recent article by Lyman. She reminds us that Joyce expanded Molly's monologue significantly from the manuscript stage to the final form in the printed text—a subject treated at length by Prescott (1964:77–105)—and she assumes that he must have done so with the intention of softening Molly's portrait. One of the means to achieve this effect is, as Lyman puts it, "to counterbalance her faults with those of her husband," such additions and insertions serving "to draw the two characters closer together by analogy." Ironically, the list of examples Lyman adduces to illustrate this particular point is headed by the very passage that, as we have seen above, refers to Boylan, not to Bloom: "Numerous passages, inserted after the composition of the manuscript, suggest that if Molly is deceitful, so is Leopold. *She wonders, 'who gave him that flower he said he bought'* (U 741), she recalls once when she 'found the long hair on his coat' (U 739), and she concludes that '1 woman is not enough for them' (U 739)" (1983:194, italics mine). A slip such as this shows, once again, that we cannot be too careful when trying to understand and, *a fortiori*, to interpret Molly's soliloquy. In this same article by Lyman there is a similar error, due not only to blatantly careless reading but also to sheer lack of empathy and of insight into the concrete setting. Having pointed out that some of Joyce's additions to the original manuscript stress Bloom's courteous nature as reflected in Molly's musings, Lyman quotes a few passages that illustrate this tendency: "Still incorporating passages into the episode, *Joyce has Molly recall the time 'when he stood up to open the door for me it was nice of him to show me out'* (U 752–53), and she acknowledges, despite her frustration with him, that 'still he had the manners not to wake me' (U 764)" (1983:197, italics mine). The irony of the matter is, once more, that the first passage Lyman quotes here does not refer to Bloom at all, but to a Mr. Cuffe. Moreover, it occurs in a context in which Bloom appears to have acted to someone else in a remarkably *discourteous* manner. Molly's train of thought that leads up to the passage in question starts at 18.503/752.12; she regrets Bloom's failure to get a regular job or even to hold on to it when he gets one, like the time he worked for Mr. Cuffe: "he could have been in Mr Cuffes still *only for what he did*" (18.510/752.19–20, italics mine). Cuffe must have fired Bloom for being impudent to a customer, if we are to trust the narrator in "Cyclops": "he was up one time in a knacker's yard. Walking about with his book and pencil . . . till Joe Cuffe gave him the order of the boot for giving lip to a grazier" (12.835–38/315.08–11). At Bloom's request, Molly went and tried to persuade Cuffe to take her husband back: "then sending me to try and patch it up I could have got him [Bloom] promoted there to be the manager he [Cuffe] gave me a great mirada once or twice *first he was as stiff as the mischief* really and truly Mrs Bloom" (18.510–13/752.20–23, italics mine). Molly remembers feeling very bad in her shabby old dress at the time, which leads to a digression of some fifteen lines, her thoughts dwelling on clothes, hats, and Bloom's behavior in shops. Then, with her characteristic "yes," she picks up the thread again, remembering she managed to catch Cuffe's eye in earnest at last and still appreciating his courtesy (although she was fully aware of his ulterior motives and despite that she had failed in her mission, after all): *"yes he was awfully stiff* and no wonder but he changed the second time he looked . . . I could see him looking very hard at my chest when he stood up to open the door for me it was nice of him to show me out in any case" (18.527–30/752.40–753.01, italics mine).

Molly's "Yes" that opens the final episode of *Ulysses* differs in nature and emotional value from her "Yes" that concludes it. What they have in common, though, is that both are responses to something Bloom had said or done, and, when we come to think of it, this is, essentially, what the whole episode is about. We call it "Molly's soliloquy," but our excuse for eavesdropping on her is our desire to hear all about Bloom.

LIST OF REFERENCES

Adams, Robert Martin. *Surface and Symbol: The Consistency of James Joyce's "Ulysses."* New York: Oxford University Press, 1962.

———.*James Joyce: Common Sense and Beyond.* New York: Random House, 1966.

———.*Proteus, His Lies, His Truth: Discussions of Literary Translation.* New York: Norton, 1973.

———."Hades." In Hart and Hayman, ed. *James Joyce's "Ulysses,"* 1974, 91–114.

———.*Afterjoyce: Studies in Fiction after "Ulysses."* New York: Oxford University Press, 1977.

Aldridge, John W., ed. *Critiques and Essays on Modern Fiction, 1920–1951.* New York: Ronald Press, 1952.

Anderson, Chester G. *James Joyce and His World.* London: Thames and Hudson, 1967.

Atherton, J. S. "The Oxen of the Sun." In Hart and Hayman, ed. *James Joyce's "Ulysses,"* 1974, 313–39.

Barrow, Craig Wallace. *Montage in James Joyce's "Ulysses."* Potomac, Md.: Studia Humanitatis, 1980.

Bauerle, Ruth, ed. *The James Joyce Songbook.* New York: Garland Publishing, 1982.

Begnal, Michael H., and Fritz Senn, eds. *A Conceptual Guide to "Finnegans Wake."* University Park: Pennsylvania State University Press, 1974.

Beja, Morris, ed. *James Joyce, "Dubliners" and "A Portrait of the Artist as a Young Man": A Casebook.* London: Macmillan, 1973.

Benstock, Bernard. *Joyce-Again's Wake: An Analysis of "Finnegans Wake."* Seattle: University of Washington Press, 1965.

———."Arthur Griffith in *Ulysses:* The Explosion of a Myth." *ELN* 4 (1966): 124–25.

———."*Ulysses* without Dublin." *James Joyce Quarterly* 10 (1972): 90–117.

———."Telemachus." In Hart and Hayman, ed. *James Joyce's "Ulysses,"* 1974, 1–16.

———.*James Joyce: The Undiscovered Country.* Dublin: Gill and Macmillan; New York: Barnes and Noble, 1977.

———.Review of Raleigh, *The Chronicle of Leopold and Molly Bloom. James Joyce Quarterly* 16 (1978): 195–98.

———."On the Nature of Evidence in *Ulysses.*" In Bushrui and Benstock, ed. *James Joyce: An International Perspective.* Gerrards Cross, Bucks.: Colin Smythe; Totowa, N.J.: Barnes and Noble, 1982a, 46–64.

————, ed. *The Seventh of Joyce*. Bloomington: Indiana University Press; Brighton: Harvester Press, 1982b.

Benstock, Shari. "Through a Glass Darkly: Déjà Vu in *Ulysses*." *James Joyce Quarterly* 13 (1976): 473–76.

————."The Evasion Principle: A Search for Survivors in *Ulysses*." *Modern Fiction Studies* 24 (1978): 159–79.

————."The Printed Letters in *Ulysses*." *James Joyce Quarterly* 19 (1982a): 415–27.

————."The Dynamics of Narrative Performance: Stephan Dedalus as Story-teller." *ELH* 49 (1982b): 707–38.

————, and Bernard Benstock. *Who's He When He's at Home: A James Joyce Directory*. Urbana: University of Illinois Press, 1980.

————."The Benstock Principle." In Benstock, ed. *The Seventh of Joyce*, 1982, 10–21.

Bidwell, Bruce, and Linda Heffer. *The Joycean Way: A Topographic Guide to "Dubliners" and "A Portrait of the Artist as a Young Man."* Dublin: Wolfhound Press, 1981; Baltimore: Johns Hopkins University Press, 1982.

Blamires, Harry. *The Bloomsday Book: A Guide through Joyce's "Ulysses."* London: Methuen, 1966.

Bolt, Sydney, *A Preface to James Joyce*. London and New York: Longman, 1981.

Boone, Joseph Allen. "A New Approach to Bloom as 'Womanly Man': The Mixed Middling's Progress in *Ulysses*." *James Joyce Quarterly* 20 (1982): 67–85.

Booth, Wayne C. *The Rhetoric of Fiction*. Chicago: University of Chicago Press, 1961.

Bowen, Zack. "Libretto for Bloomusalem in Song: The Music of Joyce's *Ulysses*." In Senn, ed. *New Light on Joyce*, 1972, 149–66.

————.*Musical Allusions in The Works of James Joyce: Early Poetry through "Ulysses."* Albany: State University of New York Press; Dublin: Gill and Macmillan, 1975.

Brandabur, Edward. *A Scrupulous Meanness: A Study of Joyce's Early Work*. Urbana: University of Illinois Press, 1971.

Brown, Carole. "Omar Khayyam in Monto: A Reading of A Passage from James Joyce's *Ulysses*." *Neophilologus* 68 (1984): 623–36.

————, and Leo Knuth. *Bloomsday, the Eleventh Hour: The Quest for the Vacant Place*. Colchester: A Wake Newsletter Press, 1981.

Bruns, Gerald L. "Eumaeus." In Hart and Hayman, ed. *James Joyce's "Ulysses,"* 1974, 363–83.

Budgen, Frank. *James Joyce and the Making of "Ulysses."* Bloomington: Indiana University Press, 1960 (rpt. of the original 1934 edition).

Burgess, Anthony. "A Paralysed City." In Beja, ed. *James Joyce: "Dubliners" and "A Portrait,"* 1973a, 224–40.

————.*Joysprick: An Introduction to the Language of James Joyce*. London: André Deutsch, 1973b.

Bushrui, Suheil Badi, and Bernard Benstock, eds. *James Joyce: An International Perspective*. Gerrards Cross, Bucks.: Colin Smythe; Totowa, N.J.: Barnes and Noble, 1982.

Cambon, Glauco. *La Lotta con Proteo.* Milan: Bompiani, 1963. German translation by W. Hartig (pp. 1–118) and H. Hofmann (pp. 119–299), *Der Kampf mit Proteus: Untersuchungen über Sprache und Sein in der modernen Litaratur.* Munich: Carl Hanser, 1970.

Campbell, Joseph, and Henry Morton Robinson. *A Skeleton Key to "Finnegans Wake."* New York: Harcourt, Brace, 1944; London: Faber and Faber, 1947.

Chace, William M., ed. *Joyce: A Collection of Critical Essays.* Englewood Cliffs, N.J.: Prentice-Hall, 1974.

Cohn, Dorrit. *Transparent Minds: Narrative Modes for Presenting Consciousness in Fiction.* Princeton: Princeton University Press, 1978.

Cope, Jackson I. "Sirens." In Hart and Hayman, ed. *James Joyce's "Ulysses,"* 1974, 217–42.

Cronin, Anthony. "The Advent of Bloom." In Chace, ed. *Joyce: A Collection of Critical Essays,* 1974, 84–101.

Davies, Stan Gébler. *James Joyce: A Portrait of the Artist.* London: Davis-Poynter, 1975.

Day, Robert Adams. "Deacon Dedalus: The Text of the *Exultet* and Its Implications for *Ulysses.*" In Bernard Benstock, ed. *The Seventh of Joyce,* 1982, 157–66.

Delaney, Frank. *James Joyce's Odyssey: A Guide to the Dublin of "Ulysses."* London: Hodder and Stoughton, 1981.

Dick, Susan. "Tom Kernan and the Retrospective Arrangement." *James Joyce Quarterly* 18 (1981): 149–59.

Douglas, Mary. *Purity and Danger: An Analysis of Concepts of Pollution and Taboo.* Harmondsworth: Pelican Books, 1970.

Duytschaever, Joris. "James Joyce's *Ulysses* in Dutch." *Revue des langues vivantes* 37 (1971): 701–11.

Ellmann, Richard. "The Limits of Joyce's Naturalism." *Sewanee Review* 63 (1955): 567–75.

———. *James Joyce.* New York: Oxford University Press, 1959. Rev. ed., 1982.

———. *"Ulysses" on the Liffey.* London: Faber and Faber, 1972. New ed., with corrections, 1974.

———. *The Consciousness of Joyce.* London: Faber and Faber, 1977.

Empson, William. "The Theme of *Ulysses.*" *Kenyon Review* 18 (1956): 26–52.

Epstein, E. L., ed. *A Starchamber Quiry: A James Joyce Centennial Volume, 1882–1982.* New York and London: Methuen, 1982, esp. 73–106.

Fischer, Therese. *Bewusstseinsdarstellung im Werk von James Joyce. Von "Dubliners" zu "Ulysses."* Frankfurt am Main: Neue Beiträge zur Anglistik und Amerikanistik 10, 1973.

Fischer-Seidel, Therese, ed. *James Joyces "Ulysses": Neuere deutsche Aufsätze.* Frankfurt am Main: Suhrkamp, 1977.

French, Marilyn. *The Book as World: James Joyce's "Ulysses."* Cambridge, Mass.: Harvard University Press, 1976.

Friedman, Melvin J. "Lestrygonians." In Hart and Hayman, ed. *James Joyce's "Ulysses,"* 1974, 131–46.

Gabler, Hans Walter, with Wolfhard Steppe and Claus Melchior. *'Ulysses": A Critical and Synoptic Edition,* 3 vols. New York and London: Garland, 1984.

Garrett, Peter K. *Scene and Symbol from George Eliot to James Joyce: Studies in Changing Fictional Mode.* New Haven: Yale University Press, 1969.

Garvin, John. *James Joyce's Disunited Kingdom and the Irish Dimension.* Dublin: Gill and Macmillan, 1976. New York: Barnes and Noble, 1977.

Gifford, Don, with Robert J. Seidman. *Notes for Joyce: An Annotation of James Joyce's "Ulysses."* New York: Dutton, 1974. Quoted as "Gifford."

Gilbert, Stuart. *James Joyce's "Ulysses": A Study.* London: Faber and Faber, 1930.

Givens, Seon, ed. *James Joyce: Two Decades of Criticism.* New York: Vanguard Press, 1948. Augmented ed., 1963.

Glasheen, Adaline. *A Census of "Finnegans Wake": An Index of the Characters and Their Roles.* Evanston, Ill.: Northwestern University Press, 1956. A *Second Census* appeared in 1963, and a *Third* (Berkeley and Los Angeles: University of California Press) in 1977.

Glowinski, Michal. "On the First-Person Novel." *NLH* 9 (1977): 103–14.

Goldberg, S. L. *The Classical Temper: A Study of James Joyce's "Ulysses."* London: Chatto and Windus, 1961.

———. *Joyce.* Edinburgh: Oliver and Boyd, 1962.

Goldman, Arnold. *The Joyce Paradox: Form and Freedom in His Fiction.* London: Routledge and Kegan Paul; Evanston, Ill.: Northwestern University Press, 1966.

Gordon, John. *James Joyce's Metamorphoses.* Dublin: Gill and Macmillan; Totowa, N.J.: Barnes and Noble, 1981a.

———. "The Secret of Boylan's Bottom Drawer." *James Joyce Quarterly* 18 (1981b): 450–58.

Groden, Michael. *"Ulysses" in Progress.* Princeton: Princeton University Press, 1977.

Hall, Vernon, Jr. "Joyce's Use of Da Ponte and Mozart's Don Giovanni." *PMLA* 66 (1951): 78–84.

Halper, Nathan. "The Boarding House." In Hart, ed. *James Joyce's "Dubliners,"* 1969, 72–83.

Halperin, John, ed. *The Theory of the Novel: New Essays.* New York: Oxford University Press, 1974.

Hanley, Miles L., ed. *Word Index to James Joyce's "Ulysses."* Madison: University of Wisconsin Press, 1951.

Hannay, John. "Coincidence and Analytic Reduction in the 'Ithaca' Episode in *Ulysses." Journal of Narrative Technique* 13 (1983): 141–53.

———. "Coincidence and Fables of Identity in "Eumaeus." *James Joyce Quarterly* 21 (1984): 341–55.

Hardy, Barbara. *Tellers and Listeners: The Narrative Imagination.* London: Athlone Press, 1975.

Hart, Clive. *Structure and Motif in "Finnegans Wake."* London: Faber and Faber; Evanston, Ill.: Northwestern University Press, 1962.

———. *James Joyce's "Ulysses."* Sydney: Sydney University Press, 1968.

———. "Wandering Rocks." In Hart and Hayman, ed. *James Joyce's "Ulysses,"* 1974, 181–216.

————, ed. *James Joyce's "Dubliners": Critical Essays*. London: Faber and Faber, 1969.

————, and Leo Knuth. *A Topographical Guide to James Joyce's "Ulysses."* I: *Text*, II: *Maps*. Colchester: A Wake Newslitter Press, 1975; 5th rev. ed., 1981.

————, and David Hayman, eds. *James Joyce's "Ulysses": Critical Essays*. Berkeley and Los Angeles: University of California Press, 1974.

Harvey, W. J. *Character and the Novel*. London: Chatto and Windus, 1970.

Hayman, David. *Joyce et Mallarmé*, 2 vols. Paris: Lettres Modernes, 1956.

————."Forms of Folly in Joyce: A Study of Clowning in *Ulysses.*" *ELH* 34 (1967): 260–83.

————."Clowns et farce chez Joyce." *Poétique: Revue de théorie et d'analyse littéraires* 2 (1971): 173–99.

————."Cyclops." In Hart and Hayman, ed. *James Joyce's "Ulysses,"* 1974, 243–75.

————."Stephen on the Rocks." *James Joyce Quarterly* 15 (1977): 5–17.

————."*Ulysses": The Mechanics of Meaning*. 2nd ed. Madison: University of Wisconsin Press, 1982.

Henke, Suzette A. *Joyce's Moraculous Sindbook: A Study of "Ulysses."* Columbus: Ohio University Press, 1978.

Hentze, Rudolf. *Die proteische Wandlung im "Ulysses" von James Joyce und ihre Spiegelung im Stil*. Marburg: Elwert, 1933.

Herr, Cheryl. "Irish Censorship and 'The Pleasure of the Text': The 'Aeolus' Episode of Joyce's *Ulysses.*" In Dennis Jackson, ed. *Irish Renaissance Annual* III. London and Toronto: Associated University Presses, 1982, 141–79.

Herring, Phillip F. "Lotuseaters." In Hart and Hayman, ed. *James Joyce's "Ulysses,"* 1974, 71–89.

Hodgart, Matthew J. C. "Aeolus." In Hart and Hayman, ed. *James Joyce's "Ulysses,"* 1974, 115–30.

————.*James Joyce: A Student's Guide*. London: Routledge and Kegan Paul, 1978.

————, and Mabel P. Worthington. *Song in the Works of James Joyce*. New York: Columbia University Press, 1959.

Humphrey, Robert. *Stream of Consciousness in the Modern Novel*. Berkeley and Los Angeles: University of California Press, 1954.

Hutchins, Patricia. *James Joyce's Dublin*. London: Grey Walls Press, 1950.

————.*James Joyce's World*. London: Methuen, 1957.

Iser, Wolfgang. *Der implizite Leser: Kommunikationsformen des Romans von Bunyan bis Beckett*. Munich: Fink, 1972. English version: *The Implied Reader: Patterns of Communication in Prose Fiction from Bunyan to Beckett*. Baltimore: Johns Hopkins University Press, 1974.

————.*Die Appellstruktur der Texte: Unbestimmtheit als Wirkungsbedingung literarischer Prosa*. Konstanz: Universitätsverlag, 1974.

————.*The Act of Reading: A Theory of Aesthetic Response*. London: Routledge and Kegan Paul, 1978. Baltimore: Johns Hopkins University Press, 1979.

Janusko, Robert. *The Sources and Structure of James Joyce's "Oxen."* Ann Arbor, Mi.: UMI Research Press, 1983.

Joly, Ralph Robert. "Chauvinist Brew and Leopold Bloom: The Weininger Legacy." *James Joyce Quarterly* 19 (1982): 194–98.

Jones, William Powell. *James Joyce and the Common Reader.* Norman: University of Oklahoma Press, 1955.

Joyce, Patrick Weston. *English as We Speak It in Ireland.* Portmarnock (Dublin): Wolfhound Press, 1979 (first published 1910).

Kain, Richard M. *Fabulous Voyager: James Joyce's "Ulysses."* Chicago: University of Chicago Press, 1947, Rpt., with corrections, New York: Viking Press, 1959.

———."The Position of *Ulysses* Today." In Staley, ed. *James Joyce Today,* 1966, 83–95.

Kaiser, Gerhard R. *Proust-Musil-Joyce: Zum Verhältnis von Literatur und Gesellschaft am Paradigma des Zitats* (chap. 4: "Joyce, *Ulysses*"). Frankfurt am Main: Athenäum Verlag, 1972, 145–225.

Kellogg, Robert. "Scylla and Charybdis." In Hart and Hayman, ed. *James Joyce's "Ulysses,"* 1974, 147–79.

Kenner, Hugh. *Dublin's Joyce.* London: Chatto and Windus, 1955.

———."Circe." In Hart and Hayman, ed. *James Joyce's "Ulysses,"* 1974, 341–62.

———.*Joyce's Voices.* London: Faber and Faber, 1978.

———.*Ulysses.* London: George Allen and Unwin, 1980.

Knight, Douglas. "The Reading of *Ulysses.*" *ELH* 19 (1952): 64–80.

Knuth, A.M.L. *The Wink of the Word: A Study of James Joyce's Phatic Communication.* Amsterdam: Rodopi, 1976.

———.Review of *(a)* Gifford with Seidman, *Notes for Joyce* (1974), and *(b)* Hart and Hayman, ed. *James Joyce's "Ulysses"* (1974). *Dutch Quarterly Review of Anglo-American Letters* 5 (1975): 298–305.

———."A Belt for Hercules" (review of Seidel, *Epic Geography* [1976]). *A Wake Newslitter* 14 (1977): 10–13.

———.*Bloomsday, the Eleventh Hour,* s.v. "Brown, Carole."

———.*A Topographical Guide,* s.v. "Hart, Clive."

Kreutzer, Eberhard. *Sprache und Spiel im "Ulysses" von James Joyce.* Bonn: Bouvier, 1969.

Levenston, E. A. "Narrative Technique in *Ulysses:* A Stylistic Comparison of 'Telemachus' and 'Eumaeus.' " *Language and Style* 5 (1972): 260–75.

Levin, Harry. *James Joyce: A Critical Introduction.* London: Faber and Faber, 1944.

Levitt, Morton P. "A Hero for Our Time." *James Joyce Quarterly* 10 (1972): 132–46.

Link, Viktor. "Bau und Funktion der Circe-Episode im *Ulysses* von James Joyce." Ph.D. diss., University of Bonn, 1970.

Litz, A. Walton. *The Art of James Joyce: Method and Design in "Ulysses" and "Finnegans Wake."* London: Oxford University Press, 1961.

———."The Genre of *Ulysses.*" In Halperin, ed. *The Theory of the Novel,* 1974a, 109–20.

———."Ithaca." In Hart and Hayman, ed. *James Joyce's "Ulysses,"* 1974b, 385–405.

Lukács, Georg. "The Ideology of Modernism." In David Lodge, ed. *Twentieth-Century Literary Criticism.* London: Longman, 1972, 474–87.

Lyman, Stephany. "Revision and Intention in Joyce's 'Penelope.' " *James Joyce Quarterly* 20 (1983): 193–200.

Lyons, J. B. *James Joyce and Medicine.* Dublin: Dolmen Press, 1973.

———.*Oliver St. John Gogarty.* Lewisburg: Bucknell University Press, 1976.

McBride, Margaret. "At Four She Said." *James Joyce Quarterly* 17 (1979): 21–39. "At Four She Said: II." *James Joyce Quarterly* 18 (1981): 417–31.

MacCabe, Colin, ed. *James Joyce: New Perspectives.* Brighton: Harvester Press, 1982.

McCarthy, Patrick A. "Joyce's Unreliable Catechist: Mathematics and the Narration of 'Ithaca.' " *ELH* 51 (1984): 605–18.

McHugh, Roland. *The Sigla of "Finnegans Wake."* London: Edward Arnold, 1976.

———.*Annotations to "Finnegans Wake."* Baltimore: Johns Hopkins University Press; London: Routledge and Kegan Paul, 1980.

———.*The "Finnegans Wake" Experience.* Dublin: Irish Academic Press, 1981.

Maddox, James H., Jr. *Joyce's "Ulysses" and the Assault upon Character.* New Brunswick, N.J.: Rutgers University Press; Brighton: Harvester Press, 1978.

Madtes, Richard E. "Joyce and the Building of 'Ithaca.' " *ELH* 31 (1964): 443–59.

———.*The "Ithaca" Chapter of Joyce's "Ulysses."* Ann Arbor, Mi.: UMI Research Press, 1983.

Magalaner, Marvin, and Richard M. Kain. *Joyce: The Man, the Work, the Reputation.* New York: New York University Press, 1956.

Mason, Michael. *James Joyce: "Ulysses."* London: Edward Arnold, 1972.

Mink, Louis O. *A "Finnegans Wake" Gazetteer.* Bloomington: Indiana University Press, 1978.

Misra, B. P. "Sanskrit Translations." *A Wake Newslitter* 1, no. 6 (1964): 8–10; 2, no. 1 (1965): 9–11.

Morton, Richard. *"Ulysses": Notes.* Rexdale, Ont.: Coles, 1970.

Moseley, Virginia. *Joyce and the Bible.* DeKalb: Northern Illinois University Press, 1967.

Mosenthal, S. H. *Deborah.* In *Gesammelte Werke,* 2 vols. Stuttgart and Leipzig: Hallberger, 1878.

Noon, William T., S. J. *Joyce and Aquinas.* New Haven: Yale University Press, 1957.

———."Song the Syrens Sang." *Mosaic* 6 (1972): 77–83.

Norris, Margot. *The Decentered Universe of "Finnegans Wake": A Structuralist Analysis.* Baltimore: Johns Hopkins University Press, 1974.

Peake, C. H. *James Joyce: The Citizen and the Artist.* London: Edward Arnold, 1977.

Pomeranz, Victory. "The Frowning Face of Bethel." *James Joyce Quarterly* 10 (1973): 342–44.

Power, Arthur. *Conversations with James Joyce*, ed. Clive Hart. London: Millington, 1974.

Power, Mary. "The Discovery of *Ruby*." *James Joyce Quarterly* 18 (1981): 115–21.

Prescott, Joseph. "Notes on Joyce's *Ulysses*." *Modern Language Quarterly* 13 (1952a): 149–62.

———."Mosenthal's *Deborah* and Joyce's *Ulysses*." *MLN* 67 (1952b): 334–36.

———.*Exploring James Joyce*. Carbondale: Southern Illinois University Press, 1964.

Quinn, Edward. *James Joyce's Dublin: With Selected Writings from Joyce's Works*. London: Secker and Warburg, 1974.

Raleigh, John Henry. "Bloom as a Modern Epic Hero." *Critical Inquiry* 3 (1977a): 583–98.

———.*The Chronicle of Leopold and Molly Bloom: "Ulysses" as Narrative*. Berkeley and Los Angeles: University of California Press, 1977b.

———."On the Way Home to Ithaca: The Functions of the 'Eumaeus' Section in *Ulysses*." In Zack Bowen, ed. *Irish Renaissance Annual* II. London and Toronto: Associated University Presses, 1981, 13–114.

Rankin, H. D. "James Joyce's Satyr-Play: The 'Cyclops' Episode in *Ulysses*." *Agora: A Journal in the Humanities and Social Sciences* 2 (1973): 3–12.

Reichert, Klaus. "Lesbarkeit oder Erhaltung der Komplexität? Thesen zur Praxis des Uebersetzens." *Akzente: Zeitschrift für Literatur* 25 (1978): 65–76.

Reynolds, Mary T. *Joyce and Dante: The Shaping Imagination*. Princeton: Princeton University Press, 1981.

Rice, Thomas Jackson. *James Joyce: A Guide to Research*. New York and London: Garland, 1982.

Schneider, Ulrich. *Die Funktion der Zitate im "Ulysses" von James Joyce*. Bonn: Bouvier, 1970.

Schoenberg, Estella I. "The Identity of the 'Cyclops' Narrator in James Joyce's *Ulysses*." *Journal of Modern Literature* 5 (1976): 534–39.

Schutte, William M. *Joyce and Shakespeare: A Study in the Meaning of "Ulysses*." New Haven: Yale University Press, 1957.

———.*Index of Recurrent Elements in James Joyce's "Ulysses*." Carbondale: Southern Illinois University Press, 1982.

Seidel, Michael. *Epic Geography: James Joyce's "Ulysses*." Princeton: Princeton University Press, 1976.

Senn, Fritz. "Seven against *Ulysses:* Joyce in Translation." *James Joyce Quarterly* 4 (1967): 170–93. Rpt. in *Levende Talen* (1970): 512–35.

———."Nausicaa." In Hart and Hayman, ed. *James Joyce's "Ulysses*," 1974a, 277–311.

———."The Rhythm of *Ulysses*." In L. Bonnerot, ed. *"Ulysses": Cinquante ans après*. Paris: Didier, 1974b: 33–42.

———."Trivia Ulysseana I." *James Joyce Quarterly* 12 (1975): 443–50.

———."Odysseeische Metamorphosen." In T. Fischer-Seidel, ed. *Neuere deutsche Aufsätze*, 1977, 26–57. Originally published in "Book of Many Turns," *James Joyce Quarterly*, 10 (1972): 29–46.

———."Die fruchtbare Illusion der Übersetzbarkeit: Bemerkungen zur

Ulysses-Übersetzung." *Akzente: Zeitschrift für Literatur* 25 (1978): 39–52.

―――."Dogmad or dubliboused?" *James Joyce Quarterly* 17 (1980): 237–61.

―――."Weaving, unweaving." In Epstein, ed. *A Starchamber Quiry*, 1982a, 45–70.

―――."Righting *Ulysses*." In MacCabe, ed. *James Joyce: New Perspectives*, 1982b, 3–28.

―――."Trivia Ulysseana IV." *James Joyce Quarterly* 19 (1982c): 151–78.

―――, ed. *New Light on Joyce from the Dublin Symposium*. Bloomington: Indiana University Press, 1972.

Smith, Paul Jordan. *A Key to the "Ulysses" of James Joyce*. Chicago: Covici, 1927. Rpt. San Francisco: City Lights ed., 1970.

Solmecke, Gert. "Funktion und Bedeutung der Parodie in Joyces *Ulysses*." Ph.D. diss., University of Cologne, 1969.

Staley, Thomas F., ed. *James Joyce Today: Essays on the Major Works*. Bloomington: Indiana University Press, 1966; Don Mills, Ont.: Midland Books, 1970.

―――, ed. *Fifty Years "Ulysses*." Bloomington: Indiana University Press, 1972. Rpt. 1974.

Stanford, W. B. *The Ulysses Theme: A Study in the Adaptability of a Traditional Hero*. Oxford: Blackwell, 1954.

Stanzel, Franz. *Die typischen Erzählsituationen im Roman*. Wien: Braumüller, 1955. Trans. James P. Pusack, *Narrative Situations in the Novel*. Bloomington: Indiana University Press, 1971.

Staples, Hugh B. " 'Composition of Place': The Setting of 'Cyclops.' " *James Joyce Quarterly* 13 (1976): 393–99.

Stewart, J.I.M. *James Joyce*. London: Longmans, Green and Co., 1960.

Strong, L.A.G. *The Sacred River: An Approach to James Joyce*. London: Methuen, 1949.

Sturdy, John. *"Numbers": Commentary*. Cambridge: Cambridge University Press, 1976.

Sultan, Stanley. *The Argument of "Ulysses*." Columbus: Ohio State University Press, 1964.

Thomas, Brook. "Not a Reading of, but the Act of Reading *Ulysses*." *James Joyce Quarterly* 16 (1978): 81–93.

Thornton, Weldon. *Allusions in "Ulysses": An Annotated List*. Chapel Hill: University of North Carolina Press, 1968.

Tindall, William York. *James Joyce: His Way of Interpreting the Modern World*. New York: Charles Scribner's Sons, 1950.

―――.*A Reader's Guide to James Joyce*. New York: Noonday Press, 1959.

―――.*A Reader's Guide to "Finnegans Wake*." London: Thames and Hudson, 1969.

―――.*The Joyce Country*. New York: Schocken Books, 1972.

Topia, André. "Contrepoints Joyciens." *Poétique: Revue de théorie et d'analyse littéraires* 7 (1976): 351–71.

Van Caspel, Paul P. J. "The Theme of the Red Carnation in James Joyce's *Ulysses*." *Neophilologus* 38 (1954): 189–98.

―――."A Plea for Intertranslation: Notes on the 'Cyclops' Chapter of

Ulysses." *Dutch Quarterly Review of Anglo-American Letters* 9 (1979a): 114–28.

———."Father and Son in the 'Lotuseaters' Episode of Joyce's *Ulysses.*" *English Studies* 60 (1979b): 593–602.

Van der Vat, D. G. "Paternity in *Ulysses.*" *English Studies* 19 (1937): 145–58.

Van Dyck Card, James. " 'Contradicting': The Word for Joyce's 'Penelope.' " *James Joyce Quarterly* 11 (1973): 17–26.

Von Phul, Ruth. " 'Major' Tweedy and His Daughter." *James Joyce Quarterly* 19 (1982): 341–48.

Vreeswijk, Harry. *Notes on Joyce's "Ulysses" Part I: A Very First Draft.* Amsterdam: Van Gennep, 1971.

Watt, Ian. *The Rise of the Novel.* Harmondsworth: Pelican Books, 1972.

Weiss, Daniel. "The End of the 'Oxen of the Sun.' " *Analyst* 9 (1955): 1–16.

Wilson, Edmund. "James Joyce." Excerpt from *Axel's Castle*, 1931. In Chace, ed. *Joyce: A Collection of Critical Essays*, 1974, 50–66.

Woods, John. *The Logic of Fiction.* The Hague-Paris: Mouton, 1974.

INDEX

Paul van Caspel taught literature at Groningen University in the Netherlands. He is the author of a book on acoustic aspects of modern poetry and has worked extensively as a translator of English and Swedish (into Dutch) and Italian and Spanish (into English).